SPEAKING THE UNSPEAKABLE IN POSTWAR GERMANY

signale
modern german letters, cultures, and thought

Series editor: Peter Uwe Hohendahl, Cornell University

Signale: Modern German Letters, Cultures, and Thought publishes new English-language books in literary studies, criticism, cultural studies, and intellectual history pertaining to the German-speaking world, as well as translations of important German-language works. *Signale* construes "modern" in the broadest terms: the series covers topics ranging from the early modern period to the present. *Signale* books are published under a joint imprint of Cornell University Press and Cornell University Library in electronic and print formats. Please see http://signale.cornell.edu/.

Speaking the Unspeakable in Postwar Germany

Toward a Public Discourse on the Holocaust

Sonja Boos

A Signale Book

Cornell University Press and Cornell University Library
Ithaca, NY

Cornell University Press and Cornell University Library gratefully acknowledge
the College of Arts & Sciences, Cornell University, for support of the Signale
series.

First published 2014 by Cornell University Press and Cornell University Library

Printed in the United States of America

Library of Congress Cataloging-in-Publication Data

Boos, Sonja, 1972– author.
    Speaking the unspeakable in postwar Germany : toward a public discourse
on the Holocaust / Sonja Boos.
        pages cm. — (Signale : modern German letters, cultures, and thought)
    Includes bibliographical references and index.
    ISBN 978-0-8014-5360-1 (cloth : alk. paper) —
    ISBN 978-0-8014-7963-2 (pbk. : alk. paper)
    1. Holocaust, Jewish (1939–1945)—Influence. 2. Holocaust, Jewish (1939–1945)—
Public opinion. 3. Speeches, addresses, etc., German—History and criticism.
4. Germany (West)—Intellectual life. 5. Public opinion—Germany (West)
I. Title. II. Series: Signale (Ithaca, N.Y.)
    D804.3.B66 2014
    940.53'180943—dc23   2014030965

Cornell University Press strives to use environmentally responsible suppliers and
materials to the fullest extent possible in the publishing of its books. Such materials
include vegetable-based, low-VOC inks and acid-free papers that are recycled, totally
chlorine-free, or partly composed of nonwood fibers. For further information, visit
our website at www.cornellpress.cornell.edu.

Cloth printing   10 9 8 7 6 5 4 3 2 1
Paperback printing   10 9 8 7 6 5 4 3 2 1

In memory of José Camejo

Strange, not to have wishes any more.
To see, where things were related, only a looseness
fluttering in space.

—Rainer Maria Rilke, *The Duino Elegies*

CONTENTS

ACKNOWLEDGMENTS

I began this project at Princeton University, where I was fortunate to have the intellectual support of many remarkable colleagues and friends. I am deeply indebted to Barbara Hahn, whose thoughtful and constructively critical commentary repeatedly renewed my enthusiasm and confidence in the project. I am especially thankful for her ability to see the potential of this project, which I was unable to fully articulate in its earlier stages. I am also extremely grateful that she remained an exceptionally accessible colleague and close friend despite her geographical and institutional remoteness. Most importantly, I want to thank her for teaching me how to write. Brigid Doherty came to this project when its conceptual framework and the composition of a first draft were already well advanced, and I am still amazed at how quickly and naturally she became not only a crucial interlocutor, who steered me toward pertinent questions and relevant literature, but the project's intellectual anchor sine qua non. I can only attribute this to her extraordinary intelligence and intellectual flexibility, as well as her truly effortless kindness and grace.

I would also like to thank Michael W. Jennings, who has been an extremely important teacher and mentor throughout these years. Words are not enough to express how grateful I am for his unending support and friendship. Thomas Y. Levin has been an inspiration, both personally and professionally, and I am very appreciative of his readiness to serve as a reader and for his outstanding intellectual generosity. Arnd Wedemeyer has read and commented on my work at regular intervals, and my writing has greatly benefited from his critical intellect and encyclopedic knowledge. Finally, I would like to thank the following colleagues and dear friends who have read and edited portions of the manuscript of this book and offered valuable criticisms, many of which I have incorporated into my text: Jutta Adams, Leora Batnitzky, Dorothee Boos, Katra Byram, Kaira M. Cabañas, Lisa Cerami, Stanley Corngold, Nikolaus Wegmann, and Tobias Wilke. Others, though not directly involved in this project, have gone out of their way to provide emotional support and intellectual stimulation (be it through ongoing conversations or professional collaborations) during my time at Princeton: Florian N. Becker, Kerry Bystrom, May Mergenthaler, Sarah Pourciau, P. Adams Sitney, and Susan Sugarman.

My sincere thanks go to those people who were involved in the final stages of this publication. My colleagues at Oberlin College—Grace An, Elizabeth Hamilton, Steve Huff, Heidi Thomann Tewardson, and Katherine Thomson-Jones—have helped me bring the manuscript to completion through their intellectual generosity and warm friendship. I also wish to thank Kizer S. Walker, managing editor of the Signale series, for his many insights and patient guidance throughout the process, and Marian Rogers for her thorough and rigorous work on the manuscript as an editor. The publication of this book was supported by the Oregon Humanities Center and the University of Oregon College of Arts and Sciences.

I am, finally, deeply indebted to my parents, Dorothee and Theo Boos, and my sisters, Katrin Back-Schück and Irene Gräfin von Schwerin, who have shaped me, and continue to shape me, in ways I am still discovering.

ABBREVIATIONS

AN   Uwe Johnson, *Anniversaries*

EA   Theodor W. Adorno, *Education after Auschwitz*

GB   Uwe Johnson, *Georg-Büchner-Prize acceptance speech*

GC   Ingeborg Bachmann, *German Contingencies*

GD   Martin Buber, *Genuine Dialogue and the Possibilities of Peace*

HC   Hannah Arendt, *The Human Condition*

HP   Peter Szondi, *Hope in the Past*

IN   Peter Weiss, *The Investigation*

IT   Martin Buber, *I and Thou*

KJ   Hannah Arendt, *Karl Jaspers: A Laudatio*

LL   Peter Weiss, *Laocoon or the Limits of Language*

ME   Paul Celan, *The Meridian*

OH   Hannah Arendt, *On Humanity in Dark Times: Thoughts about Lessing*

WP   Theodor W. Adorno, *The Meaning of Working through the Past*

SPEAKING THE UNSPEAKABLE
IN POSTWAR GERMANY

INTRODUCTION: AN ARCHIMEDEAN PODIUM

Give me a place to stand and I will move the Earth.

—Archimedes, quoted by Pappus of Alexandria,
Synagoge, book 8

In the short autobiographical prose piece *Ein sehr junges Mädchen trifft Nelly Sachs* (A Very Young Girl Meets Nelly Sachs), Esther Discherheit reimagines her first encounter with a German-Jewish poet, Nelly Sachs, which took place in 1965.[1] Discherheit remembers that she had been deeply impressed by this "meeting," which, albeit mediated through television, nevertheless had the effect of momentarily breaking her and her mother's isolation and loneliness by way of triangulating them with a person with whom they had something in common: like her mother, Sachs had been brought up as an assimilated Jew in the cultivated milieu of Berlin's affluent bourgeois society. Both Sachs's and Discherheit's mothers had responded to the anti-Semitic movement with initial disbelief, and both had survived the Holocaust at the cost of lifelong despair. As the offspring of a Jewish survivor, Discherheit had herself suffered considerably, most notably from the covert

1. Esther Dischereit, *Übungen jüdisch zu sein* (Frankfurt a. M.: Suhrkamp, 1998), 9–15; unpublished translation by Kizer Walker.

anti-Semitism and open hostility she faced growing up in postwar German society. She thus described Sachs's appearance on German television as an eye-opening and truly dramatic experience:

> I sat practically with open mouth in front of the TV, watching high-ranking German politicians giving standing ovations to a Jew. They honored her with a matter-of-factness, which was in complete contradiction to my life and experiences up to that point. That's what it was to me—I was thirteen years old. That was the first unbelievable thing I experienced in connection with this event. Next I heard Nelly Sachs speak. She, a Jew, was able to talk in Germany in a loud and clear voice, with her head raised, and the way she was speaking, Jewish in a completely obvious way, was something that had never existed, not for one day, in our house.[2]

Young as she was, Dischereit had been unaware that in 1965, Sachs's receiving and accepting a major award in Germany was by no means an exceptional occurrence. In the preceding decade, a number of Jewish Holocaust survivors had already been honored by German institutions, and many of these honorees had seized this opportunity to publicly address a broader German audience. But this does not take anything away from Dischereit's astute perception and understanding of the significance of Sachs's intervention. To the contrary, Dischereit's reflections bring to light what was—and still is—unfairly taken for granted. For the pervasive desire for normalcy and recovery had produced an atmosphere in postwar Germany that veiled how incredible it was that Sachs and others like her could speak, and speak publicly, in and about Germany. And yet Sachs's words, which are so direct and accurate that they "hit my [Dischereit's] mother's heart, so that she flushed all over and her eyes shone with sorrow," would not have been possible in 1965 had there not been a precedent.[3] Before Sachs, other major intellectual and literary figures—most notably Theodor W. Adorno, Hannah Arendt, Ingeborg Bachmann, Martin Buber, Paul Celan, Uwe Johnson, Peter Szondi, and Peter Weiss—had given (or staged, as in the case of Weiss) public speeches in Germany that in some way or another took account of the fact that millions of Jews were murdered in German concentration camps and that postwar Germany's public did not seem to care. But in contrast to Sachs, these speakers did not speak in verse but instead experimented with the form of public speech, using it as an instrument for both critical analysis and self-reflection.

For these speakers, nothing was a given when it came to Germany: not the notion of "public" nor the genre of "speech" nor even "speaking" itself. Hence nothing in their speeches conforms easily to a given tradition. To the contrary,

2. Ibid., 14–15.
3. Ibid., 15.

their public speeches are exceptions, experimentations, sometimes even accidents. For what could one possibly say when addressing those responsible for the Second World War and the Holocaust? How could one encounter a people that until recently had embodied the savagery of Nazism? How could one properly speak in the language of persecution and genocide? And most importantly, how could one address any of these questions if they were persistently ignored, dismissed, and denied by the German public?

Elaborated through a series of test cases, *Speaking the Unspeakable in Postwar Germany: Toward a Public Discourse on the Holocaust* traces the aesthetic and communicative processes inscribed in the particular practice of public speaking, while inquiring into the conditions under which various authors, scholars, and philosophers helped shape the formation of a public discourse about the Holocaust in postwar Germany.[4] Problematizing the very premise of public speaking in light of a breach in tradition that had yet to be fully understood, these public speakers unfailingly resisted conventional modes of aesthetic and rhetorical representation. Instead of trying to mend what they perceived as a radical break in historical continuity, or corroborating the myth of a "new beginning," they searched for ways to make this historical rupture rhetorically and semantically discernible and—such is the alternative the medium of public speech presents to these writers and intellectuals—literally audible.[5]

This book thus raises the question of how language failed these public speakers, or how they believed it failed them—a question of particular urgency to the exiled German-speaking Jews who figure prominently in this study, so much so, indeed, that it became their touchstone for the rhetorical and discursive organization of their public speeches. With the exception of Theodor W. Adorno (1903–69), who returned to Germany in 1949 and resumed his teaching duties at Frankfurt University soon after his arrival, as well as Uwe Johnson (1934–84), a German citizen who delivered his speech to the Jewish American Congress (JAC) while living in New York, and Peter Szondi (1929–71), a Hungarian Jew whose speech coincided with his relocation to Berlin, the speakers considered here—Hannah Arendt (1906–75), Martin Buber (1878–1965), Ingeborg Bachmann (1926–73), Paul Celan (1920–70), and Peter Weiss (1916–82)—visited Germany only sporadically. During

---

4. The present study spans the historical period that saw the gradual division of the two Germanys and the development of two separate German states. However, it takes the Federal Republic of Germany as its focal point, since the German Democratic Republic's problematical policies toward the Jews and its ideologically inflated anti-Nazi stance effectively left less room for the development of a discourse about Jewish persecution and a culture of memory. See Jeffrey M. Peck, "East Germany," in *The World Reacts to the Holocaust*, ed. David S. Wyman and Charles H. Rosenzveig (Baltimore: Johns Hopkins University Press, 1996), 447–72; and Małgorzata Pakier and Bo Stråth, eds., *A European Memory? Contested Histories and Politics of Remembrance* (New York: Berghahn Books, 2010).

5. The end of the Second World War was popularly referred to as a *Stunde Null*, a "zero hour" (at 24:00 on May 8, 1945) at which the clock of German history purportedly started ticking afresh.

these visits, then, their native language—enunciated, resisted, and reappropriated in the presence of a live audience—implicates both the speakers and their address-ees in often bizarre events of misguided and failed communication. That is, the breach in tradition caused by the war and the Nazi genocide of the Jewish people strongly and repeatedly manifests itself as a crisis of language, so that the questions of how to speak, how to speak in German, and how to speak to the German public are conveyed and enacted in the rhetorical structure, composition, and delivery of the speeches at hand.

What then is the political scope of these public speeches? While only some speakers (most notably Johnson and Weiss) in fact directly responded to current political controversies, all adopted tactics of resistance that would allow them to dismantle the "restorative" discourse that in their view dominated the Christian conservative politics of Adenauer's Germany.[6] Moreover, they reconfigured the relationship between the public sphere and the very idea of "politics" by drawing attention to the effects of the Nazi past on present-day public life. This was crucial, because, as Arendt explained, they were still under the influence of a major shock caused by the discovery of Auschwitz: "It was really as if an abyss had opened. . . . *This ought not to have happened.* And I don't mean just the number of victims. I mean the method, the fabrication of corpses and so on—I don't need to go into that. This should not have happened. Something happened there to which we can-not reconcile ourselves. None of us ever can."[7] Rather than being predicated on the ideological framework of West German postwar politics with its emphasis on economic growth, political integration, and cultural recovery, their speeches are characterized by their insistence on a historical absence and an ontological loss: the (virtual) absence of Jews and survivors and their living memory in Germany and the concomitant loss of truth and meaning, justice and ethics.[8]

Thus in addition to offering a new entry into the question of postwar Germany's public sphere, this book tackles the issue of the fractured cultural and national identities of a number of German Jews, a problem that had little political resonance in the postwar years. It was up to these individuals to untangle the iniquitous legacy of the anti-Semitic legislation of the Third Reich, which had gradually stripped away the possibility that one could be both a German *and* a Jew. This had profound implications for the public speeches they were to deliver in Germany: no longer

---

6. The epithet *restaurativ* (restorative) is applied by many left-leaning intellectuals of the postwar period.

7. Hannah Arendt, "'What Remains? The Language Remains': A Conversation with Günther Gaus," in *Essays in Understanding, 1930–1954: Formation, Exile, and Totalitarianism*, ed. Jerome Kohn (New York: Harcourt Brace, 1996), 13–14.

8. As Giorgio Agamben writes, "Almost none of the ethical principles our age believed it could recognize as valid have stood the decisive test, that of an *Ethica more Auschwitz demonstrata*." Giorgio Agamben, *Remnants of Auschwitz: The Witness and the Archive*, trans. Daniel Heller-Roazen (New York: Zone Books, 2002), 13.

could they address other Germans as fellow citizens or compatriots, nor could they take for granted a shared culture and knowledge base. In ways both subtle and astonishing, the ideological assertion of a difference thus retained its power in their public speeches. By disrupting the discursive formations of postwar society and by introducing a language that is sometimes hesitant, sometimes taciturn, but always self-consciously (anti)rhetorical, these public speakers exemplify what Alexander Kluge and Oskar Negt would come to define, in their 1972 sociological study, *Öffentlichkeit und Erfahrung* (Public Sphere and Experience), as a *Gegenöffentlichkeit* (counter-public sphere), which, in addition to arising alongside and against the bourgeois public sphere, emerges from historical breaks: "Historical fissures—crises, war, capitulation, revolution, counterrevolution—denote concrete constellations of social forces within which a proletarian public sphere develops. Since the latter has no existence as a ruling public sphere, it has to be reconstructed from such rifts, marginal cases, isolated initiates."[9] Although Kluge and Negt's concept of *Gegenöffentlichkeit* is of course predicated on the proletarian public and the revolutionary working class, it nevertheless includes all those who exist in a state of tension with the dominant public sphere while positing their specificity and differentiation with regard to the bourgeois model.[10] To the degree that the public speakers under discussion subverted the interests of West Germany's majoritarian public sphere through their highly idiosyncratic and nonconformist approaches to public speaking—by essentially breaching the unspoken agreement to remain silent about and turn the page on the mass extermination of Jews—they constitute a counter-public sphere along the lines of that defined by Kluge and Negt.

There are several reasons why Kluge and Negt's notion of a *Gegenöffentlichkeit* is a critical concept for the present study. Firstly, it provides a fitting theoretical framework for a study of public speech or speaking, given that it likewise centers on the construction of an authentic language and new discursive forms that would be genuine to the subjective experience of individuals, enabling them to creatively resist and reappropriate their horizons of experience in an oppositional relation to the bourgeois public.[11] By divulging subjective experiences that undermined the hegemonic discourse on German suffering, and by stating that they represented millions of Jews who had suffered endlessly more, the present set of public speeches became a significant threat to postwar Germany's status quo.[12] Secondly, Kluge and

9. Alexander Kluge and Oskar Negt, *Public Sphere and Experience: Toward an Analysis of the Bourgeois and Proletarian Public Sphere*, trans. Peter Labanyi, Jamie Owen Daniel, and Assenka Oksiloff (Minneapolis: University of Minnesota Press, 1993), xliii.

10. Ibid., 43.

11. Kavita Daiya, *Violent Belongings: Partition, Gender, and National Culture in Postcolonial India* (Philadelphia: Temple University Press, 2008), 12.

12. According to Gilad Margalit, the acknowledgment of German suffering was tantamount to denying German guilt during the postwar era. See Gilad Margalit, *Guilt, Suffering, and Memory: Germany Remembers Its Dead of World War II* (Bloomington: Indiana University Press, 2010). See also

Negt deemphasize the prevalence of the (Habermasian) bourgeois public sphere in order to draw attention to emerging counter-public spheres that defy alienation and fragmentation "from below." The counterpublic thereby offers, as Miriam Hansen puts it, "forms of solidarity and reciprocity that are grounded in a collective experience of marginalization and expropriation."[13] This model of two competing discursive spaces—one a "reconciliation narrative" that exercises hegemony, the other an array of unorthodox, experimental approaches to public speaking—is a useful vehicle for understanding Germany's conflicted public sphere during the postwar years. As various exiled, formerly exiled, or voluntarily exiled literary and intellectual figures began to collide with the limits and exclusions imposed on them by the official discourse of German suffering, the gaps and limitations of West Germany's public sphere began to unravel.[14] Thirdly, the fact that Kluge and Negt extend the notion of politics to all sites of social interaction legitimizes, indeed encourages, this book's focus on ostensibly "alternative" cultural sites of political production, such as literary prize addresses, academic lectures, and theatrical performances. And yet, given the extensive reach of mass media in the postwar period, as well as the concomitant loss of an obvious community of belonging, these instances of public speech are invariably experienced as mediated and volatile. This is in accordance with Kluge and Negt's concept of a counter-public sphere, whereby interventions into public culture are inevitably interpreted through a prism of otherness that is "no longer rooted in face-to-face relations and subject to discursive conflict and negotiation."[15]

This book nevertheless argues that taken together, these events of public speaking helped the formation of a counter-public sphere—to borrow the phrase of one critic, a "modern hybrid site of discursive contestation"—that beginning in the 1950s increasingly challenged the Germans' insensitivity or indifference toward Jewish suffering while calling for a broader acknowledgment of responsibility for the crimes committed by the Nazi regime.[16] It is significant that this counterpublic formed in Germany and in the German language—but through the voices of mostly Jews. This speaks to Gilad Margalit's claim that the awakening of a public discourse on the Holocaust was the product of a Jewish Holocaust narrative's penetration into German discourse. To cite Margalit, "The Jewish story entered German consciousness principally through literary and documentary works by Jews about their Holocaust experiences."[17] While it is certainly true that the work of some of the writers Margalit mentions (most notably Albrecht Goes and Paul Celan) did enter Germany's mainstream literary market, it is important to realize

---

Elisabeth Krimmer, *The Representation of War in German Literature: From 1800 to the Present* (Cambridge: Cambridge University Press, 2010), 110.

13. Miriam Hansen, foreword to Kluge and Negt, *Public Sphere and Experience*, xxxvi.

14. Margalit, *Guilt, Suffering, and Memory*, 78.

15. Hansen, foreword, xxxvi.

16. Daiya, *Violent Belongings*, 12.

17. Margalit, *Guilt, Suffering, and Memory*, 78.

that a majority of Germans did not actually read (or know how to read) their books. The prose and poetry of the theologian Goes appealed mostly to the Protestant *Bildungsbürgertum* (the educated upper and middle class) and Celan's breakthrough poetry collection, *Mohn und Gedächtnis* (Poppy and Memory), was praised for its magic, surrealist, and aesthetic qualities, and not for providing an unprecedented perspective into the inner life of a Holocaust survivor.[18] Hence it is doubtful whether these narratives played a substantial role in creating public awareness of the scope of the Nazi crimes. Public speeches by contrast provided these literary figures with a broader and more comprehensive public platform from which they could effectively divulge their individual experience and their intellectual understanding of it to a national audience that they would otherwise never reach.

Even though the contemporary audiences often failed to register the subversive potential of these public speeches, so that most of them did not have a noticeable impact at first, the speeches nevertheless set the stage for what many consider a more "revolutionary" episode in German history, the protest movement of 1968. Probing the limits of *Vergangenheitsbewältigung*—a discursive formation that centered around the claim that postwar German society could "cope with" the past by focusing on future-oriented activity—they foreshadow the intense debate over the *Vaterschuld* (silence of our fathers) incited by the generation of 1968.[19] Thus reconstructed, the public speeches to be considered here become the sign of an eruption of dissent that was already imminent in the 1950s and early 1960s but that crystallized only around 1966–67, when a younger, newly formed public of students began to participate in demonstrations, sit-ins, and protest actions arranged by the Sozialistischer Deutscher Studentenbund (SDS; Socialist German Students Union) and other radical organizations. The present book thus traces the period of postwar Germany's engagement with the Nazi past from the first public speaker to mention the Holocaust (Buber in 1953) to the first audiences (members of the SDS and the JAC, respectively, in 1967) to a refusal to listen. For the purposes of this book, the "new left's" widening focus on, and concomitant reinterpretation of, the Nazi past will come to signal the end of the postwar era, and with it the stifling of the counterpublic that is the object of this study.

The public speakers that figure in this study lacked the relatively free and open discursive space of the politicized university. For them the breach in tradition also manifested itself as the loss of a politically progressive public sphere. For while the public sphere is inherently a challenging environment, the speakers under

18. Barbara Wiedemann gives ample evidence that the vast majority of Celan's readers did not even realize that he was a Jew. Barbara Wiedemann, *"Ein Faible für Tübingen": Paul Celan in Württemberg; Deutschland und Paul Celan* (Tübingen: Klöpfer und Meyer, 2013). One critic issued a warning to German teachers making them aware that a discussion of Celan's *Todesfuge* "can easily glide over into a discussion of the persecution of Jews." See Jochen Vogt, "Treffpunkt im Unendlichen? Über Peter Weiss und Paul Celan," *Peter Weiss Jahrbuch* 4 (1995): 102–21, here 113.

19. On the controversial term *Vergangenheitsbewältigung*, see chapter 8. See also Thorsten Eitz and Georg Stötzel, *Wörterbuch der "Vergangenheitsbewältigung": Die NS-Vergangenheit im öffentlichen Sprachgebrauch* (Hildesheim: Georg Olms Verlag, 2007).

discussion faced exceptionally inauspicious circumstances because they had not previously entered the public sphere of general cultural discourse in postwar Germany. The only speaker to routinely reach a large audience with his radio lectures was Adorno: a ubiquitous presence in postwar Germany's media landscape, he was skilled in expressing his philosophical thought in a style that would be relatively accessible for a mass audience. But not one of these figures conformed to the image of the moderately left-wing (and male) German intellectual whom Jürgen Habermas, in his seminal doctoral thesis published in 1962 as *Strukturwandel der Öffentlichkeit* (The Structural Transformation of the Public Sphere), had identified as the representative of Germany's emergent public sphere.[20] As a result the speakers first had to produce the kind of public in which their speeches might take effect.

Their efforts to make a practical contribution to a public sphere from which they themselves felt alienated and excluded were accompanied by parallel attempts of left-leaning German scholars to historicize and theorize the public sphere (yet in a way that often reinscribed the division between home-grown public intellectuals and foreigners): as the number of theoretical speculations on the topic published in the postwar period indicates, the issue of the public sphere was clearly at stake. Habermas's *Strukturwandel der Öffentlichkeit* exemplifies what one might describe as a widespread pessimism among younger German theorists regarding the perceived decline of the bourgeois public sphere. As Habermas writes, "Tendencies pointing to the collapse of the public sphere are unmistakable, for while its scope is expanding impressively, its function has become progressively insignificant."[21] Arendt, whose influence is strongly felt in Habermas's book, had anticipated this renewed interest in the problem of the public sphere with the 1960 German version, *Vita Activa*, of her 1958 study, *The Human Condition*, and her book will provide some of the theoretical background for the discussion in chapter 1.[22]

Habermas's case is interesting, however, because his early work so clearly marks him as a member of a younger generation who did not experience the Third Reich as adults. In contrast to Arendt and Habermas's teachers Max Horkheimer and Theodor W. Adorno, whose confidence in human rationality had been profoundly shaken by Auschwitz, Habermas retained his confidence in the public sphere as the mainstay facilitator of democracy. Habermas to be sure continued to hold up key principles of the Enlightenment: freedom of thought, limitations on governmental

---

20. Jürgen Habermas, *The Structural Transformation of the Public Sphere: An Inquiry into a Category of Bourgeois Society*, trans. Thomas Burger and Frederick Lawrence (Cambridge, MA: MIT Press, 1989).

21. Habermas, *The Structural Transformation*, 4. And further: "Two tendencies dialectically related to each other indicated a breakdown of the public sphere. While it penetrated more *spheres* of society, it simultaneously lost its political *function*, namely: that of subjecting the affairs that it had made public to the control of a critical public" (140).

22. Hannah Arendt, *The Human Condition* (Chicago: University of Chicago Press, 1998); hereafter abbreviated as *HC*.

power, a free market economy, and a transparent system of government in which the rights of all citizens would be protected. The problem with Habermas's fairly idealized account of Germany's public sphere is that his notion of the public sphere subsumes difference by excluding groups that do not form a majority of the total population: ethnic minorities, women, and the working class. In this context, Kluge and Negt's insistence on competing public spheres, founded on the "substantial life-interests" of contradictory identities, begins to take on significance.[23] By investigating the conditions of possibility for instigating a public discourse about the Holocaust in Germany, this book sheds light on the speaker's inscription within a ritualized network of problematical—anti- or philo-Semitic and thus ultimately repressive—relationships. Following Kluge and Negt, this book does not claim to resolve the tension between these individuals' life interests on the one hand, and the public sphere's claim to represent society as a whole on the other, nor will it attempt to fill this sociocultural gap. Its purpose is neither to define the essence of a German-Jewish experience, which is invariably fractured into an array of oftentimes incompatible cultural and national identities, nor to make the experience of survivorship available to a contemporary readership. Rather it makes a contribution to the study of West Germany's public sphere by investigating its "use value" (Kluge and Negt) for a number of intellectuals who have since become canonical figures of Germany's cultural—but not political—landscape.[24] By examining whether and how these public speakers were able to articulate their experience and interpretation of past events so as to mobilize their audiences toward a major change of consciousness, *Speaking the Unspeakable* offers a new approach to the problem of the public sphere, a concept as much at stake today as it was during the postwar era.

The Public Sphere

In the 1950s and 1960s a number of intellectual figures thus entered and subverted postwar Germany's public sphere through their politically minded yet antideliberative, epideictic yet noncongratulatory speeches. As a rhetorical genre, epideictic speech is a hybrid form that does not impinge on the cultural or political context in which it occurs but instead acts upon the nature of rhetoric itself—and hence it achieves authority more from style than from meaning. Yet the charge of empty rhetorical sophistry must not be leveled against the *Preisreden* (prize addresses) considered here. While they are certainly self-referential and often display a nondialectic and monologic structure—some indeed border on the language of literary prose and even poetry—they nevertheless attracted a substantial public audience, and hence were inherently political events. Producing what Arendt defined as a "space

---

23. Kluge and Negt, *Public Sphere and Experience*, xlvi.
24. Ibid., 1.

of appearance," these speech events occasioned gatherings of a plurality of actors and speakers, which is, according to Arendt, the condition sine qua non of politics (*HC*, 199). In addition to *Preisreden*, this book will also explore other forms of (and forums for) public speaking—a university lecture by Szondi, Adorno's radio talks, Weiss's avant-garde theater, and Johnson's public speech at the Jewish American Congress, the latter embedded in narrative prose—that allowed these speakers to register and critically examine the discourses that informed their aesthetic and scholarly practice.

In each case, the question of dissent concerns both the political and the cultural structure of postwar society. Politically, some of these speakers were disappointed that the military, political, and social forces of the past were allowed to persist in the present. Adorno suggests that the conditions of repression, which had laid the psychological and ideological groundwork for the Holocaust, remained largely unchanged even two decades after the end of World War II. Both Buber and Arendt decry the rearmament of the Federal Republic and the stationing of atomic weapons in Germany, while Weiss brings the defective judicial system into the fray of public debate.[25] Worst of all, millions of committed Nazis had been integrated into the new democracy, a practice that Johnson and Szondi criticize as scandalous leadership continuity between the Third Reich and the present day, which they took as another symptom of Germany's failure to embrace an improved and truly democratic order. Looking beyond the scope of the nation's political structure, some of these literary intellectuals are also concerned with the commodification of culture and literature. Ironically tagged *Literaturbetrieb* (literary establishment), a term that echoes Adorno's *Kulturindustrie* (culture industry), the world of letters in particular seemed to be organized around a few prominent groups—most notably the Gruppe 47 (Group 47)—while avant-garde authors were either excluded or assimilated and "domesticated."[26] Symptomatic of these efforts was a trend to create and reinstate literary awards for both aspiring and recognized writers: in the period between 1950 and 1960, about sixty literary prizes were thus (re)established in the Federal Republic alone, among them the Georg-Büchner-Preis, the Literaturpreis der Freien Hansestadt Bremen, the Lessing-Preis der Freien und Hansestadt Hamburg, and the Goethepreis der Stadt Frankfurt.[27]

25. See Kluge and Negt, *Public Sphere and Experience*, 1; and Martin Buber, *Genuine Dialogue and the Possibilities of Peace* (1953), in Buber, *Pointing the Way*, ed. Maurice Friedman (New York: Harper and Brothers, 1957), 232–39; hereafter abbreviated as *GD*. See also Arendt, *The Human Condition*, 176.

26. See Hans M. Enzensberger, "Die Clique," in *Almanach der Gruppe 47*, ed. Hans Werner Richter (Reinbek: Rowohlt, 1962), 271.

27. Dieter Sulzer, Hildegard Dieke, and Ingrid Kußmaul, eds., *Der Georg-Büchner-Preis 1951–1978* (Marbach am Neckar: Deutsche Akademie für Sprache und Dichtung Darmstadt, 1978), 347–67, here 350. See also Wolfgang Schwerbrock, "Literaturpreise und Öffentlichkeit," *Frankfurter Allgemeine Zeitung*, November 4, 1961.

These literary awards and their respective prize ceremonies exemplify the multidimensionality of the German notion of *Öffentlichkeit* (public sphere), which, though commonly understood to refer to the concrete social institutions where meanings are articulated and negotiated, as well as to "the collective body constituted by and in this process," as Miriam Hansen writes, also denotes a psychosocial, ideational realm that according to Arendt "comes into being wherever men are together in the manner of speech and action."[28] That is to say, these literary prizes encouraged the public to discuss and take interest in contemporary German culture and literature. By honoring writers and intellectuals, federal and local governments would further nurture both their political reputation and their cultural prestige. Providing for the large majority of the occasions on which postwar writers and intellectuals gave public speeches, literary awards were thus used to rehabilitate Germany's status as a *Kulturnation* (nation of culture) and help determine who would best represent its standards and values when the time came to write the history of postwar Germany.

It is no coincidence that a considerable number of these literary prizes were awarded to Jewish intellectuals who were living in exile and would return only temporarily to Germany. Jews were thus being reclaimed as fellow Germans, while their previously asserted racial or ethnic "difference" was disavowed on the grounds that, after all, they had been born in Germany, spoke German as a mother tongue, or at any rate wrote for a German readership. Those exiles whom the Nazis had deprived of their German citizenship on political and racial grounds were now entitled to renaturalization according to Article 116, Paragraph 2 of the German constitution, the *Grundgesetz*.[29] Yet with the exception of Adorno, who renewed his German citizenship in 1955, the public speakers considered here did not seek to repatriate: Arendt, a secular German Jew, never reapplied for German citizenship, even though she took her German readers seriously enough to personally produce German versions of books she had originally written in English. In a similar vein, Weiss, son of a Jewish-Hungarian father and a Swiss mother, acquired Swedish citizenship in 1946 and intermittently wrote in Swedish, but nevertheless continued to "dream" in the German language.[30] Szondi, a Hungarian Jew who learned German as a foreign language, permanently settled in Berlin in 1961 but maintained his Swiss nationality. Celan, born into a German-speaking Jewish family in Bukovina, wrote German poems that were, however, infused with Hebrew expressions and terminology. A lecturer in German at the École Normale

---

28. Hansen, foreword, ix; and Arendt, *The Human Condition*, 199.

29. This new law supersedes the German principle according to which nationality is determined by blood rather than birthright, a principle that goes back to an 1842 law that served to prevent the naturalization of Jews.

30. As Weiss notes, "Takes notes in Swedish, but dreams in German." Peter Weiss, *Notizbücher: 1960–1971* (Frankfurt a. M.: Suhrkamp, 1981), 1:678–79; my translation.

Supérieure, he became a French citizen in 1955. Buber, an Austrian and later Israeli Jew, had coproduced (with Franz Rosenzweig) a new German translation—in his own words *Verdeutschung* (Germanification)—of the Hebrew Bible. And Bachmann, whose earliest poems exhibit a certain affinity with *Heimatdichtung* (local, patriotic literature), soon harbored very negative feelings toward her native Austria and gradually identified with the victims of the Holocaust.[31] Johnson, finally, born in Pomerania and much to his displeasure labeled "writer of the divided Germany," actively sought out encounters with Jewish immigrants, particularly during the two and a half years he lived in New York.[32] Addressing the Holocaust as an international, rather than narrowly German event, Johnson sheds critical light on the ramifications of Germany's so-called *Sonderweg* (special path).

This book is about public speakers, some of whom are Germans or Jews and some of whom are, or used to be, both. Given, however, the range of different conceptions of what it means to be a "German Jew" at this historical juncture, the very notion seems void of significance—but it nevertheless *matters* whether a specific speaker is Jewish or not. Devoted as they all are to the memory of the Jewish victims of the Nazi regime, these figures cannot be grouped into a single defining sociocultural or political category, and they certainly transcend the artificial pseudo-scientific racial boundaries drawn up by the Nazi regime. Instead they represent a miniature model of what Arendt defines as a "human plurality, [namely,] the paradoxical plurality of unique beings" (*HC*, 176): differing not only in terms of their ethnic or national identities but also in terms of their human essence, their absolute difference from one another is greater than their relative difference from the German nation or "race."

Although the different parts of this book organize the speeches under discussion around the three theoretical concepts of self-revelation, dialogue, and testimony, to be completed by a final section on the role of the radio, other combinations, based on the biographical affinities of, or the intellectual, even emotional, connections among these writers, would be equally valid. For instance, both Arendt and Weiss wrote books conjuring up the theatrical aspects of Nazi trials; Szondi authored some of the most canonical essays on Celan's poetry, a scholarly expertise he shared with his mentor, Adorno; Arendt asked Bachmann to translate her book on the Eichmann trial; Johnson produced a poignant story about his "pilgrimage" to Bachmann's graveside in Klagenfurt; both Buber and Arendt were associated with

---

31. Eva B. Revesz thus argues that Bachmann's "lyrical voice evolves into an increasingly traumatized realization of the horrors through a projective identification with the victims. This transferential identification becomes so strong that the distinction between self and other breaks down entirely in what the intellectual historian Dominick LaCapra has termed 'secondary traumatization and surrogate victimage.'" Eva B. Revesz, "Poetry after Auschwitz: Tracing Trauma in Ingeborg Bachmann's Lyric Work," *Monatshefte* 99, no. 2 (Summer 2007): 198.

32. Uwe Johnson, *Begleitumstände: Frankfurter Vorlesungen* (Frankfurt a. M.: Suhrkamp, 1980), 336.

the Zionist movement. A constellation of public speeches given by eight congenial yet heterogeneous intellectuals, this book proposes just one of many possible patterns or configurations. Hence the imaginary lines drawn from one public speech to the next, from books to speeches, and from Germans to Jews, reveal an intricate network of influences and interrelations. A loosely affiliated faction rather than a cohesive group along the lines of, for instance, the Gruppe 47, the public speakers who are the focus of this book constitute a counterpublic that emerges from sometimes remote and abstract relationships: the breaking of communicative rules and the absence of personal and communal certainty take the place of ritualized meetings and formal invitations. But although they are defined negatively, in terms of acts of opposition, interruption, and skepticism, there is among these figures a level of cohesion through integrity and moral conviction. The latter does not necessarily result from their being Jewish (and hence persecuted, exiled, and deprived of a proper voice during and beyond the Nazi period). Instead it is the cohesion of a shared subject position, defined by the common concern for, and the determination to give a voice to, those who had been persecuted, exiled, and deprived of a proper voice.

In that way, this book explores whether the conceptual space of a German-Jewish diaspora, defined through the experience of suffering in concentration camps or from exile, be it self-imposed or not, fulfills the premise of an objective "Archimedean" vantage point from which these speakers could help redefine the once (presumed to be) clearly demarcated parameters of Germany's public sphere. Public oration calls for a distant vantage point from which a speaker can perceive his or her object of study—in this case Germany's unresolved relationship to the Nazi past—with the largest possible degree of objectivity and a view of totality. As Archimedes's theory of the lever maintains, the greater the distance between the fulcrum of a lever and the object to be lifted, the stronger the motive force that will be applied to it. By the same token, the ability to assume a detached and independent standpoint is taken to increase a thinker's—and by extension speaker's—capability to survey his object of study and see it in relation to all other things. The question that arises from this analogy, then, concerns the possible forces set in motion by public speakers who occupy such an assumed location outside Germany's political and cultural coordinates. By avowing and mobilizing their status as Jews who are no longer Germans, and as Germans and Austrians who feel that they do not belong, they effectively retain the kind of critical distance necessary to disentangle the dense texture of Germany's public sphere, and as a result apply an unusual amount of leverage to some of its contradictions, conflicts, and problems.

Rhetoric, Event, Enunciation

Another important vector of this book is the discipline of rhetoric, a field German theorists have long not been interested in investigating. Their desire to eliminate rhetoric stands in sharp contrast to modernist cultural tendencies in France, Great Britain, and the United States that "have created . . . the conditions for a renaissance of rhetoric, which today is asserting itself in all fields of intellectual endeavor and cultural production," as John Bender and David E. Wellbery note.[33] Emphasizing the ways in which a number of public speakers distanced themselves from classical rhetoric as a coherent cultural practice or doctrine, the present study thus situates itself in a disciplinary field that Bender and Wellbery have defined as *"an age not of rhetoric, but of rhetoricality*, the age, that is, of a generalized rhetoric that penetrates to the deepest levels of human experience."[34]

One reason why rhetoric underwent significant revision in the German context is that it was wholly overdetermined at the historical juncture of post-Fascism. It is a trope of postwar German rhetorical scholarship that in light of Josef Goebbels's propaganda speeches, the very notion of "rhetoric" has become a pejorative term.[35] The demagogic power of Goebbels's *Sportpalastrede* (Speech at the Berlin Sports Palace, 1943), for instance, is clearly an effect of its rhetorical force: campaigning for the idea of a "total war," Goebbels used persuasion and a series of suggestive questions to raise his audience's level of patriotism and militancy.[36] And Adolf Hitler, in addition to dedicating an entire chapter of *Mein Kampf* (My Struggle, 1925–26) to the topic of rhetorical speech, effectively instituted an academy of rhetoric to instruct aspiring party functionaries in propaganda, political speech, and mass agitation.[37]

Yet, in the history and theory of German-language literature and philosophy since 1945, relatively little attention has been paid to the place of public speeches delivered by major figures in those fields. While ancient Greek and Latin orations play a central role in the curricula of classics departments and the time-honored *Lateinschule* (grammar school), their German successors are taught in just a handful of rhetoric departments and are rarely studied in their own right as part of an intrinsically German tradition. Existing volumes on postwar German speech often emphasize the political and propagandistic aspects of rhetoric by focusing on deliberative speeches given by politicians and state officials while neglecting

33. John Bender and David E. Wellbery, eds., *The Ends of Rhetoric: History, Theory, Practice* (Stanford, CA: Stanford University Press, 1990), 25.

34. Ibid.

35. See, for instance, Hellmut Geissner, *Rede in der Öffentlichkeit: Eine Einführung in die Rhetorik* (Stuttgart: Kohlhammer, 1969), 19; Walter Jens, *Von deutscher Rede* (Munich: Piper, 1969); Gerhard Storz, "Zur Diskussion über die verachtete Rhetorik," *Stuttgarter Zeitung*, November 31, 1964; January 9, 1965; March 27, 1965).

36. See Iring Fetcher, "Wollt ihr den totalen Krieg?," in *Joseph Goebbels im Berliner Sportpalast 1943* (Hamburg: Europäische Verlagsanstalt, 1998), 103; and Günter Moltmann, "Goebbels' Rede zum totalen Krieg am 18. Februar 1943," *Vierteljahreshefte für Zeitgeschichte* 12, no. 1 (1964): 13–43.

37. See chapter 6, "The Struggle of the Early Period—the Significance of the Spoken Word," in Adolf Hitler, *My Struggle* (London: Hurst & Blackett, 1937). For an analysis of Hitler's rhetoric, see Kenneth Burke, *The Philosophy of Literary Form* (Berkeley: University of California Press, 1967), 191–220.

other forms of public speech that are also much harder to classify. Focused on their argumentative content, these studies often judge public speeches against—rather than contrast them with—the classical discipline and conventions of rhetoric, and thus fail to pinpoint the political and cultural specificity of postwar speeches, and in particular their ostensible resistance to the discipline of rhetoric. Finally, such studies usually neglect the question of how these speeches relate to other forms of intellectual practice and do not examine it in a broader framework that embraces social, political, cultural, and aesthetic questions alike.[38]

Traditional assumptions about—and significant revisions of—Germany's long-standing rhetorical tradition are everywhere at play in the public speeches under discussion. The speakers could not help but write their speeches in response to this tradition and in an effort to interrogate its conditions and premises. This is particularly true for Arendt and Buber, both exiled German-Jewish scholars who returned during the 1950s to deliver speeches in Frankfurt's Paulskirche (St. Paul's Church), which more than any other location in Germany embodied the idea of—and hopes invested in—deliberative speech as a pillar of parliamentary democracy.[39] It is no coincidence that the German Friedenspreis des deutschen Buchhandels (Peace Award of the German Book Trade) has been awarded at this particular site, given that it housed the earliest sessions of Germany's first freely elected parliament in 1848–49. Hence Arendt and Buber were surely aware of the famous speeches given by members of the National Assembly at that time—Ludwig Uhland, Heinrich Freiherr von Gagern, Ernst Moritz Arndt, and Ludwig Simon, among others—when they stepped onto the historic podium of the secularized church.[40]

In the German tradition, public speeches often functioned as catalysts for conservative, patriotic, and militant ideologies. The speeches delivered in post–World War II Germany are, however, in no way easy allegories for the rebuilding of a more progressive and democratic nation. On the contrary, what the speeches that are the focus of this study have in common is that they stand in opposition not only to reactionary efforts of evincing patriotism and national identity through public speech, but also to the ultimately facile construction of a—supposedly—pluralistic discourse about the past in postwar Germany. With an intimation of defiance that

---

38. See, for instance, Detlef Grieswelle, *Politische Rhetorik* (Wiesbaden: DUV, 2000); Kurt Spang, *Rede* (Bamberg: C. C. Buchners, 1987). More recently, Jan C. L. König has made considerable headway in addressing the linguistic, communicative, and pragmatic idiosyncrasies of public speech while also taking into account their embeddedness in political, cultural, and physical contexts. See Jan C. L. König, *Über die Wirkungsmacht der Rede: Strategien politischer Eloquenz in Literatur und Alltag* (Göttingen: Vandenhoeck und Ruprecht, 2011).

39. Buber, "Genuine Dialogue"; and Hannah Arendt, "Karl Jaspers: A Laudatio," in *Men in Dark Times* (New York: Harcourt and Brace, 1968): 71–80; hereafter abbreviated as *KJ*.

40. For an overview of the rhetorical culture of the Frankfurter Nationalversammlung (Frankfurt Parliament) of 1848–49, see Helmut Heiber, "Die Rhetorik der Paulskirche" (Diss. masch., Berlin, 1953). A selection of national assembly speeches is published in Walter Hinderer, *Deutsche Reden* (Stuttgart: Reclam, 1973) and in Gert Ueding, *Deutsche Reden von Luther bis zur Gegenwart* (Frankfurt a. M.: Suhrkamp, 1999).

seems to emerge from a shared skepticism with regard to rhetoric as an intellectual and cultural practice per se, the majority of public speakers considered here
emancipate their literary prose or scholarly erudition from rhetorical persuasiveness. If they set their speeches apart from the discipline of rhetoric, it is, however,
not because they agree with classical Greek philosophers who contended that persuasion could undermine their quest for truth, depth, and interiority, but rather
because they reject the very idea of persuasion on the basis of principle.[41] Ambivalent about exerting influence on and control over their listeners, these speakers
engage critically with the disciplinary conventions of rhetoric. Rather than guiding
or manipulating their audience toward adopting their own ideas and convictions,
they introduce them to fundamental philosophical and theoretical problems, as
well as to unanswered and sometimes indeed unanswerable questions, doubtless
because at this point in time, straightforward opinions and tangible solutions are
simply not available to them. Some speakers dispose of rules and topoi to speak as
antirhetorically as possible, while others speak in an utterly nonargumentative language that explicitly rejects persuasiveness. What is most striking, however, is that
all of these speakers magnify the event character of their public speeches—namely,
that they are anchored both temporally (in a specific occasion) and spatially (in the
public realm). In other words, for them, "speech" is not a genre but an *event*. After
all, public speech interweaves different ontological registers (of a specific time and
place but also of less tangible—psychological and metaphysical—parameters), and
is therefore, following Josef Vogl's definition of the Deleuzian *événement*, neither
an object or item nor a referent, but rather "an aesthetic, a poetic thing."[42]

Taking up Aristotle's concern, first articulated in his seminal treatise *On Rhetoric*, with the material situations in which public speaking occurs, and putting pressure on the pragmatic aspects of their public speeches, these speakers pay increased
attention to the semiotics of discourse at the expense of the semantics of words.[43]
What matters to them is not what certain statements mean but *how* they mean—
that is, how meaning is produced in the act of speaking and through the logic of its
oral delivery and public reception. Viewing their own speeches as pragmatic, communicative events, these speakers are keenly aware of the wider social relations in

---

41. See Plato, *Phaedrus*, trans. C. J. Rowe (London: Aris & Phillips, 1999), 91; and Aristotle, *On Rhetoric: A Theory of Civic Discourse*, trans. George A. Kennedy (Oxford: Oxford University Press, 1991), 35.

42. Josef Vogl, "Was ist ein Ereignis?," in *Deleuze und die Künste*, ed. Peter Gente and Peter Weibel
(Frankfurt a. M.: Suhrkamp, 2007), 69; my translation.

43. The idea of a semiotics of discourse can be attributed to Charles Sanders Peirce, who observed
that signification is not an inherent property of the signs produced in communication, but rather a product of the relationship between the intentions of these signs and their perception and apprehension by a
listener. See on this Jacques Fontanille, *The Semiotics of Discourse*, trans. Heidi Bostic (New York: Peter
Lang Publishing, 2006), 10. On the notion of discourse, see Michel Foucault, who argues that meaning
emerges from power structures and other social and historical determinants that regulate what can be
said and thought at a given time and by whom. Michel Foucault, *The Archaeology of Knowledge*, trans.
A. M. Sheridan Smith (London: Tavistock Publications, 1972).

which their speeches take place. In this way, their activity as public speakers tallies with a contemporaneous theoretical paradigm: the increased focus on the *situatedness* of speech in the disciplines of linguistics and rhetoric of the postwar period and the concomitant insight that language is largely unintelligible outside the social conditions and purposes in which it is embedded. Most commonly associated with the Anglo-Saxon movement of new rhetoric, but equally central to communication theory and post-Saussurean structuralist linguistics of the 1950s and 1960s, the insight into the situatedness of language led to an increased preoccupation with the social and psychological conditions of discourse and the claim that rather than ever being "neutral," language is pragmatic, rhetorical, and persuasive. As Kenneth Burke writes, "Wherever there is persuasion, there is rhetoric. And wherever there is 'meaning' there is persuasion."[44]

The question of persuasion leads to another key term of this project: performativity. While it is true that the public speakers under discussion take a resistant stance toward—or seek to rise above—rhetorical persuasion, because it is naturally associated with Nazi demagogues who sought the support of the masses by appealing to popular passions and fears, this does not mean that their speeches are necessarily unpersuasive. As a matter of fact, they sometimes evince a persuasive force in a more immediate and indeed enduring manner than classical deliberative speech. Instead of trying to convince their audiences to think and feel in a certain way, which would induce them to take specific actions, the speakers, as it were, perform these actions themselves, and they do so by means of simple utterances, such as by saying, for instance, "I thank you" (Celan) or, to cite a second example, "I appeal to you" (Buber). To be sure, by shifting from locutionary to illocutionary statements, or, in the language of pragmatic linguist J. L. Austin, from constative to "performative" locutions, their speeches generate movements of force that perform concrete and immediate actions.[45] For according to Austin's definition, a *performative*, rather than conveying meaning through a representational system of signs, produces and transforms the pragmatic speech situation itself. A more direct form of linguistic activity than persuasive rhetoric, it neutralizes the antithesis of word and action by actually *constituting* the object to which it is meant to refer. Having no referent outside itself, the utterance then *is* the action.

One such performative speech is Szondi's 1961 *Antrittsrede* (inaugural address) at Berlin's Free University.[46] A young professor about to take on his first academic position in Germany, Szondi is centrally concerned with the question of the extent to which intellectual figures like Walter Benjamin were excluded from the career

44. Kenneth Burke, *A Rhetoric of Motives* (New York: Prentice-Hall, 1950), 172.
45. J. L. Austin, *How to Do Things with Words* (Cambridge, MA: Harvard University Press, 1962), 6.
46. Peter Szondi, *Hope in the Past: On Walter Benjamin*, in *On Textual Understanding and Other Essays*, trans. Harvey Mendelsohn (Minneapolis: University of Minnesota Press, 1986), 145–60; hereafter abbreviated as *HP*.

prospects offered to non-Jewish scholars by the German academy. Yet Szondi refrains from explicitly criticizing a discriminatory practice that extended from the Weimar Republic and much earlier into the postwar period. Instead he attempts to improve Benjamin's status among academics by quoting extensively from—and thus forcing them to listen to—a broad range of Benjamin's writings. It is then precisely by way of these performative quotations that Szondi obliges his audience to retrace and reflect on the material and cognitive processes that resulted in Benjamin's works while also counteracting the continuing discrimination against a Jewish intellectual.

When viewed against the backdrop of both classical Aristotelian and contemporaneous rhetorical theory, it becomes evident that there is a tension in the public speeches under consideration, between their desire to register and critique the deceptiveness and potential abuse of classical rhetoric on the one hand, and their equally powerful desire to meet the communicative challenge of public speaking on the other. By reading these speeches in conjunction with the concurrent rediscovery of persuasion as perhaps the most critical and also most problematic element of rhetoric, and the corresponding concern with the pragmatic situatedness of discourse and language, the present study explores the ways in which public speakers instrumentalize—or fail to instrumentalize—language, while describing the social, political, and psychological factors that determine how (efficiently) information is transmitted from sender to receiver in each individual case. Because these speeches are contingent on a specific social context and historical situation, there is considerable tension between the speakers' intentions and the ways in which these intentions are deflected by the enunciative event of their speech. The book thus productively extends the discussion of linguists' insistence on the conditions of possibility that determine events of enunciation.

Involving speaking subjects as well as listeners, public speech does not behave as a fixed, passive medium. With this in mind, the present study seeks to account for the semantic structure of both its performance and its reception in West Germany's public sphere. In other words, this study treats public speech as a "complicated dynamic system of interdependencies" that includes a communicator, a message, a recipient, and the medium.[47] For contrary to written communication, where the act of writing and its reception remain strictly separate, public speech occurs in the form of a bidirectional exchange whereby the reception of a speech feeds back into its presentation. This can take the form of projected audience reactions, which a speaker takes into consideration while drafting a public speech, or that of actual pragmatic feedback, which he or she receives during its delivery. In the latter case, the speaker may then choose not to abide by the script by modifying, omitting, or adding particular statements. That speeches are communicative

---

47. Grieswelle, *Politische Rhetorik*, 52.

processes constantly reshaped by the subject's experience or interpretation of the event is exemplified by Johnson's speech at the Jewish American Congress in New York.[48] According to Johnson's account, the hostile reactions of the audience made him aware of the inadequacy of his script, which he then cut short to face a question-and-answer session. By thus illustrating the role played by the audience and by staging the invasion of reception into his speech, Johnson demonstrates that his addressees, though absent from the scene of writing, are active participants in the delivery of his public address. The same holds for the process of persuasion. Taking the form of a bidirectional exchange, Johnson's speech compelled his audience to identify with his person and message, but also allowed his audience to impose their criticisms on him.

In addition to offering an operational definition of what is meant by the "speech event," the chapter on Johnson demonstrates how the novelist complicated the formal status of his original script in relation to the event of its enunciation. By fictionalizing a speech he gave in reality and by providing the reader with a revised version of the original script, which was essentially a "reading" of his proper text, Johnson raised a number of important questions regarding the relationship between writing and public speech. Which version of his address is the "original"—the script, its enunciation in 1967, or its fictionalization in the novel *Jahrestage* (Anniversaries), the first volume of which appeared in 1970? Is a public speech that is being revised for print and adapted for broadcasting still an oration? And given that public speeches survive in the form of written texts, why insist on the oral specificity of the genre? Conceived and circulated within the parameters of both orality and writing, speeches do not precede writing logically or temporally, as in most cases the spoken words are intimately bound to the properties of a preconceived and premeditated script. For unless a public speech is entirely improvised, the process of writing precedes its oral delivery. Hence the written text is neither temporally secondary nor spatially exterior to (public) speech. As a reading of Weiss's play *Die Ermittlung* (The Investigation) will demonstrate, some forms of public speaking—in this case, witness testimonies uttered in a Frankfurt courtroom and on a theater stage, respectively—are severed from their oral specificity.[49] In Weiss's play, the spoken testimony of human beings cannot compete against the factuality of written and printed artifacts, particularly since the former are ventriloquized by actors who do not act in any conventional theatrical sense. In curtailing their emotional power, the actors on stage disavow their human authenticity, which in turn makes them unable to controvert evidence against evidentiary facts.

---

48. Uwe Johnson, *Anniversaries: From the Life of Gesine Cresspahl*, trans. Leila Vennewitz (New York: Harcourt Brace Jovanovich, 1975), 167–70; hereafter abbreviated as *AN*.

49. Peter Weiss, *The Investigation: A Play*, trans. Jon Swan and Ulu Grosbard (New York: Atheneum, 1966); hereafter abbreviated as *IN*.

Most of the speeches to be considered here were recited and read word for word from a manuscript on the occasion of their original public presentation. As the site of an unpredictable interplay between a prepared script and a unique situation, these public speeches evince a series of reversals. Firstly, they subvert the Platonic principle according to which the human voice functions as the most accurate conveyer of meaning.[50] Contradicting the traditional assumption that the voice elucidates text and that spoken words interpret themselves, speakers like Bachmann and Celan fail to adapt such a "hermeneutically expressive" diction.[51] Marked by the speakers' quiet, monotonous, and seemingly disconnected tones of voice, Celan's and Bachmann's oral delivery contradicts, rather than expresses, their statements. Secondly, the majority of speeches resist the conventional conflation of voice and person(ality), being and utterance. Refuting the logocentric paradigm according to which speech functions as an unmediated vessel of meaning, they fail to reveal self-presence and being.[52] A case in point is Arendt's Lessing Prize address *Von der Menschlichkeit in finsteren Zeiten* (On Humanity in Dark Times: Thoughts about Lessing), a speech in which the speaker's voice did not "flow" directly from her "soul."[53] To the contrary, Arendt's spoken words—and specifically those that refer to the speaker herself as the subject of enunciation—suspended her person in discourse and thereby thwarted Arendt's attempt at revealing herself.

Overturning the traditional assumption that contrary to writing, oral deliberation is analogous to dialogic exchange, the speeches under discussion tend to be monologic, even self-absorbed. Instead of explaining, rephrasing, and strategically repeating in an effort to minimize or correct misunderstandings, some of the speakers refused to interact with their addressees. The oftentimes patently antidialogical character of public speech is particularly palpable in Celan's Büchner Prize address *Der Meridian* (The Meridian), where his frequent and almost compulsive use of the rhetorical figure of apostrophe—he repeated the formula "Ladies and gentlemen"

---

50. See, for instance, Hans-Georg Gadamer on the difference between interpreting written and spoken language: "In contrast to the spoken word there is no other aid in the interpretation of the written word. Thus the important thing here is, in a special sense, the 'art' of writing. The spoken word interprets itself to an astonishing degree, by the way of speaking, the tone of voice, the tempo etc, but also by the circumstances in which it is spoken." Hans-Georg Gadamer, *Truth and Method*, ed. Garrett Barden and John Cumming (New York: Continuum, 1975), 393.

51. Ingeborg Bachmann, *Ein Ort für Zufälle: Rede zur Verleihung des Georg-Büchner-Preises* [German Contingencies], in Bachmann, *Werke*, ed. Christine Koschel, Inge von Weidenbaum, and Clemens Münster (Munich: Piper, 1978), 4:278–95; hereafter abbreviated as *GC*; Paul Celan, *The Meridian: Final Version—Drafts—Materials*, ed. Bernhard Böschenstein and Heino Schmull (Stanford, CA: Standford University Press, 2011); hereafter abbreviated as *ME*.

52. Jacques Derrida, *Of Grammatology*, trans. Gayatri Chakravorty Spivak (Baltimore: Johns Hopkins University Press, 1997), 11.

53. Hannah Arendt, "On Humanity in Dark Times: Thoughts about Lessing," in Arendt, *Men in Dark Times*, 20–21; hereafter abbreviated as *OH*.

as many as twelve times—only emphasizes the hermetic, indeed antidialogical, character of his public address. By contrast, Buber's Peace Prize address represents a focused attempt to engage in a quasi-spiritual dialogue with his German audience. Responding to his audience's experienced "truth" by issuing an ontological "call," Buber clearly sought to act as a dialogical rhetor. But whereas he considered his encounter with a German audience as one that could potentially be considered "genuinely dialogical," the ensuing dialogue was effectively severed from the referential context of Buber's script. Hence his speech spawned a dialogue that communicates nothing.

One final question surfaces from the conceptual level of this study. It concerns the hypothetical difference between writing and speaking, which is in each case aligned with the operative distinction between the theory and practice of public speaking. Each part of this book thus examines a theoretical approach to the question of public speech, which it then juxtaposes with sometimes promising, sometimes failed "applications" of this theory to concrete events of public speaking: in part 1, Buber's dialogical philosophy becomes the touchstone for a public speech of his own that performs and, as it were, instantiates a German-Jewish dialogue that privileges otherness and the particularity of discrete historical moments while rejecting essentialism and the ideologies associated with it. But Buber's speech is also echoed by Celan's and Bachmann's explicitly antidialogical speeches, which foreground the flaws and agonies of engaging in such a "genuine dialogue." Hence Celan's and Bachmann's interventions gesture toward the creation of a critical rather than faith-based counter-public sphere that would pose a significant challenge to hegemonic economies of knowledge construction. In part 2, Arendt's and Johnson's ultimately futile—and in Johnson's case self-ironizing—efforts at revealing themselves in the realm of the public are read against the backdrop of Arendt's concept of "self-revelation," a concept that is as foundational for Arendt's theorization of the public sphere as it is unrealistic as regards the practice of public speech at this historical juncture. And yet, by juxtaposing the concept of "public" with that of "pariah," and by contrasting the notion of self-revelation with that of testimony, Johnson and Arendt successfully negotiate the conditions of possibility that would enable the creation of a counterpublic as defined by Kluge and Negt. In part 3, diverse instances of witness testimony, uttered in contexts that ostensibly undermine their judiciary provenance, emanate from Szondi's and Weiss's critical reflections on the hermeneutic status of textual and oral citation. This part of the book will unearth the ethical and epistemological challenges inherent to the claim of speaking "on behalf of" the "other" while arguing that this indeed points toward a viable way of creating a counter-public sphere along the lines of Kluge and Negt. Part 4, finally, revisits Adorno's theoretical writings on the radio to ask how the mass media allowed this prominent thinker to position himself in the force field between the concrete interests of public reeducation efforts and the theoretical standards of the university. Seizing on the opportunity to reach a mass audience

through the radio while also training a generation of students in critical thinking, Adorno's voice was ultimately crushed by the anti-imperialist agenda of the
increasingly militant students. It is this negotiation between theorizing and practic-
ing public speech, as well as the textually encoded frustration with, even rejection
of, these limits, that structures this book.

Part I

In the Event of Speech

Performing Dialogue

1

MARTIN BUBER

In Germany the preacher alone knew what a syllable weighs, or a word,
and how a sentence strikes, leaps, plunges, runs, runs out; he alone had
a conscience in his ears.

— Friedrich Nietzsche, *Beyond Good and Evil*

On September 13, 1960, Martin Buber and Paul Celan, two central—if fundamentally dissimilar—intellectual figures of the German-speaking Jewish diaspora,
had a brief, dissonant encounter (this was the only time they met).[1] Their dispute
revolved around the possibility and legitimacy of engaging in a dialogue with Germans.[2] Having accompanied Celan to the meeting, which took place in the lobby
of a Paris hotel, Jean Bollack recalls how deeply disappointed his friend was by

1. As an Austrian Jew who had grown up in Lemberg and Vienna and later lived in Berlin and
Heppenheim, Martin Buber left Germany in 1938 to settle in Jerusalem, Palestine, where he continued
his scholarly and educational work as a cultural Zionist. Paul Celan (born Antschel) lived in Bukovina
when it was occupied by the Soviets and subsequently, in 1941, invaded by the Germans. Celan's parents
were deported and killed, and he was placed in a labor camp. After the end of World War II Celan lived
in Bucharest until he immigrated to Paris in 1948.

2. See the report by Jean Bollack, who was present during the meeting, in Jean Bollack, *Paul Celan:
Poetik der Fremdheit*, trans. Werner Wögerbauer (Vienna: Zsolnay, 1999), 133. See also John Felstiner,
Paul Celan: Poet, Survivor, Jew (New Haven: Yale University Press, 1995), 161.

the much-revered scholar-philosopher Buber, whose viewpoints struck Celan as injudicious, even naive: "Did Buber grasp the tragic nature of the stories he was divulging in Germany? Did he grasp that his contradictory and (to Celan's mind) theological work implied that he repudiated everything, even his own language? Celan addressed Buber's contradictions by speaking of his own. His solidarity and his questions transformed into accusations."[3]

Ignorance, denial, self-contradiction—Celan's impetuous language suggests the extent to which the subject under discussion was loaded for him. The poet objected strongly to Buber's confidence in the peacemaking power of dialogue and his amicable engagement with Germany's public sphere. Buber at first refused to return to Germany, to be sure, but when he finally went in 1953 to accept the Peace Prize of the German Book Trade, he promoted his unflagging faith in a possible future of German-Jewish relations.[4] A pioneer of reconciliation, Buber gave his Peace Prize address the telling title *Über das echte Gespräch und die Möglichkeit des Friedens* (Genuine Dialogue and the Possibilities of Peace), even though his appearance in Germany occurred at a time when the 1951–52 retribution debate had only barely receded from public view:[5] at that time not a few Israelis were opposed to the idea of accepting monetary retribution from the federal government, insisting that this would bestow an undeserved sense of redemption on West Germany.[6] In the eyes of his Israeli critics, Buber's candor with regard to current political issues, and, more concretely, his readiness to accept two major awards from public institutions in Germany, amounted to perfidy.[7]

---

3. Bollack, *Paul Celan*, 133. According to James K. Lyon, Celan's criticism of Buber was linked to the philosopher's willingness to meet with Martin Heidegger in 1959. See James K. Lyon, *Paul Celan and Martin Heidegger: An Unresolved Conversation, 1951–1970* (Baltimore: Johns Hopkins University Press, 2006), 98.

4. Buber had been unable to accept the Goethe Prize of the University of Hamburg, which he received in 1951, in person.

5. Martin Buber, *Verleihung des Friedenspreises des deutschen Buchhandels 1953 in der Frankfurter Paulskirche and den Religionsphilosophen Martin Buber* (Frankfurt a. M.: Hessischer Rundfunk, 1953), audio recording; quoted from Martin Buber, "Genuine Conversation and the Possibility of Peace" in Buber, *Men of Dialogue: Martin Buber and Albrecht Goes* (New York: Funk & Wagnalls, 1969), 20–27. Buber's Goethe Prize speech, given in 1953, was published in 1962 as "The Validity and Limitation of Political Principle," in Martin Buber, *Pointing the Way: Collected Essays*, ed. and trans. Maurice Friedman (London: Routledge and Kegan Paul, 1957), 208–19. Other speeches Buber delivered in Germany include "What Is Common to All" (1956) and "The Word That Is Spoken," in Martin Buber, *The Knowledge of Man: Selected Essays*, ed. Maurice Friedman, trans. Maurice Friedman and Ronald Gregor Smith (New York: Harper & Row, 1965), 89–109 and 110–20.

6. On the retribution debate, see Constantin Goschler, *Schuld und Schulden: Die Politik der Wiedergutmachung für NS-Verfolgte seit 1945* (Göttingen: Wallenstein, 2005), 172.

7. See Schalom Ben-Chorin, *Zwiesprache mit Martin Buber: Erinnerungen an einen großen Zeitgenossen* (Gerlingen: Bleicher, 1978), 123. For a description of the affair surrounding Buber's *Friedenspreisrede*, see Martin Buber, *Werkausgabe*, ed. Paul Mendes-Flohr and Peter Schäfer (Gütersloh: Gütersloher Verlagshaus, 2001–), 6:169–71. Buber's stance toward the question of Zionism was likewise controversial. In opposition to the Orthodox Nationalist majority, Buber was in favor of a binational solution in Palestine instead of a two-state solution, and, after the establishment of the Jewish state of Israel, he pleaded for a regional federation of Israel and Arab states.

Both Buber and Celan repeatedly visited Germany during the 1950s and 1960s, yet Celan went with a greater degree of reluctance; he had experienced his first visit in 1952, which was occasioned by an invitation from the Gruppe 47, as a personal failure.[8] According to Celan's account, the audience had sneered at his poem *Todes-fuge* (Death Fugue, 1949), and one group member had commented to him that his pathos-filled inflection reminded him of Josef Goebbels's.[9] Although the group members' criticism was directed against the chant-like style of Celan's prosody—his markedly unironic performance seemed sibylline, almost enraptured—they certainly were equally perplexed by the formal features of Celan's poetry, the broken syntax and radical minimalism of which proposed that signification and meaning had collapsed in the post-Holocaust world. Where the Gruppe 47 sought realistic storytelling that would help society "cope with" the Nazi past, Celan's poetry abjured narrative cogency. And while the former vowed to modernize the German language to arrive at a new, simpler, and more direct way of telling history, the latter carefully examined each and every word, especially those tainted by the euphemistic vocabulary of National Socialism, mulling over its incommensurability and negativity and finally substituting German terms with enigmatic synonyms and neologisms that would each communicate its unique history of violence and suffering while at the same time refusing to perpetuate the language of the perpetrators. Constantly reflecting on the question of what it meant to write poetry after Auschwitz, Celan's poetry always raises the possibility of poetic failure because it is imbued with the trauma inscribed in the German language.

Despite their exile, both Buber and Celan wrote in German and hence for a German-language readership. Yet while Buber's writings are marked by the expressionist diction emblematic of the first decades of the twentieth century and a truly imposing, pathos-filled rhetoric, Celan's poetry is self-reflexive and hermetic, always bordering on, indeed performing, what Celan once tagged "a terrifying silence" in the face of "what happened" in National Socialist Germany.[10] Celan,

8. Other visits include Celan's one and only trip to Berlin in 1967 and a visit to Martin Heidegger in the same year, both of which prompted poems that corroborate Celan's dismay at the sight of various sites of death and suffering amid modern German city life in "Du liegst," from *Schneepart* (Snow-part, 1971), and at Heidegger's silence about his association with the Nazi Party in "Todtnauberg," from *Lichtzwang* (Lightduress, 1970). Paul Celan, *Gedichte* (Frankfurt a. M.: Suhrkamp, 1975), 2:334; Celan, *Lightduress*, trans. Pierre Joris (Los Angeles: Green Integer, 2005), here 62–69. See Peter Szondi, "Eden" (1972), in Szondi, *Celan Studies*, ed. Jean Bollack, trans. Susan Bernofski with Harvey Mendelsohn (Stanford, CA: Stanford University Press, 2003), 83–92; and chapter 15, "'Todtnauberg' and Its Aftermath, 1967–1968," in Lyon, *Paul Celan and Martin Heidegger*, 173–91.

9. See Sigrid Weigel, *Ingeborg Bachmann: Hinterlassenschaften unter Wahrung des Briefgeheimnisses* (Vienna: P. Zsolney, 1999), 437. See also Klaus Briegleb, "Ingeborg Bachmann, Paul Celan: Ihr (Nicht-) Ort in der Gruppe 47," in *Ingeborg Bachmann und Paul Celan: Poetische Korrespondenzen*, ed. Bernhard Böschenstein and S. Weigel (Frankfurt a. M.: Suhrkamp, 1997), 29–81, here 53–54.

10. See Celan's "Speech on the Occasion of Receiving the Literature Prize of the Free Hanseatic City of Bremen" in Paul Celan, *Collected Prose*, trans. Rosmarie Waldrop (Manchester: Carcanet, 1986), 33–35, here 34.

who had been deported to a labor camp by a rather willing Romanian government in 1942, was a deeply skeptical thinker who displayed what Arendt once
characterized as the émigré's "fundamental distrust of everything merely given."[11]
In Celan's case this includes not only "all laws and prescriptions, moral and social"
but also "the sources of authority of law [and] the ultimate goals of political organizations and communities"—most notably the discursive hegemony of National
Socialism.[12] The meeting with Buber, unsatisfactory as it seemed, pushed Celan
to revisit his own stance on the question of what it meant for a Jewish exile to
address an audience of a variety of Germans—made up of former bystanders, victims, and perpetrators, of members of the first and second generations, of individuals, too, who downplayed the significance of the Cologne synagogue desecration in
1959, and of others who came to Celan's defense against Claire Goll's plagiarism
charges.[13] In a letter to Celan, Ingeborg Bachmann had expressed her concern that
"having entered a room full of people one has not chosen oneself, whether one
is still prepared to read for those who do want to listen, and are ashamed of the
others."[14] There was no easy answer to this dilemma. But in his Büchner Prize
address, titled *Der Meridian* (The Meridian), which Celan gave only a few weeks
after his encounter with Buber, on October 22, 1960, in Darmstadt, Celan clearly
demonstrates that he found Buber's reconciliatory position toward the Germans
untenable.[15]

Although Celan decided to deliver his Büchner Prize address in Germany
and accept this German award, his accusations against Buber are inscribed in his
speech, if in an inconspicuous and oft-overlooked manner. One of the passages that
most resonates with Buber's thought, a paragraph that defines the poem as dialogue, dates from the final writing stage; Celan added it after his meeting with
Buber and just days before he delivered the final version of the speech.[16] In addition

---

11. Hannah Arendt, *The Origins of Totalitarianism* (New York: Harcourt, 1966), 435.

12. Ibid.

13. In the early 1960s and roughly coinciding with Celan's nomination and acceptance of the Büchner award, accusations by Claire Goll, who indicted Celan of plagiarizing the poetry of her late husband, Yvan Goll, cast a shadow over Celan's public persona. For a detailed description of this affair,
see Barbara Wiedemann, *Paul Celan—Die Goll-Affäre: Dokumente zu einer "Infamie"* (Frankfurt a. M.:
Suhrkamp, 2000).

14. I. Bachmann to P. Celan, December 10, 1958, in *Correspondence: Ingeborg Bachmann and Paul
Celan*, trans. Wieland Hoban (London: Seagull Books, 2010), 151.

15. Celan had already taken up several of Buber's motives in his prose piece *Gespräch im Gebirg*,
a text that features two mysterious companions, named "Gross" and "Klein," who communicate in a
language that does not converse but simply addresses: "Do you hear me, he says—I know, cousin, I
know... Do you hear me, he says, I'm here. I am here, I've come." P. Celan, "Conversation in the Mountains" (1959), in Celan, *Collected Prose*, 17–22, here 20. The text ends, much like *The Meridian*, with the
breakdown of dialogue.

16. See his note "M. Buber, in conversation" followed by the revised draft titled "Encounter." Paul
Celan, *Der Meridian: Endfassung, Vorstufen, Materialien*, ed. Bernhard Böschenstein and Heino Schmull
(Frankfurt a. M.: Suhrkamp, 1999), 131–48. Thus instead of viewing Celan's Büchner Prize address
exclusively in light of Martin Heidegger's philosophy, the present study contextualizes the speech with
Buber's philosophy of dialogue. For a canonical Heideggerian reading of Celan, see Lacoue-Labarthe's

to redirecting some of his aesthetic questions concerning the ontological possibility of poetry and language as well as the dichotomy between art and reality into the realm of ethics, Celan here articulates an unfavorable response to Buber, even if this response is never made explicit. Charged with Buber's idiosyncratic vocabulary, Celan's Büchner Prize address carefully gauges and examines the philosopher's prodialogic stance but ultimately rejects it, along with Buber's optimistic pledge to renew a long-lost German-Jewish tradition. Contrary to Buber's Peace Prize address, then, which optimistically embodies a "genuinely dialogical" and politically committed commencement, *The Meridian* is punctuated by interjections that fail to address any potential listeners. Evoking a series of textually self-referential signs, the speech is ultimately a self-recursive monologue reaffirming the historical caesura implied by the cipher of "Auschwitz." Bachmann, the third speaker to be considered in the first part of this book, shares Buber's deliberate and strategic use of the relational space between speaker and audience, yet while Buber employs it in the affirmative sense of promoting a German-Jewish dialogue, Bachmann uses it to challenge the psychological status quo that has been reached in Germany. Her 1964 Georg Büchner Prize address, *Deutsche Zufälle* (German Contigencies), not only considers the psychosocial health of the Germans—it revolves around the theme of "insanity" in Büchner's prose fragment *Lenz*—but also constitutes a deliberate response to Celan's reflections on Büchner.[17] For Bachmann both eludes and self-reflectively reinscribes her role as an unstable dialogic partner in her Darmstadt address. By thus mirroring Celan's resistance to any form of public dialogue in a German context, she demonstrates her solidarity with the Jewish poet, who had been publicly defamed around the time he gave his Büchner address.

Based on an understanding of the "public sphere" as a social site where meaning is negotiated through dialogic exchange, this chapter inquires into the qualitative dimension of public speech as a distinctive form of dialogue that can create oppositional, subaltern spheres of influence within the dominant sphere of public life. Despite their great differences in details of form and intent, the discursive interactions between Buber, Celan, and Bachmann and their respective audiences generate a counterpublic that challenges the dominant mode of reality within West Germany's public sphere. Of course this kind of contact comes at a great sacrifice. Reflecting on the challenge of articulating subjective experience in a public

essay "Catastophe," in Philippe Lacoue-Labarthe, *Poetry as Experience*, trans. Andrea Tarnowski (Stanford, CA: Stanford University Press, 1999), 41–70, here 45. Lyon, while mentioning Celan's other addressees (Gottfried Benn, Ernst Robert Curtius, Gustav René Hocke, Hugo Friedrich, Claire Goll, even Martin Buber), also underscores Celan's borrowings from Heidegger; see chapter 11, "*The Meridian*: An 'Implicit Dialogue with Heidegger,' 1960," in Lyon, *Paul Celan and Martin Heidegger*, 122–34. See also Martin Jörg Schäfer and Ulrich Wergin, eds., *Die Zeitlichkeit des Ethos: Poetologische Aspekte im Schreiben Paul Celans* (Würzburg: Königshausen & Neumann, 2003), 115.

17. See Ingeborg Bachmann, *Georg-Büchner-Preis 1964 der Deutschen Akademie für Sprache und Dichtung* and *Ingeborg Bachmann, Dankesrede* (Frankfurt a. M.: Hessischer Rundfunk, 1964), audio recording.

dialogue, the speakers sometimes unwittingly reproduce the structures that they confront. This is especially the case with Celan and Bachmann, who, by critically revisiting Buber's notion of dialogic relations, exert a modicum of pressure on themselves and/or their interlocutors.

Speech as Dialogue

"I do not philosophize more than I must," Buber once stated in response to critics who disapproved of his unconventionally "optimistic" and "concrete" approach to philosophy.[18] Although he was a scholar, and as such was confronted with the rules and conventions of academic discourse, Buber was opposed to logical elaboration in its detached, erudite form. His teachings, so he insisted, needed to be "transmittable"; contrary to scientific treatises, they had to be persuasive and universally engaging: "My philosophy serves, yes, it serves, but it does not serve a series of revealed propositions. It serves an experienced, a perceived attitude that it has been established to make communicable."[19] With this statement, Buber not only recapitulates his discontent with respect to what he saw as the self-absorbed logicizing practiced in the academy, but he also sums up his own philosophical mission, namely, his continuing effort to reach out to a general public—in Buber's language, the *Gemeinschaft* (community)—rather than addressing university professors or other independent scholars like himself. Buber was a constructive thinker who took his sociopolitical role as a public intellectual and teacher extremely seriously; he was not only the foremost advocate but also an eminent practitioner of communication: "I am not teaching a lesson," Buber thus informed his interlocutors, "but I carry on a conversation."[20]

Buber habitually used public speech as a means to promulgate his dialogical philosophy.[21] It allowed him to convey and clarify speculative lines of argument for his often nonacademic audiences. But more importantly, Buber favored the genre of public speech because of its compatibility with the very essence of his philosophy, as this form of *spoken* communication provided him with the adequate means to demonstrate, indeed perform, the most fundamental principle of his philosophical thought: that human existence is inherently dialogical in nature. Privileging

---

18. Martin Buber, "Replies to My Critics," in *The Philosophy of Martin Buber*, ed. Paul Arthur Schilpp and Maurice Friedman (LaSalle, IL: Open Court, 1967), 698–744, here 702.

19. Ibid., 690–91.

20. Ibid., 693.

21. Kenneth N. Cissna and Rob Anderson have examined the relation between Buber's conception of genuine dialogue and his own, practical attempts at realizing dialogue in his public appearances. Contrary to the present study, however, these commentators focus on actual dialogues—that is, face-to-face encounters between two individuals, as, for instance, academic panel discussions or television interviews—rather than Buber's public speeches. Kenneth N. Cissna and Rob Anderson, *Moments of Meeting: Buber, Rogers, and the Potential for Public Discourse* (Albany: State University of New York Press, 2002), 2.

intersubjective relations between the self and the other over all other kinds of relationalities (i.e., between the self and the world or the absolute, respectively), Buber's
philosophy is deeply concerned with the anthropological and ontological dimension of spoken language. Buber indeed considered the primary form of language
its concrete spokenness and not its capability to signify.[22] Opposed to conventional
theories of language that define words as containers of *logos*—that is, meaning,
cosmic reason, a divine plan—Buber conceived of words as empty shells whose
primary function was not to transmit ideas, but to function as a medium. Words,
when spoken out loud for the sake of genuine dialogue, could engender intersubjective encounters regardless of what they said. Hence in Buber's view truth resided
not in the words or communicative content of such dialogues but in the process—in
the event—of language itself: "[Dialogue] is completed outside contents, even the
most personal, which are or can be communicated. Moreover it is completed not
in some 'mystical' event, but in one that is in the precise sense factual, thoroughly
dovetailed into the common human world and the concrete time-sequence."[23]

In the treatise *Das Wort, das gesprochen wird* (The Word That Is Spoken), first
published in 1960, Buber defined this dialogical event as *aktuelles Begebnis* (actual
occurrence), referring to the spokenness of language in the event of spontaneous
communication.[24] Contrary to other, less genuine modalities of language—namely,
präsenter Bestand (present continuance), which includes all that which is sayable at
a given point in time, and *potentialer Besitz* (potential possession), which comprises
all that which has ever been said insofar as it can still be recuperated—*aktuelles
Begebnis* denotes language that is realized in the form of spoken, interpersonal
dialogue—its real occurrence in human life. As Buber elaborates, "Existence and
possession, presuppose an historical acquisition, but here nothing else is to be presupposed than man's will to communicate as a will capable of being realized. This
will originates in men's turning to one another; it wins gesture, vocal sign, the word
in the growing fruitfulness of this basic attitude."[25] This latter form of language is,
like public speech, context bound, ephemeral, and, most importantly, dialogical. As
Buber declares, "Language never existed before address."[26] Language, which is first
and foremost a dialogical *event*, brings forth, and from its first instance effectively
constitutes, response. It follows that, as Emmanuel Levinas contends, "truth is not
a content" for Buber, and "words do not contain it."[27] In saying "I" Buber's subject
does not put words to his use, nor does he grasp a thing; rather, his words become

22. See Martin Buber, "Dialogue" (1929), in Buber, *Between Man and Man*, trans. Ronald Gregor
Smith (New York: Macmillan, 1965) 1–39, here 4.
23. Ibid.
24. Martin Buber, "The Word That Is Spoken" (1960), in Buber, *The Knowledge of Man*, 110–20,
here 110.
25. Ibid., 111.
26. Ibid., 115.
27. Emmanuel Levinas, *Proper Names*, trans. Michael B. Smith (Stanford, CA: Stanford University Press, 1996), 19.

a container for a different, *averbal* kind of dialogue that arises between the "I" and the subject and thing that this "I" encounters. Dialogical encounters are thus diametrically opposed to information exchange, persuasion, and intentionality, and involve presenting oneself in such a way that one is open to hearing the other's "otherness." As Levinas writes, for Buber

> the word is not true because the thought it states corresponds to the thing, or reveals being. It is true when it proceeds from the *I-Thou* relation, which is the ontological process itself. . . . The static notion of truth, which is to be that which reappears as long as the truth can be said, is destroyed in this conception. . . . Buber describes a being no narration could grasp, because that being is living dialogue between things who do not relate to one another as contents: *one being has nothing to say about the other*. The acuity of the *I-Thou* relation is in the total *formalism* of that relation.[28]

Paradoxically, it is precisely this "total formalism" that for Buber makes actual, genuine dialogue possible. As a thinker who always strived to transform his writings into speech and speech into genuine dialogue, Buber believed that the latter could be realized, but only through the nonsubstantive character—the emptiness—of the *I-Thou* relation.[29]

But how was Buber able to carry out his mission as a public lecturer and prophet of genuine dialogue over into a period when ethical life—and God—was, in his own words, "eclipsed" by the historical reality of the Holocaust?[30] In a world devoid of divine signs, how could Buber maintain his faith in the absolute? In the absence of God, how could he hope to make him present through genuine dialogue? Finally,

---

28. Ibid., 27.

29. In *I and Thou*, Buber juxtaposes two primary relations—defined as the word pairs *Ich-Du* (I-Thou) and *Ich-Es* (I-It), respectively—which are also based on two different conceptions of alterity. In the *Ich-Du* encounter, the "I" does not conceptualize or cognize the other's identity: "Whoever says You," Buber writes, "does not have something for his object." Martin Buber, *I and Thou*, trans. Walter Kaufmann (New York: Charles Scribners' Sons, 1970), 55; hereafter abbreviated as *IT*. The *Ich-Du* can involve persons, animals, or even a stone, since it rises above the technicalities of human language: "We hear no You and yet feel addressed; we answer—creating, thinking, acting: with our being we speak the basic word, unable to say You with our mouths" (*I and Thou*, 57) The second word-couple, *Ich-Es*, describes a nonessential relation of alterity. Here, the "I" encounters the Other by way of cognition and experience: "Man goes over to the surface of things and experiences them. He brings back from them some knowledge of their condition—an experience. He experiences what there is to things" (55) According to Buber, this relation is inferior, since the Thou to which the I refers is not a particular person but an intrinsic plurality: "For what they [the experiences] bring to him is only a world that consists of It and It and It, of He and He and She and She and It" (55). The "It" denotes a multiplicity of potential participants who are insubstantial and substitutable. As Buber notes, the *Es* is but a lacuna: "Every It borders on other Its; It is only by virtue of bordering on others" (55). Buber's two-pronged investigation of an essential, nonconceptual and a mediated, cognitive relation of alterity, respectively, goes back to his predialogical period. See Paul Mendes-Flohr and in particular the chapter "Buber's Epistemology," in Mendes-Flohr, *From Mysticism to Dialogue* (Detroit: Wayne State University Press, 1989), 72–75.

30. Martin Buber, *The Eclipse of God: Studies in the Relation between Religion and Philosophy* (New York: Harper and Brothers, 1953).

in the aftermath of a crime against humanity, how precisely did Buber envision man's return to humanity and to human goodness, especially as this concerned the German perpetrator nation?

There is no better place to explore these questions than Buber's 1953 Peace Prize address, since Buber here evokes, indeed attempts to ontically *realize*, an event of dialogical saying in the face of a German audience who for him epitomized the full range of "otherness" of the dialogic "other." This is not to deny that the speech also signifies, persuades, and deliberates. In fact, the present chapter seeks to demonstrate that the speech is in fact both: an act of "saying" that actualizes the kind of genuinely dialogical encounter Buber prescribes in his philosophy (most notably in his magnum opus, *Ich und Du* [I and Thou], written in 1923), as well as a classical deliberative speech.[31] As a matter of fact, for Buber these two modalities of (public) speaking do not preclude one another, since men are always at once exposed (to the ontic existence of the other) and functionally bound (to a historical hour). Buber's conflation of speech and saying thereby speaks to a central insight of classical rhetoric—namely, that the political import of deliberative rhetoric is inseparably bound up with the spokenness of public speaking.[32]

Buber's Peace Prize address has many of the qualities of a political intervention. But its true significance lies in the implications of a public speech that was conceived as an ontic event and as such lays emphasis on its unique and unpredictable quality. In the language of French linguist Émile Benveniste, Buber's speech is *discours* (discourse) that goes beyond a mere didactic, constative purpose; it is "language put into action . . . between partners," and as such it alters the pragmatic speech situation itself.[33] It is thus a speech riven with contradiction. Founded on spiritual claims that run counter to the secular premises of postwar European culture and thought, Buber's Peace Price address nevertheless participates in the latter. It resonates with and in fact becomes legible through Benveniste's notion of "discourse" and J. L. Austin's definition of "performative" speech acts precisely through its difference from such pragmatic concepts. The speech indeed gains critical purchase by rejecting some and underpinning other foundational principles of the pragmatic linguistics from the 1950s. By examining Buber's dialogical philosophy in the context of a real event of public speaking that is subject to its own

31. Buber, *I and Thou*, 170.

32. See Aristotle, *On Rhetoric: A Theory of Civic Discourse*, trans. George A. Kennedy (Oxford: Oxford University Press, 1991), 38.

33. Émile Benveniste, *Problems in General Linguistics* (Miami, FL: University of Miami Press, 1973), 223. For a comparative study of Buber's dialogical philosophy and Austin's speech act theory, see Andreas Hetzel, "Das schöpferische Wort: Bubers Sprachdenken und die Tradition der Logosmystik," *Im Gespräch: Hefte der Martin Buber-Gesellschaft* 8 (2004): 41–47. For an overview of the parallels between Buber's and Benveniste's conceptions of language, see Stéphane Mosès, "Émile Benveniste et la linguistique du dialogue," *Revue de Métaphysique et de Morale* 4 (2001): 97–98. It should also be noted that neither Austin nor Benveniste ever cited Buber's work.

semantic and hermeneutic vicissitudes, the relevance and accuracy of these contemporaneous theoretical approaches to the problems of "speech" and "dialogue" will thus be put to a practical test.

The Orator

There is a way in which the figure of Buber contradicts the premise of this study, which is concerned with the fallacies of public speech in the historical context of postwar Germany, as well as the failures experienced by a set of public speakers who sought to challenge the prevailing silence about the Holocaust in Germany. Contrary to Arendt, Johnson, and Celan (and ultimately also Bachmann and Szondi), whose public interventions through the medium of speech betrayed their skeptical attitude toward political engagement, Buber was a confident and commanding public speaker. He was well aware of how to make use of rhetoric, and the genre of speech was indeed his preferred form of writing.

Buber began his practice as a public speaker in 1909 in Prague with the delivery of his historic *Drei Reden über das Judentum* (Three Speeches on Judaism)—which would be followed by many other speeches—advocating a spiritual revival of Judaism.[34] Apparently these speeches hit the nerve of contemporary culture. As one commentator observes, "Buber was only 31 years old at the time, but he appeared to his listeners as a great, wise man."[35] During the Weimar Republic, Buber taught at Franz Rosenzweig's Freies jüdisches Lehrhaus (Free Jewish School) and later directed the Mittelstelle für jüdische Erwachsenenbildung (Center for Jewish Adult Education), an institution founded to reeducate Jewish teachers who had been driven out of the general school system by the Nazis.[36] Even under the desolate conditions imposed by National Socialism, Buber continued to lecture there, and his talks were attended not only by the Jewish community but also by non-Jewish intellectuals.[37] During this period, Buber was also active as an itinerant lecturer, traveling the country to revive the word of the Bible. Driven by the conviction that the Bible had to be transformed from a book to concrete, indeed *spoken*, teaching, Buber insisted on its apostrophic

34. Rivka Horwitz notes that Buber sometimes tested his ideas in an oral setting before committing them to a final, printed form. See Rivka Horwitz, *Buber's "Way to I and Thou": The Development of Martin Buber's Thought and His "Religion as Presence" Lectures* (Philadelphia: The Jewish Publications Society, 1988), 7. Horvitz also emphasizes "the impact of the audience on Buber: At times it helped him formulate his thinking in difficult matters" (11).

35. R. Welsch, "Einleitung," in Martin Buber, *Der Jude und sein Judentum: Gesammelte Aufsätze und Reden* (Gerlingen: Lambert Schneider, 1993), xxiii.

36. See Yitzhak Arad, Israel Gutman, Abraham Margaliot, eds., *Documents on the Holocaust: Selected Sources on the Destruction of the Jews* (Lincoln: University of Nebraska Press, 1999), 51–52.

37. Ernst Simon, *Aufbau im Untergang* (Tübingen: Mohr, 1959), 35.

quality: "The biblical word is inseparable from the situation of its spokenness, without which it loses its concreteness, its corporality. A command is not a sentence but an address."[38]

Buber's intellectual endeavor combines theological inquiry with social and political responsibility—his teachings represent a form of peaceful, communal, and at the same time religious activism that promotes faith and passive resistance.[39] In his 1933 inaugural speech at the Free Jewish School, Buber thus defined his project as one that was inherently pedagogical. Determined to unite and educate the Jewish people, his teachings were to meet three criteria: teach wisely, impart the Jewish tradition, and admonish in the manner of the prophets.[40] As a public speaker, Buber thrived on all three: he deciphered biblical psalms with impassioned scholarly insight and endowed his audience with a wealth of folkloric Hasidic tales, but beyond teaching, he also *embodied* the figure of the prophet. Although Buber was not a rabbi, he spoke exaltingly to stir his constituents' conscience and urged them to turn to God. Buber's chanting orations were indeed filled with verbal and aural expressivity. Not only was his voice penetrating; his physiognomy was also rather prophet-like. And of course his personality served as a valid petition for this public speaker.[41] For as Aristotle maintained, a major conditioning factor for a speaker's authority is his *ethos*, his moral character. Surely Buber's success in Germany resulted as much from his commanding, incorruptible presence as from the argumentative value of his teachings.[42] A rabbi through example, Buber stood by and for his words; he was a living example of the values he was preaching.[43]

While Buber's rhetorical style can seem antiquated, even pompous, to present-day readers, for the German witnesses to the delivery of his Peace Prize address in 1953, Buber's pathos-laden rhetoric and the distinctive cadences of an Eastern European Jew may have added urgency and weight to his statements. Buber did not shy away from such grandiose terms as *Heilsmächte* (powers of salvation), *Herzenswandel* (change of heart), and *Wiedergeburt* (rebirth), thus providing the German public with the kind of hope-inspiring and redemptive rhetoric it surely

38. Martin Buber, "Ein Hinweis für Bibelkurse" (1936); quoted in Buber, *Werke* (Munich: Kösel/ Lambert Schneider, 1962), 2:1183–86; my translation.

39. As Buber puts it, "This work, done under great difficulty, was intended to give the Jews, and especially the youth, unswerving stability in face of Hitler's will to grind them down." Martin Buber, *Reden über Erziehung* (Heidelberg: Lambert Schneider, 1953), 8–9.

40. Buber distinguishes between the *weisende* (guiding), *mahnende* (urging), and *überliefernde* (preserving) objectives of teaching. M. Buber, "Aufgaben jüdischer Volkserziehung: Frankfurter Lehrhausrede zur Wiedereroffnung des Jüdischen Lehrhauses am 19. November 1933," in Buber, *Der Jude und sein Judentum*, 588–91, here 589.

41. See, for instance, Hermann Hesse, *Gesammelte Werke* (Frankfurt a. M.: Suhrkamp, 1951), 8:324.

42. On the notion of *ethos*, see Aristotle, *On Rhetoric*, 37 and 120.

43. On the link between *vita* and *verbum*, see Rüdiger Schnell, "Von der Rede zur Schrift: Konstituierung von Autorität in Predigt und Predigtüberlieferung," in *The Construction of Textual Authority in German Literature of the Medieval and Early Modern Periods*, ed. James F. Poag and Claire Baldwin (Chapel Hill: University of North Carolina Press, 2001), 95.

yearned for during this period of gloom and dejection. Buber's language no doubt differed from the rhetoric that dominated the political culture of West Germany, a plain and unadorned rhetoric that expressed the greatest possible distance from the emotional amalgam of Nazi mass propaganda with its ideologically inflated, triumphalist pathos. In this historical context, Buber's Peace Prize address stands out as a wisely and cautiously deliberative speech in the garb of conventional epideictic rhetoric. Buber, while using the expected polite formulas to express his thanks for the honor of receiving the Peace Prize, does not waste much time on preliminaries but quickly issues a vigorous criticism of the Cold War. He refrains, however, from submitting a concrete political analysis or polemicizing against specific individuals or governments. Yet in a move that is uncharacteristically up-front and bold even for him, Buber submits that the current political culture is corrupt not because of particular individuals or policies, but because of the way politics are communicated: "The debates between statesmen which the radio conveys to us no longer have anything in common with human conversation: the diplomats do not address one another but the faceless public. Even the congresses and conferences which convene in the name of mutual understanding lack the substance which alone can elevate the deliberations to genuine talk: candour and directness in address and answer" (*GD*, 237).

In this passage, Buber draws a distinction between the insubstantial debates and negotiations of statesmen, which he aligns with self-interest and ideology, and unbiased, genuine dialogue, which he believes to transpire among pious individuals. Producing a comparison that foreshadows Kluge and Negt's distinction between a dominant and a subaltern sphere of discursive interaction, Buber suggests that the debates between statesmen have no constructive political purpose, as statesman neither speak to one another nor do they properly address the *Öffentlichkeit*. Rather they talk *at* a faceless, anonymous public. Their speeches never actually enter the modality of genuine face-to-face dialogue but instead rebound from those to whom such dialogue is ostensibly directed. They are only a pretense of address.

In Buber's view, even the success of political debates between statesmen is tied more to specific formal attributes than to the substantive content of the debates. These debates lack significance because of *how* rather than *what* they communicate: they provoke no answers, and thus fail to stimulate deliberation and pluralist debate. Diametrically opposed to genuine dialogue, such discourse is fossilized speech. For Buber, the inability to speak in a genuine, dialogical manner is not, however, restricted to modern statesmen and rulers. It is a problem that pertains to all people and peoples: "That peoples can no longer carry on authentic dialogue with one another is not only the most acute symptom of the pathology of our time; it is also that which most urgently makes a demand of us" (*GD*, 238). The battle cries of war have drowned out genuine human dialogue, particularly the dialogue between Germans and Jews.

Often taken to be the chief contribution of his Peace Prize address, Buber's reflections on the Cold War barely conceal what is truly at stake for him when giving his acceptance speech. Far more interesting and revealing than these reflections is that Buber mentions the words "Auschwitz" and "Treblinka." Indeed he was the first recipient of the Peace Prize ever to do so and thereby break the taboo of silence.[44] Buber came to speak the unspeakable, and yet not to attack. For he welcomed the occasion to deliver a speech in Germany, believing it would open up a way to overcome what he perceived as "a faceless public" (*GD*, 237). This is yet another sign of his unflinching determination to advance German-Jewish reconciliation. He would not be defeated by the challenge of facing the German public even if it meant encountering those who had, "under the indirect command of the German government and the direct command of its representatives, killed millions of my people in a systematically prepared and executed procedure whose organized cruelty cannot be compared with any previous historical event" (*GD*, 232). But neither was he going to pretend that they had not. Buber's opening remarks are unique and groundbreaking in their directness and simplicity, not only for Buber but for postwar German discursivity in general. For Buber openly and plainly stakes out the conditions of a German-Jewish encounter and concludes with a powerful imperative to reinstate a genuine dialogue: "Let us not allow this satanic element in men to hinder us from realizing man! Let us release speech from its ban! Let us dare, despite all, to trust!" (*GD*, 239). Convinced that noncommunication is a curable disease, Buber hopes to bring about a change of heart in a critical mass of German individuals—to be achieved through the example of a single leader: "Can such an illness be cured? I believe it can be. And it is out of this, my belief, that I speak to you. I have no proof for this belief. No belief can be proved; otherwise it would not be what it is, a great venture. Instead of offering proof, I appeal to that potential belief of each of my hearers which enables him to believe" (*GD*, 238). Buber hereby avows his aim to actualize a German-Jewish dialogue, as daring as it is necessary, by way of his Peace Prize address: ironically referring to himself as a "surviving arch-Jew," he addresses the German public and thereby initiates a process that most of his contemporaries deem undesirable or unfeasible (*GD*, 234). Explicitly stating that he is calling out to them, even in a sense invoking them, his rhetoric produces a movement of force that performs rather than simply "constates" an action. It thus corresponds to Austin's definition of a "performative" utterance: "To utter the sentence (in, of course, the appropriate circumstances) is not to describe my doing of what I should in so uttering to be doing or to state that I am going it: it is to do it."[45] The use of two *verba dicendi*—"I speak to you" and

---

44. See Lothar Müller, "Der abgesperrten Weltluft den deutschen Raum weit öffnen," *Frankfurter Allgemeine Zeitung*, July 1, 1999, 44.
45. Austin, *How to Do Things with Words*, 6.

"I appeal to you"—indicates that Buber moves beyond the paradigm of persuasive rhetoric and, accordingly, the expectation that a speech, when properly argued, will induce people to act in a desired manner. Buber's speech is more ambitious, its effect more immediate. For it affects the present state of affairs *in that* he is speaking to his audience, so that with his speech, and in particular with the above-cited opening invocation, this essential dialogue would indeed transpire.

Uttered in the first-person singular, present tense, indicative active, Buber's sentence is an illocutionary utterance that performs an action rather than describing it. Given that the action achieved through this utterance is itself that of speaking, Buber would be indulging a tautology by telling this to his audience. Instead, Buber's utterance takes place in—and affects—the here and now. Because of its performative nature, it is inseparable from the social relations and purposes in which it is uttered, just as the speech in which it is embedded affects (and is affected by) the historical event of its public delivery. It follows that once this moment has passed and his statement is no longer contained in the respective speech event, it inevitably becomes meaningless and at least to some degree unintelligible. As Jacques Derrida elaborates, "The performative does not have its referent (but here that word is certainly no longer appropriate, and this precisely is the interest of the discovery) outside of itself or, in any event, before and in front of itself. It does not describe something that exists outside of language and prior to it. It produces or transforms a situation, it effects; [this productivity] constitutes its internal structure, its manifest function or destination."[46]

Does Buber's speech act have such a desired effect and produce the reality stated? According to Austin, speech acts must meet certain "felicity conditions" to succeed, such as the "executive condition," which determines whether "the procedure is executed by all participants both correctly and completely."[47] By calling on the potential faith of his listeners, Buber anticipates the possibility that some or all listeners might not answer his call and therefore render his speech act of "speaking to them" pointless and incomplete—after all, for Buber a conversation has to be dialogical in order to be genuine. And so he does not address "them" directly but instead calls on their faith, a faith that is itself not a given but, as he states explicitly, merely a potentiality. And yet it is worthwhile, not only because their faith, even as a potentiality, supersedes their intellectual or even moral contribution (since faith is superior to reason), but also because his philosophy is based on the premise that faith is performatively produced (through dialogue).[48] This is possible because, as

46. Jacques Derrida, "Signature Event Context" (1971), in Derrida, *Limited Inc* (Evanston, IL: Northwestern University Press, 1988), 1–23, here 13.

47. Austin, *How to Do Things with Words*, 15.

48. See Jacques Derrida, "Faith and Knowledge: The Two Sources of 'Religion' at the Limits of Reason Alone" in *Religion*, ed. Jacques Derrida and Gianni Vattimo (Stanford, CA: Stanford University Press, 1998), 1–78.

Buber's friend and collaborator Rosenzweig maintained, the faith of the Jew is, like language for Buber, content-less and "more than words."[49] It is not based on the knowledge (of, for instance, the coming of Christ for the Christian), but rather it is the perpetual *Erzeugnis einer Zeugung* (product of begetting) of something.[50] For Buber, the presence of faith is an effect of genuine engendered dialogue, itself proof of the powerful immediacy of the faith of the Jewish people.

Hence the faith to which Buber appeals is not a secular faith—a kind of faith in our cognitive powers. What is at issue is, instead, the spiritual faith of his audience. Buber is convinced that even if some or all of his Christian German listeners lack the religious fervor to participate in his performative dialogue, he can still address their spiritual, human core and therefore create the space for a unique encounter. This is not because he is such a gifted orator (which he surely was), but because any encounter between men intrinsically and permanently holds the possibility of divine revelation. Thus the functional and hermeneutic specificity of Buber's concept of "genuine dialogue" gestures toward an entirely new, unmediated register of reality that would exist independently of the pragmatic and mundane aspects of communication.

The Single One

Then how could such a dialogical event occur during a public address where only one individual rises to speak? Can interpersonal dialogue arise from a ceremonial speech, can a conversation be a public, collective affair? And to what degree can Buber involve the addressees as his genuine dialogic other? Crucially, for Buber, delivering public speeches and engaging in dialogue are by no means conflicting modes, since as a public speaker he does not address a crowd but a variety of discrete faces. As he once explained, the only way in which he found himself capable of delivering a public address was by envisioning it as a direct contact with worthy individuals: "The indispensable presupposition for my speaking publicly: being able to regard every face that I turn toward as my legitimate counterpart."[51] Of course public speech involves more than an effort of imagination. In his treatise *Die Frage an den Einzelnen* (The Question to the Single One, 1936), Buber asserted that a public speaker must be able to accept and acknowledge each audience member individually: "Even if he has to speak to the crowd he seeks the person, for a people can find and find again in truth only through persons."[52] As a public speaker, Buber

49. Franz Rosenzweig, *The Star of Redemption*, trans. Barabara E. Galli (Madison: University of Wisconsin Press, 2005), 363.

50. Ibid.

51. M. Buber to Bruno Snell, January, 25, 1952; quoted in Maurice Friedmann, *Buber's Life and Work: The Later Years, 1945–1965* (New York: E. P. Dutton, 1983), 111.

52. Martin Buber, "The Question to the Single One" (1936), in Buber, *Between Man and Man*, 40–82, here 64–65.

sought to engage in a plurality of genuine dialogues, and he did so by attempting to speak to an audience of many, as if he were addressing one participant at a time. In each distinct encounter, Buber explained, he singles one person out from the crowd, making him or her the "partner" in a unique—if only temporary—exchange. That is to say, in his ideal scenario the speaker converts a crowd into a multiplicity of separate participants who are, however, not conceived as stable, clearly defined human individuals but rather as distinct, indivisible "things"—no longer faceless but not yet individualized.

For there is but one ethically responsible way to connect with the other without instrumentalizing his alterity. First, one must resist the urge to emphatically identify with the other, since this would crush his concrete individuality and reduce him to a mere reservoir of otherness.[53] Second, one has to ignore those calls that are, as one commentator puts it, merely "pragmatic—to define situations, to resolve problems, to achieve specific goals."[54] For genuine dialogue amounts to an existential, world-disclosing bearing that has nothing to say. It arises whenever someone responds to an address by acknowledging the other in light of his or her own experienced truth, independently of what is said and whether or not the addressee responds verbally. What is more, genuine dialogue rests upon religious fervor and a sacred stance, since it constitutes the response to a spiritual call and thereby effectively molds a space for divinity. As Buber explains, "When I confront a human being as my You and speak the basic word I-You to him, then he is no thing among things nor does he consist of things. . . . Neighborless and seamless, he is You and fills the firmament. Not as if there were nothing but he; but everything else lives in *his* light" (*IT*, 59). As a practitioner of speech and theoretician of dialogue, Buber conceived of the medium of public speech as a potentially "genuine" form of dialogue. This is remarkable, given that the latter stands at a remove from content and meaning and has such strong religious underpinnings. Yet it is precisely public speech, and his Peace Prize address in particular, that Buber employs to reconcile the sociopolitical and spiritual realms of society. It is quite obvious that Buber constantly shifts registers, making a critical point about the crisis of present-day human social relations, but also commanding his audience to lead a religious life and to resist the forces of Satan. Hence for Buber both registers are related:

> Therefore, the fact that it is so difficult for present-day man to pray (note well: not to hold it to be true that there is a God, but to address Him) and the fact that it is so difficult for him to carry on a genuine talk with his fellow-men are elements of a single set of facts. This lack of trust in Being, this incapacity for unreserved intercourse with the other, points to an innermost sickness in the sense of existence. One symptom of

---

53. Ibid., 63–65.
54. Jeanine Czubaroff, "Dialogical Rhetoric: An Application of Martin Buber's Philosophy of Dialogue," *Quarterly Journal of Speech* 86, no. 2 (2000): 174.

this sickness, and the most acute of all, is the one from which I have begun: that a genuine word cannot arise from the camps. (*GD*, 238)

Thus, rather than "instilling" religious faith in his audience, Buber strives to generate genuine dialogues that would become the site of God's actualization. For Buber believes that God inserts himself into truly dialogical—reciprocal and ontic—encounters between human individuals, encounters that defy cognition and rest on grace. Rejecting the idea of a mystical union with God, Buber instead believes that dialogical encounters transpire in the physical reality of the everyday.[55] Buber's point then is not to lift his Frankfurt audience out of their quotidian lives and thus deny their existence in reality, but to intuit their ontological dimension, which would in turn transcend the individual and collective social identities of all participants. The ensuing dialogue would revive their human essence and allow for a glimpse of the absolute. As Buber explains to his Frankfurt audience,

> Harkening to the human voice, where it speaks forth unfalsified, and replying to it, this above all is needed today. The busy noise of the hour must no longer drown out the *vox humana*, the essence of the human which has become a voice. This voice must not only be listened to, it must be answered and led out of the lonely monologue into the awakening dialogue of the peoples. Peoples must engage in talk with one another through their truly human men if the great peace is to appear and the devastated face of the earth to renew itself. (*GD*, 235)

Buber suggests that despite the moral decay of humanity, genuine dialogue could appear in flashes, for fleeting, serendipitous moments—even in a public speech, and even in Germany. In this way, Buber's speech is consistent with his lifelong endeavor to counter the perpetually regressive motion of history. Buber envisioned the world on a simultaneously upward and downward spiral that would culminate in messianic redemption.[56] As Buber writes in *I and Thou*, "History is a mysterious approach to closeness. Every spiral of its path leads us into deeper corruption and at the same time into more fundamental return" (168). The final stage of the world's "corruption" will be the end of history, a point at which humankind's turn to God will coincide with a divine response: "The God-side of the event whose world-side is called return is called redemption" (168). Seen in the light of his prophetic messianism, Buber's Peace Prize address reveals itself as a project complicit with Jewish eschatology: it prepares the world for the impending Day of Atonement.

---

55. As Buber notes with regard to his earlier mystical experiences, "Since then I have given up the 'religious' which is nothing but the exception, extraction, exaltation, ecstasy; or it has given me up. I possess nothing but the everyday out of which I am never taken." Buber, "Dialogue," 14.

56. On Buber's messianism, see Jacob Taubes, "Buber and Philosophy of History," in *The Philosophy of Martin Buber*, ed. Paul Arthur Schilpp and Maurice Friedman (LaSalle, IL: Open Court, 1967), 398–413.

Such confidence in the power of genuine dialogue marks Buber as a member of an older generation that has its intellectual roots in the decades preceding World War I. Spanning the period from his formative years at the turn of the century to the end of the postwar era, Buber's work is contained in a time capsule, preserving precisely that kind of historical (and moral) continuity that thinkers like Arendt and Adorno believed to be irretrievably lost. Accordingly, Buber is more concerned with what he vaguely describes as "the suffocation of the living word of human dialogue" than with real and specific human catastrophes, signal among them the Shoah. This is not to suggest that Buber's attitude was marked by historical indifference. According to his own account, the Holocaust deeply shook the foundations of his beliefs.[57] What it means is that instead of focusing on the uniqueness of that concrete event in recent history, Buber presents it as one among many symptoms of the much older and steadily expanding "disease" of secularization and modernity, a diagnosis that is as valid to him in 1953 as it had been fifty years in the past. This then is the context of Buber's invitation to return to a more immediate, primordial voice: "Harkening to the human voice, where it speaks forth unfalsified, and replying to it, this above all is needed today" (*GD*, 234). Countering a contemporary disease with a discourse that he had begun to develop in the second decade of the twentieth century, Buber proposes that the answer to the current crisis of human life, as it is laid out in his Peace Prize address, can be found in his dialogical thought.

Presence and Absence

In his Peace Prize address, Buber maintains a tension between the theorization of dialogue's demise and the claim to retrieve a certain ideal of it. This is typical of the prophet as a mediating figure. As a "prophet of religious secularism," Buber naturally calls on heaven and earth to listen and experience how his discourse, as much vision as hypothesis, generates genuine dialogue.[58] Drawing on the prophetic tradition of the efficacious sign, his speech acts on the addressees and does what it signifies: it inaugurates a dialogue and hence takes a first step toward the process of reconciliation. In other words, the Peace Prize address comes to function in the here and now as it unfolds within the precarious setting of Buber's historical visit to Germany. By putting his trust in the spontaneous force of the present moment— namely, the sociopolitical and historical context of his public speech—Buber thus endows the latter with considerable agency. Hence the success of his public speech is determined less by the content of his script alone than by the unfolding of a specific performance: it depends on the significance of the occasion, the composition of

---

57. See Martin Buber, "The Dialogue between Heaven and Earth," in *On Judaism*, ed. Nahum N. Glatzer (New York: Schocken Books, 1972), 214–25.
58. Donald J. Moore, *Martin Buber: Prophet of Religious Secularism* (New York: Jewish Publication Society of America, 1974).

his audience, and their reaction," as well as the professional and psychological circumstances by which he (the speaker) may in turn be affected. In other words, as an activity that is inseparable from the peculiar social relations in which it finds itself placed, Buber's public speech lives off the specific communicative situation in which it is uttered without thereby being brought to completion. And while this holds true for any public speech, Buber's speech is a particularly pointed example, since for him this situation is just the beginning, a departure that will be magnified indefinitely by the process Buber has set in motion.

And yet all begins here, not just with his performative utterance but with what Benveniste calls the "special circumstances" in which it was made: "The performative utterance . . . cannot be produced except in special circumstances, at one and only one time, at a definite date and place. . . . This is why it is often accompanied by indications of date, of place, of names of people, witnesses, etc. In short it is an event because it creates the event."[59] For both Buber and Benveniste, there is an unavoidable alliance between an utterance and its contextual setting, which together produce an excess of meaning. Speech then emerges as an inherently polysemic and unpredictable activity. The meaning of an utterance, of what Benveniste terms an "instance of discourse," is dependent on the reality to which it refers. Situated within the semantic dimension of speech, enunciations are diametrically opposed to linguistic signs, which belong to the semiotic dimension of language. They occur as a speaker appropriates—and in the act of appropriation actualizes—language, which thus, for an instant, ceases to be a virtual system of signs to constitute a unique and unpredictable event. According to Benveniste such an event is in turn the actual utilization—the very enactment—of language, even though it effaces itself as soon as it is spoken. In addition to being transitory, dialogue is inherently intersubjective. According to Benveniste, this is less the case because it is bound to a subject (for as such it might still be "enclosed in solipsistic subjectivity") than because it consists of allocutions, which naturally postulate an addressee: "*I* posits another person the one who, being, as he is, completely exterior to 'me,' becomes my echo to whom I say *you* and who says *you* to me."[60] Discourse depends on the presence of a communicative partner whose participation must be active and deliberate. It is oriented toward the other, and thus it is constitutionally, structurally dialogic. As Benveniste writes, "This polarity of persons is the fundamental condition of language, of which the process of communication, in which we share, is only a mere pragmatic consequence."[61]

In a compelling article unraveling Benveniste's "linguistics of dialogue," Stéphane Mosès has made a case for Benveniste's extreme sensibility to the philosophical

---

59. Benveniste, *Problems in General Linguistics*, 236.
60. Ibid., 225.
61. Ibid.

dimension of language. Despite his being a linguist in "the most technical sense of the word," Benveniste was, according to Mosès, highly aware of the problem of subjectivity, specifically as it emerged in the discursive act.[62] This becomes apparent if his work is compared to that of Buber's longtime collaborator Rosenzweig, who in his *Der Stern der Erlösung* (The Star of Redemption, 1921) developed a philosophy of language that centered on the irreducible presence and singular reality contained in the first- and second-person pronouns "I" and "Thou." As Mosès notes, the structural similarities between Benveniste and Rosenzweig's thought cannot, however, be an effect of a direct engagement of the French linguist with the German-Jewish philosopher. In France, Rosenzweig's work was not discovered until the 1980s.[63] How, then, can we account for the equally strong affinities between Benveniste's linguistics and Buber's philosophy of dialogue? Buber's *I and Thou* had been translated into French by 1938; however, Benveniste never cites or even mentions Buber. And yet both depart from a split foundation that is based on the distinction between deixis and anaphora, presence and absence, actuality and property. Where Benveniste differentiates between two kinds of intersubjective relations ("Every man taken as an individual sets himself as *me* in relation to *you* and *him*"), Buber distinguishes between two relationalities: *Ich-Du* (I-Thou) and *Ich-Es* (I-it).[64] As Buber writes, "The world is twofold for man in accordance with his twofold attitude" (*IT*, 53). Buber's *I-Thou* is marked by presence and wholeness, while the *Ich-Es* embodies absence and void: "The basic word 'I-Thou' can only be spoken with one's whole being. The basic word 'I-It' can never be spoken with one's whole being" (*IT*, 54). Similarly, Benveniste differentiates between an *I-he* relation, denoting an encounter that never really takes place, because neither participant is present or an actual person, and an *I-you* relation, describing a direct, physical encounter during which the *I* and the *you* are present and attest to their presence in every single one of their utterances.[65] Like the *I-Thou* of Buber's system, Benveniste's *I-you* thus denotes a primary, truly interpersonal relation:

> As soon as the pronoun *I* appears in a statement it evokes, explicitly or implicitly, the pronoun *you* and the two together evoke and confront *he*. In this moment a human experience is relieved, revealing the linguistic instrument on which it is founded. . . . The pronoun *I* is transformed from an element of a paradigm into a unique designation which produces a new person each time. This process is the actualization of a basic experience for which no language can conceivably fail to provide the instrument.[66]

---

62. Mosès, "Émile Benveniste et la linguistique du dialogue," 108.
63. Ibid.
64. Émile Benveniste, "Language and Human Experience," *Diogenes* 51 (Fall 1965): 1–12, here 1.
65. As Benveniste states, "The 'third person' is not a 'person', it is really a verbal form whose function is to express the *non-person*." Benveniste, *Problems in General Linguistics*, 198.
66. Benveniste, "Language and Human Experience," 2.

Yet these similarities also mark a sharp distance between Benveniste's and Buber's respective conceptions of the speech event. Benveniste's analysis, specifically his distinction between two kinds of speaking relations (and two kinds of speaking subjects), is an inquiry into how language constructs subjectivity through the indexical trace of participant deixis (*I-you*). The agent or subject of a given discourse embodies the shifter *I* in any given moment of speaking. Buber's analysis of speech, by contrast, rather than being premised on the construction of subjectivity—be it as a linguistic or philosophical category—explores how the act of speaking shifts the intersubjective relations between the respective participants to ultimately annul their individuality. So rather than constituting them as subjects, the act of speaking here voids the significance of the participants. For Buber relegates their agency to a third, transcendental term—God—whose all-encompassing presence renders obsolete the creaturely distinction between *Ich* and *Du* or *Es*.

Yet much is at stake for Buber in the difference between *Du* and *Es*, a difference that has real ramifications for his encounter with a live German audience. Again, this difference is not a problem of linguistic meaning or philosophical exactitude but one of the pragmatic effect of this particular speech event, which is in turn coupled with its spiritual, eschatological impetus. Buber carefully stakes out the limits of his dialogical address by dividing his audience into worthy and unworthy addressees: the latter group, while not coterminous with the *Ich-Es* relationality, is equally considered—indeed, treated—as absent and void, whereas the former group supplies the potential partners for an *Ich-Du* relation:

> When I think of the German people of the days of Auschwitz and Treblinka, I behold, first of all, the great many who knew that the monstrous event was taking place and did not oppose it. But my heart, which is acquainted with the weakness of men, refuses to condemn my neighbor for not prevailing upon himself to become a martyr. Next there emerges before me the mass of those who remained ignorant of what was withheld from the German public, and who did not try to discover what reality lay behind the rumours which were circulating. When I have these men in mind, I am gripped by the thought of the anxiety, likewise well known to me, of the human creature before a truth which he fears he cannot face. But finally there appears before me, from reliable reports, some who have become as familiar to me by sight, action, and voice as if they were friends, those who refused to carry out the orders and suffered death or put themselves to death, and those who learned what was taking place and opposed it and were put to death, or those who learned what was taking place and because they could do nothing to stop it killed themselves. (*GD*, 233)

Buber distinguishes between several groups of Germans, which are structured according to their knowledge of and participation in the Holocaust. These different groups represent various strata of society and their corresponding degrees of guilt and responsibility—but more than that, they symbolize entirely different dimensions of human existence. As Buber states, he considers those who "carried out orders" monstrous and subhuman, and thus he cannot speak to them: "I, who am one of those who remained alive, have only in a formal sense a common humanity with those who took part in this action. They have so radically removed themselves from the human sphere, so transposed themselves into a sphere of monstrous inhumanity inaccessible to my conception, that not even hatred, much less an overcoming of hatred, was able to arise in me" (*GD*, 232). To Buber the murderers and collaborators are situated in an extrahuman realm. Even though "alive"—and it is not unlikely that some of them were scattered among the audience assembled at Frankfurt's Paulskirche—they have compromised their status as human beings and are thus no longer present to him. On the other hand, those heroic individuals who refused to obey orders and paid with their lives to uphold their superior principles are miraculously present as if they had been capable of surviving persecution: "I see these men very near before me in that especial intimacy which binds us at times to the dead and to them alone. Reverence and love for these Germans now fills my heart" (*GD*, 233).

By claiming to share a common realm with the deceased martyrs of Nazi Germany while excluding living individuals from his address, Buber reverses the poles of absence and presence, which are so central for both his own and Benveniste's conceptions of speech and their respective definitions of alterity and subjectivity. Buber thereby sets the stage for a legitimate *Ich-Du* encounter: he announces that it is not their material presence, as Benveniste claims, that determines who does or does not function as a dialogic partner in the act of speech. Rather it is a kind of spiritual kinship between him and a select group of German individuals, some of who are admittedly no longer alive. Hence genuine dialogue, albeit requiring the undivided presence of each involved individual, does not hinge on their actual, physical presence. The human world converges on a transcendental realm; genuine dialogue reunites the dead with the living.

Das Zwischen

There is a common trope, philosophical, social, and literary, that describes dialogue as a means of continuing conversation between two equal partners. But even if one partner is the speaker and the other, one (or more) interlocutor(s), as in Buber's Peace Prize address, dialogue can occur in an atmosphere of egalitarian give-and-take. Buber's conception of dialogue is more complex, however, since he implements a third term, which he dubbed *das Zwischen* (the sphere of the between), that would infuse this dialogue with sacredness.[67] In Buber's system, the *Zwischen* represents the temporal and spatial enabler of genuine dialogue but simultaneously

---

67. Martin Buber, "What Is Man?," in Buber, *Between Man and Man*, 118–205, here 203.

causes its infinitely elusive character, for it does not engender a common, collective realm or a shared, mundane reality. While the *Zwischen* gives shape to an instance of dialogue, this dialogue is deeply interiorized by way of a reversal of consciousness itself: it begins as a quasi-intuitive, nonintentional, and almost arbitrary encounter, but immediately collapses into itself and thereby throws the participants back upon their individual consciousnesses. The very moment the participants become aware of their alterity, their dialogue breaks off abruptly. Consequently, the *Zwischen* can never engender a permanent and cohesive form of communality. And yet it is easy to imagine how, in its fluidity and almost filmic character of interconnected moments, it could instantiate a counter-public sphere in which these individual "snapshots" could loosely adhere. The capacity to collapse—and, more specifically, the prerequisite formal distinction between two qualitatively different realms coupled with the impossibility of a dialectical correction despite their repeated convergence—represents a common ground between Buber's dialogical philosophy and Celan's poetology. The *Zwischen* in particular, as a category that makes the paradox of a "momentary immersion" in the redemptive act possible, is structurally analogous to what was to become the central motif in Celan's Büchner Prize address: the figure of the "meridian."

Buber's *Zwischen* is a truly groundbreaking philosophical category. It involves all essential relationalities immanent to reality, enabling the *Ich* to enter into relations with the "other," the world, and God. Buber indeed conceives of the *Zwischen* as a sphere where all these categories naturally converge: "It is rooted in one being turning to another as another, as this particular other being, in order to communicate with it a sphere which is common to them but which reaches out beyond the special sphere of each."[68] As this citation suggests, the *Zwischen* is a sphere that is common to the *Ich* and the *Du*, thus allowing them to meet and enter in dialogue. Without such a common site, the actualization of their relation would never occur. Buber further proposes that the concrete reality of the *Zwischen* bridges the gap between the subject and the natural world. And more than that, although it has the character of an almost tangible, existent location in human reality, it is also the "site" that links humanity to a transcendental beyond. For in the *Zwischen*, the human being encounters God in the form of "a presence as strength" (*IT*, 158). As Buber writes, "I am there as whoever I am there. That which reveals is that which reveals. That which has being is there, nothing more. The eternal source of strength flows, the eternal touch is waiting, the eternal voice sounds, nothing more " (*IT*, 160). The *Zwischen* represents the "narrow ridge" between the "I," the world, and the absolute; it is, in Buber's words, a "third" that draws the circle around the dialogic happening: "In the most powerful moments of dialogic, where in truth 'deep calls unto deep,' it becomes unmistakably clear that it is not the wand of the

---

68. Ibid.

individual or of the social, but of a third which draws the circle round the happening. On the far side of the subjective, on this side of the objective, on the narrow ridge, where *I* and *Thou* meet, there is the realm of 'between'."[69]

. The *Zwischen* regulates the coexistence of human beings in society and at the same time functions as a site of theophany. As Buber explains, "It is not man's own power that is at work here, neither is it merely God passing through; it is a mixture of the divine and the human" (*IT*, 166). In other words, the reality of men's relation with God as an exclusive relation includes and encompasses the possibility of relation with all otherness. At the same time, the *Zwischen* subverts received notions of mediacy. Undermining teleological and dialectical models of philosophy, Buber's third term fails to mediate the *Ich-Du* relation, as it simultaneously relates and separates the "I" and the "Thou," which, given their irreducible antinomy, remain suspended in an in-between.

Buber further complicates his ontological inquiry by stating that each word pair possesses its own peculiar temporality. The *Ich-Es* relation is a permanent plane that corresponds to the continuity of human time and space. It is essentially the common realm of shared reality that enables us to interact with and exist within the complex and diverse environment of the world. It corresponds to the public sphere insofar as it is a space bound by individual agency and the networks of communication among its participants. By contrast, the *Ich-Du* relation, which embodies the spontaneous encounters between an "I" and a "Thou," disrupts the permanence of the *Ich-Es* relation. As Buber writes, "In this firm and wholesome chronicle the You-moments appear as queer lyric-dramatic episodes" (*IT*, 84). It is important to note that the *Ich-Du* relation, albeit epitomized by the personal and indeed intimate meeting of "I" and "Thou," is by no means restricted to the private sphere between two individuals. Even if the *Ich-Du* relation communicates no content, it is a practice that concerns everyone within the public realm. As Buber's notion of reciprocity exceeds the position of two interlocutors in the act of speaking, the whole community will benefit.

Providing momentary access to a parallel realm that exists beyond time and space, the *Ich-Du* "does not hang together in space and time" (*IT*, 84). For this reason, Buber calls these *Ich-Du* instances *Beziehungsereignisse* (events of relation), a term that, much like *aktuelles Begebnis*, emphasizes the inherently event-like structure of the encounter. A *Beziehungsereignis* is characterized by the fact that two partners each encounter the "other's" alterity: "The only thing that matters is that for each of the two men the other happens as the particular other, that each becomes aware of the other and is thus related to him in such a way that he does not regard and use him as his object, but as his partner in a living event."[70] This

---

69. Ibid., 204.
70. Martin Buber, "Elements of the Interhuman," in Buber, *The Knowledge of Man*, 72–88, here 74.

mutual *Beziehungsereignis*, albeit a fleeting instance in mortal time, touches on infinity. However, it cannot last, for as soon as the "I" realizes the "other's" alterity, it recognizes itself as a subject and reflects on its own identity. It will then inevitably also cognize and perhaps even address—seek to communicate with—the "other," and by that disrupt the *Beziehungsereignis*. For human language transforms the *Ich-Du* into an *Ich-Es* relation; the fact that human beings speak and articulate, that they conceive words in their brains, then move their tongues and actually produce sounds in their throats, is what makes their expulsion from the realm of the infinite inevitable. If it were not for this linguistic—literally, lingual—speaking faculty of humankind, the *Ich-Du* relation might never end. We would simply and eternally stand in language, a mystical, preverbal, and spiritual language that is not yet and will never be contained in *logos*. As Buber notes, "In truth language does not reside in man but man stands in language and speaks out of it " (*IT*, 89).

Yet in Buber's view, it is not the verbal response that actualizes a dialogical address, but the moment prior to it: namely, the reception of a prelinguistic call. Men enter into essential *Ich-Du* relations because they are spiritual beings. It is in the nature of these essential relations that they issue forth a prelinguistic call, or, to be precise, this call *is* the *Ich-Du* relation. This call cannot remain unanswered, yet any answer to it is incommensurate with its magnitude and significance. For as the "I" responds to the call of the "Thou," he binds the latter by and into a different, verbal, and conceptual language, so that in this precise moment the nonverbal *Ich-Du* relation gives way to the conceptual and cognitive continuum of the *Ich-Es*. In Buber's words, "All response binds the You into the It-world" (*IT*, 89). One can respond to the call of the "Thou" only qua language, but to thus respond is to alter the "Thou" and to equalize his or her alterity, since language cognizes, identifies, and reflects. At that point, the "Thou" is no longer the "other": "In a genuine dialogue each of the partners, even when he stands in opposition to the other, heeds, affirms, and confirms his opponent as an existing other. Only so can conflict certainly not be eliminated from the world, but be humanly arbitrated and led towards its overcoming" (*GD*, 238).

What then does Buber hope to achieve with his Peace Prize address? Conceived as a spiritual call that would instill the German people with religiosity, it also inevitably binds his dialogic other and thus destroys his essential relation with him or her. For as soon as Buber addresses the "Thou," the *Ich-Du* is converted into an *Ich-Es* relation and carried over into the temporal continuum of the social. As Buber writes, "The individual You *must* become an It when the event of relation has run its course" (*IT*, 84). But perhaps this "experience" will teach his audience to continue a different, more mundane, but equally important dialogue: "Those who build the great unknown front across mankind shall make it known by speaking unreservedly with one another, not overlooking what divides them but determined to bear this division in common" (*GD*, 238). What is more, the spiritual relation that terminates with the collapse of the *Ich-Du* dialogue comes to an end only in the realm of human reality. It will continue to persist outside the coordinates of space and time, where it has existed all along. For even if the *Ich-Du* relation appears to us as unstable and elusive, it is always there already, and thus it will not disappear. As Buber writes, "In the beginning is the relation—as the category of being, as readiness, as a form that reaches out to be filled, as a model of the soul; the *a priori* of relation; *the innate You*" (*IT*, 78). Unlike a relation between two preexisting entities, the *Ich-Du* relation precedes the thinking of "I" and "Thou." As partners who constitute one another by way of their dialogue, the "I" and "Thou" are derivative of their relation. By thus dissolving the authority of its elements, Buber's system replaces the *Ich-Du* with the relation itself.

Buber believes that the *Ich-Du* and *Ich-Es* planes cannot be translated into one another but remain strictly separate. And yet he refrains from privileging one over the other, insisting that both represent essential aspects of human existence. As Buber states, "One cannot live in the pure present: it would consume us " (*IT*, 85). Some of his critics have found the twofold character of Buber's primary word pairs to result in another polarization or, as Walter Kaufmann contends, a Manichaean dualism "that is unworthy of Buber."[71] But even though his philosophy is based on a structural dualism, Buber's word pairs are not meant as extreme poles of good and evil, but rather as ideal types between which human life oscillates. For Buber it is not a matter of choosing the just one but of balancing their dialectic tension without dissolving it.

The two word pairs should not be seen as antitheses. Rather they constitute a regulative concept that negotiates the possibility of contact between the social and religious realms of human life.[72] Essentially, for Buber, society and metaphysics depend on one another in a complex but often inscrutable way. Religiosity, for instance, is not simply a function of social life, but rather a metaphysical fact that bears major significance for both the political and the private life of the community. (This is why his Peace Prize address can rightly be considered both a sermon and a deliberative speech.) Also, while Buber promotes the *Ich-Du* because it makes theophany possible, he maintains that the continuum of the *Es*-world is not inherently immoral: "The basic word I-It [only] comes from evil. . . . When man lets it have its way, [then] the relentlessly growing It-world grows over him like weeds" (*IT*, 95–96). As Buber goes on to emphasize, it is indeed indispensable: "Man's communal life cannot dispense any more than he himself with the It-world" (*IT*, 97). Hence Buber replaces the unifying principle of sublation with the disruptive power of alterity: a genuine dialogue does not mediate the encounter of the self and the "other" but instead separates them. As a result, they are never subsumed under a

71. Walter Kaufmann, *Discovering the Mind* (New York: McGraw-Hill, 1980), 264.
72. On the relationship between the social and religious aspects of *I and Thou*, see Horwitz, *Buber's Way to "I and Thou,"* 11–12. See also Paul Mendes-Flohr on Buber's use of the term religiosity; Mendes-Flohr, *From Mysticism to Dialogue*, 79.

higher principle, an all-encompassing Hegelian *Weltvernunft* (reason of the world). Buber's model of human existence is thus not susceptible to historical transformation. In fact, the philosopher remained critical of Hegel's attempt to once and for all overcome human solitude. Buber's *Zwischen* provides but temporary reprieve from solitude and individuation; it is not a step in a predestined teleology but a process without end or beginning. To be precise, it is a process that is punctuated by so many ends and beginnings that it can hardly be considered a "process" in the conventional sense. Contrary to the Paulinian notion of *Heilsgeschichte*—the interpretation of history stressing God's saving grace—which Buber criticizes for ignoring the possibility of an inner transformation of man that would precede the apocalypse, Buber's prophetic messianism submits that history does not follow a set course of events but is free and open to alternatives. As Buber writes, "The future is not fixed, for God wants man to come to Him with full freedom, to return to Him even out of a plight of extreme hopelessness and then to be really with Him."[73]

Despite its theological character, which clearly contradicts the secular basis of Kluge and Negt's social theory, there is a way in which Buber's philosophy of dialogue provides an instructive model of how isolated discursive interactions can generate a counter-public sphere that is inclusive but not comprehensive, and alternative without making itself obsolete. Mapping out a form of dialogue associated with an inherently pluralist, nonhegemonic stance, Buber's approach takes a prophetic view that is by definition opposed to the dominant sphere, which is invested in reason and dogma at the expense of progress and faith. Buber's idea of social transformation rests on an alternative vision: however fragmented and incomplete the universe, every single dialogic encounter has the potential to effect improvement and portend a radical change in human destiny.

---

73. Martin Buber, "Prophecy, Apocalyptic and the Historical Hour," in Buber, *Pointing the Way*, 192–207, here 198.

2

PAUL CELAN

Paul Celan's Büchner Prize address is saturated with the terminology of Martin Buber's *I and Thou*, a work Celan had extensively studied and reread around the time of his meeting with Buber. This is evident in Celan's use of terms such as *Atemwende* (turn of breath) and *Atempause* (pause for breath), which strongly resonate with Buber's notion of *Atemholen* (drawing a deep breath) and *Atemanhalten* (holding one's breath) (*ME*, 7, 8; *IT* 65, 168). Also, where Buber writes, "Whoever says You . . . stands in relation," Celan responds, "The poem . . . stand[s] in the encounter" (*IT*, 55; *ME*, 9). And where the philosopher declares, "Experience is remoteness from You," the poet states, "Art creates I-distance" (*IT*, 59; *ME*, 6). Finally, the "meridian" metaphor itself echoes similes Buber borrowed from the vocabulary of geography and astronomy, such as *Weltachsendrehung* (the rotation of the world's axis) and *Koordinatensystem* (system of coordinates), to name but a few (*IT* 81, 145).

Given the manifold references and allusions to Buber's *I and Thou*, which add extra dimensions to Buber's thought while also revealing Celan's underlying ambivalence, it is imperative to recognize Celan's deep unity with the mind of the older thinker without, however, neglecting the considerable differences in his own approach to the problem of public speaking. This chapter will read *The Meridian* as a metatext to Buber's *I and Thou*, but as one that tells a very critical story. Seen through Celan's pessimistic lens, the conceptual premise of Buber's dialogical philosophy is simply not tenable, and neither is there a pragmatic basis for what Buber terms a "genuine dialogue." Specifically, Celan's direct confrontation with the German public in the context of an award ceremony conveys that the possibility of his engaging with them in a German dialogue is contingent on a non-euphemistic, hyperliteral language that might reach the inconceivable reality of the concentration camps. Until that particular dialogue, in that exact language, can be had, no other dialogue can be real and viable. Thus if Buber's positively and optimistically constructive speech enacts a genuine dialogue between himself and members of West Germany's public sphere, Celan's negative response performs the sheer impossibility of reaching that audience. It is not that Celan would intentionally counteract Buber's ambition. Rather he arrives at a similar position (on the question of a counter-public sphere in which the experience of survivorship could be recognized in its collective dimension) by taking the reverse path, substituting reticence (for pathos) and hypothesis (for faith). Even though it is predicated on silence and the failure to communicate, Celan's speech nevertheless postulates an alternative, relational sphere of individual lived experience: *Erfahrung*. The latter is qualitatively distinct from the immediate but isolated experience that thinkers like Benjamin and Adorno had linked to the proliferation of *Erlebnis* under the conditions of modernity. As Miriam Hansen writes, "*Erfahrung* crucially came to entail the capacity of memory—individual and collective, involuntary as well as cognitive—and the ability to imagine a different future."[1] Celan's distinction between art and poetry, as conveyed in the following pages, is founded on this very idea.

Subtle as it is, the weight of Celan's rhetorical rejection of Buber's notion of dialogue is only fully perceivable by hearing the speech out loud. More than any other example of public speaking considered here, *The Meridian* must be read, indeed listened to, *as a speech*, for it is only when one hears Celan's voice enunciating his difficult prose that the full extent of its opacity becomes apparent. As the original transcript of the speech shows, Celan had painstakingly underlined the words he planned to emphasize, and he articulated his text in a meticulous and acoustically lucid manner.[2] And yet the expressiveness of his enunciation only underscores the transcript's semantic obscurity. Celan's language abounds with cryptic references, paradoxical metaphors, and metonymic shifts that generate infinite regress

---

1. Miriam Bratu Hansen, *Cinema and Experience: Siegfried Kracauer, Walter Benjamin, and Theodor W. Adorno* (Berkeley, CA: University of California Press, 2012), xiv.
2. See the facsimile of typescript "L" in Celan, *The Meridian*, 281.

or circularity, delineating the circumlocutious quality that generates the speech's evocative title: the speech is itself a "meridian." Concerned with the limits to what could and what could not be said after Auschwitz—with what Celan refers to as "the borders language draws" (*ME*, 9)—poetic language for Celan can only ever represent (and only hypothetically so) a sphere of linguistic artifice. Contrary to Buber's genuine dialogue, then, which dispenses with the semantic function of language, Celan's relies on language in its semantically most elaborate form. And yet, despite their differences, both speeches are equally premised on the futility of making a meaningful *statement* all the while pinning their hope on the transformative power of performative *speech*.

It is hard to conceive that Celan wrote *The Meridian* as a public address to be delivered to a general audience at the Büchner Prize ceremony. There is no precedent for Celan's speaking for over half an hour in highly abstract and often disjointed sentences replete with cryptic messages that even the quickest thinker might capture only upon reading and rereading the text. It is a strange way of positioning himself as a poet laureate, for the less he explains the less he divulges.

What further complicates matters is that Celan at one point self-reflexively contemplates the opaque quality of his speech in a language that is, however, equally cryptic. In a passage that comments on a familiar criticism leveled at contemporary poetry—that it is deliberately unintelligible—Celan likewise withholds his mite of meaning. The passage begins with an *unvermittelt* (immediate) allusion to the sudden appearance of a mysterious *etwas* (something). And then, quoting Pascal in a foreign language (French) and via the less-canonical, lesser-known intermediary Lev Schestov (an antisystematic philosopher whose often paradoxical thought, instead of solving problems, emphasizes life's enigmatic qualities), Celan provides a definition of this "something" that explains nothing. The passage is worth quoting in full: "'Ne nous reprochez pas le manque de clarté puisque nous en faisons profession!'—This is, I believe, if not the congenital darkness, then however the darkness attributed to poetry for the sake of an encounter from a—perhaps self-created—distance or strangeness" (*ME*, 7). Instead of clarifying, Celan here validates poetry's "darkness" as something that is congenital and yet, paradoxically, has been "attributed to" it, rightfully allocated from a "perhaps self-created," and thus maybe imaginary, maybe nonexistent "distance or strangeness." All for the sake of some unexplained "encounter" that may or may not transpire within (or result from?) the realm of poetry. So at least Celan "believes."

As a public speaker, Celan is diametrically opposed to Buber, whose every sentence expresses with utmost clarity, *is*, what it is saying. In contrast to Buber's Peace Prize address, then, Celan's *Meridian* seems almost impenetrable. Situated in the realm of the hypothetical, its winding, circuitous rhetoric often alludes to a particular meaning, which it then fails to convey. While Buber practices a seemingly effortless form of public speech that purports to instantiate dialogue by way of genuine "saying," Celan ultimately founders on the generic constraints of public speech. Like his poetry, *The Meridian* tests the semantic range of his native language and as it were performs the boundaries of the unsayable through a language that borders on hermeticism. However, as Celan delivers a public speech in Germany, the problem of verbal representation gains in dimension and implication. For lack of the ability to state explicitly the knowledge he has about the Holocaust and for want of an ideal, sympathetic listener who would be able (and willing) to hear it, he is painfully aware of the sheer impossibility of living up to the task of confronting a German audience and speaking to them. And yet Celan produces fragment upon fragment, even if these fragments are provisional and lacking in rhetorical confidence. His speech, albeit premised on Buber's philosophical system and the concept of genuine dialogue, approaches the philosopher's questions from the opposite end of the spectrum. Imposing rhetorical constraint where Buber removes himself from the precepts of what is considered sayable, Celan gives an infinitely more provisional, indeed apprehensive, public address.

But what specific aspects of Buber's philosophy of dialogue does Celan adopt? With endless variety, a rhetorical and highly artificial language is set up against one that is spoken, intersubjective, and unpredictable. This pervasive theme reiterates Buber's dichotomy between inauthentic, fossilized speech and unmediated, genuinely dialogical "saying." Revisiting the romantic trope of poetry as dialogue, Celan equates the latter, dialogical form of speech with poetry: "The poem is lonely. It is lonely and *en route*," Celan notes in *The Meridian*; and then adds: "The poem wants to head toward some other, it needs this other, it needs an opposite. It seeks it out, it bespeaks itself to it" (*ME*, 9). Buber had likewise drawn an analogy between poetry and dialogue in his lecture *The Word That Is Spoken*, delivered in July 1960 in Munich (note again the temporal proximity to Celan's Büchner Prize address). Yet contrary to Celan, who maintains that the poem's quest for a dialogical other must inevitably fail, Buber suspects such interlocutors to *wesen* (be) virtually anywhere. As Buber's archaism, which incidentally predates Heidegger's use of the word, suggests, they are permanent, abundant, and readily available: "For the poem is spokenness, spokenness to the Thou, wherever this partner may be."[3] The poem is dialogue and thus positively connoted. Conversely, *Kunst* (art) is negative, as it binds and cognizes, indeed reconstructs. Buber writes: "All response binds the You into the It-world. That is the melancholy of man, and that is his greatness. For thus knowledge, thus works, thus image and example come into being among the living. . . . Art too: as he beholds what confronts him, the form discloses itself to the artist. He conjures it into an image" (*IT*, 89–91). Arising when "a human being confronts a form that wants to become a work through him," artworks result from creative acts that mold *Gestalt* (form) into a *Gebilde* (image) (*IT*, 60, 91). Whereas for Buber poetry seeks out genuine dialogue, art is based on the artist's individual,

3. Buber, "The Word That Is Spoken," 118.

indeed individuated, experience—*Erlebnis*. Understood as the fragmented, alienated, and hence inferior form of experience, *Erlebnis* disturbs the smooth flow of what Buber referred to as "cosmic reality."[4]

Celan presents a similarly critical, if more drastic, version of Buber's rationale against the process of representation and mimesis when quoting a prominent passage from Büchner's prose fragment *Lenz* (1835):

> Yesterday as I was walking along the valley, I saw two girls sitting on a rock: one was putting up her hair, the other helping her; and the golden hair was hanging free, and a pale, solemn face, and yet so young, and the black peasant dress, and the other one so absorbed in her task. The finest, most heartfelt paintings of the Old German School scarcely convey an inkling of this. At times one wishes one were a Medusa's head in order to turn a group like this into stone, and call everybody over to have a look. (*ME*, 5)

According to Celan's reading of the passage, Büchner's protagonist, who is based on the historical playwright J. M. Reinhold Lenz, rejects the kind of artistic process embodied by the Medusa's head because it transforms and effectively freezes nature into its other—namely inauthenticity, automation, and artifice: "This is a stepping beyond what is human, a stepping into an uncanny realm turned toward the human—the realm where the monkey, the automatons and with them . . . oh, art too, seems to be at home" (*ME*, 5). Art is, for Büchner as for Celan, the equivalent of a reified form of experience. It is also, like Buber's realm of the *Ich-Es*, both ubiquitous and uncanny.

In his *Meridian* speech, Celan aligns art not only with mimesis and artifice but also with rhetoric, while poetry stands for authentic saying (*ME*, 3).[5] In Celan's own terms, art is the equivalent of monological *Sprechen* (speaking), and poetry corresponds to genuine *Reden* (saying). This is a clear reference less to Heidegger's phenomenological project than to Buber's dialogical philosophy.[6] As Celan writes in his prose narrative *Gespräch im Gebirg* (Dialogue in the Mountains, 1959), itself a text that strongly resonates with Buber's thought, "[The stone] does not talk, he speaks, and whoever speaks, sibling child, talks to nobody, he speaks, because nobody hears him, nobody and Nobody."[7] In contrast to *Reden*, which calls for response and thus

---

4. Martin Buber, *The Letters of Martin Buber: A Life of Dialogue*, ed. Nahum N. Glatzer and Paul Mendes-Flohr (New York: Schocken Books, 1991), 12.

5. See Lacoue-Labarthe, *Poetry as Experience*, 48–49.

6. Against the dominant approach that interprets Celan's Büchner Prize address as an effect of his engagement with Heidegger's philosophy, the present study emphasizes the influence of Buber on Celan's canonical text.

7. Paul Celan, *Gesammelte Werke in fünf Bänden*, ed. Beda Allemann and Stefan Reichert (Frankfurt a. M.: Suhrkamp, 1983), 3:169–73, here 171; my translation. Lyon notes that Celan "disclaimed any connection between the title of his own 'Gespräch im Gebirg' and an early work by Buber entitled

actively involves the addressee, *Sprechen* rejects and ultimately rebounds from the other because here the *I* is not open to encounter the other's alterity. Like Buber, Celan believes that the latter, self-absorbed, and antidialogical form of speaking dominates human dialogue.

In the *Meridian* speech, ubiquitous *sprechen*, which is exemplified by what Celan defines as Camille and Danton's "artful words," is the force that propels Celan's speech away from genuine dialogue (*ME*, 3). For Celan makes inflated use of rhetorical tropes and shuns the idiosyncratic vocabulary of verbal communication, thus impeding the dialogical encounter that might otherwise result.[8] We have then two prose texts about dialogue that are poles apart. On the one hand, there is *Conversation in the Mountains*, a written narrative that lays claim to an oral tradition by recounting a dialogue (that was originally spoken in Yiddish)—or so the conceit goes. On the other hand, there is *The Meridian*, a speech that refutes its status as an actual oral event by emphasizing its scriptive, rhetorical economy.[9] In what emerges as another layer of irony, Celan's oft repeated invocation "Ladies and gentlemen" in *The Meridian* bespeaks the habit of Jews from Eastern Europe to fill awkward conversational silences with courtesy phrases.[10] Used as a quintessentially Yiddish idiom, uttered by a Jew from Czernowitz who spoke German, not Yiddish, and who did not identify with Eastern European Jewry, the phrase subverts the audience's preconceived notions concerning Jews, by effectively invoking and provoking their own hidden anti-Semitic tendencies.

'Gespräch in den Bergen,' to which I [Lyon] had called attention. But he went on to confirm that there were other parallels, among them the dialogical underpinnings of their works." Lyon, *Paul Celan and Martin Heidegger*, 227 n. 21.

8. The *Meridian* includes, but is certainly not limited to, the following rhetorical figures: *anamnesis* ("Art, you will remember" [2]); *climax* ("Art . . . is . . . a problem . . . a mutable, tough and long-lived, I want to say, an eternal problem" [2]); *anadiplosis* ("The poem is lonely. It is lonely and *en route*" [9]); *anaphora* ("It is the counterword, it is the word that cuts the 'string.' . . . It is an act of freedom. It is a step" [3]); *litotes* ("that I don't let this go unsaid" [4]); *epanalepsis* ("probably is in the air—the air we have to breathe today" and "I search for Lenz himself, I search for him . . . I search for his shape" [5 and 6]); *parenthesis* ("Doesn't Büchner—I now must ask—doesn't George Büchner" [5]); *paradox* ("A calling-into-question to which all of today's poetry has to return, if it wants to question further" [5]); *oxymoron* ("go with art into your innermost narrows. And set yourself free" [11]); *synonym* ("I have anticipated, reached beyond" [5]); *refrain* ("Long live the king" [3]); *apostrophe* ("But the poem does speak!" [8]); *correction* ("it speaks always only on its own, on its own behalf" [8]); *conduplicatio* ("permit me . . . permit me" [8, 9]); *annomination* ("But not just language as such, nor, presumably, just verbal 'analogy' either" [9]); *parallelism* ("And the human being? And the creature?" [10]); *metaphor* ("I find . . . a *meridian*" [12]); *anticipation* ("I have anticipated, reached beyond" [5]); *citation* ("permit me to quote here a phrase by Malebranche" [9]); and finally in a citation from *Lenz* an *elision* ("And so he lived on . . ." [6]).

9. For a listing of the Yiddish and oral elements in *Conversation in the Mountains*, see Stéphane Mosès, "Wege, auf denen die Sprache stimmhaft wird," in *Argumentum e silentio*, ed. Amy C. Colin (Berlin: W. de Gruyter, 1987), 43–57, here 48.

10. See Richter, "Die politische Dimension der Aufmerksamkeit im *Meridian*," *DVjs* 77 (2003): 659–76, here 665. Richter cites a diary entry by Franz Kafka as evidence for the "Eastern-Jewish habit of inserting, when speech halts, 'Honorable Ladies and Gentlemen' or just 'Dear.'" Franz Kafka, diary entry of January 24, 1912, in Kafka, *Tagebücher 1910–1923* (Frankfurt a. M.: Fischer, 1994), 177.

The phrase is interesting, too, because it is simultaneously a remnant of a vernacular tradition and a standard rhetorical trope. And in that latter function, as part of the disembodied rhetoric of written tradition, it further destabilizes the oral status of Celan's speech. In a paradoxical inversion of speaking and writing, which *The Meridian* itself fails to fully grasp, the speech leaves its actual oral provenance in question by mobilizing the artificiality and scripted character of rhetorical eloquence, whereas Celan's *Conversation in the Mountains* is presented as the transcript of a fictional conversation that is itself a rumination on the possibility of an impending dialogue. By continually drawing attention to its own rhetoricity, Celan's self-consciously rhetorical speech performs the ubiquity of art's artificiality and at the same time gradually consumes its other—poetry and dialogical saying.

It has been noted that Celan stages several attempts to break away from rhetorical redundancy.[11] Speaking about the so-called *Kunstgespräch* (dialogue about art) in Büchner's play *Dantons Tod* (Danton's Death), he suggests that it is so empty and formulaic that it could be continued ad infinitum if it were not to be interrupted: "if nothing interfered" (*ME*, 2). As if testing whether rhetorical artifice could give way to poetic saying or an event of genuine dialogue, Celan suggests that it ultimately can: "Something does interfere" (*ME*, 2). But while in Büchner's play, Danton is called out and the conversation comes to a halt, there is no such disruption in Celan's speech.[12] Here the potential break, the breaking in of essence and genuine dialogue, never takes place, and Celan instead resumes, indeed resigns himself to, his futile, art-bound soliloquy, noting laconically, "Art returns" (*ME*, 2). The *Meridian* speech is itself a *Kunstgespräch*, self-consciously aware that, at least in Buber's terms, a *Gespräch* about *Kunst* is an oxymoronic construction. As if incapable of changing the discursive register of his speech, Celan alludes to but in the same breath rejects the possibility of a radical departure from art and rhetoric.[13] Although the latent possibility of *Dichtung* resurfaces time and again (most notably in his discussion of Lucile's exclamation "Long live the king" and in the allusion to Lenz's "falling silent," both examples of speech acts that eschew signification), such precious, liberating, and quintessentially human instances of poetry appear highly improbable (*ME*, 3, 7).[14] This is not to deny that Celan gestures toward the possibility that a shared emotional experience may arise from his public address. At one point he even asserts suggestively, "It takes away his—and our—breath and words" (*ME*, 7).

11. See, most recently, Schäfer and Wergin, *Die Zeitlichkeit des Ethos*, 125 and 134.
12. See Georg Büchner, *Danton's Death* (1835), act 2, scene 3, in *Georg Büchner: The Major Works*, ed. Matthew Wilson Smith, trans. Henry J. Schmidt (New York: Norton, 2012), 17–82, here 49.
13. See Schäfer and Wergin, *Die Zeitlichkeit des Ethos*, 121.
14. Paul Celan reads Lucile's *Gegenwort* "Long live the king" as a word that actualizes itself outside of the referential or semantic function of language. Articulating a truth that "stands outside all relation to an expressible What" (Buber, "The Word That Is Spoken," 118), her statement is pure communication in which words *embody* rather than signify truth. In that way, it could be defined as an instance of genuine dialogue, "a saying without a said." Levinas, *Proper Names*, 40.

Yet Celan's measured and not in the least breathless enunciation of this very statement refutes the validity of the projected stance. Hence the phrase must be understood as a trope and not as an emotive move. It speaks to Celan's reticent elocution,
which is so introverted that it even suppresses identification and empathy, be it
with Büchner's characters or with the speaker himself. Mobilizing the trope of
reading as a solitary labor, Celan's speech leaves no room for a dialogical *uns* (us). In
contrast to Buber, who sought to provoke a dialogue with his Paulskirche addressees through his reconciliatory rhetoric and hope-inspiring imagery, Celan never
breaks through to his audience. Projecting the end of a German-Jewish dialogue
(if one ever did exist), *The Meridian* implies a trajectory that foreshadows and ultimately leads to Celan's withdrawal from Germany's public sphere, which in his
view perpetually replayed the historical violence of National Socialism.

Dialogue's recession deep into a hypothetical sphere significantly lowers the
stakes of Celan's public speech in Germany. As he wrote in a letter to Otto Pöggeler
on August 30, 1961, his goal in Darmstadt was simply to bring dialogue *back to
memory*: "It seemed to me a matter of—among other things—evoking the memory
of dialogue as the (perhaps sole) possibility of the towardness of men (and only
then the poets)."[15] A threefold concession to the improbability of a German-Jewish
dialogue: access is not immediate, but rather through "memory"; likewise, it is a
"possibility" rather than an actuality; furthermore, even this tentative access is not
guaranteed, but may only "perhaps" occur. Maybe a more forceful trigger for memory recall would be requisite than the one Celan opted for in his speech. The persistent in*script*ion (the use of the word here is deliberate) of the apostrophe "Ladies
and gentlemen" hardly suggests authentic, anthropomorphically based dialogical
exchange, but seems rather to be founded on a rhetorical conceit reflective of unrealized intent. Indeed, it rings out almost like the call of a carnival barker.

The Meridian

In 1959, the year before Celan received the Büchner award, poet laureate Günther
Eich concluded his Büchner Prize address with a conventional expression of gratitude: "Ladies and gentlemen, I thank you for your attention."[16] The next year a
surreptitiously mocking Celan countered the conventions of the Büchner Prize—
and epideictic rhetoric sui generis—by thanking his audience for their *attendance*:
"Ladies and gentlemen, I thank you for your presence" (*ME*, 13). By substituting *Anwesenheit* (attendance) for *Aufmerksamkeit* (attentiveness), Celan intimates

15. P. Celan to Otto Pöggeler, August 30, 1961, in Otto Pöggeler, *Spur des Worts: Zur Lyrik Paul Celans* (Freiburg: K. Alber, 1986), 156; my translation.

16. Günther Eich, "Rede zur Verleihung des Georg-Büchner-Preises" (1959), in *Jahrbuch: Deutsche
Akademie für Sprache und Dichtung Darmstadt* (Heidelberg: Lambert Schneider, 1953–), 170–82, here
182; my translation.

that they may not have listened properly and that while they were surely physically "present," they may have been mentally elsewhere. As will become obvious later, this suggestion is perfectly in line with Celan's critique of technology, whereby mass media (including the radio broadcasting technology used to transmit his speech) are detrimental to forging relationships and meaningful connections across disparate discursive spaces.

When Celan casts into doubt his audience's concentration and attentiveness, this is not a light accusation, given that *Aufmerksamkeit* is a conceptual cornerstone of *The Meridian*. A superior mental state of undistracted concentration on both sensory impressions and historical facts, attentiveness is for Celan the source and precondition of poetry: "The attention the poem tries to pay to everything it encounters, its sharper sense of detail, outline, structure, color, but also of the 'tremors' and 'hints,' all this is not, I believe, the achievement of an eye competing with (or emulating) ever more precise instruments, but is rather a concentration that remains mindful of all our dates" (*ME*, 9).

There is, in what Celan describes as *Aufmerksamkeit*, a close link to the primary relation, the *Beziehung*, which forms the foundation of Buber's dialogical philosophy. Situated outside of the permanence of the everyday, the *Beziehung* is, according to Buber, always already there; it is a timeless relation that reaches into the infinite, yet it can be actualized as a *Beziehungsereignis*, an instance or *event* of genuine saying. Celan likewise conceives of a permanent, primal, and, at the same time, elusive state of being that precedes dialogue—and by extension, poetry. Defined as the complete openness toward the otherness of the other, this heightened state of "attentiveness" antedates experience and cognition. But while Celan's notion of *Aufmerksamkeit* is likely inspired by Buber's *Beziehung*, it is stripped of its theological implications and redemptive sentiment. For contrary to Buber's spiritual, indeed sacred, notion of *Beziehung*, Celan's *Aufmerksamkeit* is a secular concept that is grounded in human consciousness, emphasizing the creaturely and the abject. Thus where Buber's *Beziehung* gives way to an instance of divine grace, Celan's *Aufmerksamkeit* conjures the radical forces of (human) nature. Quoting Malebranche—again via an intermediary, Walter Benjamin—Celan refers to it as the "natural prayer of the soul" (*ME*, 9).

Another pointed difference relates to how Buber and Celan respectively define and construe the domain of art. While both situate art in the realm of artifice, only Celan deems it uncanny. In Buber's view, the work of art, albeit a representation and thus a derivative of the original (as mentioned earlier), bears the potential to restore its essence and thus renew the instance of dialogue or poetry that has inspired it: "All response binds the You into the It-world. . . . But whatever has thus been changed into It and frozen into a thing among things is still endowed with the meaning and the destiny to change back ever again" (*IT*, 89–90). Celan, who defines poetry as a radical and harmful—but not irrevocable—intervention, likewise submits that the boundaries separating art and poetry are flexible: art results from instances of—and thus contains as its unrealized potential—poetry, just as poetry is always already transformed into art. As Celan notes, "The poem stands fast at the edge of itself; it calls and brings itself, in order to be able to exist, ceaselessly back from its already-no-longer into its always-still" (*ME*, 8). Identifying poetry as another instance of art, as both its origin *and* potential, Celan contends that art and poetry interrelate and replace one another in a sort of two-pronged exchange. Art is the teleological endpoint in which poetry culminates: "Art would be the route poetry has to cover" (*ME*, 6). And poetry in turn follows in the footsteps (read: complies with the conventions) of art: "poetry which does have to tread the route of art" (*ME*, 6). Yet in direct opposition to Buber, Celan associates both poetry *and* art/rhetoric with *das Unheimliche* (the uncanny) and suggests that neither one provides relief or escape. In a passage of *The Meridian*, Celan indeed collapses the very difference between the two by conflating them at once constatively and performatively: like Lucile's "Long live the king" in Lenz, art is "a terrifying falling silent. . . . Poetry . . . the abyss *and* the Medusa's head, the abyss and the automatons, seem to lie in one direction" (*ME*, 7).[17]

Is this the language of poetry, or is it rhetorical virtuosity? By sheer generic convention, Celan's Büchner Prize address, an epideictic speech written for the purpose of accepting a literary award, is located on the margins between poetry and rhetoric, but it defines itself negatively in relation to both domains. Not only is poetry unattainable and the rhetorical regressive, they are both conflated and thereby reduced to a condition of indistinction. This at least is what the above quote performs as a communicative act: the conjunction *und*, emphasized in the text with italics ("Poetry . . . the abyss *and* the Medusa's head"), thrusts the speaker away from poetry and into the negative space of ellipsis. Beyond its often overrated concern with poetology, *The Meridian* is thus less a speech about poetry than a speech taking recourse to—or rather gesturing toward—the language of poetry to deflect the incommensurability of public speaking. Specifically, it is a speech about the conditions of possibility of public speech in the face of a German post-Fascist audience. In self-reflexively referring to itself, *The Meridian* exposes the genre of public speech as a medium unsuitable for approaching the task of accepting the dubitable honor of a German literary award. Accordingly, it ends with a foregone conclusion: "I find . . . a *meridian*" (*ME*, 12). In what Stanley Corngold has defined as a "medial intrusion," the speech here self-consciously refers back to "the archive"— the transcript from which it emerges—and thereby denies any importance to the enunciative event that has actualized it.[18] In the end, there is no instance of poetry that could momentarily breach the artifice of representation through mystical

---

17. See Thomas Schestag, *Buk* (Munich: Boer, 1994), 10.
18. Stanley Corngold, *Lambent Traces: Franz Kafka* (Princeton, NJ: Princeton University Press, 2004), 56.

openness and totality. There is only its scriptive counterpart: a text that has been scripted already, *The Meridian*. Consequently, the speech concludes in a recursive loop of self-reference by which it collapses into itself and thereby annihilates whatever modicum of meaning it may have produced along the way. And yet this final phrase may offer a unique truth about Celan's rhetorical sensibility: it reveals his resistance to the production of definite meaning.

After all, *The Meridian* is not only the title of Celan's script (and later published speech) but also its central metaphor. A geographical term denoting an imaginary circle on the earth's surface that passes through the North and South geographic poles, the meridian functions as an allegory of self-recursiveness, for it denotes an axis that has two poles but no definite beginning or end. In a deeper sense, it describes a precise and unique geographical denomination that in itself consists of an infinite number of points that despite having a meaningful reference in reality are, mathematically speaking, identical. That at least is how the meridian metaphor applies to Celan's speech. Like a meridian, the speech has no internal signification, nor even narrative directionality, for the order of the paragraphs could be inverted without doing violence to their textual (il)logic. Inverting the sense of reading the speech would be inconsequential, as this inversion would produce neither return nor closure but instead result in the same state of alienation and absurdity that otherwise occurs. But neither is there a referential context outside of the reality of the speech. In *The Meridian* (and the same is true for Celan's poetry), signifiers thus seem to emerge with an entirely new sense and relation to reality. They are, in Celan's own words, *aktualisierte Sprache* (language actualized), which is to say that their meaning is not an inherent property but a pragmatic *function* of the literary text (*ME*, 9). Dependent on the specific context in which it is being uttered, the *Meridian* speech is an event of saying, the meaning of which emerges not from the text itself but from its presentation and reception in Germany's public sphere. Peter Szondi's quote regarding Celan's poetry is equally applicable to his *Meridian* speech: "Celan's language does not speak *about* something, but 'speaks' itself."[19]

Stripped of revelatory power and continually pushing communicative boundaries, *The Meridian* fails to provide a dialectical correction of the world, a world that has been turned upside down—historically, spiritually, and ethically. Contrary to Buber, then, who in his Peace Prize address explored the potential this occasion had in store for him, Celan did not consider the Büchner award ceremony a propitious hour for conjuring change and redemption. Just the opposite is true: his speech protracts the experience of chaos and negativity. As Celan puts it pithily (and in reference to the madness that has befallen the protagonist of Büchner's novella *Lenz*): "He who walks on his head, ladies and gentlemen—he who walks on his head, has the sky beneath himself as an abyss" (*ME*, 7).

---

19. Peter Szondi, "The Poetry of Constancy" (1971), in Szondi, *Celan Studies*, 1–26, here 13.

If there is a point of connection it lies elsewhere. There certainly is a vague form of dialogue emerging from his cryptic, almost solipsistic, speech, yet it involves the speaker and his alter ego rather than an extratextual listener. Not surprising, given that Celan knew that no one who had not been there would be able to grasp the reality of the camps. Celan's persistent use of the apostrophe "Ladies and gentlemen," a poetic figure of exclamatory address, suggests that Celan expected his testimony to bounce back from his audience. For each instance of apostrophe signals that the speaker momentarily turns away from some other interlocutor to address his audience—the *Damen und Herren*—as if he were, or suddenly became, aware of them. The speech thereby suggests that the speaker is not in active pursuit of a dialogue with them, but rather addresses someone else. But who is this other interlocutor if not the poet himself?[20] Like many of Celan's poems, the speech is conceived as a dialogue that "speaks on behalf ... *of a totally other*" (*in eines Anderen Sache zu sprechen*, ME, 8). Yet this other is, paradoxically as it may seem, Celan's proper persona. That is, not his biographical person per se, but some vacillating version of the speaker: Celan's self-projection as a *lyrisches Ich* (lyrical self).[21] In that way, Celan's *Meridian* speech is less of a departure from his poetry than has been suggested elsewhere. Like those poems in which Celan posits a *Du* to inaugurate a dialogue with a person who habitually no longer exists, the *Meridian* speech addresses someone who is merely a hypothetical entity, a lyrical more than real interlocutor, a construction rather than an actual person. This extremely fragile and arguably virtual *Du* is ultimately a placeholder for the speaker's *Ich*.

In his notes for the *Meridian* speech, Celan makes this relation explicit: "The poem ... is solidary; it stands with you, as soon as you, reflecting on yourself, turn toward it" (*ME*, 201). And in another preliminary draft, Celan suggests that it is through poetry that he constitutes himself: "The poem as the I becoming a person" (*ME*, 191).[22] Dialogue, by contrast, is the counterpart of poetry, since it is associated with the perception of otherness ("awareness of the other and the stranger," *ME*, 191). As in his poems, Celan makes extensive use of the second-person pronoun *Du* in the *Meridian* speech without actually interacting or communicating with anyone outside the text. For Celan repeatedly breaks off to emphatically address his

---

20. Irene Kacandes defines apostrophe as a figure that "involves the act of an orator turning away from his normal audience" to address someone else, who could, according to Kacandes, be a dead person, since "the ancients did not distinguish among types of apostrophe based on the ontological status of the apostrophized." Irene Kacandes, *Talk Fiction: Literature and the Talk Explosion* (Lincoln: University of Nebraska Press, 2001), 146.

21. Szondi first made this point in his essay "Reading 'Engführung'": "And so the opening lines of 'Engführung' give us to understand that ... it is not true that the poet is addressing the reader directly (as is the case in a great many poems), nor even that the words have anything to do with him." Peter Szondi, "Reading 'Engführung'" (1971), in Szondi, *Celan Studies*, 27–82, here 29. See also Bollack, *Paul Celan*, 16–17.

22. Bollack emphasizes how crucial this process was for Celan, who sought to secure his biographical continuity through these alter egos. Bollack, *Paul Celan*, 16.

audience yet at each occasion fails to break through to them. Celan thus admonishes these "ladies and gentlemen" as inadequate listeners: "someone who hears and listens and looks . . . and then doesn't know what the talk was all about" (*ME*, 3).

A reluctant public speaker, Celan insinuates that the "ladies and gentlemen" attending his speech have but a faint idea of the self-exploratory process they have come to witness, a process during which he seeks, but ultimately fails, to reclaim his biography. A series of tentative steps and rhetorical questions that gradually replace the speaker's biographical self with a fictitious persona, Celan's Büchner Prize address embodies what Celan terms "a sending oneself ahead toward oneself" (*ME*, 11). Projecting the poet's lived and suffered reality into the realm of rhetoric, the speech illustrates the poet's experience of individuation: "I had . . . encountered myself" (*ME*, 11). As the ellipsis severing the "I" from the "myself" suggests, the self-encounter failed to afford him an experience of self-identity, but resulted instead in Celan's awareness of his incommunicable alienation and alterity. The latter is again symbolized by the figure of the meridian: "Ladies and gentlemen, I find something that consoles me a little for having in your presence taken this impossible route, this route of the impossible. I find what connects and leads, like the poem, to an encounter. I find something—like language—immaterial, yet terrestrial, something circular that returns to itself across both poles while—cheerfully—even crossing the tropics: I find . . . *a meridian*" (*ME*, 12). The significance of the meridian metaphor goes further. Its use here echoes a very different use of the metaphor, which Celan had encountered in a letter from Nelly Sachs: "Dear Paul Celan . . . Between Paris and Stockholm runs the meridian of grief and of comfort."[23] As a semicircle that stretches from Celan's home in Paris to Sachs's own home in Stockholm, Sachs's meridian symbolizes a self-regulating movement between two major poles of emotional experience, consolation and suffering. Sachs accords it the power to provide mediation and emotional equilibrium. Celan, by contrast, envisions the meridian as a loop that not only stretches from one pole to the other but extends through both poles to come full circle again ("something circular that returns to itself across both poles" *ME*, 12).[24] Both eternally extending and infinitely recurring, Celan's meridian is not a pendulum but a circle, a tractionless spinning wheel. It is evidently a figure that refutes any prospects of mediation.[25]

Celan's use of the meridian metaphor not only differs from Sachs's; it is also diametrically opposed to Buber's notion of a *Himmelsbahn* (celestial orbit), which

---

23. N. Sachs to P. Celan, October 28, 1959, in P. Celan and N. Sachs, *Briefwechsel*, ed. B. Wiedemann (Frankfurt a. M.: Suhrkamp, 1999), 25. *Paul Celan, Nelly Sachs: Correspondence*, trans. Christopher Clark, ed. Barbara Wiedemann, intr. John Felstiner (Riverdale-on-Hudson, NY: Sheep Meadow Press, 1995); quoted in Felstiner, *Paul Celan*, 156 n. 27.

24. See Jean Bollack, "Paul Celan und Nelly Sachs: Geschichte eines Kampfs," *Neue Rundschau*, 1994, 121. On the term *meridian*, see also Schestag, *Buk*, 5.

25. As Schestag points out, Celan eliminated the notion of consolation when he cited the metaphor in a response to Nelly Sachs. Schestag, *Buk*, 7.

represents the natural course of human history: "The path is not a circle. It is the way" (*IT*, 168). A perpetually dwindling spiral that never touches the same point twice, Buber's *Himmelsbahn* invokes a progressive motion that suggests closure and ultimately promises deliverance. Conversely, Celan's meridian touches and perpetually overshoots the poles of consolation and suffering. That it to say, it symbolizes life *after* it has culminated in an endpoint of history—the complete blockage of experience. Celan's meridian figures both as the impossibility of transcendence and as the existential void experienced by a subject standing in the catastrophe's aftermath. Hence it embodies the fate of the *Ich* who is ontically suspended and can therefore neither converge with his biography nor encounter—let alone engage in a dialogue with—the other. Deprived of what Alexander Kluge and Oskar Negt have defined as a *Lebenszusammenhang*—the capacity to recognize and construct relationality in an increasingly fragmented world—Celan cannot insert himself into a preexisting community, or a politically constructed nation-state such as the Federal Republic of Germany. As a substitute he posits the existence of a conspiratorial counter-public sphere that arises among (and in the memory of) those exceptional revolutionary individuals who fought against (and fell victim to) right-wing nationalist and National Socialist ideologies.

Automation

There is another tragic biography buried in *The Meridian*. Early on in the text, Celan reminisces about the anarchist and Socialist leader Gustav Landauer, a friend and colleague to Buber who was beaten to death in 1919 by paramilitary Reichswehr and Freikorps troops controlled by the forces of reaction. Landauer, one of whose "most tragic and childish mistakes" it was, according to Celan, to believe that "his Germanness and Judaism do each other no harm and much good," continued to be a victim of right-wing Nationalist violence even beyond his death.[26] After the Nazis seized power in Germany, they destroyed his grave and sent his remains, together with a bill for relocation costs, to the Jewish congregation in Munich. It was only in 1954 that Landauer's remains were put to final rest in Munich's Neuer Israelitischer Friedhof (New Israeli Cemetery). Celan, faced with an analogous case of homelessness, was also deprived of a *Herzland* ("shoreline of the heart"), a concrete terrain and intimate place that would be the geographical focus of his identity.[27] Yet in contrast to Landauer's, Celan's loss of a home marks a traumatic turning point in his childhood rather than the culminating point of his death. In 1941 his native Bucovina, a northern province of Romania, was invaded

26. Quoted in Felstiner, *Paul Celan*, 262.
27. "Speech on the Occasion of Receiving the Literature Prize of the Free Hanseatic City of Bremen," in Celan, *Collected Prose*, 33–35, here 35.

by the Nazis, who subsequently began to ghettoize and deport all Jewish people. In 1947, the Paris Peace Treaty forced Romania to formally cede the northern part of Bukovina to the USSR. Celan's homeland ceased to exist.

There is yet another way in which Landauer and Celan's fates were to become intertwined. They also share the destiny of being *totgeschwiegen* (silenced to death)—of being muted by forces of verbal abuse. As Celan writes in a letter to Erich von Kahler: "Maybe you remember that back in the day in Darmstadt I mentioned Gustav Landauer—which not only the press but even, right then and there—be astonished, don't be astonished—, the microphones of the highly perfected loudspeaker system silenced to death (I am tempted to say: to life)."[28] Celan thus suggests that during his speech in Darmstadt the audio technology failed to properly amplify a passage in which he mentioned Landauer's name precisely because of said mention. A technological failure with consequences that are evident even today: paragraphs 1 to 9 of Celan's speech were neither transmitted on the radio nor recorded for prosperity.[29] Was this odd moment of technological "censorship" caused by an innocuous technological glitch, or was it the result of a reactionary plot against two Jews, one a former anarchist and Socialist leader, the other a foreign "rhymester," as Celan seems to imply? Conversely, is Celan's above-quoted comment a strike at his critics, or his paranoid projection, based perhaps on the fact that he was under heavy attack during the time of the Büchner address? Whatever his reasons, the result is that the audience misses Landauer's story, and with it the story of Celan, who resembles Landauer in the sense of being himself reminiscent of the one he remembers.

Then what does Celan mean by "silenced to life"? The comment can surely be read as an allusion to Claire Goll's defamation campaign. Having received vast amounts of negative publicity, Celan may be suggesting that silence surrounding his name is precisely the opposite of death: it secures his survival in West Germany's cultural establishment and literary sphere. But the comment also implies that one's proper name is structurally related to death. As Derrida has argued, the proper name speaks the singularity of death, since it holds the possibility that the one who bears the name will be absent from it.[30] God calls by name, but so did the deportation lists. Did Celan hope to secure his survival by renouncing his name? Did "Celan" hope to keep "Antschel" alive by preventing others from naming him thus? Is language literally the sphere that disembodies?

---

28. P. Celan to Erich von Kahler, July 28, 1965, in Paul Celan and Gisèle Celan-Lestrange, *Correspondence (1951–1970)*, ed. Bertrand Badiou and Eric Celan (Paris: Seuil, 2001), 1:259; my translation.

29. See Paul Celan, *Georg-Büchnerpreis 1960 der Deutschen Akademie für Sprache und Dichtung an Paul Celan, Laudatio und Dankesrede "Der Meridian"* (Frankfurt a. M.: Hessischer Rundfunk, 1960), audio recording.

30. Jacques Derrida, *The Work of Mourning*, ed. Pascale-Anne Brault and Michael Naas (Chicago: University of Chicago Press, 2001), 14.

This is certainly the case when it is transmitted through a "highly perfected speaker system" such as the one Celan came upon as he delivered his Darmstadt address. Celan, like many of his contemporaries, was alarmed by the prospect of a cybernetic age and the related horror of technological encroachment, subjugating humankind to its own fabrications. Did he perhaps find himself unwilling to speak into a microphone that was hooked up to speakers and a recording device?[31] The irony that he was to elaborate on the theme of uncanny automatons through a piece of technical equipment that was linked both psychologically and phenomenologically to this effect could not have escaped this profound and serious thinker. With his voice transmitted to the receivers and radio stations, and thus effectively multiplied (and fragmented) as if he were himself hooked up to one of the automatons he critiques in his speech, is Celan not unwittingly complicit with this unnatural and alienating form of communication?

Seen in this light, one as yet underexplored question raised by Celan's *Meridian* speech thus concerns the metareflexive dimension of his critique of technology as it pertains to the abuses of mass media power offered by public service broadcasting. For Celan not only speaks explicitly about his contempt for automatons and "thinking machines," which allowed no connections to authentic existence, but also rhetorically and performatively enacts the impossibility of making such connections and mediating dialogic exchange. In that way, Celan's speech points to the large-scale dangers and indeed the systemic failure of radio broadcasting. His Büchner Prize address prefigures a critique of television and radio that Kluge and Negt were to articulate a decade later when they contended that mass media were but a unidirectional, noninteractive mode of communication that offered nothing but "regulatory forms of communication that do not entail response."[32] Celan knows that from their inception, television and radio were not conceived as forms of communication between free individuals. Instead they were characterized by the fact that "a large heterogeneous audience more or less simultaneously exposes itself to utterances transmitted via media by an institution, whereby the audience is unknown to the station."[33]

As someone who felt himself completely and helplessly exposed to Goll's well-orchestrated, slanderous media campaign, Celan was surely sensitive to the political implications of mass media and communication technologies. Celan's speech, rather than opening up possibilities of communication and debate within the public sphere, foists itself on its recipients without invoking or responding to the demands of his interlocutors. But this is not because Celan would not have been invested

31. See Lyon, *Paul Celan and Martin Heidegger*, 125.

32. Kluge and Negt, *Public Sphere and Experience*, 101.

33. Otto N. Larsen, "Social Effects of Mass Communication," in *Handbook of Modern Sociology*, ed. Robert E. L. Faris (Chicago: Rand McNally: 1966), 348; quoted in Kluge and Negt, *Public Sphere and Experience*, 99 n. 3.

in being understood and appreciated by the German public. It is only that he was more invested in positing the paradox of broadcasting media, which created an illusion of immediate and authentic experience but effectively failed to correspond to any actual level of social cooperation. As Kluge and Negt were to put it in 1972, at a time when a depersonalizing technological shift had fully materialized, "To grasp how unnatural this state of affairs is, just imagine that one could use the telephone only if one were prepared to employ prefabricated phrases."[34] In a way, this is exactly what Celan does in his Büchner Prize address: by retrieving stock phrases and rhetorical expressions and presenting them without mediation or commentary, he comments on the absurdity of anyone expecting purposeful and authentic discourse from a public speech or the radio.

The speaker system is an automaton that amplifies and multiplies the power of a voice but at the same time severs it from human corporeality, thereby exemplifying what Sigmund Freud, in his seminal essay *Das Unheimliche* (The Uncanny, 1919), had described as the uncanny effect of an inanimate object coming to life: "When we proceed to review the things, persons, impressions, events and situations which are able to arouse in us a feeling of the uncanny in a particularly forcible and definite form, the first requirement is obviously to select a suitable example to start on. Jentsch has taken as a very good instance 'doubts whether an apparently animate being is really alive; or conversely, whether a lifeless object might not be in fact animate.'"[35]

The speaker and recording equipment used for Celan's speech allowed for a multiplicity of auditors to tune in and thereby promoted virtually unlimited proximity, immediacy, and synchronicity. All of the German-speaking world could partake in the event, and Celan would truly "go public." Yet as the medium breaks down, and the illusion of immediacy is disrupted, the unbridgeable distance between the speaker and his addressees—and the unfeasibility of their encounter—becomes painfully obvious. After all, the audio technology used to amplify and record Celan's Büchner Prize address operates on the margins of distance and proximity, presence and death. It simultaneously enables and undercuts communication, for it is designed to strengthen and multiply the speaker's voice in the public sphere, but it nevertheless makes him speechless simply by ceasing to function. In that way, the incident with the malfunctioning loudspeaker system magnifies both the challenges and the promises of public speech, particularly as it is transmitted via radio. *The Meridian* was broadcast and widely heard on public radio, the medium that had emerged from the war as the best-preserved and most broadly available means of mass communication. Given that in the early 1960s,

34. Kluge and Negt, *Public Sphere and Experience*, 102.
35. Sigmund Freud, "The 'Uncanny,'" in *The Standard Edition of the Complete Psychological Works of Sigmund Freud*, trans. James Strachey (London: Hogarth Press, 1959), 17:218–52, here 226.

85 percent of German households owned a radio transmitter, Celan's speech surely reached a larger public than his books of poetry. Celan did not, however, take his exposure to the mass audience of radio broadcasting casually. For he knew that the more accessible and consumable a voice is made, the more potentially devastating the effects of its successful transmission.

A fundamental aporia, then, of Celan's speech is that its dissemination depends on the very medium that suddenly interferes with it, along with the fact that a medium is involved at all. In this chilling, dystopian tale of technology, a voice by itself is apparently no longer enough. But what if is there *is* no voice beyond the audio system, no speech without a medium, and no language beyond automation? Then humankind has reached the point where the possibility of commencing a genuine human dialogue has been annihilated by the actuality of another truly murderous technology—the one used to carry out the "final solution."

3

INGEBORG BACHMANN

Representation demands to be radical and results from coercion.

—Ingeborg Bachmann, *German Contingencies*

Where Paul Celan points to the technological dimension of public speaking, most notably through his mystification at the loudspeakers' "censorship" of his Büchner address, Ingeborg Bachmann reacted to the obligatory use of electro-acoustic and radio-transmission technology in public speeches with a much more ambivalent attitude. The Austrian poet once offered a forceful critique of modern mass media, which she believed to be responsible for the condition of contingency that defines modernity: "I would agree with Benjamin, because it is this shrinkage of experience, that arises more and more, through the development of the mass media, through the second-hand life."[1] Yet her objections did not keep Bachmann from producing audio recordings of works that she recited herself. Bachmann's long-standing commitment to auditory media is also manifest in her continuing participation and

---

1. Ingeborg Bachmann, *Wir müssen wahre Sätze finden—Gespräche und Interviews*, ed. Christine Koschel and Inge von Weidenbaum (Munich: Piper, 1983), 140; my translation. Bachmann here alludes to Benjamin's essay "Experience and Poverty" (1933), in Walter Benjamin, *Selected Writings*, ed. Michael W. Jennings (Cambridge, MA: Harvard University Press, 1999), 2:731–72.

professional activity in radio broadcasting. After graduating from the University of Vienna, Bachmann worked as a scriptwriter and editor at the Austrian radio station Rot-Weiss-Rot (1951–53) and subsequently as a correspondent for Radio Bremen (1954–55). In addition, she coauthored the radio series *Die Radiofamilie* (The Radio Family) and wrote and published the radio plays *Ein Geschäft mit Träumen* (A Business with Dreams, 1952), *Die Zikaden* (The Cicadas, 1955), and *Der gute Gott von Manhattan* (The Good God of Manhattan, 1958).

Commentators of her audio plays have praised Bachmann's skilled and innovative handling of audio technology, maintaining that the author made creative use of sound effects to enhance her narratives with a variety of aural illusions.[2] Despite her attentiveness to the technical potential of the newly developing genre of radio play, however, Bachmann's 1964 Büchner Prize address, *Deutsche Zufälle* (German Contingencies), falls short of any obvious aural performativity. Although Bachmann devised an imaginary soundtrack including a variety of sounds—emanating from, for instance, airplanes, church bells, humans, and animals—she delivers her speech in a pointedly nondramatic prosody. Reciting a text that simulates an urban shock experience through a protoexpressionist montage, Bachmann never so much as raises her voice. On the contrary, her diction seems almost impassive. The recording suggests that Bachmann sought to minimize the amount of life the audio technology would extract from her (voice) to be transmitted to an anonymous, perhaps threatening, public. Contrary to Celan, then, who felt menaced by a sudden breakdown of the electro-acoustic system, Bachmann appears to be discouraged by the very flawlessness of the audio technology, capable of overpowering her cautiously introverted elocution. For, as Bachmann writes in her 1956 essay, "Musik und Dichtung" (Music and Poetry), the former was no doubt superior to the human voice, which, albeit lively and genuine, lacked the infallibility and precision of an acoustic apparatus:

> For it is time to forgive the human voice, that voice of a bound creature, not capable of fully saying what it suffers, nor of fully singing what high and low pitches there are to measure. There is nothing but this organ without final precision, without final trustworthiness, with its low volume, the threshold high and low—far from being a device, a sure instrument, a successful apparatus. But there is something of the plainness of youth in it, or the timidity of age, warmth and cold, sweetness and hardness, every virtue of the living. And this distinction to serve hopeless approximation![3]

---

2. See Peter Weiser, *Wien: Stark bewölkt* (Vienna: Christian Brandtstätter, 1984), 104; quoted in Joseph G. McVeigh, "Ingeborg Bachmann as Radio Scriptwriter," *German Quarterly* 75, no. 1 (2002): 42. See also Weigel, *Ingeborg Bachmann*, 260.

3. Ingeborg Bachmann, "Musik und Dichtung" (1959), in Bachmann, *Werke*, 4:59–62, here 62; my translation.

The audio technology used to record and transmit her speech is analogous to a vocal organ, but with "final precision" and unforgiving exactitude. As an acoustic device it reveals not only Bachmann's thoughts and ideas but indeed the very materiality of her living voice in the public sphere. It transmits every quiver and break in her (at least initially) anxious recital, thereby calling attention to the poet's mortality. Like the phonograph, it is a memento mori.[4]

However, the primary interest in the voice recording of Bachmann's Büchner Prize address is not the question of whether or not it serves the "hopeless approximation" of a "bound creature," as Bachmann contends, nor whether or not it is the site of unadulterated authentic expressivity that provides better, more direct access to her human essence than a written text. Rather, the interest lies in the discrepancy between the innocuous tone of Bachmann's performance and the confrontational style and calamitous subject matter of her speech. The live recording of Bachmann's Büchner Prize address provides evidence that Bachmann was a reluctant and by far less prolific and self-assured public orator than, for instance, Buber, who, incidentally and curiously, often refused to be audiotaped, even if his Peace Prize address was as a matter of course broadcast by Hessischer Rundfunk (the public broadcasting station of Hessia).

Yet while Bachmann seems to display what members of the Gruppe 47 had described as a resigned, anxious attitude and awkwardness when reading her poetry, she did take advantage of the Büchner award ceremony, which she clearly understood as a unique opportunity to communicate with West Germany's public.[5] Hence the timidity of Bachmann's voice is deceptive. The speech is a powerful intervention that experiments with and subverts the role of radio broadcasting. Like the radio play *The War of the Worlds*, which Orson Welles aired over the Columbia Broadcasting System radio network in October of 1938, subjecting its listeners to a simulated news bulletin about a supposed Martian invasion, Bachmann's 1964 Büchner Prize address challenges the audience with a provocative feature that implies, through a continuing series of manic scenes and lurid fantasies, that the city of Berlin might still be under siege.[6] Superimposing an apocalyptic vision of

---

4. See John Durham Peters, "Helmholtz und Edison: Zur Endlichkeit der Stimme," in Friedrich Kittler, Thomas Macho, and Sigrid Weigel, *Zwischen Rauschen und Offenbarung: Zur Kultur- und Mediengeschichte der Stimme* (Berlin: Akademie Verlag, 2002), 289–312, here 312.

5. Hans Werner Richter, *Im Etablissement der Schmetterlinge: Einundzwanzig Portraits aus der Gruppe 47* (Munich: Hanser, 1986), 47.

6. On the negative impact of Bachmann's Büchner Prize address, see Weigel, *Ingeborg Bachmann*, 376 n. 49. See also Anna M. Parkinson, "Taking Breath: The Ethical Stakes of Affect in Ingeborg Bachmann's *Ein Ort für Zufälle*," in *Re-acting to Ingeborg Bachmann: New Essays and Performances*, ed. Caitríona Leahy and Bernadette Cronin (Würzburg: Königshausen und Neumann, 2006), 65–79, here 70; and Elke Schlinsog, *Berliner Zufälle: Ingeborg Bachmanns "Todesarten"-Projekt* (Würzburg: Königshausen und Neumann, 2005), 109. For a survey and analysis of references to other important historical and political contexts of the speech, such as the Cold War, see Jost Schneider, "Historischer Kontext und politische Implikationen der Büchnerpreisrede Ingeborg Bachmanns," in *Über die Zeit schreiben*, vol. 2, *Literatur- und Kulturwissenschaftliche Essays zum Werk Ingeborg Bachmanns*, ed.

a war-ridden Berlin on an equally dystopian imagery of the contemporary city, Bachmann transports her audience into a surreal landscape of grotesque artifice— truly an *Ort für Zufälle* (Place for Contingencies), as the title of the published speech conveys.[7]

Bachmann's depiction of Berlin thereby undermines the institution of the Büchner Prize, and with it one of the most prestigious institutions of West Germany's literary landscape: the Akademie der deutschen Sprache und Dichtung (Academy of German Language and Poetry). Instead of praising the German literary tradition, or its poster child Büchner, Bachmann stirs up horrors that the German nation had arguably just begun to forget. Yet the discussion, raised by previous commentators, of whether Bachmann really intended her Büchner Prize address as a public speech, or if she instead had resolved to merely present her latest prose, is ultimately irrelevant. Bachmann's hyperbolic rhetoric as well as her use of blame as a hortative device is fully compatible with the noninstrumental, display rhetoric of epideictic speech.[8]

The question, then, is not whether or not the speech is an example of epideictic rhetoric, but rather what kind of an epideictic speech it is, if it so obviously pushes the generic boundaries to new limits. Insofar as it is incoherent and wavering in its assignment of blame—after all it remains ambiguous whether Bachmann blames the medical staff, the military, the population of Berlin, East or West Germany, or herself, an Austrian citizen—*German Contingencies* fails to construct a politically viable argument or a socially and ethically "appropriate" narrative. Instead it performs, like any classical epideictic speech, the rhetorical self-annihilation of rhetoric by doubling itself metadiscursively in a way that results in a paradox: the rhetorical effect of Bachmann's speech on her listeners depends on their metadiscursive recognition that the speech produces a projective identification with the speaker *as* listener. At the same time, the speech stages a battle for mastery between two rivaling voices that in their dialogical interrelation become self-consciously aware of this dual perspective.

Given its hyperexplicitness as well as its thorough rejection of symbolism, most notably its ostensible lack of metaphorical or figurative speech, Bachmann's Büchner Prize address corroborates her decision to abdicate poetry in favor of prose. It is a well-known fact that after the publication of her prose collection *Das dreißigste Jahr* (The Thirtieth Year) in 1961, she never published another work of poetry. What is more, the speech inaugurates Bachmann's *Todesarten-Projekt* (Manners of Death Project), an unfinished novel trilogy the author conceived as a comprehensive

---

Monika Albrecht and Dirk Göttsche (Würzburg: Königshausen und Neumann, 2000), 127–39. See also Christian Däufel, *Ingeborg Bachmanns "Ein Ort für Zufälle": Ein interpretierender Kommentar* (Berlin: de Gruyter, 2013).

　7. Such is the title of the print version of the speech, first published by Wagenbach in 1965.

　8. See, most recently, Schlinsog, *Berliner Zufälle*, 110–11.

record of the suffering that results from the hidden or socially acceptable crimes committed in and by patriarchal society.[9] As Bachmann writes in a preliminary draft of *German Contingencies*, the prose fragment *Sterben für Berlin* (Dying for Berlin, 1961–62), "And the threat does not occur during war, in times of naked violence, of dominating survival, but before and after, that is, during peace."[10] Bachmann effectively considered the patriarchism and chauvinism of postwar society a continuation of National Socialism.

Seen from Bachmann's perspective, present-day Berlin appears as bleak and amorphous as it was during the area bombings of World War II. Reconfiguring the city's topography by reimagining its most representative sites, such as Gedächtniskirche, Kadewe, Checkpoint Charlie, Krumme Lanke, and Bahnhof Zoo, to name but a few, the speech depicts the perversion and insanity of a society at war while resonating with Bachmann's sometimes sarcastic, sometimes terrified, but always intellectually elusive investment in a city that, even more so than her hometowns Vienna and Klagenfurt, embodied the perils of National Socialism for her. For Bachmann, who had spent 1963–64 in Berlin with a fellowship from the Ford Foundation, viewed the former capital of Nazi Germany as a site of trauma that made its aesthetic representation impermissible. As Bachmann states in her Büchner Prize address, "The damaging of Berlin, the historical conditions of which are familiar, does not allow for mystification or elevation into a symbol," unless, Bachmann concedes and reflects cryptically, this representation is radical "and results from coercion" (*GC*, 279).

Darstellbarkeit

Concluding the first poetologically oriented and introductory section of Bachmann's speech, the above statement implicitly situates what is to follow within the debate of post-Holocaust art.[11] Although Bachmann neither mentions the genocide of the Jews nor directly links Austria's National Socialist past with the kind of patriarchal oppression she still sees at work in present-day society, as she does in her novels, both are unambiguously implied in her graphic language and the violent imagery of her speech. Avoiding a sensationalist tone from which one could

---

9. Ingeborg Bachmann, *"Todesarten"-Projekt*, ed. M. Albrecht and D. Göttsche (Munich: Piper, 1995). For a thorough study of Bachmann's *Schreibwerkstatt* and the development of her *Todesartenprojekt* in Berlin see Ekkerhart Rudolph, "Interview mit Ingeborg Bachmann," and Gerda Bödefeld, "Interview mit Ingeborg Bachmann," in Bachmann, *Wir müssen wahre Sätze finden*, 57 and 111, respectively.

10. Ingeborg Bachmann, *Nachlass*: TA1/ 175, Österreichische Nationalbibliothek, Vienna; my translation. See also Schlinsog, *Berliner Zufälle*, 16.

11. See, most recently, Stephanie Bird, *Women Writers and National Identity: Bachmann, Duden, Özdamar* (Cambridge: Cambridge University Press, 2003), 90. See also Kirsten A. Krick-Aigner, *Ingeborg Bachmann's Telling Stories: Fairy Tale Beginnings and Holocaust Endings* (Riverside, CA: Ariadne Press, 2002).

detect pleasure in her voice, she represents horrors without belittling the experience of suffering or offering a falsely redemptive solution. Instead, she lets nothing but pure, untainted language do the work of recollection:

> We have so many sick here, says the night nurse and fetches the overhanging patients, who are all moist and shaking, back from the balcony. Once again the night nurse looks right through everything, she knows of the balcony thing and applies "the hold" and gives a shot that goes through and through and gets stuck in the mattress so that one can no longer get up. . . . Someone yells that the churches have to go, the patients scream, flee to the corridor, there is water running from the rooms to the corridor, there is blood mixed in, because some have bitten through their tongues, because of the churches. . . . Everyone coughs and hopes and has a thermometer in the armpit, under the tongue, in the rectum, and the needles ten centimeter long in the flesh. (*GC*, 281–82)

This is Bachmann at her most intense. As in the notoriously violent dream sequence in her novel *Malina*, Bachmann experiments here with the limits of *Darstellbarkeit* (representability), an endeavor coinciding temporally and conceptually with her "conscious abdication of poetry in Adorno's terms," which one commentator locates in this period.[12] Bachmann's answer to the problematic status of art and poetry in the wake of Nazi barbarism, as it is expressed here, is radical in its consequence: her speech submits and demonstrates that it is indeed possible to represent the horror, provided that this is done under the same or *psychologically analogous* conditions to those that caused the original dreadful experience. By staging a scene of writing—or rather, *speaking*—that reveals itself as a psychoanalytical session during which a patient not only (neutrally, that is) articulates "unspeakable" horrors, but actually reexperiences them insofar as she is equally frightened and horrified by the coercive process that generates her speech, Bachmann's Büchner Prize address performatively reproduces the coercive conditions under which her text has emerged. In ways both unexpected and obvious, the speech thereby purports to be a spontaneous, hysterical utterance instead of a conventional public address.

Bachmann allegorizes the problem of *Darstellbarkeit* by submitting an argument not *for* the unspeakability of the Nazi terror, but rather *against* the alleged *un*speakability used to deny a voice to those who were subjected to it. She makes this critique within the paralinguistic dimension of her reading, on the level of her *performance*. For the speaker's voice is not only fearful, but stifled and gradually suppressed by the hypnotic voice of an other, a cruel and torturous therapist-figure who emerges as the source of the speaker's coercion. Indeed, the only way to explain

---

12. See Revesz, "Poetry after Auschwitz," 195.

the emotional detachedness and restrained timbre of Bachmann's elocution, which stands in such sharp contrast to its macabre content, grotesque language, and accusatory character, is to differentiate between two competing agencies, one situated on the ontic level of Bachmann's voice, the other on the semantic level of her text. The transcript of the speech represents a trauma text that revolves around Bachmann's stay at a mental institution in Berlin while also alluding to a prior hospitalization in Klagenfurt. But its delivery exhibits the aural and rhetorical qualities typically associated with hypnosis therapy, signal among them repetitiveness, monotony, overstimulation, and a singsong quality that results from its droning, paratactic syntax: "It is aside from the streetcar, is also in the hour of silence, [there] is a cross in front of it, is a crossing in front of it, it is not so far, but also not so close, is—wrong guess!—a thing also, is not an object, is by day, is also by night, is used, has people inside, has trees around it, can, doesn't have to, shall, doesn't have to, is carried, is dropped off . . ." (*GC*, 279).

To the extent that the first and last sections of the speech are presented under the guise of hypnosis, the middle part can be read as a response uttered under the coercive power of a hypnotist. To be sure, the text, which is an incongruous, hysterical discourse consisting of an incessant stream of uncanny hallucinations and morbid fantasies, is marked by a protohysterical collapse of meaning and coherence on the spatial and temporal planes: Berlin trembles and tumbles, Potsdam folds into the buildings of Tegel, the streets lift by forty-five degrees. At the same time, major historical incidents merge with an apocalyptic "now": a flood of veterans returning to Berlin at the end of World War I, the assassination of Walther Rathenau in 1922, the hanging of members of the Kreisau circle in 1944 in Plötzensee. Recounting a military intervention from the perspective of an observer in a hospital, Bachmann here alludes to her own witnessing of the arrival of Hitler's troops in Klagenfurt, an experience that coincided with her sojourn in a hospital. In an oft-cited interview with the German women's magazine *Brigitte*, Bachmann described this as an event so traumatic that with it began her memory:[13]

> There was a specific moment which destroyed my childhood. The entry of Hitler's troops into Klagenfurt. It was something so terrible, that my memory begins with that day: with that early sorrow, whose intensity was perhaps never to be repeated. Naturally, I didn't understand all this at the time, in the way an adult would understand it. But this enormous brutality, which could be sensed, this screaming, singing and marching—the origin of my fear of death. A whole army intruded on our quite peaceful Carinthia.[14]

---

13. Scholarship remains divided over whether this statement is true. For an overview of the discussion see Weigel, *Ingeborg Bachmann*, 24.

14. Bödefeld, "Interview mit Ingeborg Bachmann"; translation by Marjorie Perloff, *Wittgenstein's Ladder: Poetic Language and the Strangeness of the Ordinary* (Chicago: University of Chicago Press, 1996), 264 n. 4.

Bachmann was hospitalized in 1938, at the historical juncture of the Anschluss, because she suffered from diphtheria. It seems likely that the memory of this first, traumatic "fear of death" was triggered again as Bachmann found herself in another hospital in Germany (and in a context that, for reasons that will appear later in their proper sequence, reminded her of Germany's violent past): in 1963, Bachmann underwent treatment at the Martin Luther Hospital in Berlin. Thus Bachmann's Büchner Prize address dramatizes her wartime "trauma" by conflating history with an autobiographical memory, except that in this particular literary reiteration, the agency of the aggressor is displaced onto the clinical staff and some unspecified military power (the Allies, perhaps), while scores of other victims are substituted for her own subjectivity. There is no first-person narrator who figures as a stable witness of this military and/or medical assault. Dramatizing an array of incongruous events and perspectives, the speech retains no stable focus or center of agency. Instead it alternates among what appear to be random competing responses to the chaos, including aggression, panic, and blame. The implications of this highly emotional confrontation are at least twofold. First, it reveals the contradictory logic of Bachmann's childhood trauma while simultaneously objectifying it. Second, it nevertheless compels the audience to think about the nature of this trauma as it extends into their own experience.

The speech's disjuncture between voice/elocution and language/text, which simultaneously exposes and adulterates Bachmann's autobiographical experience, conveys a complexity that is structurally analogous to the composite nature of the authorial stances shaping Bachmann's *Todesarten* texts. As in *Malina* (Malina: A Novel) and *Das Buch Franza* (The Book of Franza), the performance of Bachmann's Büchner Prize address is divided between two competing subject positions, which can be understood to represent a victimized female patient and a patriarchal therapist figure, respectively.[15] In the novels, these subject positions are negotiated among various narrators and characters. In *Malina*, the female first-person narrator eventually surrenders her voice to a male narrator who likewise figures as a character in the novel, while in *Das Buch Franza* the female protagonist occasionally assumes, and arguably merges with, the voice of the male narrator who is telling her story.

In her Büchner Prize address, Bachmann likewise explores the conditions of possibility of female narration and of making audible a voice that is ultimately her therapist's object of mastery. Representing a tortured body as well as a truly frantic text, Bachmann's voice is a political site that itself embodies a traumatic experience. The audio recording of Bachmann's speech can be understood as the literal record of this trauma. For it reveals telling instances of parapraxis—the Freudian mistakes or "slips," which, according to Freud, "have a meaning and can

---

15. On the subject position in *Das Buch Franza* and *Malina*, see Hans Höller, *Ingeborg Bachmann: Das Werk von den frühesten Gedichten bis zum "Todesarten"-Zyklus* (Frankfurt a. M.: Athenäum, 1987), 210.

be interpreted."[16] The following misspeak, for instance, conveys that Bachmann's perspective may be even more profoundly nihilistic than it would seem judging from the script of the speech itself, suggesting that Bachmann was unconsciously convinced that while things went on (as usual), nothing would transpire ever again: "Es geht weiter. Es wird nicht*s* [instead of "nicht," emphasis added] mehr vorkommen." (It goes on. *Nothing* will [instead of "It will not," emphasis added] happen again.) Another psychologically revealing slip is the following, oddly performative error: "Die Fußgänger *er*fangen [instead of "verfangen," emphasis added] sich . . ." (The pedestrians are caught . . .) Bachmann here literally—aurally—stumbles over an inseparable prefix, a verbal trap that she (the text's author) has set herself and that could be said to indicate a repressed memory linked to her fear of performing.

Clearly, it is the speaker's human voice itself—that is, the voice in the sense of the sound produced in her vocal cords rather than in the metaphorical sense of her voice as a function of narration or as a lyrical self—that provides the critical cues for reading Bachmann's Büchner Prize address, not least because the two rival speakers are resuming their battle here. Enacting the gradual silencing of the patient's voice through a fictitious therapist, Bachmann's performance is based on the conceit that the narrative is generated and simultaneously destabilized by her therapist's intervention. Contrary to Bachmann's novels, then, which are interspersed with a number of dialogues investing men with the roles of therapists, *German Contingencies* relegates the latter to the text's exteriority. Rather than being textually inscribed in the narrative, the therapist is the one who "performs" Bachmann's text and thereby exercises ultimate control over it. Hence Bachmann's peculiar delivery and her quiet, monotonous, indeed hypnotizing voice simulate a therapeutic intervention that involves her and, by extension, every member of her audience. The latter must go beyond simply appreciating her speech as a literary experiment and instead recognize it as a speech that aims to affect its listeners. By hearing Bachmann's voice, the listeners serve as unwitting subjects of a hypnosis experiment in the form of a public speech. It resembles a twofold exercise in auditory experimentation: therapeutic and literary.

The Talking Cure

Simulating a therapy session during which an imaginary psychoanalyst, who is embodied by the speaker's droning voice, cures an unconscious trauma that the author of the speech shares with her audience, Bachmann's Büchner Prize address gestures toward the possibility of "talking away" traumatic memories that have been repressed by the German public. Read in the suggestive yet monotonous voice of a hypnotherapist, the text of Bachmann's speech thus figures as her response

---

16. Sigmund Freud, *An Autobiographical Study* (1925), ed. James Strachey (New York: W. W. Norton: 1952), 52.

to the hypnosis analysis: it conveys how a patient discharges certain affects and memories that she associates with her trauma. In so doing, Bachmann's literary experimentation takes a scientifically informed approach to hypnosis theory. It is with great ease and efficiency that Bachmann, a former intern at a neurological clinic, the Nervenheilanstalt Steinhof near Vienna, who had also attended lectures on psychology at the university, engages Sigmund Freud's and Josef Breuer's early experimentations with hypnosis therapy. Specifically, her speech builds on Freud's and Breuer's observation that their patients tended to relive previous experiences when put under hypnosis, experiences that could be associated with the symptomatic expression of their illnesses. In a lecture they coauthored in 1893, titled "On the Psychic Mechanism of Hysterical Phenomena," Freud and Breuer define the aim of hypnosis as bringing the sources of these memories and emotions to consciousness: "It is necessary to hypnotize the patient and to arouse his memories under hypnosis of the time at which the symptom made its first appearance; when this has been done, it becomes possible to demonstrate the connection in the clearest and most convincing fashion."[17]

The first attempts to treat what was then called "hysterical paralysis" with hypnosis therapy originated in Breuer's work with patient "Anna O.," whose hysterical symptoms allegedly declined when the patient, under hypnosis, provided her therapist with a precise account of the circumstances under which each symptom had initially emerged.[18] Breuer argued that by tracing the final symptom back to the traumatic circumstances of its first occurrence, he was able to cure his patient of an array of hysterical symptoms. In her speech, which is framed as a treatment in which the patient is placed under hypnosis so that she may remember a traumatic event, Bachmann likewise recalls a series of memories and traces them back to the original trauma. The resulting narrative is a racing and disjointed account of events she ostensibly has a hard time remembering: "The fluff, the feathers, everyone lost, it is long ago, it is not long ago. It is a celebration, everyone is invited, people drink and dance, must drink, so as to forget everything, it is—wrong guess!—is today, was yesterday, will be tomorrow, [there] is something in Berlin" (*GC*, 292).

One way to characterize this passage is through a medical idiom. Bachmann chooses a language of sickness and pain that is also devoid of empathy. This is a rhetoric of hysteria that structurally reproduces the effects of a therapeutic session. Just as in the hypnosis therapy described in Breuer's and Freud's article, Bachmann's account stages a gradual discharge that recapitulates, in reverse chronology but

---

17. Josef Breuer and Sigmund Freud, "On the Physical Mechanism of Hysterical Phenomena: Preliminary Communication" (1893), in Freud, *The Standard Edition*, 2:1–17, here 3.

18. As Mikkel Borch-Jakobsen has pointed out, Breuer never actually used hypnotic induction on his patient Anna O: "In reality, it was not Breuer but Freud himself who, bolstered by the hypnotic experiments of Charcot, Janet and Delboeuf, first used direct hypnosis in order to recover and 'talk away' traumatic memories." Mikkel Borch-Jakobsen, *Remembering Anna O.: A Century of Mystification*, trans. Kirby Olson (New York: Routledge, 1996), 19 n. 7.

by no means systematically, every occurrence that led to her illness. But does it also claim to eliminate her hysterical symptoms? The speech begins in medias res, with the hospital scene cited above and an apocalyptic scenario of fighter planes crashing through the hospital. After an insistence on adverbs of time that signal immediacy—*jetzt* (now), *dann* (then), *schon* (already)—the narrative gradually slows down to alternate between depictions of the chaos on the streets and in the hospital, and finally illustrates the effect of the war on "die Kinder"—the children of Berlin—whose innocent and lighthearted response to the military intervention not only recalls the romance between the then fifteen-year-old Franza and a British officer described in the *Todesarten* cycle, but also sharply contradicts the logic of Bachmann's "primal scene" from her childhood, which she evoked in the *Brigitte* interview. The text ends on the following significantly less destructive and chaotic note: "No one knows if there is hope, but if there is no hope, then it is not so horrible after all, it dampens itself, it doesn't have to be hope, it can be less, it is nothing, it is . . . the last airplane has approached, the first one approaches after midnight, everything flies rather high up, not through the room. It was a turmoil, was nothing after all. It will not happen again" (*GC*, 292–93).

Bachmann's speech—and, by extension, the hypnotic session that is invoked by it—concludes with a set of conflicting statements. Culminating in the paradoxical assertion that "it was nothing after all" and "will not happen again," this final paragraph superimposes two fundamental psychological processes on Bachmann's public address. The first assertion reflects the mental mechanism of *Verdrängung* (repression), which Freud defined as the function of keeping something out of consciousness and thus inhibiting the development of affect connected with the repressed idea.[19] Unable to integrate the ideas and emotions associated with the traumatic experience into her consciousness, the patient continuously reexperiences the traumatic incident mentally and physically until therapy helps her revisit and cope with the origin of the trauma. The second assertion has two implications. Firstly, it substantiates the (former) presence of a trauma, the occurrence of a traumatic incident, and secondly, it insinuates the possibility that the hypnotic therapy has indeed provided a cure. By stating that "it" will not recur, the patient—or the analyst (in these final sentences, their stances are hard to discern)—confirms that the trauma has successfully been brought to consciousness under psychologically safe conditions. As a result, the patient would be cured, and the audience of Bachmann's public address would emerge as the witness to a therapeutic session that they, too, require in order to work through their own repressed traumas and memories.

By thus exposing the West German public to a group therapy session that would help them acknowledge their Nazi past, Bachmann's address portends Alexander

---

19. Sigmund Freud, "Repression" (1915), in Freud, *The Standard Edition*, 14:141–58.

and Margarete Mitscherlich's *Die Unfähigkeit zu trauern* (The Inability to Mourn), a study diagnosing the German nation with a collective trauma reinforced by government failure to address it seriously: "Official policy remains anchored to nebulous fictions and wishful thinking and has, to this day, failed to make any searching attempt—even if only for the sake of its own political health—to understand the terrifying past and, among other things, the terrifying influence which Nazi promises were able to acquire over the German people."[20] Citing these seminal assertions in 1981, Alexander Kluge and Oskar Negt added that while some Germans may well have individually, if passively, mourned the downfall of Nazi Germany and Hitler's death, the German public had yet to build a collective memory of National Socialism. As Kluge and Negt write with regard to what they consider the undergoing "process of irrealisation," "It is rather the case that people in reality are slaving away *like the dead*, responding to each new fracture, each one of the numerous breaks, as if they were dead, robot-like, while pulling that which is alive back into themselves, into the smallest group, instead of developing an awareness of the losses within the public sphere."[21]

The Mitscherlichs and Kluge and Negt agree that given the grand, national scope of Germany's historical trauma, a cure must be achieved collectively.[22] Hence the urgent need for a counter-public sphere that could provide the framework or forum for a collective effort at *Trauerarbeit* (mourning). In a similar vein, Eric L. Santner argues that "mourning, if it is not to become entrapped in the desperate inertia of a double bind, if it is to become integrated into a history, must be witnessed."[23] But how could such a large-scale cultural project be integrated into the psychoanalytic process, which is traditionally conceived as a profoundly *private* act? After all, it is no coincidence that the private sphere—deemed the sphere of emotional intensity—is conceived of as separated from the public sphere, where reason and fact are meant to prevail. Reversing the bifurcation of "public" and "private" to which psychoanalysis had given legitimacy, Kluge and Negt's concept of the counter-public sphere acknowledges and indeed privileges the conscious and unconscious fantasies of individuals and subaltern subjects.

By using her public speech in Darmstadt and its radio transmission to put herself and the West German citizenry in a state of increased suggestibility and imaginative activity, and by subsequently excavating and talking through what the public has denied and forgotten, Bachmann's speech gestures toward the possibility of providing a "talking cure" that would effectively operate on a collective basis.

20. Alexander Mitscherlich and Margarete Mitscherlich, *The Inability to Mourn*, trans. Beverly R. Placzek (New York: Grove Press, 1975), 10.

21. Alexander Kluge and Oskar Negt, *Geschichte und Eigensinn* (Frankfurt a. M.: Zweitausendeins, 1981), 581–82; my translation.

22. Mitscherlich and Mitscherlich, *The Inability to Mourn*, 25.

23. Eric L. Santner, *Stranded Objects: Mourning, Memory, and Film in Postwar Germany* (Ithaca, NY: Cornell University Press, 1990), 28.

A provocative yet decidedly unironic public address, Bachmann's Büchner Prize address performs the dialogue between a plurality of patients and a mysterious, all-powerful doctor-figure. Bachmann's "dialogue" thereby subverts the balance of reciprocity and immediacy that was the marker of Buber's spirited dialogical encounter with a German audience. In Bachmann's dialogue, power is manifest and favors the anonymous, patriarchal, Fascist authority embodied in Bachmann's voice. In this way, Bachmann takes Celan's response to Buber one step further by acknowledging that the realities of oppression are inherent in the form of public speech itself, which is in turn defined as an inherently false and alienating form of dialogical engagement.

As a public speech, *German Contingencies* thus goes beyond merely scandalizing West Germany's public sphere: it involves the audience in a psychoanalytical session that could be beneficial to them, provided they observe and cogitate on this "analytical dialogue" while experiencing its effects.[24] That is to say, as the listeners attend to this hypnotic narrative, they might themselves feel its gruesome effect either through empathy with the subject of the hypnosis or as subjects under hypnosis in their own right. By posing the question of who or what causes their respective responses, they might activate memories that in turn elicit a chain of associations similar to the ones produced by the text itself. They would then link the medical and military themes, embodied by the syringes and fighter planes, to Nazism and patriarchy, just as they are linked, in *Das Buch Franza*, through the figure of *SS-Hauptsturmführer* (captain) Dr. Kurt Körner, a participant in the Nazi euthanasia program for the mentally ill by whom Franza demands to be killed with a deadly injection to escape her husband's tyranny.[25]

Thus forced to negotiate their own involvement and role in the process of speaking and listening, the listeners may ponder the question of whether they partake in the coercion by listening or, on the contrary, are themselves coerced by having to listen. There is a contradiction of double coercion in this act of listening, since it is not evident whether the listener is affected by the hypnosis or whether it is her act of listening that forces the speaker to carry on. Thus rendered ambiguous, the speech's situation creates a self-reflexive moment that justifies the classification of *German Contingencies* as epideictic speech—the rhetorical genre where persuasion is achieved through precisely this kind of self-reflexive, metadiscursive uncertainty. As Richard Lockwood has convincingly argued, epideictic rhetoric "is about the present, about what is happening at the moment, and if what is happening at the

---

24. See Tasco Horman, who recently articulated the question of whether and how it might "be possible to organize a process of public education so that it resembles the psychoanalytic process of working through." Tasco Horman, *Theaters of Justice: Judging, Staging, and Working through in Arendt, Brecht, and Delbo* (Stanford, CA: Stanford University Press, 2011), 4.

25. On the detailed references to the euthanasia program in Bachmann's work, which are based on her reading of Alexander Mitscherlich's documentation of the Nuremberg trial, see Krick-Aigner, *Ingeborg Bachmann's Telling Stories*, 134–35.

present, right now, is a speech . . . then epideictic rhetoric must always also be about itself: about its own function or effect."[26]

It is this moment of self-reflexivity that further links Bachmann's epideictic speech back to its relatively covert psychoanalytic framework. In Freudian psychotherapy, the term *Übertragung* (transference) refers to the redirection of a patient's previous object-relationships onto the analyst, and so, like epideictic rhetoric, transference inheres unique enunciative relations that involve a speaker, a listener, and a referent. And similar to the process by which the listeners of a public speech are to introject the speech and adhere to its contentions, and thereby become ready to consciously act or think differently, the recognition of the transference relationship represents the vital turning point in the analytic situation, as it is by acknowledging and analyzing the fact that she has made a false connection and projected unconscious emotions on the very real person of her analyst that a patient can begin to effect change in her mental life. In the case of Bachmann's listeners, this might play out as the recognition that they are projecting emotions connected with their own repressed ideas of guilt and victimhood onto the persona of the speaker, who found herself traumatized by the same events.

To pursue the same, fundamental aspiration of thorough self-analysis, Bachmann's listeners must construct their own postwar (and posttherapy) personae based on their individual moral responsibility for the collective crimes of their culture. But as much as every one of Bachmann's listeners is implicated in the historical realities at the heart of her address, there is nevertheless no simple way of separating the agents from the victims, and the oppressors from the oppressed.[27] After all, it is the (female) night shift nurse whose syringe thrusts her patients into the same echelon as both the victims of the Nazi euthanasia program and Franza—who ironically desires to share their fate.

Against an essentialist notion of gender and nationality, Bachmann's scenes of trauma mobilize a pathology of victimhood that includes men and women, Jews, Germans and Austrians, and finally all those who may suffer from the oppressive conditions of past and present societies. Contrary, then, to Buber and Celan, who take a principled and nuanced stance of victimhood in their public speeches, Bachmann eschews straightforward victimhood by conflating different kinds of victimization and by presenting herself more complicatedly as a double agent of coercion *and* subjection.[28] Given that she avoids the use of the pronominal persons

---

26. Richard Lockwood, *The Reader's Figure: Epideictic Rhetoric in Plato, Aristotle, Bossuet, Racine and Pascal* (Geneva: Librarie Droz, 1996), 70.

27. See Weigel on the "synthesis of guilt and victimhood" in Bachmann's poetry. Weigel, *Ingeborg Bachmann*, 237.

28. Bachmann's identification with the victims of the Holocaust and her conflation of different kinds of victimhood are, of course, rather problematic. This is particularly the case in the *Franza* novel fragment where the protagonist not only identifies herself as belonging to an inferior race and class but effectively compares her own suffering with that of aboriginal Australians, the Papuans, the Incas, and blacks.

"I" and "you," Bachmann's listeners have to constantly renegotiate their own shifting positions in relation to her enunciative practice of speaking: it is simply not clear who sends, who receives, and who is the speech's referent. The challenge is to resolve this intricate enunciative puzzle, which aligns Bachmann's Büchner Prize address with both psychoanalysis and epideictic speech.

The result is a parable of national trauma, which is simultaneously also a fantasy about the curative power of public speech that echoes the myth of the "talking cure"—the belief, proliferated by the Freudian school of psychoanalysis, that the memories obtained through therapy reflect the true state of a patient's psyche. Its performative force is not, however, a matter of linguistic meaning, semantic property, or rhetorical impetus, as in Buber's and Celan's public speeches, but an effect of its theatrical presentation. Still, Bachmann's speech substantiates what Lacan and the American narrativists consider "the reconstructive and 'hermeneutic' character of memory."[29] For rather than asserting the factual, historical accuracy of the story obtained under hypnosis, Bachmann's speech uncovers this very story *as a narrative* that performs—and through this performance *produces*—truth. Hence the speech is based on a twofold theatrical operation: the theatricality of her voice mimics the droning voice of a hypnotherapist, whereas the (to some) shocking textual performance dramatizes a range of hysterical symptoms. Given that these very symptoms, represented through a disjointed, incongruous narrative, are compatible with the Adornian dictum of post-Holocaust art, Bachmann's hysterical speech, itself the expression of a trauma that relates to Nazi torture and abuse, produces the symptoms expected from her and hence truly "exists for the sake of the cure."[30]

Despite its discordant and surreal rhetoric, *German Contingencies* is a very personal and, at the same time, Bachmann's most directly political text, for it challenges the psychological—and by extension political and moral—status quo that has been reached in Germany. Its hidden implications are provocative: according to Bachmann, the entire nation suffers from a collective trauma.

---

29. Borch-Jakobsen, *Remembering Anna O*, 6.
30. Ibid., 83.

Part II

"Who One Is"

Self-Revelation and Its Discontents

4

Hannah Arendt

Is it true Jacob about the concentration camps? . . .
Impossible to live with that. It's useless.
How can you answer for that?

—Uwe Johnson, *Speculations about Jacob*

Gesine Cresspahl, the protagonist of Uwe Johnson's novel *Anniversaries*, is an unusual female antihero. Johnson paints the picture of a woman who seems both strangely receptive to the ramifications of (violent) past events and aloof to the unfolding implications of current affairs. Yet Johnson partially redeems his character from the charge of political compliance and immaturity by granting her access to a genuine public intellectual through her personal acquaintance with the philosopher Hannah Arendt. Arendt, with whom Johnson became acquainted when he lived in New York in 1966–68 (working as a textbook editor and subsequently doing research for *Anniversaries*), exemplifies through her role in the novel how a public intellectual or, in her specific case, a public philosopher can reach beyond an academic audience to challenge society's conventional certitudes about matters as diverse as politics, history, and social justice. By having Arendt enter his fictional world as herself and by having her play the role of an intellectual mentor and personal educator for his protagonist, Johnson gestures toward the possibility of bridging the gap between the public intellectual and the private citizen. He has "Arendt" instruct the German secretary: "We must not nourish our lives on bread alone; we need proofs, too, child" (*AN*, 56).[1] Through such candid relationships, current political and social questions could potentially find their way into communities of political equals. Ensuing debates could help the latter develop a liberal consciousness and motivate their responsible civic engagement.

Arendt's character thus figures as the site where the private and public spheres merge in a politically productive and ethically appropriate manner. She moves freely and independently in the world and thinks for herself and thereby demonstrates how philosophers can provide intellectual guidance for the general populace and even contribute to the formulation of policy. As Arendt writes, politics should not be decided by statesmen alone but by "those who know how to act in concert" (*HC*, 324). By including a prominent public intellectual like Arendt in his novel, Johnson offers a scaled-down version of the kind of public realm the philosopher had herself envisioned. For Arendt's life and work are driven and held together by her advocacy of a *vita activa* and her rejection of the self-absorbed and apolitical *vita contemplativa* propagated by traditional Western philosophy. Of course Arendt's own life serves as an example of the emphasis she placed on political action and speech, for she had one foot in the academy and one in the public realm of media and publishing, often holding an academic position while maintaining a relationship with a variety of public channels that sought to influence government politics.[2] Most importantly, her writing was not bound to the academic environment. Instead of preaching from within the ivory tower, Arendt often wrote articles for the popular press and was thus widely read by the general public.

Whereas Arendt's character epitomizes the intellectually and morally superior, and therefore inspiring, public intellectual in *Anniversaries*, Uwe Johnson, who likewise figures as himself in the novel, represents intellectual and moral defeat, most conspicuously in the diary entry of November 3, 1967, where a German author identified as "Uwe Johnson" delivers a speech to the Jewish American Congress at the Roosevelt Hotel in New York.[3] There is enormous heuristic value in the juxtaposition of Arendt and Johnson in the novel because both figures represent varying degrees of moral attributes in accordance with Johnson's larger social and political themes. But even beyond *Anniversaries*, the juxtaposition of Arendt and Johnson allows for a new, more practice-oriented point of entry into the question

1. Arendt appears under her real name only in a preprint of *Anniversaries*, published in *Merkur* 7 (1970): 664. Her character is named "Countess Seydlitz" in the book edition.

2. See Elizabeth Young-Bruehl, *Hannah Arendt: For the Love of the World* (New Haven, CT: Yale University Press, 1982), 389–90.

3. The correct name of the organization, founded in 1919 by Zionist and immigrant community leaders to provide a voice at the peace conference at Versailles, is American Jewish Congress.

of postwar Germany's public sphere, as it is refracted through the prism of Arendt's and Johnson's critical experience. Most notably, the way in which Johnson presents his speech at the Jewish American Congress in the novel, where he recounts a speech he had actually delivered several months earlier, on January 16, 1967, at the same Manhattan location, reveals Johnson's skepticism toward the possibility of constructing a politically meaningful discourse in the medium of public speech. The reason put forward initially is both simple and practical. His ability to speak clearly and persuasively was severely tested by his (Jewish American) audience because they were distrustful and unsympathetic.

Although the diary entries of which *Anniversaries* is composed are set in present-day New York City, the novel is deeply concerned with the state of German society, where the weight of the past is omnipresent. It can, for instance, be felt in the repressive, undemocratic way in which the governments of both Germanys conduct politics. But the dark legacy of Fascism is also manifest on a global scale. Gesine Cresspahl knows that the world she lives in has been obscured by wars and genocide and that ideology has become a facade behind which people conceal themselves. Johnson continuously ironizes his protagonist as a sensation-hungry consumer of dreadful stories about political affairs and social and cultural decline. But the novel nevertheless does take very seriously Gesine's anxiety about the burden of the past. If there is one question that drives Gesine Cresspahl it is the one cited in the epigraph to this chapter: "How can you answer for that?" Addressed to Jakob Abs, a refugee from Pomerania, whom Gesine meets and falls in love with as a teenager, the question is triggered in the summer of 1945 by two events: the young Gesine witnesses the ghastly mass burial of World War II refugees in her fictitious hometown "Jericho" and sees her first photographic representation of a concentration camp. After this traumatic discovery of the reality of the Nazi genocide, which she was too young to experience firsthand, Gesine is hopelessly guilt-ridden, since she feels that as a German, she cannot delete these events from her own biography: "I am the child of a father who knew of the systematic killing of the Jews. . . . I belong to a national group that has slaughtered another group in numbers that are too high."[4] Not only is her consciousness permanently invaded by memories from her childhood and youth under two totalitarian regimes—National Socialism and Stalinism, respectively—but the bitter awareness of Germany's status as the perpetrator nation also emerges whenever she reads about nominations of former Nazi officials for government positions and belated Nazi trials that strike her as insufficient in scope.

Gesine constantly thinks about Germany's violent past and even seeks mental help from a real-life thinker and psychoanalyst, Alexander Mitscherlich, to cope

---

4. Uwe Johnson, *Jahrestage: Aus dem Leben von Gesine Cresspahl* (Frankfurt a. M.: Suhrkamp, 1970–83), 232; my translation.

with her trauma symptoms. Her guilt only intensifies through her acquaintance with members of the German-Jewish diaspora in New York City, her adoptive home since 1961, where her fixation on the past is set against her fascination with the eruption of the student revolts and the climax of the civil rights movement, as well as the escalation of the Vietnam War and the crushing of the "Prague Spring" through the Soviet invasion of Czechoslovakia. By combining a collage of newspaper clippings, Gesine's memories, and present-day events that are filtered through her consciousness, the novel blurs the distinction between the personal experience of its protagonist and current social and political affairs. The novel is indeed structured so as to mediate between these two perspectives. Gesine's biography is tied to contemporary history in such a way that the great political and ethical problems of the day have a bearing on her everyday state of mind.[5] She constantly thinks about history and contemporary politics, yet her reflections are not always founded on the firm premise of objective data (or that which the *New York Times* considers "fit to print") but are often occasioned by her memories and the personal stories of acquaintances and relatives.

Although Gesine is an attentive reader who, laudably, pays considerable attention to any available report about Germany's Nazi past, her ability to perceive the present world is entirely dependent on the media. She literally "needs" her daily reading of the *New York Times*, here anthropomorphized as a "stubborn old aunt," which on some days constitutes her only form of adult exchange. In the context of the novel, Gesine's reading habits exemplify that the medium of the newspaper and its readers are mutually dependent—she devours articles that confirm her views, which have in turn been shaped by her previous readings. As a figure who is evidently rendered passive by forms of mass spectacle and the mediatization of experience, Gesine represents Germany's post-Fascist citizenship as it slips into reified cultural definitions and conformity with dominant social conditions.

The question the novel poses in its strategic inclusion of multiple newspaper clippings concerns the uneasy triangle among the media, the citizen, and the public intellectual in a country where only decades before, the *Gleichschaltung* (forcible coordination) of all aspects of society and government had both facilitated the repression of political decision making and driven the assault on the apolitical private sphere of the individual.[6] In the Third Reich, the relationship between the public and the private spheres had indeed been turned on its head as open debate

5. See Bernd Auerochs, "'Ich bin dreizehn Jahre alt jeden Augenblick': Zum Holocaust und zum Verhältnis zwischen Deutschen und Juden in Uwe Johnsons 'Jahrestagen,'" *Zeitschrift für deutsche Philologie* 112, no. 4 (1993): 595–61. See also Ulrich Fries, *Uwe Johnson's "Jahrestage": Erzählstruktur und politische Subjektivität* (Göttingen: Vandenhoeck u. Ruprecht, 1990), 128–29.
6. See Ralf Dahrendorf, *Society and Democracy in Germany* (Garden City, NY: Anchor Books, 1969), 401.

and intellectual exchange were forced to retreat from the public sphere into the private, and the private virtues of the individual (fortitude, discipline, sacrifice, etc.) were shoved into the eye of the public. This is one of the reasons why political thinkers like Arendt and Johnson, who were concerned with the continuous repression that characterized the political landscape of postwar Germany's public sphere, looked critically at the legacy of the Third Reich.

While both Johnson and Arendt are motivated by a shared conviction (namely, that it is their obligation as citizens and intellectuals to maintain democratic responsibility and uphold real principles of justice and truth), their work is also informed by a deep-seated doubt regarding the prospect of creating a public space—or what Arendt termed an "in-between"—that would lie between people and bind them into a liberal body politic. Nowhere is this more apparent than when Arendt and Johnson, a philosopher and a novelist, respectively, are faced with the task of giving a public address: as if to compensate for the naive optimism that drives them in front of a public audience, the trajectory of their speeches exposes a shift away from political engagement toward a silence that shows, rather than states, what can otherwise not be communicated. At the same time, their language displays acute rhetorical ambiguity. Unable as they are to establish a stable border between self and other, between private and public spheres, Arendt and Johnson fail to reveal themselves to their respective audiences. And yet their speeches involve significant personal breakthroughs—and ideological breaks as well. By discursively reenacting her alienating experience as a marginalized German-Jewish intellectual and by mobilizing her concept of the pariah, Arendt effectively asserts a counternarrative against the hegemonic discourse of postwar Germany's public sphere. In a similar vein, Johnson stages a discursive disruption that subverts our understanding of the relation between dominant and dominated, hegemonic and marginalized perspectives. At the same time, he redefines Arendt's concept of self-revelation by examining and effectively changing the circumstances that hinder the participation of his interlocutors. That said, this chapter appropriates Kluge and Negt's concept of *Gegenöffentlichkeit* to demonstrate that Arendt's and Johnson's self-critical interventions make considerable headway toward the conception of an alternative practice of public speech.

The Social

Arendt gave her Lessing Prize acceptance speech *Von der Menschlichkeit in finsteren Zeiten* (On Humanity in Dark Times: Thoughts about Lessing) in 1958, almost a decade before Johnson addressed the Jewish American Congress in New York. And while Arendt's speech, a fairly publicized event at the time, has become firmly emplaced in the existing framework of Arendt scholarship, Johnson's address has been and still is a puzzle for Johnson commentators: apart from a newspaper clipping announcing the event, there exists no documentation of its precise circumstances.[7] We simply do not know what happened that night in New York and what brought Johnson to satirize the predicament of his public address. But we do know that in the novel, Johnson repeatedly thematizes a point that Arendt famously theorized in *The Human Condition*: the problem of the fading boundaries between the public and private realms, which results in the absorption of their very difference (*HC*, 68–69). One clue to this problem consists in the frequent reference to a story run by the *New York Times* on Svetlana Stalin, whose insipid and ultimately sentimental musings fascinate Gesine. Johnson also incorporates a polemic against Hans Magnus Enzensberger, who in 1968 published an open letter to the president of Wesleyan University in the *New York Review of Books* explaining why he had given up his fellowship there and left the United States for Cuba in open protest against the Vietnam War.[8] Through this pointed criticism, the novel contends that it is preposterous of Svetlana Stalin and Enzensberger to assume that their personal views could be relevant to the general public.

The continuing conflation of public and private matters and the troublesome ramifications of this issue are highlighted through the juxtaposition of Arendt's and Johnson's speeches. For what is at stake in both is that the speakers miscalculate the phenomenological boundary between their self-perception, which is formed by an experiencing gaze directed to themselves, and their public personae, dictated and explicated by other individuals. Because of the sweeping loss of privacy in modernity, their attempts at controlling their public images while at the same time realizing a form of Arendtian "self-revelation" through the medium of public speech shrink to a relatively hopeless effort.

Another point of reference between the two speeches is that both Arendt and Johnson falter on the problem of alterity, which—while surely at issue in any direct confrontation between a public speaker and an audience—only intensifies with the peculiar cultural constellation provided by the structure of these specific speech events: Arendt, a German-Jewish intellectual who had exiled herself to New York, delivered her speech in Hamburg to a West German audience, while Johnson, a German writer who temporarily lived in New York, spoke to the local Jewish community and one of the most important political organizations of American Jews. And whereas Arendt felt co-opted by the social obligations and pressures that are attached to receiving such a prestigious award in Germany, Johnson felt redundant as a speaker whose audience allegedly did not care to listen to a German speaker.

What further connects Arendt's and Johnson's public speeches is that Johnson, who had experienced the Jewish American community as unreceptive, indeed antagonistic, employed Arendt as a mediating figure who would facilitate his

7. See Alfons Kaiser, "Der 16. Januar 1967 oder Können wir uns auf Johnson verlassen?," *Johnson-Jahrbuch* 2 (1995): 256–58, here 257.

8. See also Uwe Johnson, "Über eine Haltung des Protestierens" (1967), in Johnson, *Berliner Sachen*, Kursbuch (Frankfurt a. M.: Suhrkamp, 1975), 95.

political project and support Gesine's personal quest. Mindful of her privacy, his depiction of Arendt in the novel is, however, so schematic that she emerges as an ideal type whose personal life is important only insofar as it exemplifies that of an exiled German-Jewish intellectual (and this is precisely the role she involuntarily inhabited during her Lessing Prize address), just as Mrs. Ferwalter, another Jewish acquaintance of Gesine's, exemplifies the fate of an Auschwitz survivor.

Gesine's life is marked by her struggle to come to terms with her own past, which is inextricably linked to the recent events in German history. This struggle also motivates her attempts to learn about Jewish culture and acknowledge German responsibility for the loss of millions of Jewish lives. For Gesine—and for Johnson—individual fates and history are not separate entities but belong together, just as personal culpability and national guilt are interconnected. In the context of the novel, "Arendt" represents the exiled German-Jewish intelligentsia, while "Comrade Writer" stands for Gesine's compatriots and her fatherland, Germany. By juxtaposing these competing spheres of influence, Johnson tests the possibility of constructing a collective memory that would be sustained by a plurality of German and Jewish lives.[9] Moreover, the fictional conversations between Gesine and the philosopher embody the primary vehicle of the kind of pluralist society Arendt had envisioned in *The Human Condition*. Gesine and "Arendt" represent a citizenry that would scrutinize the media and take an active interest in politics, while their conversations, based on respectful friendship and solidarity, would represent the most basic and most ideal modality of human relations. As Arendt writes in her Lessing Prize address, "We are wont to see friendship solely as a phenomenon of intimacy, in which the friends open their hearts to each other unmolested by the world and its demands. . . . But for the Greeks the essence of friendship consisted in discourse. They held that only the constant interchange of talk united citizens in a *polis*" (*OH*, 24).

Arendt contends that the debates, even conversations, between friends should not be banned from the public sphere, since they are of major political significance: they represent one way to transform our intrinsic alterity, a principle that separates us from one another and aligns us with organic and even inorganic life, into a plurality—a concept that in Arendt's eyes pertains exclusively to humankind (*HC*, 176). As friends who are uniquely distinct from one another, we realize and complete ourselves as human beings.

And yet the fictional dialogues between Arendt and Gesine did not make it into the novel. In the diary entry of September 11, 1967, which includes the conversation cited above, Gesine converses with a "Countess Seydlitz" instead. Arendt had refused Johnson's request to include her as a character in his novel. Apparently the

---

9. See Michael Hofmann, "Die Schule der Ambivalenz: Uwe Johnsons 'Jahrestage' und das kollektive Gedächtnis der Deutschen," *Johnson-Jahrbuch* 10 (2003): 109–19, here 111–12 and 117.

conversations in the novel failed to meet Arendt's criteria for "speaking together" in the public realm: Johnson had collapsed the distinction between the public and the private spheres by having Arendt appear as the same person with whom he had conversed in reality. By incorporating citations from their private debates in fictitious dialogues, and thus ultimately quoting her out of context, Johnson made Arendt liable for opinions she had not explicitly and voluntarily made public through the controlled process of writing and publishing. And while Arendt's character in the novel does not sound like the biographical Hannah Arendt (she speaks Johnson's unmistakable ironic idiolect), the conversations between "Arendt" and Gesine Cresspahl could be perceived as extracts from real conversations between Arendt and Johnson. For readers who would assume that the dialogues in the novel were based on actual quotes, they would have the thrilling appeal of news.

The novel does still reveal that Arendt's apartment on the Upper West Side is frequented by an eclectic crowd of artists, academics, and intellectuals, and that despite its prohibition, Arendt feeds the pigeons in Manhattan's Riverside Park. Did Arendt object to figuring in Johnson's novel because he surely would represent her in an intimate and thus ultimately noncivic, apolitical manner? Does Johnson's larger project of capturing the correlation between the public and private sides of human experience conflict with the tenets of Arendt's concept of self-revelation and her critique of intimacy?[10] Unaware of the precise nature of her role in the novel, Arendt resisted, fearing that Johnson would divulge private information about her and thereby allow for the intrusion of matters of sheer existence into the public domain (of the novel).[11] And as such everyday trivia—Arendt's penchant for pigeons—encroaches on *Anniversaries*, a novel that is clearly marked as a politically engaged project, it would become complicit with the rise of "the social," a realm that failed to inspire *humanitas*, the willingness to share the world and by that constitute it as a reality. For, as Arendt contends, the expansion of "the social" damages republican democracy as it tends to standardize each individual and prevent "spontaneous action or outstanding achievement" (*HC*, 40).[12]

While Arendt has made the point that friends share the world by talking about it, this does not mean that every dialogue is necessarily productive. For speech to be sustained by a spirit of humanity and openness, it must recognize the specific

---

10. Intimacy has, in Arendt's view, "no objective tangible place in the world" (*HC*, 39). It only breeds radical subjectivism, and thus it interferes with self-revelation.

11. Commenting on Arendt's distinction between privacy and intimacy, Seyla Benhabib clarifies, "By *privacy* . . . Arendt means primarily the necessity that some aspects of the 'domestic-intimate' sphere be hidden from the glare of the public eye." Seyla Benhabib, *The Reluctant Modernism of Hannah Arendt* (New York: Rowman & Littlefield, 2003), 212.

12. As Hanna Fenichel Pitkin has demonstrated, Arendt's notion of "the social" must not be equated with "society" or with what is typically associated with "the social." The concept most closely resembles Marx's notion of alienation. Hanna Fenichel Pitkin, *The Attack of the Blob: Hannah Arendt's Concept of the Social* (Chicago: University of Chicago Press, 2007).

potentiality given to the individual by the sheer fact of her being. As Arendt writes, "With word and deed we insert ourselves into the human world, and this insertion is like a second birth, in which we confirm and take upon ourselves the naked fact of our original physical appearance" (*HC*, 176–77). Speech and action are expressions of our bodily existence, but they are also more than that; they are "the modes in which human beings appear to one another" (*HC*, 176). If Arendt protested against appearing in the novel, it is because in the domain of fiction her character would be severed from her beingness—in the sense of both her physical presence and that which transcends it—and consequently her conversations with Gesine could hardly disclose her unique distinctness as an individual. In *Anniversaries*, "Arendt" is merely a name, a name without a being attached to it, and thus an individual incapable of sending speech and action forth into the world to achieve self-disclosure.

It is thus that the anecdote about Johnson's inopportune use of Arendt in *Anniversaries* highlights the problematic relationship between private conversations and public debates, which intersects with the equally complex relationship between book publications and public speeches. Arendt was reportedly not at ease with the deliberate and premeditated act of publishing. She admits in a letter to Johnson: "I am never quite comfortable when someone quotes what I have written; it is a kind of divestment of one's freedom, as if one wanted to commit me—although naturally I have committed myself."[13] Arendt is even more skeptical with regard to her ability to give interviews, let alone deliver a public address.[14] Her Lessing Prize speech testifies to her misgivings about the medium of speech, where the enunciation and the reception of a discourse coincide temporally and spatially, so that the persona of the speaker registers immediately—and hence more forcefully—as its agent. Arendt knows that as a speaker she cannot detach her biographical person from her text, but will be identified with the point of view she communicates. In a way that is both necessary and inevitable, she will be held responsible for it by the public.

And yet this is also the sense in which for Arendt, public speech can potentially serve as a productive conduit for pluralist "speech," that most powerful modality of the human condition that allows a person to enact her unique life story and reveal herself in (and to) the world. For lack of a more stable terminology in *The Human Condition*, the present study will indeed employ a dual definition of Arendt's notion of "speech." It incorporates the more unmediated and unpremeditated form of

---

13. H. Arendt to U. Johnson, July 6, 1970, in Hannah Arendt and Uwe Johnson, *Der Briefwechsel*, ed. Eberhard Fahlke and Thomas Wild (Frankfurt a. M.: Suhrkamp, 2004), 39; my translation.

14. In a letter to Jaspers, Arendt writes: "In no case can [an interview] be printed as I spoke it because, when I speak extemporaneously, I make grammatical mistakes, repeat too much, tend to sloppiness. Speaking just isn't writing." H. Arendt to K. Jaspers, September 7, 1952, in *Hannah Arendt/Karl Jaspers Correspondence, 1926–1969*, ed. Lotte Kohler and Hans Saner, trans. Robert Kimber and Rita Kimber (New York: Harcourt Brace Jovanovich, 1992), 431.

public speaking Arendt associated with the rhetorical culture of classical Greece, a form of speech that afforded (adult male) citizens the possibility of communicating their ideas and, more importantly, *themselves* in the public realm. But it also comprises a more formalized type of speech that, as Arendt's own example will show, is not always conducive to revealing "who one is" and does not necessarily rest on unalloyed initiative. For there is, in the modern era, an increased utilitarian need for public discourse, and public speakers are often instrumentalized. And yet figures like Arendt and Johnson must nevertheless be regarded as political actors, for they composed their own speeches instead of using professional speechwriters, and thereby inserted themselves into the world through their proper words. Even if their speeches were inflected by certain forces or pressures, their utterances are still purely and authentically *theirs*.

The *Daimōn*

Such distinctiveness defines the exemplarity not only of speech, but also of the public intellectual who utters it. In her *Laudatio an Karl Jaspers* (Karl Jaspers: A Laudatio), an address she gave in 1958 when the German Book Trade's Peace Prize was awarded to Karl Jaspers, Arendt goes to great lengths to explain the distinctive stakes of maintaining an authentic and affirmative appearance in the public realm.[15] In her view, no person is better suited to represent this ideal than her former friend and teacher: "Jaspers's affirmation of the public realm is unique because it comes from a philosopher and because it springs from the fundamental conviction underlying his whole activity as a philosopher: that both philosophy and politics concern everyone. This is what they have in common; this is the reason that they belong in the public realm where the human person and his ability to prove himself are what count" (*KJ*, 74). According to Arendt, Jaspers had mastered the public realm because he was able to translate his scholarly integrity and his objective, philosophical language into a discourse that was relevant to the general public. But beyond his book publications, Jaspers was an exemplary intellectual because of his outstanding ability to represent nothing but his own existence—the sum total of his "having proved [him]self"—in the public eye (*KJ*, 71, 73). Indeed, Jaspers epitomized the kind of ideal thinker Arendt could not be, as he had a real passion for the light of the public and was enthusiastic about answering its call, while she herself could not stand such a level of uncertainty.[16] Arendt's self-perceived incompetence as a public speaker, as well as her more general frustration with the modern-era

---

15. Arendt, "Karl Jaspers," 71–81.
16. For Arendt, this problematic was captured in Jaspers's notion of a "venture into the public realm." See Hannah Arendt, "'What Remains? The Language Remains': A Conversation with Günther Gaus," in Arendt, *Essays in Understanding, 1930–1954: Formation, Exile, and Totalitarianism*, ed. Jerome Kohn (New York: Harcourt Brace, 1996), 1–23, here 22.

public realm, is textually encoded in her *laudatio* of Karl Jaspers and her Lessing Prize address, both haunting examples of the problems involved in translating her theoretical concept of self-revelation into a viable political reality that is also relevant to the German public. As will become evident, Germany's public sphere did not provide the kind of "space of appearance" where she could "reveal herself" as a genuine and distinct individual. Yet Arendt's speech suggests that the formation of a counterpublic, which she effectively initiates by momentarily reinhabiting the role of a pariah, could compensate for the added risk of disclosing herself to the German public. Paying tribute to a true public intellectual, Gotthold E. Lessing, the Lessing Prize address betrays Arendt's struggle to define her own role as a public figure. At its core lies an apologia for her withdrawal from Germany's public sphere: the speech oscillates between her determination to speak in Germany and her tendency to reinscribe and theorize the very impossibility of doing so. As a result, it becomes apparent why Arendt preferred writing books to giving public speeches, regardless of the emphasis she placed on speech as a form of pluralist action.

In Arendt's threefold distinction between labor, work, and action, the modes of labor and work are identified with biological life; they correspond to our bodily qualities, our fertility, vitality, talents, and shortcomings, as well as our ability to endure pain.[17] By contrast, speech and action endow us with the possibility of fulfilling the potential of human life beyond our physical limitations and qualities, as every speech and action contains "the question asked of every newcomer: 'Who are you?'"—through speech we disclose our intrinsic self (*HC*, 178). While both modes of human existence go hand in hand with the principle of self-revelation, speech has a greater affinity to self-revelation than does action, since, as Arendt writes, "through the spoken word [one] identifies [oneself] as the actor, announcing what [one] does, has done, and intends to do" (*HC*, 179).[18] Rather than referring to our physical features, characteristics, qualities, and inclinations, this "who" signifies "the unique and distinct identity of the agent"—in other words, our human essence (*HC*, 180). Every time we speak or act in public, our spoken and lived words escape into the unknown and unprecedented to reveal us to ourselves and to others.

Given the primacy of self-revelation in Arendt's conception of the public realm, it would be a mistake to reduce the latter to a purely objective and anonymous entity. As Arendt writes in her *laudatio*, "Caught up in our modern prejudices, we think that only the 'objective work,' separate from the person, belongs to the

---

17. In *Anniversaries*, Mrs. Ferwalter epitomizes the modes of labor and work, since her existence harbors "the irrelevant" and thereby corroborates the reification of human life (*HC*, 51). Sustained by the banal and undifferentiated language of the social realm, her speech is "mere talk" and thus the opposite of self-revelation (*HC*, 180).

18. However, this is not a strict binary opposition. Action and speech are closely related, since, as Arendt concedes, "many, and even most acts, are performed in the manner of speech. . . . Speechless actions would no longer be action because there would no longer be an actor" (*HC*, 178).

public; that the person behind it and his life are private matters, and that the feelings related to these 'subjective' things stop being genuine and become sentimental as soon as they are exposed to the public eye" (*KJ*, 72). While the public realm connotes a conceptual space encompassing civic institutions, conventions, and the law, it does not preclude the individuals who constitute it and uphold its significance. For Arendt, it is a tangible and dynamic space populated by real people. It is a platform for political agency and a composite of individuals who have "proved [themselves] in life" as well (*KJ*, 71). As a person enters the public realm, she not only brings her objective work but also her intrinsic "person" along. Paradoxically, our distinctiveness, the fact that we are unique in who we are, represents not only the most deeply individual but also the most public and objective quality of the human condition.

In the attempt to reconcile the tensions between self-revelation and privacy, subjecthood and plurality, Arendt introduces a new dichotomy between those aspects of the human condition that are *persönlich* (personal) and those that are *personhaft* (individual). The "personal" and the "individual" aspects belong to the private-social and public spheres, respectively. As she explains in her *laudatio*, the "personal" includes a person's preoccupations, inclinations, and feelings, which should be kept private, as they are merely subjective. By contrast, the category of the "individual" encompasses that which has objective social and political value and belongs to everyone. According to Arendt, it is put forward in the form of the "living act and voice," uttered in public and in a clearly objective context, yet still attached to the agent himself in that it exposes his unique existence (*KJ*, 73). Although not yet on its way to the "uncertain, always adventurous course through history," the living act and voice are already beyond the control of the individual: "The personal element is beyond the control of the subject and is therefore the precise opposite of mere subjectivity. But it is that very subjectivity that is 'objectively' much easier to grasp and much more readily at the disposal of the subject" (*KJ*, 71).

Although she praises Jaspers for his strong presence in the public realm, Arendt's *laudatio* is infused with a personal undertone that hints at something not fully articulated. There is a risk associated with disclosing oneself in the public realm. One has to make a leap toward the other, the cognizer who is other than oneself, that plurality of human beings to whom one is bound in the self-disclosing act. Hence self-revelation is fraught with uncertainty: "[Personality] is very hard to grasp and perhaps most closely resembles the Greek *daimōn*, the guardian spirit which accompanies every man throughout his life, but is always only looking over his shoulder, with the result that it is more easily recognized by everyone a man meets than by himself" (*KJ*, 73). The self that is revealed in the encounter between individuals, or between an individual and the public, is by its nature intangible and mercurial. Self-revelation can thus neither be achieved willfully nor be avoided unless one remains in "complete silence and perfect passivity" (*HC*, 179). Finally, self-revelation is an effect of—and as such is limited to—the perception of the other. While the "*daimōn*" appears clearly and unmistakably to the human world, it remains hidden from the person herself (*KJ*, 73; *HC*, 179).

The phenomenon of self-revelation then entails an epistemological paradox: the moment we want to define the unique "who" that has revealed itself, we begin to describe "qualities he necessarily shares with others like him" (*HC*, 181). But such descriptions never reach the essence of a human being. "Who" we are is so unique that it defies human language, which functions by analogy and comparison rather than by distinction and individuality. Because the most essential is utterly elusive and volatile, Arendt employs the metaphor of the *daimōn* so as to visualize how self-revelation occurs. To describe it in words would be to eschew an essence impossible to define or capture verbally, for, as Arendt knows, sensory perceptions and cognitive acts are by no means interchangeable.[19] Given that it happens promptly and intuitively in the form of spontaneous "looking over [one's] shoulder" rather than evolving logically and over time, self-revelation cannot be translated into human language (*HC*, 180). According to Arendt the "who" (one really is) is revealed in words and deeds and bound to a specific narrative. And yet it transcends verbal expression.

Arendt's claims are of considerable magnitude. Self-revelation is the primary and exclusive path to leading a *vita activa*. Yet it undermines our sovereignty and self-determination, since we can neither actively trigger nor prevent it. Furthermore, we cannot observe it in ourselves, nor could we ever explain it to others. The essence of who we are reveals itself only as we are intuited by someone else; however, this someone would then be deprived of the cognitive certainty that would allow her to differentiate it from our physical features and outward characteristics. For our intrinsic uniqueness as actors in the common world and in history is always already overridden by "what" we are—namely, our "qualities, gifts, talents, and shortcomings" (*HC*, 179). The sheer sight of our bodies is more revealing than a verbal expression of our life experience: somatic substance supersedes linguistic signification. While Arendt insists that speech is the key agent of self-revelation, and that action needs speech so as to complete itself, it is hard to fathom how our speech could ever beat others' visual cognition of us. The *daimōn* is always already there, sitting on our shoulder, and winking at our foes.

Arendt admonishes us that as we step out into the bright light of the public stage, we are recognized and thus also reduced to our physical appearance before we even set out to speak. The semantic content of our speech is invaded—if not completely overridden—by our bodily appearance, by our visual and aural manifestation in

---

19. "What is heard cannot be represented (pictorially) for the eye, what is seen cannot be adequately represented (verbally) for the ear. Hence where truth is experienced primarily as something that is seen—for the Greek in the [εἶδος]—, it has to become [ἄρρητος], unsayable; where it is experienced primarily as something that is heard—for the Jews as the word of God—, its visual representation must be prohibited." Hannah Arendt, *Denktagebuch*, ed. Ursula Ludz and Ingeborg Nordmann (Munich: Piper, 2002), 2:600; my translation.

the world. Details as marginal and inadvertent as "the unique shape of the body and sound of the voice" sustain our action and speech (*HC*, 179). As Arendt progresses, her critique of self-revelation renders her *laudatio* ever more oblique. Ultimately, she suggests that her praise of Jaspers is diluted by the visual and aural qualities attributed to the speaker—herself—and thus implies that in the attempt of conjuring up Jaspers's manifold qualities, she reveals more about her own possibilities and limitations.

Arendt's speech can be read as a scrupulous and yet provocative justification for her reluctance to deliver Jaspers's *laudatio*. But its true significance is that it foreshadows Arendt's second encounter with a postwar German audience on the occasion of her Lessing Prize address, where Arendt's negative premonitions were to prove only too sound. For the reception of this second German speech was indeed inflected by the aural aspects of Arendt's delivery: the commentator who covered the event for the *Frankfurter Allgemeine Zeitung*, for instance, effectively failed to acknowledge the substance of the address but instead focused on the "charming" pitch of the speaker's voice: "Her voice was low and full, as she decried tyranny. How she attacked things that darken our times—a Hecuba of freedom! How infinitely confusing her peripeties, then, gentle and half an octave higher when she gives herself up to irony; when she becomes sarcastic, she is charming."[20] Given that Arendt's human essence here all but disappears behind her aural delivery, her speech cannot be considered a new beginning, a singular and fresh encounter that would enable Arendt's self-revelation and her audience's authentic response. The image that asserts itself is that of Arendt standing alone, in front of a foreign audience, her speech annulled beforehand by her *laudator* Hans Biermann-Ratjen, Hamburg's senator for culture, who co-opts Arendt's identity before she even begins her speech:[21]

> We wish to reclaim you as our own, and it would be a great and moving honor for us, if you allow us to do so, although it is understood that it is not you who returned to us, but us who returned to you! But if you accept this, then you as a German have done a great deal to help us contemporary Germans through your work to, albeit not pay off our unmeasurably great moral guilt to our Jewish fellow citizens, to whom we owe so much in the development of German culture—for this is impossible—, but to meet them, to integrate them in our lives, our future.[22]

---

20. "Hannah Arendt," *Frankfurter Allgemeine Zeitung*, September 29, 1959; quoted in Sara Eigen, "Hannah Arendt's 'Lessing Rede' and the 'Truths' of History," *Lessing Yearbook* 32 (2000): 309–24, here 319; my translation. While Arendt did not deny that a person's tone of voice could be a true expression of her personality, she nevertheless insisted that it should have no place in intellectual debate. Arendt, "Was bleibt?," 16.

21. Hans H. Biermann-Ratjen, "Politische Kultur und Kulturpolitik (Laudatio auf Hannah Arendt)," in V. F. W. Hasenclever, *Denken als Widerspruch: Plädoyers gegen die Irrationalität oder ist Vernunft nicht mehr gefragt?* (Frankfurt a. M.: Eichborn, 1982), 33–38; my translation.

22. Ibid., 37.

As Biermann-Ratjen concedes, Arendt's German-Jewish origin, the fact that she is not foreign but also not exactly one of them, makes her the perfect laureate. It allows the city of Hamburg to reclaim her as a long-lost compatriot, a gesture that would simultaneously help redeem Germany's national guilt toward the Jewish people. This was a simple scheme, too simple for the complexities of German-Jewish victimhood, and not a little naive given that Arendt was sharply opposed to the idea of returning to Germany as a German (Jew). As she once wrote in a letter to Jaspers, "It seems to me that none of us [Jews] can return (and writing is surely a form of return) merely because people again seem prepared to recognize Jews as Germans or something else. We can return only if we are welcome as Jews."[23] What makes matters worse is Biermann-Ratjen's comment to the effect that since Arendt is a woman, having chosen her as a laureate could advance the cause of Germany's civic rights by promoting equality between men and women: "I doubt anyone has acted more 'Lessing-like' than you, to carry the light of a spiritual order into our turbid times. But you don't seem to know yet that given our thoroughness, we Germans are at the moment very strict with regard to the observance of basic constitutional law, and so I must rebuke your doubting statement, because it contradicts the political equality of men and women."[24] Reduced to a threefold symbol, what could Arendt possibly say? How is it possible to respond to—let alone accept—a prize that is awarded to a German, a Jew, and a woman, but not to her person as such?

Written in 1959, one year after she completed *The Human Condition*, Arendt's Lessing Prize address has a completely different status and impetus from her *laudatio* of Jaspers, in which she described the stakes of self-revelation in a relatively objective and intellectually distanced manner. In the Lessing Prize address, this concept becomes the invisible center that organizes the speech. It is, after all, an acceptance speech that serves to reveal the laureate who has been awarded the prize. (This would have been Arendt's chance to prove herself worthy if that was what she was concerned about.) But the speech betrays a different outlook on the significance of the occasion. Arendt occasionally substitutes the first-person singular form *Ich* for the impersonal *man* (one), and these moments indicate that Arendt struggles to make the audience aware of who she really is. These are attempts to break into a testimonial register—testimony is always given in the first person—which would serve as a corrective for her inability to reveal herself to her audience. That the occasion of the Lessing Prize address ultimately does not support such a high purpose is reflected by the cultural-critical metadiscourse on the conditions of possibility of self-revelation contained therein. Based on the awareness that there is always a differential burden when a Jewish speaker addresses Germany, the Lessing Prize acceptance address ultimately negates Arendt's concept of self-revelation.

23. H. Arendt to K. Jaspers, January 29, 1946, in *Hannah Arendt/Karl Jaspers Correspondence*, 31–32.
24. Biermann-Ratjen, "Politische Kultur und Kulturpolitik," 37–38; my translation.

The Pariah

Arendt's Lessing Prize address is a lucid scholarly text that resembles a lecture more than a classical epideictic speech. Arendt does not rejoice in praise, nor does she express gratitude; indeed, she neither thanks her audience nor actually—formally—"accepts" the award by performing the speech act that would acknowledge it. The speech reads as a kind of counterhistory of the Lessing Prize, not only because it breaks with the thematic conventions of epideictic rhetoric but also because, contrary to Lessing's dialogical, almost colloquial, style of writing, Arendt's language is rather dispassionate and objective.[25] Meandering through her own writings on political theory and philosophy, Arendt delves into a number of topics that align with Lessing's thought, and the figure of Lessing, himself a thinker who had command over a variety of topics and disciplines, appears repeatedly in the text. Lessing's presence allows Arendt to weave political theory, philosophy, history, and literature into a commentary on Lessing, his work, and his relationship to German society. Reaching from antiquity to the Enlightenment to the twentieth century, Arendt covers the major periods of European intellectual history in order to probe Lessing's place within Germany's cultural tradition and to define his intellectual legacy. By tracing the influence of the Enlightenment, rationalism, and sentimentalism on her own age, Arendt further illustrates Lessing's impact on modernity and on her own political philosophy.

Yet a more hesitant undertone lies beneath Arendt's assertive and rational voice. As she effortlessly explores her ostensibly neutral *sujet*, her speech recedes to a rhetorical vanishing point, a seemingly inarticulable crisis that is projected toward the end of her text. This crisis is not linked to Lessing's enlightened philosophy but rooted in the racial doctrines of the Third Reich, a topic Arendt withholds until the final paragraphs of the address. It is not that these two disparate rhetorical registers are unconnected—they indeed converge thematically on the concept of "worldlessness"; however, the worldlessness of Lessing's time is nothing but a harmless prelude to the complete destitution of the public realm during the Hitler regime, marked, as it was, by the "atrophy of all the organs with which we respond to [the world]" (*OH*, 13).

According to Arendt, postwar Germany was still under the influence of this catastrophe. After the complete collapse of civic order during the Third Reich, the public realm was devoid of its "power of illumination," and German citizens were still distrustful of one another and the world (*OH*, 4). As she stands on her Hamburg podium, Arendt deliberately rubs postwar Germany's sore spot. Worldlessness, the phantom of the restoration era, had overruled the public sphere, and the common world was receding: "The question is how much reality must be retained

---

25. Jens, *Von deutscher Rede*, 69–70.

even in a world become inhuman if humanity is not to be reduced to an empty phrase or a phantom. Or to put it another way, to what extent do we remain obligated to the world even when we have been expelled from it or have withdrawn from it?" (*OH*, 22).

It is in the formulation of precisely this question that Arendt's two distinctive speeches intersect. The question is important to the historical figure of Lessing, whose life Arendt frames as a relentless struggle against his contemporaries. But Lessing never turned his back on the world: "Lessing never felt at home in the world as it then existed and probably never wanted to, and still after his own fashion he always remained committed to it" (*OH*, 5). Arendt thereby complicates the accepted view of Lessing as a rationalist thinker who embodies the Enlightenment's penchant for scientific truth and a fixed reality (*OH*, 5). Her Lessing comes closer to the "tramp" as which the thinker reportedly perceived himself.[26] Lending Lessing an air of worldlessness, of distance from the public realm, Arendt's description is thus itself "put another way" (*anders gewendet*), as it triangulates Lessing's political malaise with her own quandaries about her role as a public intellectual. Arendt in fact "reverses" (*um-wendet*) the problem of "worldlessness" and "applies" (*an-wendet*) it to her unstable status as a German-Jewish thinker in postwar Germany. Aligning her experience with Lessing's intellectual space, which is staked out by the binary between "world" and "worldlessness," Arendt likewise finds it difficult to maintain an unequivocal position with regard to the public.

As in other sections of the speech, Arendt's language here resonates with earlier formulations from her 1958 study *The Human Condition*. Far from a fragile yet ideal "space of appearance" that "holds men together" in dialogue, the modern-day public sphere was deeply threatened by the realm of "the social," a space of necessity that was continually expanding and caused the gradual disintegration of the public realm through an unseemly obsession with private affairs. Arendt is thus cautious as she proves the "platform" of Germany's public sphere; however, her reasons for caution extend beyond the mere degeneration of the public realm instigated by the rise of the social. The figure of decline that dominates her Lessing Prize address is "worldlessness," a category Arendt first used to describe Heinrich Heine and Rahel Varnhagen's loss of reality in nineteenth-century Germany. The term thus denotes a more intense form of alienation that is specific to the situation of Jews in Germany. Hence if Arendt cannot concretely situate herself "in" the public realm, this is not because the latter has been overridden by the social, but, more specifically, because she was speaking as a Jew in Germany. Arendt's focus has shifted from the stern ideal of true citizenship as it is sketched out in *The Human Condition* to a thin rationale for inhabiting the world despite the concrete historical realities of post-Fascist Germany.

26. K. Jaspers to H. Arendt, September 11, 1959, in *Hannah Arendt/Karl Jaspers Correspondence*, 378.

In a letter she wrote to Jaspers in 1946, Arendt alluded to the dire existential conditions she experienced as a Jewish pariah in the United States: "A decent human existence is possible today only on the fringes of society."[27] That the problem persisted in Arendt's mind, and that it persisted well into the 1960s, especially in Germany, is clear even if Arendt refrains from providing a detailed firsthand account of her experience of displacement and statelessness in her Lessing Prize address. Arendt, whose attitude is marked by scholarly matter-of-factness and the presentation of a sense of neutrality (however deceptive) even as she speaks about the concrete ramifications of anti-Semitism in the lives of individuals, submits a subversive interpretation of the historical phenomenon of the pariah instead of testifying to it. Suggesting that pariahs possess a unique, indeed more intense, sense of humanity precisely because they are excluded, Arendt argues that genuine humanity emerges from a space external to the common world. From her perspective, inside and outside are thus completely reversed. The Jews who had been denied the status of human beings in Nazi Germany salvaged the idea of humanity while they were being banned from an increasingly inhumane world. As pariahs, they could not directly intervene in politics, yet they were not utterly disenfranchised either. As Arendt explains, truth emerges from the limits of society and from people who have broken ties with convention. In that way, the realm of the pariah is not located on the fringes of the world but constitutes instead the very epicenter of humanity. And yet the pariah's experience is not accessible through cognition or empathy. One must be a pariah to understand how this status grants survival and protects the notion of humanity. In a similar vein, Arendt also makes the point that the humanity of the pariah does not survive to testify to itself: "The humanity of the insulted and injured has never yet survived the hour of liberation by so much as a minute" (*OH*, 16). Once the repression has ended, the pariah will reamalgamate with the common world, leaving no tangible trace of her heightened humanity. As Arendt concedes, given the evanescence of her remembered experience, the truth of her account is impossible to verify.

What is ultimately at stake for Arendt in the speech is the question of political responsibility. A former pariah herself, Arendt was possibly still under the shock of an experience of persecution that began with the sweeping and quick demise of her intellectual milieu in 1933.[28] By comparing herself to Lessing, Arendt asks whether or not she carries an obligation toward the German public and whether she is required to accept the Lessing award: "In awards, the world speaks out, and if we accept the award and express our gratitude for it, we can only do so by

27. H. Arendt to K. Jaspers, January 29, 1946, in *Hannah Arendt/Karl Jaspers Correspondence*, 29.

28. Arendt's own experience as an exile was hardly marked by anonymity or worldlessness: an active member of New York's German-Jewish community, she was involved in the aid of Jewish refugees, wrote a column for the German-language Jewish newspaper *Der Aufbau*, and finally traveled in her capacity as a researcher for the Commission of European Jewish Cultural Reconstruction.

ignoring ourselves and acting entirely within the framework of our attitude toward the world, toward a world and public to which we owe the space into which we speak and in which we are heard" (*OH*, 3).

Overshadowing the remainder of the text, this preliminary reflection is of particular urgency, since it concerns the articulation, the very event of her Lessing Prize speech. Arendt asks whether she ought to choose the intimacy and brotherhood of the pariah or (re)enter Germany's common world and speak to her former persecutors—and thereby risk appearing as a politically malleable parvenu. There is a certain irony in the institution of a Lessing Prize named after a thinker who was conscientiously involved, yet, like Arendt, "allergic to public relations."[29] At least until this point, Arendt's split existence between two continents and two languages had afforded her a modicum of freedom, humanity, and integrity. As she travels to Germany, however, she can no longer sustain this ambiguous position. Either she can accept the prize, address the Hamburg Senate, and thereby redeem the German people's guilt toward her, or she can refuse to give her speech, reject the award, and thereby insist on her solidarity with the Jewish people. Hence her critical designation of the Lessing Prize: it is a "Columbus' egg," a clever yet unscrupulous device through which the Hamburg Senate simply seeks to redeem Germany's past crimes.

The Lessing Prize puts Arendt in a double bind. On the one hand, she cannot fail to mention the wrongs she suffered as an exiled German Jew, since her address, which makes a strong case for adhering to reality, would descend into hypocrisy if she herself failed to remain faithful to her proper reality as a former pariah. She must call attention to her personal experience with Germany's anti-Semitic past and name herself as a Jew, even though she knows that mentioning the word "Jew" is no small gesture in postwar Germany. This, then, is Arendt's dilemma: for the sake of reality, she must bear witness to her historical status as a German Jew. Yet she can do so only in her function as a laureate of a German literary award—that is, in a role that denies her identity as a Jewish pariah, given that a "pariah" is defined precisely in terms of her being barred from the common world, the space in which Arendt is now invited to speak and be heard in her function as a "citizen of the world, as a savant."[30] By accepting this privilege instead of undercutting an award ceremony intended as an easy reconciliation of perhaps irresolvable differences, she would compromise her very unique personality and thereby betray herself. For Arendt, her wavering speech and her equally wavering plea for humanity must inevitably take the form of denial, even if the negativity of such a denial is undoubtedly offset by the chance to contribute to the formation of a counter-public sphere in postwar Germany.

---

29. Quoted in Young-Bruehl, *Hannah Arendt*, 392.
30. Biermann-Ratjen, "Politische Kultur und Kulturpolitik," 37; my translation.

The crux of Arendt's Lessing Prize address is her own dilemma as a German-Jewish intellectual: the fact that she is torn between her solidarity with the pariahs of the world on the one hand, and her increasing exposure as a public intellectual on the other. To testify for herself, Arendt would have to split herself into two separate entities and adopt the position of a pariah as well as that of a witness who speaks on behalf of the pariah, since only the latter has a place and voice in the world. In other words, she would have to serve simultaneously as the subject and object of her public speaking. In that way, her split subject position corresponds to the structure that is peculiar to testimony: for testimony presupposes at least two subjects or voices, that of a witness who suffered an event and that of a "neutral" observer.[31]

The subtext of Arendt's speech testifies to both, the impossibility of giving a complete testimony and the fundamental contradictions inherent in her attempt at public speaking. For there are only a few instances in the Lessing Prize address in which Arendt speaks about herself, instances marked by the use of the first person singular in an otherwise impersonal narrative. The first example occurs at the beginning of the speech where she employs the first person only to question the premise of her public address. Arendt indeed suggests that she has a hard time accepting the Lessing award: "I admit that I do not know how I have come to receive it, and also that it has not been altogether easy for me to come to terms with it" (*OH*, 3). Who, then, is making this confession? The laureate who cannot "come to terms with" an honor that disavows both her uniqueness and her historical status as a German Jew? Or the pariah who cannot fathom why her life is esteemed worthy of such a prestigious award?

The apologetic tone of Arendt's statement must not be confused with defensiveness. The purpose of this "confession" is not primarily to question her worthiness, but rather to expose the hidden implications of the Lessing Prize, as in her eyes, such public distinctions are the equivalent of an ambush. They are merely a different kind of discrimination in disguise, since they repeat the gesture of judging and ultimately subordinating her as an individual on the basis of her worldly achievements. As Arendt comments laconically, "An honor gives us a forcible lesson in modesty; for it implies that it is not for us to judge our own merits as we judge the merits and accomplishments of others" (*OH*, 3). Taken literally (and a literal reading is suggested by the analytical, scholarly attitude she maintains throughout her speech), the statement defines the Lessing award as a device that deprives Arendt of independence and sovereignty. She would once again be caught in an aporetic structure: just as the privilege of speaking in Hamburg retroactively denies her status as a pariah and hence annuls her past suffering, the privilege of the Lessing

---

31. As Agamben contends, "Not even the survivor can bear witness completely, can speak his own lacuna." Agamben, *Remnants of Auschwitz*, 39.

prize, Arendt suggests, denies her the faculty to judge (herself) and thereby challenges her intellectual integrity. Taken at face value, Arendt's opening statement thus announces her twofold resignation. Having compromised her authority to speak both as a Jewish pariah and as a public intellectual, Arendt can no longer speak, because she cannot speak as herself.

Discourse and Desubjectification

It is possible to trace this dilemma through the remainder of the Lessing Prize address. There is abundant negative evidence for Arendt's reluctance to speak about herself: she uses the first-person singular form very scarcely. But even more telling are the moments in which she attempts to break into a testimonial register, occasions on which her language is framed in such a way that it corroborates the distance between herself as the subject and herself as the object of her elaboration. Instead of revealing who she is, Arendt here enters into a metalinguistic register that thematizes the event of enunciation, which it claims to literalize. This is a complicated language used less to communicate than to mediate, for it triggers a reflection on the meaning or code of testimony rather than realizing the latter. In other words, Arendt never articulates the fact that she is herself a Jewish pariah, yet she continually clears the way for such a statement and thereby effectively negotiates the conditions of possibility of giving her own testimony in postwar Germany. In doing so, her language performs the unsettling logic of testimony; it draws attention to the aporetic experience of the witness by indirectly testifying to an instance of testimony that could not be realized otherwise.

A first example of such a structurally ambivalent testimony occurs several paragraphs into the Lessing Prize address, where, in speaking of a certain "group to which I belong," Arendt indirectly attests to the fact that she is Jewish: "These and similar questions of the proper attitude in 'dark times' are of course especially familiar to the generation and the group to which I belong" (*OH*, 17). In this utterance, Arendt refers to herself in an attributive clause, hence by means of a syntactic device that relates Arendt to the noun in the main clause, "group," which it qualifies (and which her physical presence on the podium embodies). This relation is meaningful enough to be expressed twice over, once semantically and once grammatically: the subordinate clause identifies "I" as a person who "belongs to" (*angehöre*) the "group," just as the attribute "belongs" to the noun of the main clause, which it qualifies. Despite this doubling, however, the statement enacts, rather than explicitly states, the relation between Arendt and her respective "group." Arendt never literally refers to *herself* as "Jewish."

In the essay *Report from Germany*, Arendt described the "irritation that comes when indifference is challenged," as when one "state[s] *expressis verbis* what the other fellow has noticed from the beginning of the conversation, namely, that you are a Jew."[32] But her awareness of the taboo did not prevent Arendt from mentioning that she was Jewish in Germany—to be exact, it did not prevent her from rendering her Jewish identity "readable" to her audience, for this admission is the cryptic but profound *effect* of her Lessing address. After a digression, in which she stresses the difficulty of preserving one's humanity in the public realm in more general terms, Arendt returns to the concrete ramifications of this challenge: "I so explicitly stress my membership in the group of Jews expelled from Germany at a relatively early age because I wish to anticipate certain misunderstandings which can arise only too easily when one speaks of humanity (*OH*, 17)."

Here, then, Arendt seems to finally make the deliberate statement that explicitly reveals her Jewishness and draws attention to the difference that separates her from the German audience. By "explicitly stress[ing]" that she is a member of a group of Jews who were displaced at an early age, she also introduces a further distinction separating her from older exiles, from emigrants who left voluntarily and from exiled Jews of non-German origin. Not all Jews should be lumped together, Arendt suggests, for no people and no personal fates are alike. At the same time, she plausibly explains why her emphasis and boldness are necessary: they are meant to anticipate "certain" misunderstandings. Arendt is careful to use the term "anticipate" rather than "prevent," as if to suggest that misunderstandings are generally inevitable, perhaps because there is an inaccessible reality beneath the surface of her spoken text.

It is, however, precisely by way of this explicit emphasis that Arendt complicates her testimony. Semantically, the personal pronoun "I" of this sentence refers to a specific and autonomous individual—the same Hannah Arendt who is delivering a public address. However, at the very moment of this enunciation—to be precise, in the act of thematizing the moment of enunciation—this "I" distances itself from the speaking subject, so that it is no longer defined in real, psychosomatic terms. As Giorgio Agamben has argued (taking his cues from Émile Benveniste), the statement "I speak" is contradictory, since it opens up a distinction between "the flesh and blood individual and the subject of enunciation."[33] The open transition from the speech text to the speech delivery—that is, the action of stating that she is making a statement, specifically the phrase "I so explicitly stress"—shifts her statement away from the oral register of testimony to an instance of rhetorical metadiscourse. The sentence thus only appears to be a basic event of deictic language, in which the personal pronoun "I" would be relative to the extralinguistic context of the utterance referring to "who" is speaking. In reality, the testimony it announces is not actually attached to that external reality. As Agamben maintains, testimony, as it

---

32. Hannah Arendt, "The Aftermath of Nazi-Rule: Report from Germany," *Commentary* 10 (1950): 342–53, here 342.
33. Agamben, *Remnants of Auschwitz*, 117.

passes from language into discourse, is a paradoxical act that both subjectifies and desubjectifies:

> One the one hand, the psychosomatic individual must fully abolish himself and desubjectify himself as a real individual to become the subject of enunciation and to identify himself with the pure shifter "I," which is absolutely without any substantiality and content other than its mere reference to the event of discourse. But, once stripped of all extra-linguistic meaning and constituted as subject of enunciation, the subject discovers that he has gained access not so much to a possibility of speaking as to an impossibility of speaking.[34]

In other words, the empirical reality of Arendt's testimony is not that of a "real individual" in Agamben's sense but merely that of language. There is no essential reality contained in the event, person, or location her statement refers to, nor is there an "outside" of the deictic language. In metadiscourse, Agamben writes, "the subject of enunciation is composed of discourse and exists in discourse alone."[35] By using the structure of testimony as a foil to Arendt's statement, it becomes evident that she gains access not so much to a possibility as to an impossibility of speaking in the face of the German audience. For at the very instant in which Arendt makes herself the object of her enunciation, she desubjectifies herself. As a result, she "is discourse, can say nothing, cannot speak."[36] Her attempt to attest to her difference and publicly affirm her identity as a Jew fails because she is unable to speak unambiguously and without any mediation in the voice of and *on behalf of* herself.

Arendt makes one final attempt to attest to her Jewishness by pouring the whole weight of her polemical stance into a dialogue that operates as her personal credo: "In this connection I cannot gloss over the fact that for many years I considered the only adequate reply to the question, Who are you? to be: A Jew" (*OH*, 17). Despite its vehemence and surprising candor, the brief exchange is not an authentic dialogue—hence the lack of quotation marks in the printed version—but a rhetorical device in which Arendt assumes the voice of a hypothetical interlocutor without so much as attempting to create the illusion of a real exchange. A performative act rather than a positive statement about her (non)identity, this dialogue is wildly cryptic, for it leaves open who the interlocutor might be and when the exchange took place. It is also unclear whether it is hypothetical, real, or imaginary. Is it a question she once struggled with or one that she would have wanted to be asked? Is it perhaps an inner dialogue similar to those Gesine Cresspahl entertains almost constantly? Does it even matter if we know if it really occurred?

---

34. Ibid., 116.
35. Ibid.
36. Ibid., 117.

The mysterious "dialogue" is followed by a second exchange that is now clearly identified as a citation from Lessing's drama *Nathan the Wise* (1779): "[Nathan] countered the command: 'Step closer, Jew' [with] the statement: I am a man" (*OH*, 17–18). Read in the context of the Lessing citation, Arendt's answer rests on two inversions. The first inversion is that Lessing's legendary advocacy of religious tolerance and his critique of sectarianism are pitted against Arendt's claim that she embodies alterity for her listeners. While the drama's centerpiece, the Ring Parable, defends the idea that we are human before we belong to a confession or race, Arendt makes the controversial suggestion that she is first and foremost a Jew. Her unexpected response "A Jew" to the question "Who are you?" raises serious questions about the credibility of her commitment to the concept of human plurality, which she defined as a "plurality of unique beings" (*HC*, 176). The second inversion of Lessing's dialogue brings to light the aporia contained in the principle of religious tolerance as it pertains to postwar Germany. Arendt, to be sure, challenges her interlocutors to answer the following implied question: can they continue to assume the inherent worth of every person regardless of her religious orientation (or race) after the Jewish population was decimated through the kind of atrocities for which anti-Semitism became a catalyst under Hitler?

With the exception of her book about Rahel Varnhagen, in which she explored the specifically Jewish aspects of the human condition, Arendt was careful not to accentuate her Jewish perspective but rather to maintain a neutral authorial stance.[37] And in her Lessing Prize address, she situates herself outside of the discourse she is examining and does not take the standpoint of "exemplary Jewishness." She does, however, demonstrate that as a writer and thinker, she cannot be oblivious to that experience, since the terms of a German-Jewish encounter had altered considerably since 1933.[38] In the totalitarian context of the Third Reich and in its aftermath, identifying oneself in terms of an externally imposed group identity was neither an escapist gesture nor a political pose but a matter of facing the reality of persecution so as to defeat its purposes. As Arendt contends in her Lessing Prize address, "Unfortunately, the basically simple principle in question here is one that is particularly hard to understand in times of defamation and persecution: the principle that one can resist only in terms of the identity that is under attack" (*OH*, 18).

Arendt's statement resonates strongly with the message put forward by her *laudator*, who coined her identity in the most simplified and unspecific terms:

---

37. See Barbara Hahn, *Die Jüdin Pallas Athene: Auch eine Theorie der Moderne* (Berlin: Berlin Verlag, 2002), 227–28. Karl Jaspers criticized Arendt's portrayal of Rahel Varnhagen for subsuming Rahel's individual existence under the universal experience of Jewish identity. See K. Jaspers to H. Arendt, August 23, 1952, in *Hannah Arendt/Karl Jaspers Correspondence*, 193–94. On the question of Arendt's "Jewish perspective," see also Richard J. Bernstein, *Hannah Arendt and the Jewish Question* (Cambridge, MA: MIT Press, 1996).

38. See H. Arendt to K. Jaspers, December 6, 1945, in *Hannah Arendt/Karl Jaspers Correspondence*, 27–28.

German—Jew—Woman. Taking the form of an anticipatory defense, Arendt's Lessing Prize address embraces this preordained identity even though it reduces her to a threefold symbol that would cancel out the self-revelatory potential of her public speech. For her German audience, Arendt is a German Jewess who fulfills a concrete sociopolitical function. To them, she epitomizes alterity as a counter-concept to their own identity, allowing them to substantiate who *they* are: Germans are *not* Jewish; however, they have abandoned the National Socialist racial doctrines and have become thoroughly philo-Semitic. At stake is that the Lessing Prize is not awarded to a unique and irreplaceable person and intellectual, but to a function—namely, to the symbolic relation of one exemplary Jewish exile to the German nation at this historical juncture. Functioning as a synecdoche for the otherness of Jewish culture, tradition, and society, "Arendt" is just a concrete proper name given to the Jew as "the other." As such, she could be replaced by any other writer or thinker of German-Jewish provenance: Ilse Aichinger, Nelly Sachs, or Mascha Kaléko, who, only one year later, in 1959, would decide to turn down the Fontane Prize, doubtless because it was used as a political tool for demonstrating commitment to an exiled German-Jewish author.[39] In that way, Arendt's Lessing Prize address also showcases alterity as a concept of substitutability. Her *laudator* points out that she is "a Jew," a construct that subsumes her uniqueness as an individual. As if complicit with this oversimplification, Arendt conveys nothing personal about herself except for one thing that truncates her own defense of the unique distinctiveness of each human being (a claim for which her address ostensibly makes a case): Arendt invokes her Jewishness and thereby risks reducing herself to being just that. The price for this is, of course, the chance to create a space of appearance, for herself and for others, in Germany. For how can there be such a common world if there is no actor who would begin to give shape to it?

And yet it is precisely by interrogating the possibility of self-revelation that Arendt helps establish, or at least gestures toward, an alternative political realm that would resist normative structures through its tentative nature and volatility. Such a space would be less prolific and less constructive than the space of appearance Arendt saw actualized in ancient Greece. Motivated by resistance rather than agreement, and shaped by the reality of the pariah rather than the ideal of plurality, it could, however, evolve into a suitable political framework for Germany's

---

39. According to Sarah van der Heusen, the jury of the Fontane Prize selected Kaléko mainly because she was a Jewish emigrant. Friedrich Lambart's nomination letter for Kaléko mentions her "connections to the USA" and the "expected ramifications of her receiving the prize," while taking no account of the author's literary accomplishments. Lambart also attached several newspaper articles that give a romanticized account of Kaléko's exile from and return to Germany. See Sarah von der Heusen, "Mascha Kaléko und der Fontane-Preis: Ein Fallbeispiel," in *Berliner Hefte zur Geschichte des Literarischen Lebens* 8 (2008): 222–31, here 225 and 228. Von der Heusen further demonstrates that Kaléko declined the Fontane Prize because the jury included Hans Egon Holthusen, a former member of the SS.

post-Holocaust modernity. The stakes of the Lessing Prize address are much lower than in *The Human Condition*, where Arendt maps out a phenomenology of "self-revelation"—that highest form of human activity, achieved through action and speech in the public realm. It would be too ambitious to think that she could disclose her most specific and unique self in the face of a postwar German audience, but her speech certainly attempts to give testimony, even if this testimony consists in nothing more than an articulation of the plain fact that she, too, is a Jewish pariah. But as a pariah who articulates her subjective experience, Arendt makes significant headway toward the creation of the kind of *Gegenöffentlichkeit* German society denies her group. In that way, Arendt's Lessing Prize speech effectively illustrates how a counter-public sphere can emerge when hegemonic discourse is undermined through the articulation of subjective experience that resists being subsumed by the dominant sphere—precisely because in Arendt's case, the articulation is of course staged as a failure. Given her refusal to participate in the rhetoric of (self-)praise, as well as her insistence on her difference and the very incommensurability of it, her speech clearly contains what one commentator has called "the raw material of protest."[40]

By developing a self-reflexive critique of her—a former pariah's—participation in postwar Germany's discursivity, Arendt interrogates the practical boundaries of public speaking. Never is the style of Arendt's argumentation apodictic, but her Lessing Prize address in particular provides a rationale for her rejection of categorical statements and the very idea of an incontrovertible truth. Adopting a deconstructive mode of analysis, Arendt's speech indeed renounces the rationalizing rhetoric of the Enlightenment. Like Lessing, whom she essentially attempts to decanonize in her speech, Arendt hopes to strew *fermenta cognitionis* (germs of cognition) into the German public sphere so as to probe the "best-known truths," which secretly scarcely anyone still believes in (*OH*, 11).[41] Instead of offering a truth that could be neatly dissolved, and tying herself down to a single perspective, Arendt thus insists on the kaleidoscopic nature of reality. Hence she can submit only an opinion, a highly individualistic perspective on a reality whose integrity is ultimately subjective: "Let each man say what he deems truth, and let truth itself be commended unto God!" (*OH*, 31).

By thus refusing to take recourse to a language of knowledge and power, Arendt makes a tentative step in the direction of what Kluge and Negt came to envision as an oppositional, nonhierarchical counter-public sphere that would function outside of the intellectual and epistemological limits imposed by the Enlightenment and bourgeois society. For, as Kluge and Negt contend, "A counterpublic sphere that

---

40. Christopher Pavsek, "History and Obstinacy: Negt and Kluge's Redemption of Labor," *New German Critique* 68 (1996): 137–63, here 139.

41. See Georg Mein, "Fermenta cognitionis: Hannah Arendts 'Hermeneutik des Nach-Denkens,'" *DVjs* 77, no. 3 (2003): 481–511, here 490.

is based on ideas and discourses with progressive content cannot develop effective weapons against the combined elements of illusion, the public sphere, and public power."[42] In light of Kluge and Negt's theorization of the public sphere, Arendt's speech may still be a failure, but failure defined as a necessary condition for the transformation of the status quo. Arendt offers a substantial critique of postwar German society, a critique that goes beyond her theoretical reflections on the problem of "the social" in the age of modernity. While the conflation of the public and private is symptomatic of every modern society that is based on wage labor and advanced capitalism, there persists a deeper problem pertaining specifically to postwar German society. In the former Nazi state, historically real and persistent violence was veiled in justifications serving to provide the nation with an aura of "respectability" and "moral legitimacy." In themselves such phrases reveal that Germany was still under the sway of totalitarian power, a claim Arendt insinuates but never fully spells out. They clearly epitomized the country's historical self-production as a victim rather than a key instigator in relation to its ideological associations with the Nazi past.

---

42. Kluge and Negt, *Public Sphere and Experience*, 79.

5

UWE JOHNSON

> Words tell us less than accent,
> accent less than physiognomy,
> and the inexpressible is precisely that
> with which a sublime actor brings us acquainted.
>
> —Madame de Staël, *On Germany*

Whenever Uwe Johnson appears as a character à clef in his novel *Anniversaries*, there is an intensely ironic but also urgent political impetus. In the diary entry of November 3, 1967, Johnson parodies himself as a maladroit intellectual who falls into the kind of apologetic, reconciliatory discourse that he himself criticizes. By restaging a public speech that he had given in reality, a speech that according to his account was interrupted and heckled by a deeply unsympathetic Jewish audience, Johnson weaves an alarming political narrative that indirectly interrogates the value systems governing any communicative exchange between Germans and Jews in the "post-Holocaust universe."[1] As a public speaker, Johnson nevertheless

---

1. See Robert Fine and Charles Turner, eds., *Social Theory after the Holocaust* (Liverpool: Liverpool University Press, 2000), 234.

turns a repressive and repressed German discourse into a source of transgressive and potentially liberating power. Producing conditions whereby Jewish survivors can articulate their subjective experience with utmost verbal economy, his speech mobilizes a counter-public sphere that would alter the German discourse around guilt and survivorship.

The speech is occasionally disrupted by fragments of Gesine Cresspahl's inner dialogues, in which she admits to Johnson that she was embarrassed by his public appearance, which she witnessed as a member of his audience: "*Where did you sit, Gesine? Close enough to be able to see you, Comrade Writer. At the back. Yes, way back, close to a door*" (*AN*, 167). Like Johnson himself, Gesine is nervous about the possible impact of this confrontation between a German intellectual and Jewish Holocaust survivors in America. And yet it is precisely in this precarious, self-consciously ironized dialogue accompanying the speech that Gesine and Johnson negotiate their roles as conarrators of *Anniversaries*. The scene indeed thematizes a narrative pact between the author, alternately identified as "Uwe Johnson" and "Comrade Writer," and his protagonist. Hence Gesine's claim that she is likewise a narrator: "*Who's telling this story, Gesine? We both are. Surely that's obvious*" (*AN*, 169). Establishing the narrative conceit of the novel—that Gesine has appointed "Comrade Writer" to write her, and her family's, story—the diary entry of November 3, 1967, functions as a key to the entire novel.[2]

The scene at the Jewish American Congress also represents the kernel of *Anniversaries* in that it suggests that the novel is a compensatory device, conceived as a corrective for a public speech that failed miserably. Johnson, who was unable to acknowledge German guilt when personally confronting victims of the Holocaust, professes to put his expertise as a writer at his protagonist's service. Instead of reiterating his attempt at oral communication with the victims of Nazi persecution, Johnson thus creates his own double who would—at least allegorically—bear the shame of the German nation on his behalf.[3] In an ambiguous, roundabout way, Johnson questions his authorial power to penetrate the reality of the heinous crimes committed during the Nazi past. In this respect, the scene at the Jewish American Congress is as crucial for understanding Uwe Johnson's self-definition as a German intellectual as it is for comprehending the novel. On the one hand, it shows that Johnson conceived of *Anniversaries* instrumentally. Maximizing his own responsibility and accountability as a German writer, the novel is aimed at addressing the concrete political realities prevailing at the time it appeared. On the other hand, Johnson delivers this reality into the realm of fantasy. For the narrative pact between "Comrade Writer" and Gesine is a ludic strategy by which he transfers

2. Fries, *Uwe Johnson's "Jahrestage,"* 52.
3. Kurt Fickert, "The Identity of 'Der Genosse Schriftsteller' in Johnson's *Jahrestage,*" *Monatshefte für Deutschsprachige Literatur und Kultur* 91, no. 2 (1999): 256–67, here 261.

his agency as an author to a fictitious narrator figure, while reiterating the claim that Gesine exists independently of himself. In that way, the novel plays with but ultimately rejects the idea of his active engagement in the public arena. Extending beyond the novel's narrative conceit, Johnson's reluctance to take a stance as a public figure and his unwillingness to participate in mass or protest movements openly conflicted with the more revolutionary zeitgeist of the 1960s. As an at most peripheral member of the Gruppe 47, Johnson did not partake in the growing zeal for political activism common among his peers. Increasingly disenchanted with politics in a world where political interventions seemed to be motivated by ideological exhibitionism and vainglorious self-display rather than serious and sincere conviction, he ultimately announced his decision to retreat from political engagement.[4]

Given that Johnson published a fictionalized treatment of his speech at the Jewish American Congress in lieu of the script itself, the former account must be read in its context-embedded immediacy as an event that unfolded under shifting circumstances and thus exists as the sum of its manifold contingencies. Rhetorical lapses and slips of tongue are as much part of this speech as the ideas it inspired and the responses it elicited from the audience. Johnson's critical retelling of his public speech effectively captures it as a profoundly unpredictable event that revolves around a nonhierarchical set of details, including the speaker's style of clothing, his less than accent-free command of English, and the rhetorically determined ambiguities that lead to dissent and misinterpretation. Given that it was transmitted, indeed staged, from the perspective of the speaker himself, who ironized his participation in it, the account is indeed *eine Darstellung* (a representation), a rhetorical operation that, in the tradition of German romanticism, evokes its subject—best referred to in the ever-elusive term of *Vergangenheitsbewältigung*, or precisely the lack thereof—in a material and visual sense, but not in terms of making it present as an essential, absolute continuity.

On the contrary, the point of Johnson's *Darstellung* is that it is impossible to impart knowledge about Germany's political reality, and specifically its handling of the Nazi legacy, to Jewish individuals: "He will no longer try to explain his singularities as a single."[5] This is so because the event of Auschwitz had caused a chasm in civil life that severed the value systems and collective memories of German Jews from those of other Germans, a chasm that German society, looking for historical closure, failed to acknowledge. For Johnson as for Arendt, the possibility of a German-Jewish dialogue thus depends on the construction and mobilization of a public discourse that would cut through the ambiguities and disavowals that to

---

4. See Uwe Johnson, "Rede zur Verleihung des Georg-Büchner-Preises 1971" [Druckfassung], in Arendt and Johnson, *Der Briefwechsel*, 253–77, here 255; my translation; this work hereafter abbreviated as *GB*.

5. Johnson, *Jahrestage*, 257; my translation (this section was omitted from the published translation).

their minds governed Germany's public sphere. While this discourse would have to acknowledge that the Nazi terror caused a radical "breach in civilization," this very recognition was impeded, so Arendt argues, by her contemporaries' incapability of comprehending, or even noticing, the events that had shaken Western society to its foundation.[6] As Arendt writes, "The breach was prefigured in the generational break after the First World War, but it was not carried out, insofar as the awareness of the breach still presupposed the memory of the tradition and rendered the breach in principle reparable. The breach only transpired after the Second World War, when it was no longer registered as a breach."[7] Hence in Arendt's view, it is not the catastrophe itself but the lack of conscious awareness of it that corroborates the breach. The breach is final because it overflows any conceptual or cognitive framework and thus cannot register. The breach *is*, because at least in our conscious minds, it has ceased existing.[8]

For Arendt and Johnson, who not only theorize the impossibility of a German-Jewish dialogue but also undertake the challenging task of initiating one, the medium of public speech entails a series of difficulties. As a form of dedicated discourse, it manifests itself within the public sphere provided (and tainted) by cultural institutions and mass media, requiring both speakers to cut through layers of denial, apathy, and acquiescence. More specifically, it challenges Arendt and Johnson to overcome two predicaments. Firstly, they need to find an authentic voice and a valid subject position with respect to their listeners, who act—at least nominally—as their (however unresponsive) interlocutors. Secondly, they have to articulate the most horrifying events without taking recourse to denial, clichés, and "constructs that 'explain' everything by obscuring all details," as Arendt suggests in *Eichmann in Jerusalem*.[9] In other words, they are confronted with the problem of how to (rhetorically or aesthetically) represent the Holocaust, a unique and uniquely horrendous event, which in its very singularity arguably defies human reason and comprehension and thus is, like the Kantian sublime, prevented from being cognitively assimilated, let alone aesthetically represented.[10] Although the scene at the Jewish American Congress comes to expose the vexing problem of

6. The term *Zivilisationsbruch* was coined by Dan Diner in response to Hannah Arendt's first reaction to hearing about the Holocaust. See Dan Diner, ed., *Zivilisationsbruch: Denken nach Auschwitz* (Frankfurt a. M.: Suhrkamp, 1988), 9.

7. Arendt, *Denktagebuch*, 1:300; my translation.

8. See Barbara Hahn, *Hannah Arendt—Leidenschaften, Menschen und Bücher* (Berlin: Berlin Verlag, 2005), 68.

9. Hannah Arendt, *Eichmann in Jerusalem: A Report on the Banality of Evil* (New York: Viking Press, 1965), 297.

10. Kant's notion of the sublime judgment provides Lyotard with his notion of "the differend"—pointing to the irresolvable conflict between the faculties of reason and imagination. According to Lyotard it applies to the victims of the Holocaust, whose experience of being wronged shatters rational thought. Jean-François Lyotard, *The Differend: Phrases in Dispute* (Minneapolis: University of Minnesota Press, 1988).

representation as a false problem, it does play a crucial role in the rhetorical staging of Johnson's speech. In the end, both Arendt and Johnson break the epistemological barrier of Holocaust representation precisely by staging their speeches as a failure, even though in Johnson's case this failure is of course framed in the language of parody. The speeches also fail in a structurally analogous manner—namely, by suggesting that as public speakers Arendt and Johnson fail not because of *what* they say but because of the phenomenological modalities of public speaking.

The practice of public speaking is thus tested in a range of different conceptions and experiences of alterity. In Arendt's speech, the Jews were given their rightful dues as victims who were forced into the degrading condition of the pariah. By contrast, in Johnson's speech, a German public intellectual embodies the antagonistic, threatening other in relation to the worldless pariah whom the former perceives as obdurate and ultimately uncivilized. Hence the relations of alterity in which Arendt and Johnson engage are disturbed by prejudice and a deeply ingrained enmity. But they are also determined, indeed undermined, by the structuring principle of the genre of public speech. For the way in which speeches are spatially organized inherently underscores differences in perspective. Standing alone facing the audience assembly from above her podium, a public speaker is always in a remote position analogous to that of an interloper. She remains isolated as an individual who answers to a group of people that form a collective, specifically in their orientation toward her.

Arendt's Lessing speech, as was noted above, showcases alterity as a concept of plurality and substitutability, since it suggests that her audience failed to encounter the uniqueness of her person. The same conception of alterity as plurality is also applied in the novel where Johnson's listeners reject him purely because he is German—or so he suggests. Johnson appears in the semiofficial capacity of a well-respected *Schriftsteller* (novelist) whose detached, impartial perspective ostensibly affords him, and by extension his audience, insight into Germany's political situation. Like the keynote speaker of the event, Rabbi Joachim Prinz, who had just returned from a tour of West Germany, Johnson would provide the Jewish community of New York with a firsthand report of the alarming presence in the government of former Nazi functionaries who had retained their right-wing ideologies and been spared in the process of denazification. Indeed, the lecture, entitled "Germany—What Is Happening and What It Means," alluded to a recent political controversy. In 1967, Chancellor Kiesinger appointed a former member and civil servant of the Nazis, Günther Diehl, as the chief of the West German Press and Information Service: "The Chancellor of West Germany, member of the Nazi Party, accomplice of the murderers of the Jews, has remembered a friend from the same government department. And while it is true that the latter did not join the Nazi party until 1938, the fact remains that he never resigned his membership. Just the man to be press chief of the West German Government" (*AN*, 170). Instead of voicing his firm disapproval of reemploying personnel of the former Nazi state, a trend that speaks to the much-contested continuity between the regime of the Third Reich and the government of the Federal Republic, Johnson here adopts Kiesinger's perspective and voice as his own as if to empathize with him. What this litotic phrase seems to suggest, then, is that the speaker condones the chancellor's iniquitous decision to appoint a former Nazi friend. Johnson of course adopts other consciousnesses in the novel, sometimes precisely in order to expose the mind-set of individuals who behave as a repository of bigoted feelings and destructive intolerance. For instance, this is the case in the following remark made by one of the individuals who invade Gesine's consciousness: "Negroes may not buy houses here or rent apartments or lie on the white course-grained sand. Jews are not welcome here either" (*AN*, 3). Just as this racist statement of course does not express the contents of Cresspahl's thought, the above-quoted comment does not convey Johnson's or Cresspahl's approval of Kiesinger's decision. While rhetorically more ambiguous, it scorns the chancellor's nepotistic mind-set and lackadaisical attitude toward his responsibilities as West Germany's head of state.

However, the following remarks bring "Comrade Writer" dangerously close to the complacent official discourse he appears to satirize. In the attempt to restore confidence in the West German state, he argues that the latter is not in the process of resuscitating a Nazi-like regime but instead lays claim to a place among civilized nations; it is only that the Germans are ignorant about how such practices are perceived abroad. Attempting to explain the difference to his Jewish audience, the speaker asserts, "It wasn't meant as a slap in the face of surviving victims, though the world felt it was" (*AN*, 168).[11] Again, Johnson does not directly critique West Germany's unfinished denazification or condemn Kiesinger's historical irresponsibility, but instead alludes to the *Sonderweg* (special path) argument, first presented by conservative German politicians in the nineteenth century who praised the merits of an authoritarian German state distinct from neighboring European countries. "Comrade Writer's" assertion that "it wasn't meant as . . . though the world felt it was" not only implicitly accepts the notion of a German exceptionality—suggesting that the state followed a unique course that would naturally be misunderstood by the "normal" nations to the West—but indeed reproduces the patriotically inflected articulations and expansionist ideology that had served to justify the hegemonic practice of imperial Germany's political system on the basis that it followed a special, predestined course.

This apologetic explanation of the speaker's failure to communicate the intricacies of German politics is followed by a defensive one. To them, he is a "German" and hence a "Nazi" and an "enemy" (*AN*, 167, 170). His audience simply does not care to hear the opinion of some German who explains "his singularities

---

11. Given that this is the only section given in English in the diary entry, the statement appears to be a quotation from Johnson's actual address.

as a single." They express their hostile attitude by first showering him with cries of "Louder!" and then appearing to doze off: "Now the back half of the hall adjusted to the rhythm of the front half, lagging only slightly behind in the cry of 'Louder!!' . . . After he had shouted, the audience appeared to doze off and left him in the belief that he could be heard, and understood" (*AN*, 168). This, then, is how the public speech at the Jewish American Congress performs the collapse of communication in the medium of public speech. "Comrade Writer" is forced to break off his speech and is further humiliated by the fact that Rabbi Prinz has to intervene and reason with the audience members, who retort with the following accusations: "He's one of them . . . He's doing nothing about the new Nazis . . . He's not supposed to do it in his profession but as a human being . . . He ought to be ashamed" (*AN*, 169–70). Johnson's account provides two rationales for "Comrade Writer's" inability to negotiate the chasm between the German speaker and his Jewish audience. One concerns the epistemic condition by which the speech fails. The Jews discriminate against the German solely on the basis of their sensorial perception of his physique and the sound of his utterances. "Comrade Writer" is perceived—or more precisely, Johnson suggests that he is perceived—as a typically humorless, clumsy German. Not only are his sentences "too long, too German," but he also "lapsed into the wrong vowels, the wrong emphasis, into [a] pseudo-British accent," and he wears "a black-leather jacket such as otherwise only Negroes wear" (*AN*, 168–70). Their prejudiced focus on *him* rather than on the substance of his speech completely overrides his attempt at self-revelation. There could be no better application of Arendt's metaphor of the *daimōn* to the practice of public speech.

The other rationale presents the speech as rhetorically doomed because, as Johnson concedes, it was delivered in the wrong context: "Time and place had deprived him of the innocence of a tourist guide and twisted every analytical word on his lips into a defensive one" (*AN*, 169). Of course, this is itself a rhetorical statement and not a neutral evaluation of his predicament. The personification of time and space to which Johnson attributes conscious agency; the unexplained and (given its historical context) outrageous assumption that the "tourist guide" is (personally? inherently?) innocent; and finally his way of offhandedly postulating "Comrade Writer's" analytic objectivity—all these assertions reveal problems in Johnson's argumentative logic and thereby betray his projected anxiety and defensiveness. Johnson's account thereby implicitly reveals why "Comrade Writer" inevitably had to fail as a public speaker.

But the scene suggests yet another reason. "Comrade Writer's" error is that he denies his addressees precisely what he requests from them. Eager to communicate his uniqueness as a German, he is not receptive to the individuality of the members of his audience. Intent on lecturing the "5,936,000 Jews in America, two million alone in the city in which we live," he encounters them as "the roomful of Jews," and while at first he is still able to make out "individual listeners who quietly and narrowly observed the German," the individuals who make up his audience are purely and simply stripped of their individuality as they swell into an overwhelming acoustic exuberance of delight in his humiliation (*AN*, 170, 167). The conception of alterity as one of plurality and substitutability is thus not only applied by the audience who, as Johnson suggests, judges "Comrade Writer" simply because he is German, while completely ignoring his effort to bridge his difference and otherness. It is also applied by the speaker himself, who fails to establish a common ground between Germans, who are confidently looking ahead, and Jews, many of whom are still grieving their losses, because he neglects the *individual* fates of the latter. Consequently, "Comrade Writer's" confidence that he alone, a single insignificant German, could bridge such an abyssal gap between two peoples appears incredibly naive. Ironically, the final paragraph of the diary entry confirms the futility of his intervention when it paraphrases the *New York Times*' quotation regarding the affair concerning Chancellor Kiesinger, cited above. By coming full circle, the diary entry of November 16 demonstrates that "Comrade Writer" managed to accomplish nothing with his public address, at least not as far as West Germany's hegemonic ambitions are concerned. And yet Johnson's account does open up a discursive space—a German-Jewish counter-public sphere in nuce—in which his listeners are able to reappropriate the experience of survivorship through their almost averbal responses to the German speaker.[12]

Parables

Anniversaries abounds with biblical analogies and allusions, but the diary entry of November 16 in particular is preoccupied with a question that has a palpable scriptural dimension. As an ironic exhortation to accept Johnson's misguided message, which is paradoxically paired with a fundamental distrust of the power of self-revelation, it carries significant interpretative weight. Exemplifying a speech situation that is directly thematized in the gospels' "parable of the sower," Johnson here aligns his lack of rhetorical skill with Jesus's concern about the futility of his preaching: "Listen! A sower went out to sow. And as he sowed, some seed fell along the path, and the birds came and devoured it. Other seed fell on rocky ground, where it did not have much soil, and immediately it sprang up, since it had no depth of soil. And when the sun rose, it was scorched, and since it had no root, it withered away. Other seed fell among thorns, and the thorns grew up and choked it, and it yielded no grain" (Mark 4:3–7 [ESV]). The analogy between Johnson's speech and Jesus's sermon reveals an intricate net of theological and political allusions. Jesus concedes that he is routinely misunderstood when he addresses crowds, many of whom are infidels. His words fall on barren ground, since the majority of his listeners, albeit able to hear, cannot grasp the meaning of his parables. Hence his

12. Daiya, *Violent Belongings*, 12.

words yield insight and truth, but only to a small minority: "And other seeds fell into good soil and produced grain, growing up and increasing and yielding thirty-fold and sixtyfold and a hundredfold. And he said, 'He who has ears to hear, let him hear'" (Mark 4:8–9). The "parable of the sower" suggests that Jesus's speeches are so hermetic that they exclude the unfaithful and nonbelievers from the privi-lege of insight and truth: "To you has been given the secret of the kingdom of God, but for those outside everything is in parables, so that they may indeed see but not perceive, and may indeed hear but not understand, lest they should turn and be for-given" (Mark 4:11–12).

If Jesus's parables are deliberately cryptic, understanding them is reserved exclusively for those who are capable of instantaneous and transcendent cogni-zance. For divine knowledge is distributed differentially by way of privilege and initiation rather than by tradition or right. This critique has another central feature in that it inaugurates a new form of parable that cannot be decoded and need not be interpreted. By professing to speak to the crowds in parables, while secretly, in pri-vate, explaining himself to his disciples, Jesus raises two very distinct doctrines, one hermeneutic, one eschatological. The first is contained, indeed performed, in the structure of the parable of the sower, which is, after all, "a parable of parable."[13] It states that the form of the parable serves to simultaneously conceal and reveal truth, defer and bring forward meaning, since it contains at its heart a prohibition against unveiling Jesus's messianic character.[14] Jesus's identity, which is both the essence and the source of the parable's truth, is deliberately hidden so that it can and has to be made manifest. All of Jesus's parables converge toward this moment of mes-sianic self-revelation as the key to Jesus's secret messiahship. The second doctrine is one of structural and discursive deferral, suggesting that the time is *not yet* ripe for it. Until speculation gives way to faith, and hermeneutic uncertainty is resolved through an act of direct revelation, the messiahship of Jesus retains its mystery.

Although Johnson does not explicitly name the parable of the sower, the scene at the Jewish American Congress clearly invokes this biblical parallel. Like Jesus's discourse, Johnson's speech is narrated in the form of a parable, but one in which paradox—or logical contradiction, caused by spiraling self-referentiality—takes the place of a didactic message. Serving to seal his narrative pact with Gesine, the diary entry alludes to a messianic secret, for it is concerned with the identity of a mysterious sower-like figure—"Comrade Writer"—who tries to disseminate truth among a crowd of skeptics and ignorants. At the same time the episode obscures and withholds facts that are essential for understanding him, thereby effectively cor-roborating the Christian doctrine of the messiah's irreducible incommensurability.

---

13. Kirk Wetters, *The Opinion System: Impasses of the Public Sphere from Hobbes to Habermas* (New York: Fordham University Press, 2008), 115.
14. Wilhelm Wrede, *Das Messiasgeheimnis in den Evangelien: Zugleich ein Beitrag zum Verständnis des Markusevangeliums* (Göttingen: Vandenhoeck & Ruprecht, 1901), 56–66.

Johnson's audience misconstrues his speech because they fail to comprehend his discourse and profoundly misapprehend his "messianic" character. Yet, in this ironized retelling of the parable, the uncertainty of meaning is caused by a set of details that are less esoteric than they are abstruse. Vacillating between sarcasm and ignorance, profound naiveté and tactlessness, Johnson adopts a series of competing identities that are as unstable as they are indeterminate. Conversing with his imaginary protagonist, "Comrade Writer" becomes Chancellor Kiesinger, who is an African American man turned goodwill ambassador of German humility. Hence the hermeneutic uncertainty couched in Johnson's allegorical technique is an effect of his performance as a public speaker and a consequence of his highly programmatic vaudeville interpretation of the dubitable part of the "public intellectual from Germany." The biblical doctrine of dissemination has transformed into a political farce about the fallacies of self-revelation.

The paradoxical effect of Johnson's public address results from its being staged under the guise of a secret. Like Jesus, "Comrade Writer" acts and speaks in riddles to hide the significance of his teaching and to conceal his "messiahship." Ironically, however, Johnson's version of the parable of the sower suggests that his listeners fail to recognize the profound truth contained in his public address only because, essentially, there is none to be found. If they are mistaken about who (or what kind of a person) he is, it is his own fault, for *he* is unable to construct a solid identity for himself. Stuck in a web of self-referentiality, "Comrade Writer" is unable to articulate a coherent doctrine or even so much as a strategy of self-promotion. Johnson's modern retelling of the parable of the sower thereby deconstructs the redemptive biblical theory of messianic self-revelation. In the hyperrational world of secular modernity, public discourse is neither a vehicle for spreading faith nor even a catalyst for public opinion.[15] Presenting himself as a parodically exaggerated embodiment of a German intellectual, "Comrade Writer" escapes unrecognized. He is essentially too weird to decipher.

But before Johnson leaves the assembly, the episode takes another turn. Unlike Jesus's listeners, who are portrayed as submissive and voiceless recipients of his divine secrets, Johnson's audience responds to the speaker by subjecting him to their own set of issues and problems, countering "Comrade Writer" with an extremely pointed and merciless question-and-answer session. Having lost its distinctiveness and dignity in the eyes of the German speaker, the Jewish community now turns against him to confront him one individual at a time: "Employees of the hotel set up two microphones in the central aisle of the ballroom, and behind each one of them waited ten or eleven people to comment on Johnson's presentations,

---

15. For a reading of the parable of the sower in the context of literary figurations and political conceptions of "public opinion," see Kirk Wetters, *The Opinion System: Impasses of the Public Sphere from Hobbes to Habermas* (New York: Fordham University Press, 2008), 115–21.

considerations, revelations. And they said: My mother. Theresienstadt. My entire family. Treblinka. My children. Birkenau. My life. Auschwitz. My sister. Bergen-Belsen. Ninety-seven years old. Mauthausen. At the age of two, four, and five. Maidenek" (*AN*, 169).

Compared to the hermetic language of Jesus's parables, the language of the Jewish respondents, as it is presented here, conveys a full measure of utterly unambiguous information that need not be deciphered. The Jewish speakers articulate sentences and fragments of sentences that consist of nothing but subjects and locations and yet express with utmost clarity the most horrifying aspect of their existence. They are Holocaust survivors whose family members were murdered in concentration camps. In that way, they stand at the opposite pole of Johnson's narrative. Contrary to "Comrade Writer," whose shifting identity is condensed into a riddle much as Jesus's divinity was concealed in a messianic secret, they are formidably explicit about who *they* are. Their language is reduced to bare communication, presenting the most unequivocal possible view of reality: "My mother" and "Theresienstadt" mean exactly that: "My mother" and "Theresienstadt." It is pure expression that is focused on the object world, submitted in a language in which the referential function is dominant. Thus it leaves no room for denial, debate, or interpretation.

With this succinct yet comprehensive, and completely *direct*, account of Jewish suffering, Johnson presents an ethically acceptable way to embody an artistic response to the Holocaust without reducing its scope, desecrating the victims, or trivializing its unthinkable horror. By posing the problem of representation through an intricate combination of direct speech as a form of practiced, indeed publicly performed, testimony and metadiscursive interruptions that refer back to the dilemma of public speaking, Johnson offers a possible way to counter, perhaps even overcome, the problem of *Darstellung* as it pertains to the post-Holocaust world. Although their informative, utterly unrhetorical language essentially foregrounds death, this death is left *unspoken*—it is left to the listener to name. According to the force of the missing verbs and prepositions that the listener automatically fills in, "My mother" and "Theresienstadt" also mean something different—namely, "My mother . . . died at / was brutalized / dehumanized / murdered / exterminated / starved to death at . . . Theresienstadt." Given this essential implied participation at the level of filling in missing linguistic elements, the above citation emerges as yet another level of interpretation of this parable. Concrete narratives whose meaning remains implicit and unspoken, parables convey an abstract argument that teaches us what to believe and how to behave. To arrive at such a hidden prescriptive context, "Comrade Writer" (and the readers of his novel) must hear, grasp, and take seriously the fragments uttered by his Jewish interlocutors. Statements that are so literal that they are an abstraction, so reduced that they become self-evident, these phrases are coded by means of absent parts of speech and by acts of naming persons as family members, and death camps by their now familiar names, names mostly taken from locations in central Europe now known in effect *as* the camps that were built and operated there.

The momentum of their responses impels "Comrade Writer" and his readers to understand, instantaneously. These dead are the uncountable people who perished in Nazi concentration camps. They cannot be ironized like the victims of the Vietnam War registered in the *New York Times*, whom Gesine sardonically acknowledges as the war's "official dead." Johnson's account thus emerges as a respectful and compassionate gesture toward the Jewish people, whom he encountered as a nameless and threatening "other" at first, but whom he elevates to the status of equal interlocutors in the course of the question-and-answer session. By doing so, he opens up a space for the witnesses to name persons as family members and thus deanonymize at least some of the victims. By representing the experience of the listeners through their own lens of reality, the communicative structure of Johnson's public speech, in which only he had the authority to speak, is thus completely reversed. "Comrade Writer," a false prophet of sorts, is unwittingly reduced to an agent whose sole purpose is to receive and transmit their utterances to his kind. Once his listeners have finished speaking, "Comrade Writer" concedes: "It has all been said" (*AN*, 170). There is no adequate response that he, a self-appointed representative of the German people, could possibly articulate. Auschwitz is, as Maurice Blanchot put it, "an event without response."[16]

Johnson's diary entry is itself a parable about the impossibility of (self-)revelation in the medium of public speech. By contrasting the demetaphorized responses of his audience with his own language, which is irreducibly metaphorical and indeed consists of "washproof, lightfast, airthick lies," Johnson exposes himself as an inadequate public interlocutor.[17] It is not that his addressees are inattentive or prejudiced. Rather, Johnson deliberately obscures his statements so as to sabotage their cognitive efforts. From him, the Jewish community will gain no insight into German politics. Thus Johnson's seemingly forthcoming and reconciliatory speech falls into a familiar pattern. It echoes the language of denial that Johnson found typical of the way in which most Germans, centered as they were on the claim to a normalized existence, responded to their Nazi past. Such a reading is supported by the following sarcastic remark: "Johnson would have done better to say nothing about what had been forgotten" (*AN*, 169). Given that Johnson fails to break through the layers of psychological denial and sociopolitical apathy, his parable tells the story of his humbling as a public intellectual while at the same time identifying a critical lacuna in the hegemonic discourse of German national identity.

16. Maurice Blanchot, "The Last One to Speak," trans. Joseph Simas, in "Translating Tradition: Paul Celan, in France," ed. Benjamin Hollander, special issue, *ACTS: A Journal of New Writing*, 8/0, 1988, 229–39, here 238.

17. Johnson, *Jahrestage*, 257; my translation—section omitted.

In the novel *Anniversaries*, Johnson finally offers an alternative communicative model. Oral transmission, as it is practiced between Gesine Cresspahl and her daughter Marie, is one way of redeeming and gaining access to a meaningful collective memory. In the model house Marie has reconstructed from her mother's stories, Gesine finds the material proof that the act of narration can function as a bridge between the past and the present. Marie's model of the house relies solely on her mother's detailed description of her childhood home in Jerichow. She has never actually seen it herself: "I just wanted to try out what it would be, what you are telling me about. What it looks like."[18] The model reconstructed from Gesine's narrated memory will help Marie visualize the setting of her mother's narrative and thus enable her to connect with her family's story. In turn, Marie's model will allow Gesine to reconstruct specific details of the past that she might otherwise forget and would surely neglect to narrate. In other words, the question of whether the past can survive in the form of a narrative is affirmed at the moment in which Marie produces a concrete, material representation of the house in which Gesine's family lived. Considering then that the miniature model is not offered as a Christmas or New Year's Eve present but for Hanukkah, the Jewish holiday that marks the rededication of the temple in Jerusalem, the scene gives an inkling of what a shared German-Jewish history might look like.[19] For Hanukkah also symbolizes the defense of cultural identity in times of diaspora by commemorating resistance to persecution as well as persecution itself. The miniature house offered by a German girl for Hanukkah links Gesine's own "temple" in Jerichow to the Jewish temple in Jerusalem and thereby also connects the German and Jewish spheres.

Like the narrative pact between the author, Johnson, and his protagonist Gesine, the ongoing narrative between mother and daughter serves to overcome the impression of a communicative void produced by Johnson's public address. The proposition that narratives may be able to bridge the past and advance historical understanding provides the only—if tentative—optimistic conclusion of the novel. In that sense, Johnson's narrative project is in line with Arendt's conception of story-telling, an act she defined as one that is always and intrinsically embedded in an already existing web of human relationships and thus an alternative to theoretical elaboration. Arendt writes:

> The disclosure of the "who" through speech, and the setting of a new beginning through action, always fall into an already existing web where their immediate consequences can be felt. Together they start a new process which eventually emerges as the unique life story of the newcomer, affecting uniquely the life stories of all those with whom he comes into contact. It is because of this already existing web of human

---

18. Ibid., 540; my translation—section omitted.
19. Thomas Schmidt, "'Es ist unser Haus, Marie': Zur Doppelbedeutung des Romantitels Jahrestage," *Johnson-Jahrbuch* 1 (1994): 143–60, here 148.

relationships, with its innumerable, conflicting wills and intentions, that action . . . "produces" stories with or without intention as naturally as fabrication produces tangible things. (*HC*, 184)

According to Arendt, human life, as well as historical truth, is revealed to us through the language of stories, which, contrary to analogical thinking, make no generalizations and stay open toward the unexpected. But while Arendt claims that after the "totally unexpected event" of the collapse of Europe "there simply was no story left that could be told," Johnson—who is, after all, a novelist—sets out to tell the story of it all.[20] As the ongoing dialogues between Arendt, Gesine, Marie, and "Comrade Writer" respectively demonstrate, his narrative can account for the manifold incidents of these subjects' *Lebenszuammenhang* (context of living) and thereby help create a coherent and at the same time pluralistic image of the events that shook Germany, the United States, and the entire world in the twentieth century.[21] The participatory and critical renegotiations of memory and remembrance resulting in Johnson's speech resist the desire for premature completion and withstand any ideology that takes historical reconciliation for granted. With the continual deferral of self-revelation redeemed through the resounding impact of a collective testimony, and the lack of authorial agency compensated for by a participatory web of narrative relations, Johnson's novel is a critical answer to the call of the public sphere. By creating a resonance between subjective and suppressed experiences of Germans and German Jews, it envisions a counterpublic that would dispel myth and resist simplistic generalization.

The "Jewish Question"

A passage from a letter Georg Büchner wrote to his family in April 1833 concludes Johnson's 1971 Büchner Prize acceptance speech: "If I do not take part in whatever has happened or might happen, I do so neither out of disapproval nor out of fear, but only because at present time I regard any revolutionary movement as a futile undertaking, and I do not share the delusion of those who see in the Germans a people ready to fight for its rights. In the interim, I consider writing as my only occupation."[22] This passage reveals Büchner's pessimistic assessment of the revolutionary literary movement of the Junges Deutschland (Young Germany), which led him to temporarily abandon his participation in the struggle against Metternich's restorative and reactionary politics and its fight for a unified, postfeudalist German

20. Hannah Arendt, *Between Past and Future: Six Exercises in Political Thought* (New York: The Viking Press, 1961), 6.

21. Kluge and Negt, *Public Sphere and Experience*, xlvi.

22. Georg Büchner, *Complete Works and Letters*, trans. Henry J. Schmidt, ed. Walter Hinderer and Henry J. Schmidt (New York: Continuum, 1986), 250.

Republic. By citing Büchner, Johnson calls attention to his intellectual affinity with the young revolutionary. The biographical parallel proposes that his own "retreat" into literature is, like Büchner's, not necessarily a political capitulation. Another way to read this statement is to consider how Johnson actually refutes the myth according to which Büchner was torn between political commitment and revolutionary activism on the one hand, and his "apolitical" literary, philosophical, and scientific work on the other. Such a reading would be in line with the argument of Hans Mayer, who, it bears mentioning, was Johnson's academic adviser when Johnson was a student of German literature at the university in Leipzig. According to Mayer, all of Büchner's work—his plays, political publications, and scientific treatises—shares the purpose of addressing current political predicaments through a range of different approaches.[23]

But upon closer inspection the analogy fails to recognize an important difference between Büchner's and Johnson's biographies. Büchner voided his claim of disengagement from the political scene with the publication of the revolutionary pamphlet *Der Hessische Landbote* (The Hessian Courier, 1834).[24] As a matter of fact, Büchner's ostensible withdrawal from the revolutionary scene prompted a pamphlet that represents not only the climax of Büchner's political career, but also the most prominent and incendiary among the revolutionary publications of the Junges Deutschland. Written and secretly circulated in an edition of approximately one thousand copies, the pamphlet gives a passionate and sarcastic description of the peasant's and worker's economic plight and appeals to the German people to revolt against their oppressors and overthrow the ruling class. It is clearly an example of Büchner's unambiguous, uncompromising, and relentless political engagement. By contrast, Johnson's Büchner Prize address is not a manifesto by any measure, in spite of its undeniable political implications. Still, there is heuristic value in the analogy between Johnson and Büchner. Büchner's critical assessment of his contemporaries' lack of revolutionary fervor speaks to Johnson's frustration with postwar Germany's public sphere and points to some of the possible ramifications of their work as writers and intellectuals in the context of a restorative political environment. Like Büchner, Johnson does not believe that the German people are ready to pursue a genuine democracy. But while Büchner, speaking from the moment prior to the reactionary backlash of the restorative movement, suggests that Germans are "not ready yet," Johnson, speaking from the aftermath of an arguably more repressed repressive experience, amends it to "not any more."

There is another way in which Johnson's declaration is misleading. His plan to concentrate on writing and his rejection of direct political action complicate a topos often found in statements of the Gruppe 47—namely, the idea that literature

---

23. Hans Mayer, *Georg Büchner und seine Zeit* (Frankfurt a. M.: Suhrkamp, 1972), 19.
24. Georg Büchner, "Der Hessische Landbote" (1834), in Büchner, *Werke und Briefe* (Munich: Deutscher Taschenbuch Verlag, 1988), 39–65.

could not only incite, but actually *is*, a form of resistance.[25] Johnson does not share their conviction that literature changes the course of a political struggle and that a political struggle can and must be fought through pen-rather than gunmanship. In Johnson's case, the "work" of "writing" is thus neither a sign of his political disillusionment nor the conduit for a revolutionary campaign, but rather a practice that informs Johnson's self-definition as a public intellectual. Contrary to Büchner, Johnson was not confined by censorship and could write freely about political issues once he had immigrated to West Germany. Yet Johnson's case illustrates that censorship is not the only practice that leads to the restrictions imposed by hegemonic paradigms. In the German Democratic Republic, any discussion of Jewish suffering was stifled from the outset by Communist Party ideology, which held that the Holocaust as an event was defined by the oppression of Communism. Hence official doctrine regarded the persecution of Jews as a merely peripheral phenomenon of National Socialism and the latter merely an outgrowth of capitalist exploitation.[26] In the Federal Republic, political practice generated a very different kind of blindness. While the German people's responsibility for the Holocaust was officially—if tentatively—acknowledged as early as 1951, when Chancellor Adenauer admitted that "unspeakable crimes had been committed in the name of the German people," the knowledge of these crimes was by no means embedded in the nation's cultural fabric or collective consciousness.[27] On the contrary, a collective form of self-censorship extended to the point where the majority of Germans refused to acknowledge what was so obvious.

Johnson's derision of the Büchner Prize is thus a sharp criticism registering broader tendencies in German society. For according to Johnson, this kind of cultural dullness is tied to a pervasive form of political indifference that ultimately renders any effort at intervening in public affairs impractical or even farcical. In his Büchner Prize address, Johnson thus establishes an ironic link between the consumerist attitude of his readers, which the Mitscherlichs in *The Inability to Mourn* found to be symptomatic of the postwar generation's denial and repression of guilt, and the mundane, ordinary tasks shaping his life as a *Schriftsteller*, a life marked by satisfaction derived from material things and distraction from true purpose. Johnson's self-denial as an author and intellectual nevertheless comes alongside considerable radicalism. He effectively fails to deliver a festive epideictic address and instead presents a parody of the institution of the Büchner Prize and the genre of the acceptance speech, both of which he believes to contradict the revolutionary

25. For a definition of "literature of resistance," see Bertram Salzmann, "Literatur als Widerstand: Auf der Spur eines poetologischen Topos der deutschsprachigen Literatur nach 1945," *DVjs* 2, no. 77 (2003): 330–47, here 334.

26. Georg Schuppener, ed., *Jüdische Intellektuelle in der DDR: Politische Strukturen und Biographien* (Leipzig: Arbeitskreis Hochschulpolitische Öffentlichkeit beim StuRa der Universität Leipzig, 1999).

27. Cabinet sitting of September 27, 1951, in *Documents on the Foreign Policy of Israel*, vol. 6, *1951* (Jerusalem: Government Printer, 1991), 666.

spirit epitomized by its namesake patron. Conceived as a derision of the Büchner Prize, Johnson's acceptance speech is interspersed with an expense report detailing how he has (already) spent the monetary award he is about to receive: "The author does not want to accept such an amount as a simple kindness, or yet as honorarium for the speech that is expected from any recipient of this award. He feels obliged to write to you how he has invested the larger part of this money, even before he possessed it; he is convinced that the attendees can lay claim to such an expense report. The author requests the patience of those among the attendees who find the discussion of money inappropriate" (*GB*, 253). Although it may seem that Johnson provides his "expense report" in the spirit of Büchner and Weidig's original intent (the authors had included a statement in the *Hessische Landbote* detailing the Grand Duchy of Hesse's tax income and expenses), he actually subverts this critical purpose (of calling attention to the excessive demands of the feudal lords) by conflating personal trivia and historical data. Moreover, Johnson treats the former as the only valuable inside a social economy that considers the price of a cup of coffee as more significant than the bits of information shared over it.

In contrast to Arendt, Johnson explicitly accepts the prize that is awarded to him. Yet he does not fail to specify that the monetary award is the equivalent of the monthly salary of a mayor—evidently a commentary on the disputable value of his (a literary writer's) service to the public. In another subversive statement Johnson intimates that he perceives the writing of an acceptance speech as a chore that he performs only because it is bundled with a profitable financial transaction: "Of his Büchner award speech the author still did not know the one sentence which he would find in the press, let alone its third sentence. Occasionally he might have liked to wake up from a dream about an express letter, arrived from Straßburg, sender a certain Gg. Büchner: dispensed from the public speech" (*GB*, 268).

As a speech that refutes its own status as a speech by challenging its claim to originality and creativity, Johnson's Büchner Prize address is neither a political manifesto in the style of Büchner's *Hessische Landbote* nor an attempt to position himself as an heir of Büchner's literary legacy. To Johnson, the institution of the Büchner award is a prime example of the many misguided appropriations of Büchner during the postwar era where Büchner's work, which had been banned during the Third Reich, was revived by the mainstream culture of both East and West Germany, and the image of Büchner used as a foil for various political and literary schemes.[28] Johnson critiques contemporary appropriations of the celebrated young revolutionary by assuming and at the same time undermining Büchner's legacy. His speech is a calculated and provocative break with the rhetorical and social conventions of the Büchner Prize in which he cites Büchner's words without

---

28. For a collection of literary adaptations and essays on Büchner's work dating from the postwar period, see vol. 2 of Dietmar Goltschnigg, ed., *Georg Büchner und die Moderne: Texte, Analysen, Kommentar* (Berlin: Erich Schmidt Verlag, 2002).

giving him credit for the quotation and without demonstratively—and ultimately hypocritically—singing the revolutionary's praise.[29]

Like Arendt, who criticized the "restorative" atmosphere of present-day Germany in her Lessing Prize address, Johnson disrupts and challenges West Germany's public sphere. Yet while Arendt spoke in rather abstract terms—for instance, she states that restoration cannot replace the foundation of a new state, yet she never explicitly refers to a German restoration—Johnson provokes his audience with a sweeping blow against everything they may take for granted, including the social and cultural discourses that had become mainstream after 1968. For instance, in order to defy his co-optation through a literary award that would align him with Germany's most popular and most romanticized revolutionary figure, Johnson partly ignores, partly ironizes the cultural legacy of the German *Kulturnation*. He does so by giving a detailed description of various political, cultural, and social aspects of American life, while mentioning the issue of Germany's historical development and role in world politics only in passing and only critically: "The neighbor, rather of Skandinavian type, began to quietly, then obtrusively whistle the so-called German national anthem between his teeth. Then again the expansion of the Germans from the Maas to the Memel or unity plus right plus freedom?" (*GB*, 262). Like Gesine Cresspahl, who is so annoyed and embarrassed by her German compatriots that she rejects the idea of ever returning to her fatherland, Johnson seems appalled by a number of quintessentially Germanic idiosyncrasies, as for instance the "obtrusive affectation" displayed by many Germans, their contrived "conception of pedagogy," as well as their impudent habit of constantly reminding other peoples of the German wars (*GB*, 263).[30]

Paying no heed to the celebratory framework of this high-profile literary prize (with its paradigmatically German sense of literature as a pillar of high culture), Johnson time and again confronts his listeners with cultural and historical trivia about life in the Jewish diaspora. And more than that, the speech effectively functions as an inventory of sentences that were deemed taboo during the postwar era: "[The corner of 83rd St. and South Mall] is the site for the American Memorial to the heroes of the Warsaw Ghetto Battle, April–May 1943, and the six million Jews of Europe martyred in the cause of Human Liberty" (*GB*, 273, quote in English). Forcing them to acknowledge the genocide of the Jewish people, Johnson reminds his audience that for New York exiles—and the speech treats Gesine Cresspahl as one of them—World War II is all but resolved: "Additional conjectures by the author about Mrs. C.'s refusal to return to Germany: Even in the midst of loving hospitality and during relaxing evenings, the German emigrants, whether Jewish

---

29. See Judith S. Ulmer, *Geschichte des Georg-Büchner-Preises: Soziologie eines Rituals* (Berlin: de Gruyter, 2006).

30. Johnson notes, "The Germans cannot quit reminding the other peoples ever anew of the German wars" (*GB*, 261–62).

or not, keep speaking of their escape from Germany, of the camps, the intrusion of the Germans in one host country after another, of renewed escape, narrow rescue. They did it with him, they surely will do it with Mrs. C." (*GB*, 261). And yet there is a slight redemptive streak to Johnson's renegade intervention. Gesine actively seeks out personal encounters with Jewish individuals, thus counteracting what she perceives as the outward indifference and denial of her fellow Germans described in the passage above. Johnson thereby proposes that one appropriate way of responding to the national guilt resulting from the Jewish genocide is to establish personal connections to Jewish individuals.[31] For intellectual kinship and friendship (rather than appeasing publicity campaigns and rhetorical self-display) are the only acceptable means to confront the crimes committed by German nationals. Hence Johnson's and Arendt's rapport embodies a third concept of alterity. Relating to one another as complementary counterconcepts to their own identities, theirs is a relationship not of essence and substitutability but of human plurality. Valuing the distinctiveness of individuals, it corresponds to Kluge and Negt's concept of a counter-public sphere that lends force and expression to oppressed groups and marginalized individuals, thereby setting the framework for emancipatory practice.

Striking an almost impish, irreverent tone, Johnson's Büchner Prize address nevertheless has both descriptive power and analytical weight. In an effort to understand how his nation could have embarked on the genocide of the Jewish people, Johnson once again turns to Arendt: "If it was true that only the Germans had been capable of doing to the Jews what they did to the Jews. The proof was: The Germans' loyalty to the alphabet. Whoever has said A, without even noticing, will also say B. The murderous alphabet. . . . The author asks for the permission to use such remarks" (*GB*, 265).[32] According to Arendt, it is not surprising that the German people went so far as to build concentration camps, for once they had embarked on resolving the "Jewish question" stipulated by the Wannsee Conference, following through was just a matter of principle and superior organization. But Arendt's insight into this dark side of the German psyche does not prevent her from engaging in conversations with German individuals (and Johnson was among her longest-lasting and closest German interlocutors). In another dialogue fragment cryptically embedded in Johnson's Büchner Prize address, Johnson thus quotes from another one of their conversations: "The girlfriend said: There is no more Jewish question for you. Henceforth this is our question, an exclusively Jewish one" (*GB*, 260). Arendt's contention that Germany is no longer interested in the "Jewish question" has been read as a two-pronged allusion.[33] On the one hand,

---

31. See M. Hofmann, "Das Gedächtnis des NS-Faschismus in Peter Weiss' *Ästhetik des Widerstands* und Uwe Johnsons *Jahrestagen*," *Peter Weiss Jahrbuch* 4 (1995): 54–77.

32. Johnson here alludes to a remark by Arendt on the coercive logic of ideology: "You can't say A without saying B and C and so on, down to the end of the murderous alphabet." Arendt, *The Origins of Totalitarianism*, 472.

Arendt refers to the "Jewish question," which was a rhetorical question raised by the National Socialist propaganda machine to direct the German people toward its "preordained destiny" of "purging the world of Jews." On the other hand, Arendt also seems to allude to Jürgen Habermas's avowal that after World War II, the "Jewish question" had turned into a "German" dilemma:

> If there were not extant a German-Jewish tradition, we would have to discover one for our own sakes. Well, it does exist; but because we have murdered or broken its bodily carriers, and because, in a climate of an unbinding reconciliation, we are in the process of letting everything be forgiven and forgotten too (in order to accomplish what could not have been accomplished better by anti-Semitism), we are now forced into the historical irony of taking up the Jewish question without the Jews.[34]

While both Habermas and Johnson remind the Germans of their obligation to reflect on the "Jewish question," they offer conflicting scenarios of how such a practice would play out in postwar Germany. Rather contentiously, Habermas submits that since no "unbroken" Jews are left (in Germany, he probably means to say—although even that is not meant literally, of course), the question must be addressed without consulting Jews and thus at the exclusion of eyewitnesses and experts' testimony.[35] Johnson by contrast argues—and in fact demonstrates—that it could be resolved only by way of encounters and dialogues between individual Germans and Jews. Corroborating Arendt's conviction that the "Jewish question" first and foremost belongs to the Jews, Johnson asks whether he (and by extension his German readership) could be involved in *their* deliberations. While Johnson does not credit Arendt for the quotation, his statement is indicative of their shared vision of their roles as public intellectuals. It is by seeking out encounters with individuals and thus by relating to the singularity of the other qua *other*, and not by way of public lectures or—at the other extreme—political apathy, that one can meet the challenge of human speech as a form of political action. What differentiates Arendt's and Johnson's public appearances from those of other contemporary public intellectuals is that they uphold a distinction between the public and private spheres precisely by way of embracing the *personhafte* elements of lived, authentic experience—what Kluge and Negt would refer to as the allegedly counterproductive activity of *Fantasie* (fantasy) in the sense of subjective everyday

---

33. Alexandra Richter, "Die politische Dimension der Aufmerksamkeit im *Meridian*," *DVjs* 77 (2003): 659–76, here 675.

34. Jürgen Habermas, "The German Idealism of the Jewish Philosophers" (1961), in *Philosophical-Political Profiles* (Cambridge, MA: MIT Press, 1983), 21–44, here 42.

35. This resonates with Seyla Benhabib's claim that in opposition to Arendt's conception of the public as one that is "bound to topographical and spatial metaphors," Habermas's use of the term public "becomes increasingly desubstantialized [and virtual in the] process." Benhabib, *The Reluctant Modernism of Hannah Arendt*, 200.

experiences that cannot be instrumentalized. While Arendt and Johnson oppose the infiltration of the public sphere by petty personal interests, as well as the over-valuation of trivial markers of difference and identity, they focus on those aspects in a person that belong to and sustain what would be a collective German-Jewish memory: they juxtapose the experience of being persecuted with the feeling of belonging to the perpetrator nation, and the experience of loss and trauma with the feelings of shame and guilt.

This dialogic process could not mend the breach in civilization that had trans-pired in recent history. Yet the web of human relations arising from Gesine and Johnson's explorations of New York's diasporic community, from Arendt's evening receptions, and from Arendt and Johnson's friendship and correspondence indi-cates the potential points of contact connecting the subjective experiences of diverse individuals. By privileging intersubjective dialogue over conventional notions of discursive power, the novel suggests that these personal connections could provide access to a participatory renegotiation of collective memory and hence support the formation of a counter-public sphere that would substitute subjective meaning for the status quo of dominant power relations.

Part III

SPEAKING BY PROXY

The Citation as Testimony

6

PETER SZONDI

Definitions of basic historical concepts:
Catastrophe—to have missed the opportunity.
Critical moment—the status quo threatens to be preserved.
Progress—the first revolutionary measure taken.

—Walter Benjamin, *The Arcades Project*

In 1936, Walter Benjamin published an anthology titled *Deutsche Menschen: Eine Folge von Briefen* (German Men and Women: A Sequence of Letters). It contained twenty-five letters sent or received by German poets and thinkers between 1783 and 1883.[1] These included, for instance, a letter from Georg Büchner to his publisher, Karl Gutzkow, another from Johann Heinrich Kant to his brother, Immanuel, and a third by Franz Overbeck for Friedrich Nietzsche. Conjuring the bygone era of Germany's high bourgeois culture, Benjamin's anthology charts the rise and the climax of the *Kulturnation* while at the same time foreshadowing its dramatic

---

1. Walter Benjamin, *German Men and Women: A Sequence of Letters*, in *Selected Writings*, ed. Howard Eiland and Michael W. Jennings, trans. Edmund Jephcott, Howard Eiland, et al., vol. 3, *1935–1938* (Cambridge, MA: Belknap Press of Harvard University Press, 2002), 167–235.

culmination in a sociohistorical process that lead to the triumph of the National Socialist Party and Adolf Hitler's rise to power in 1933. Written at the moment in which, as Benjamin writes, "the German bourgeoisie had to place its weightiest and most sharply etched words on the scales of history," *German Men and Women* is proposed as a cryptic intervention against the mystico-irrational ideology of Fascism.[2] Of course the collection ultimately proved ineffective in protecting what many believed to be the nation's impervious intellectual and moral value system. As T. W. Adorno notes, those who read it were "in any case opponents of the regime, and the book would scarcely have created new ones."[3]

Published first as a feuilleton series in the *Frankfurter Allgemeine Zeitung* in 1933 and subsequently as the 1936 anthology, Benjamin's *German Men and Women* was reissued again in 1962 by Suhrkamp Verlag through Adorno's initiative. But the book had already resurfaced roughly a year earlier, albeit in a less visible manner. On February 22, 1961, Peter Szondi included sections of it in his *Antrittsrede* (inaugural speech) at the Free University of Berlin.[4] Szondi's speech, titled *Die Suche nach der verlorenen Zeit bei Walter Benjamin* (In Search of Lost Time in Walter Benjamin), is a meditation on Benjamin's intellectual and moral integrity that ponders the following question: "What was Benjamin thinking of when he justified his refusal to emigrate overseas with the assertion that 'in Europe [there are] positions to defend?'"[5] Szondi surmises that Benjamin was driven by a fundamental, almost biblical hope: "For this ark was not intended to save only itself. It sailed forth in the hope that it could reach even those who viewed as a fecund inundation what was in truth the Flood" (*HP*, 159). Conceived at a time when the catastrophe of war and

2. Ibid., 3:167.

3. T. W. Adorno, "On Benjamin's 'Deutsche Menschen,' a Book of Letters," in *Notes to Literature*, ed. Rolf Tiedemann, trans. Shierry Weber Nicholsen (New York: Columbia University Press, 1992), 2:329. Benjamin had initially published the letters in the *Frankfurter Allgemeine Zeitung* under the pseudonym Detlef Holz. On the anthology's different editions, see Gert Mattenklott, "Benjamin als Korrespondent, als Herausgeber von *Deutsche Menschen* und als Theoretiker des Briefes," in *Walter Benjamin*, ed. Uwe Steiner (Bern: Lang, 1992), 273–82.

4. Szondi's speech first appeared as an article, entitled "Walter Benjamin und die Suche nach der verlorenen Zeit," in *Neue Zürcher Zeitung* (Literary Supplement, October 8, 1961) and subsequently in *Zeugnisse: Theodor W. Adorno zum 60. Geburtstag*, ed. Max Horkheimer (Frankfurt a. M.: Suhrkamp, 1963), 241–56, as well as in Szondi's essay collection *Satz und Gegensatz*, in Szondi, *Schriften*, ed. Jean Bollack (Frankfurt a. M.: Suhrkamp, 1978), 2:79–97. In the same year, Szondi created a radio broadcast that was based on his inaugural lecture: *Hoffnung im Vergangenen: Walter Benjamin und die Suche nach der verlorenen Zeit* (Frankfurt a. M.: Hessischer Rundfunk, 1961). Szondi further published a revised version of the speech: "Die Städtebilder Walter Benjamins," *Der Monat* 166 (1962): 55–62, which was also reissued as the epilogue to Benjamin's *Städtebilder* (Frankfurt a. M.: Suhrkamp, 1963). Finally, this new version appeared once more as "Hoffnung im Vergangenen: Über Walter Benjamin," in *Deutsche Literaturkritik der Gegenwart*, ed. H. Mayer (Frankfurt a. M.: Goverts, 1972), 115–31.

5. The present study focuses on the original, spoken presentation of Szondi's lecture version of the speech, yet given that the latter was neither recorded nor archived by the Freie Universität, all citations are derived from one of its subsequent printed versions: Peter Szondi, *Hope in the Past: On Walter Benjamin*, in Szondi, *On Textual Understanding and Other Essays*, trans. Harvey Mendelsohn (Minneapolis: University of Minnesota Press, 1986), 145–60, here 159.

genocide was already imminent, and published once the scope of the disaster had already begun to surpass even the most pessimistic of expectations, Benjamin's *German Men and Women* was an anachronism almost from the date of its inception. At the time of its publication, the German audience for which it was initially intended was incapable of heeding the book's warning and grasping its significance. But would postwar Germany's now democratic public sphere be receptive to an admonition they had received with silent unconcern less than three decades ago? Would Szondi find an eager and appreciative audience among the faculty and students of a German university? Would he be able to convey his deep concern over the haunting influence of Germany's oppressive history?

Through his nonconformist approach to lecturing, Szondi not only breaches the university's unspoken agreement to remain silent about the mass extermination of Jews, but effectively initiates the formation of a counter-public sphere within academia. Undermining the hegemonic discourse on German suffering, his address articulates the as yet unrepresented experience of persecution and expropriation "from below." Obviously Szondi's preoccupation with Benjamin's book project is not incidental. Like the first edition of the book, which was published in Switzerland before reaching its intended audience in Germany, Szondi was in the process of trading his home in politically neutral Switzerland for a new residence in German territory, so that his path from Zurich to Berlin effectively replicated the somewhat erratic itinerary of Benjamin's *German Men and Women*. Much was at stake for Szondi, whose inaugural speech simultaneously marked his arrival in Germany and his acceptance of a position as professor of comparative literature at one of Germany's leading research universities. The extraordinary promotion of a thirty-three-year-old Jew of Hungarian descent was also a test of Szondi's ability to live among the perpetrators of the Holocaust. The difficulty was further exacerbated by the fact that Germany and Berlin in particular had once again become the focal point of an international war. On August 13, 1961, only six months after Szondi's address, the East German government closed all east-west traffic lanes as well as the border between East and West Berlin by erecting what eventually became the most concrete symbol of the Cold War, the Berlin Wall.

These geopolitical complications represent just one point of intersection between Szondi's and Benjamin's texts. Their formal resemblance is equally striking, since Szondi's inaugural speech and Benjamin's anthology share the same structuring principle. Like Benjamin, who, instead of writing a conventional cultural history about Germany's bourgeois culture, chose to compile letters that would embody it, Szondi assembled a heterogeneous collection of Benjamin citations that allow the texts to speak for themselves. As such, Szondi's project corresponds to Noah's task of saving examples of all the animal species on the ark. Drawing from the full range of Benjamin's oeuvre, Szondi quotes his prose memoir, *Berliner Kindheit um neunzehnhundert* (A Berlin Childhood around 1900); his habilitation thesis, *Ursprung des deutschen Trauerspiels* (The Origin of the German Mourning Play); his literary and theoretical studies *Zum Bilde Prousts* (On the Image of Proust), *Paris: Die Haupt-stadt des 19. Jahrhunderts* (Paris, the Capital of the Nineteenth Century), *Einbahn-straße* (One-Way Street), and, finally, *Geschichtsphilosophische Thesen* (Theses on the Philosophy of History). Additional sources include Marcel Proust's *In Search of Lost Time* and T. W. Adorno's *Minima Moralia: Reflexionen aus dem beschädigten Leben* (Minima Moralia: Reflections on a Damaged Life). Szondi's commentary, which is more exploratory than argumentative, gathers this heterogeneous assembly of quotes into a loose but comprehensive constellation.

Alternating between comment and citation, Szondi's speech is structured so as to persuade his Berlin audience that the reception of Benjamin's work and legacy must now begin—with them. Hence the speech is an elaborate rescue operation that establishes the precise moment, the institutional setting, and the addressees of Benjamin's reception. Given that this scholar's name had only recently been reclaimed from relative obscurity, no more than a few audience members might have been familiar with the theories affiliated with his thought. So far Benjamin had had no *Wirkungsgeschichte* (effective history).[6] The first compilation of his writings, which was edited and published by Gretel and T. W. Adorno in 1955, had largely been ignored by the academy and the public.[7] Deploring Benjamin's implausibly prolonged anonymity among German academics, Szondi is one of the first scholars to recognize the conceptual power and theoretical significance of Benjamin's thought. By explicitly dedicating his inaugural speech at the Free University to this relatively unknown, marginal figure who did not fit into the discursive configurations of the university, Szondi anticipates and promotes the gradual integration of Benjamin's thought into the academic disciplines of literary theory, media studies, and philosophy of history during the 1970s and 1980s. At the same time, however (and the coincidence is not accidental), Szondi distances himself from the conventions of academic rhetoric by substituting an experimental approach for dialectical reasoning, an approach that also sets this particular speech apart from Szondi's other writings. Like the other speeches discussed in this book, *Hope in the Past* makes visible the challenges of organizing and synthesizing knowledge about even just one life lost to the Holocaust. But how are we to read an academic address that transmits its meaning primarily through the use of multiple citations (a strategy borrowed from the historical avant-garde and from Benjamin himself) and that gives voice to a figure whose writings are no longer (and arguably never were) present in the academy? How are we to determine the status of these fragmentary and heterogeneous citations?

6. The term *Wirkungsgeschichte* (effective history), central to Hans-Georg Gadamer's conception of philosophical hermeneutics, refers to the relationship between the reality of a story or historical object and the reality of its interpretation in view of its historicity. Hans-Georg Gadamer, *Truth and Method*, ed. Garrett Barden and John Cumming (New York: The Seabury Press, 1975), 267.

7. Walter Benjamin, *Schriften*, ed. T. W. Adorno and Gretel Adorno (Frankfurt a. M.: Suhrkamp, 1955).

Szondi's inaugural speech is an ark, headed into an indeterminate future with the goal of rescuing Benjamin's legacy from oblivion. The biblical metaphor is apt to convey two distinct ideas; it illustrates both the structural principle and the symbolic significance of Szondi's speech. But the metaphor also corresponds to Benjamin's anthology *German Men and Women*, the very book in which Szondi had initially encountered it. While still in Zurich, Szondi had come across a copy of its first edition that contained a handwritten dedication to Benjamin's sister: "This ark, built on the Jewish model, for Dora—by Walter" (*HP*, 159). Like Benjamin's anthology, which was meant to protect the precarious legacy of German culture after Hitler had seized power, Szondi's inaugural speech aims to preserve the unwelcome legacy of a Jewish intellectual who had faced lifelong exclusion from the academy. It is a well-known fact that during the Weimar Republic and earlier, it was almost impossible for a Jew to gain the appointment of full professor. A case in point is Benjamin, whose habilitation thesis, *The Origin of the German Mourning Play*, was rejected for political reasons in 1925—that is, years before the Nuremberg Laws officially sanctioned the ban of Jewish employees from German institutions.[8] But even after the Second World War, the practice of exclusion and omission was never formally revoked, nor was it stopped effectually. The majority of professors who had adopted the racist and hegemonic Nazi ideology and consequently also sabotaged the reception of works by Jewish thinkers kept their appointments after the collapse of the Third Reich and resumed untroubled and successful careers, while Jewish scholars were often unable or reluctant to return to Germany.[9] It was not until the late 1960s that a young generation of German students demanded a confrontation with those professors who had been allowed to remain in the academy and even held chairs at German universities although they never officially revoked their association with the Nazi Party. Such discontent is expressed in Szondi's pertinent words "[The] ideological delusion . . . is rooted in all too real circumstances for it to merit oblivion" (*HP*, 147). While this line is the closest Szondi comes to issuing a call to remember the crimes of the Nazi past, his speech implicitly recounts a human crisis that Arendt and Buber had evoked before him, but which Szondi now adapts for the specific conditions of academia, taking into account its bearing on the contexts of hermeneutic practice and inquiry.

---

8. See Burkhard Lindner, "Habilitationsakte Benjamin: Über ein 'akademisches Trauerspiel' und über ein Vorkapitel der 'Frankfurter Schule' (Horkheimer, Adorno)," *LiLi: Zeitschrift für Literaturwissenschaft und Linguistik* 53/54 (1984): 152.

9. See Frank-Rutger Hausmann, *Die Rolle der Geisteswissenschaften im Dritten Reich 1933–1945* (Munich: R. Oldenbourg, 2002); and Wilfried Barner, "Literaturgeschichtsschreibung vor und nach 1945: Alt, neu, alt/neu," in *Zeitenwechsel: Germanistische Literaturwissenschaft vor und nach 1945*, ed. Wilfried Barner and Christoph König (Frankfurt a. M.: Fischer, 1996), 119–49. See also Silke Seemann's compelling study, *Die politischen Säuberungen des Lehrkörpers der Freiburger Universität nach dem Ende des Zweiten Weltkriegs (1945–1957)* (Freiburg i. Breisgau: Rombach, 2002).

Although Szondi's inaugural address marks his habilitation at the Philosophische Fakultät of Berlin's Free University, it simultaneously articulates a critique of the university as an institution. In this unconventional lecture, Szondi endorses an alternative, more "personal" canon of Germany's intellectual history, one that remonstrates against an establishment that had excluded Benjamin despite his superior qualifications and deliberately undermined the reception of his writings in the academy. Indicting those philologists who had removed seminal scholarship from syllabi simply because it was written by Jewish authors, Szondi presents a montage specifically of those voices that had been suppressed on the basis of such racial discrimination. One of these voices belongs to Proust, whose *In the Shadow of Young Girls in Flower* (1933) Benjamin had translated in collaboration with Franz Hessel. As Szondi notes, Kurt Wais, then a distinguished professor of comparative literature at Strasbourg University, whose scholarship essentially consisted of glorifying "völkisch-Aryan" national literature, responded to its publication with a scathing review that was permeated with racial slurs.[10] (Szondi was, it bears mentioning, a devoted collector of literary "scholarship" from the Nazi era.[11]) Flaunting his hatred of Proust's "Talmudical ultra-intelligence," Wais drew heavily on the National Socialist rhetoric and ideology of parasitism, describing Proust's novel as an "incubator" and "morass" that sought to "penetrate" and "suck the blood of" the treasured remnants of the Aryan culture (*HP*, 147). Given that Wais still held a chair at Tübingen University in the 1960s, Szondi's decision to cite this particular scholar signals both his unease with and his emerging defiance of the institution he was about to enter.[12]

Although it is intended for an academic audience, *In Search of Lost Time in Walter Benjamin* undermines the kind of literary scholarship Germany's established echelon of scholars and Szondi's future colleagues engaged in. Indeed, the review by Wais, which is the only quotation stemming from the pen of an antisemitic professor, is used as a negative counterpart among the other citations. Speaking through its formal structure, Szondi's speech thus breaks with both the privileged contents and the rhetorical and methodological conventions of the academy. As a speech that consists to nearly forty per cent of citations, *In Search of Lost Time in Walter Benjamin* appears to be a deliberately incongruous choice for the occasion of an inaugural lecture or any academic lecture for that matter, as it is unlikely that Szondi would have been able to aurally separate his own voice from Benjamin's

10. See, for instance, Kurt Wais, *Die Gegenwartsdichtung der europäischen Völker* (Berlin: Junker und Dünnhaupt, 1939), an anthology that vigorously endorsed the racist ideology of National Socialism.
11. See Andreas Isenschmid, "Emil Staiger und Peter Szondi," in *1955–2005—Emil Staiger und Die Kunst der Interpretation heute*, ed. Joachim Rickes et al. (New York: Peter Lang, 2007), 173–88, here 179.
12. Szondi once noted that his professional relationships with other departments of comparative literature were deeply troubled by the fact that "Kurt Wais's shadow is cast upon the German school of Comparative Literature." P. Szondi to René Wellek, September 10, 1966, in Szondi, *Briefe*, ed. Christopher König and Thomas Sparr (Frankfurt a. M.: Suhrkamp, 1993), 201; my translation.

without the typographical markers available to him in the written version. Bearing a closer resemblance to a literary reading than to a scholarly lecture, the speech arguably fails to comply with the academic standards of scientific merit and originality.

Szondi was certainly aware of the text's unacademic quality. In a letter to his editor Siegfried Unseld, he defended the stylistically "slightly problematic" accumulation of citations in *Hoffnung im Vergangenen*, the published version of his inaugural address.[13] Yet the citations were necessary "for the sake of reasoning," Szondi argued, since they furthered "the unified tone of demonstration" of his essay collection *Satz und Gegensatz*, a compilation of early essays that includes his inaugural address.[14] The use of citations is part of Szondi's project of creating polyphony. In the print version of the speech, he again refrained from rigorously separating citations from the rest of the text, using single rather than double quotation marks. Nor did Szondi use typographical means such as indentation to set the quotes apart, a strategy that likewise finds its equivalence in Benjamin's texts, where, as Szondi notes, individual voices and lives sometimes merge into one another: "Is Benjamin speaking here of both Proust and himself?" (*HP*, 154). Szondi's voice is thus never isolated or privileged over the voices of the other "speakers." In what seems like a collaborative effort of representation, the speech modulates its theme through a chorus of voices that all share equal status. As Szondi alternately cites and reflects on his predecessors' works, the speaker's identity and scholarly authority are beginning to fade.

Listening

The inaugural address *In Search of Lost Time in Walter Benjamin* has an exceptional status in Szondi's oeuvre, not only because the young scholar here couples unconventional methodology with an experimental mode of representation, but also because he is caught both literally and figuratively between two chairs: the chair of his doctoral adviser, Emil Staiger, at Zurich University and the chair of Adorno at Frankfurt University, institutional home of critical theory.[15] For although Szondi never studied with Adorno, he more than once professed his academic and intellectual affinity to the prominent Frankfurt school thinker.[16] Finally, Szondi occupies a third theoretical position, one that is not institutionally bound and not yet

13. P. Szondi to Siegfried Unseld, November 21, 1964, in Szondi, *Briefe*, 175; my translation.

14. Ibid.

15. On the growing difference between Staiger's and Szondi's views, particularly in light of the *Züricher Literaturstreit* controversy, see Isenschmid, "Emil Staiger und Peter Szondi," 173–88.

16. On the occasion of a guest lecture given by Adorno on July 7, 1967, at the Free University of Berlin, Szondi issued the following statement to defend the speaker against student protesters: "Although I was never able to study with [Adorno], I would not hesitate a minute to answer the question as to whose student I am, by committing to him also in an academic sense." Peter Szondi, *Über eine "freie (d.h. freie) Universität"* (Frankfurt a. M.: Suhrkamp, 1973), 56; my translation.

organized within the territory of literary studies in Germany. It derives from Benjamin's conception of philosophical hermeneutics.

Paradoxically, Szondi moves away from traditional methodologies and established literary categories at the precise moment of his professional entry into the German university—following his *Ruf* (formal invitation) to take a vacant chair as a professor. Like Benjamin, who had once declared that he had "nothing to say. Only to show," Szondi explicitly endorses the hermeneutic primacy of the citation when he states,[17] "We have quoted abundantly and now need only comment briefly" (*HP*, 153). Thus instead of offering his own interpretation of Benjamin's texts, Szondi allows their meaning to emerge through the structure of his speech— that is, through the numerous and lengthy citations from mostly literary but also some theoretical texts, which are assembled to take the place of, and through their assembly bring out, a number of philosophical postulates. In that way, Szondi's speech offers a new kind of theoretical perspective. Here is a scholar who, like Benjamin, reflects on the problem of rhetorical *Darstellung* in academic writing, a problem that, as Barbara Hahn notes, had no place in German intellectual history until 1925, when Benjamin issued his *Erkenntniskritische Vorrede* (Epistemo-Critical Prologue) to introduce his groundbreaking study of the German mourning play.[18]

What further sets Szondi's inaugural speech apart from the status quo of postwar German literary studies is his distance from the kind of causal explanations with which positivistic historical and philological scholarship had been concerned since the nineteenth century. Although Szondi appears to rely on the tried-and-true practice of *Parallelstellenanalyse* (parallel passage method) (after all, he includes citations from Benjamin's works that are similar to each other), he nevertheless subverts the traditional assumption that a comparison of these citations would ensure a successful interpretation and necessarily lead to a consummate comprehension of the literary text.[19] For Szondi neither explains nor interprets the many citations permeating his inaugural speech. His innovative theoretical stance is perhaps most clearly expressed in a recurring figure of thought that serves to highlight the tenets of Benjamin's philosophy of history. Speaking of a mysterious trace of the future, which is paradoxically imprinted on the mind in the form of a memory, Szondi quotes the following line from Benjamin's *A Berlin Childhood around 1900*: "Like ultra-violet rays, memory points out to everyone in the book of life writing which, invisibly, glossed the text as prophecy" (*HP*, 154). Elsewhere in the speech, Szondi cites the following aphorism, drawn from the same

---

17. Walter Benjamin, *The Arcades Project*, trans. Howard Eiland and Kevin McLaughlin (Cambridge, MA: Belknap Press of Harvard University Press, 1999), 460.

18. B. Hahn, "Außenseiter: Eine Skizze," in *Wissenschaftsgeschichte der Germanistik in Porträts*, ed. Christoph König et al. (Berlin: W. de Gruyter, 2000), 273–79, here 278.

19. See Peter Szondi, *Introduction to Literary Hermeneutics*, trans. Martha Woodmansee (Cambridge: Cambridge University Press, 1995).

autobiographical text: "The past carries with it a temporal index, according to which it is assigned to salvation" (*HP*, 157). Finally, there appears a third version of Benjamin's figure of thought, now compared to the déjà vu: "Just as the forgotten muff allows us to infer that some unknown woman has been there, so certain words or pauses allow us to infer the presence of that invisible stranger, the future, who left them behind with us" (*HP*, 154).

By drawing his listeners' attention to a recurring motif in Benjamin's work, Szondi seems to suggest that each of these citations might refer to the same idea or phenomenon. His commentary implies that a juxtaposition of the work's parallel sections might shed light on the ways in which they express the same thought, and hence allow them to mutually elucidate each other. But while Szondi obviously gestures toward the traditional analysis of parallel sections, which he calls "one of the oldest hermeneutical stratagems," he ultimately rejects the method because it tends to neglect the individual passages' hermeneutic cogency.[20] As Szondi writes, "However valuable parallel passages may be for an interpretation, the latter may not be based on them as if they were evidence independent of it."[21] Szondi almost demonstratively refrains from interpreting the individual elements of his montage and thereby reveals much about his nonconformist approach toward literary analysis. Citing parallel sections without actually comparing them to each other, Szondi calls attention to a possible resemblance between them but at the same time refuses to interpret, or even acknowledge, the significance or meaning of these correspondences. Szondi provides the following rationale for his reluctance to construct a meaning from the individual parts: "Considering the great difficulties that a reader of Benjamin's theoretical writings confronts, a brief look at his remaining work can offer no more than hints which may serve as signposts in a terrain in which hastily cleared shortcuts are of no use" (*HP*, 157). Instead of offering a conclusive interpretation of Benjamin's texts, Szondi guides his listeners toward points of departure from which they may begin their own analyses. Hence Szondi does not deny that there may be "parallel sections" in Benjamin's works, but he prioritizes their "setting," arguing that the individual sections are merely signposts in a terrain perhaps too difficult to negotiate. Refusing to penetrate deep into the essence of the literary text to construe a latent, esoteric content, Szondi thus distances himself from his teacher Staiger (whose apolitical form of literary criticism, it bears mentioning, was thoroughly compatible with Germany's "restorative" culture).[22] Where Staiger's *werkimmanente Interpretation* (work-immanent interpretation) sought to free the

---

20. Szondi, *On Textual Understanding*, 18.
21. Ibid.
22. See, most notably, Emil Staiger, *Die Kunst der Interpretation: Studien zur deutschen Literatur* (Zurich: Artemis, 1950). Wögenbauer defines Staiger's strand of *werkimmanente Interpretation* as the exemplary "intellectual attitude of the postwar period, which is shaped by the scheme of totalitarianism: the ideology of being ideology-free." Werner Wögenbauer, "Emil Staiger (1908–1987)," in König et al., *Wissenschaftsgeschichte der Germanistik in Porträts*, 239–49, here 239; my translation.

literary artifact from its historical and moral imbrications, Szondi insisted on situating it in historical and cultural contexts. And where Staiger strove to protect the autonomy of the literary work, Szondi sought to create an objective but fluctuating context of signification wherein cultural and historical phenomena would become legible and recognizable to the reader. Szondi, in other words, refrains from spelling out what he thinks the text means and what he believes he knows about Benjamin.

Szondi's reluctance to engage in traditional interpretation is obvious from the outset. The speech's introductory sentence is followed by a citation from *A Berlin Childhood* that spans almost a full printed page. It consists of several variations on a figure of thought that are folded into one another as if there were an inherent logic to the sequence. But with its layers of ambivalent meaning, Benjamin's figure is by no means self-explanatory. And yet Szondi provides neither commentary nor elucidation as he nonchalantly traverses this difficult terrain as though its status was entirely unambiguous. It is thus easy to overlook the complexity of the passage. On the one hand, it emerges as an autobiographical topography that links the individual experience of a young Walter Benjamin to historically relevant and geographically specific sites and locations: "The way into this labyrinth, which did not lack its Ariadne, led over the Bendler Bridge, whose gentle arch was my first hillside. Not far from its foot lay the goal: Friedrich Wilhelm and Queen Luise" (*HP*, 145). On the other hand, however, this almost photographic recreation of Berlin gives way to a completely different and essentially ahistorical representation of the city, which is now characterized as a protosurrealist, urban dreamscape that evokes mysterious and unconscious perceptions in the passerby: "But to lose one's way in a city, as one loses one's way in a forest, requires practice. For this the street names must speak to one like the snapping of dry twigs, and the narrow streets of the city center must reflect the time of day as clearly as a mountain valley" (*HP*, 145). Finally, in a subsequent sentence, Benjamin approaches Berlin's cityscape by means of yet another metaphor. By associating the urban labyrinth with the awakening sexuality of a youth, Szondi suggests that both epitomize disorientation: "Here or not far from here must have been the bed of that Ariadne in whose proximity I first grasped, never to forget it, what only later came to me as a word: love" (*HP*, 146). The next passage is yet another variation on the recurrent theme: "I learned this art [of losing one's way] late in life: it fulfilled the dreams whose first traces were the labyrinths on the blotters on my exercise-books" (*HP*, 145). Here, the figure goes beyond the mere attempt to describe a never-resting cityscape or the mental and emotional bafflement of a child. Exceeding the factual significance of the image itself, the labyrinth represents the narrator's course of life as well as the utopian idea of alternative life plans unfolding beyond the limitations of chronological time.

But how are we to understand Szondi's choice to cite this particular passage in full? Perhaps he chose it because it effectively offers a thematic cross-section of Benjamin's oeuvre, showcasing his intellectual depth and breadth (given that his works range from essays on surrealism to theses on the philosophy of history and from autobiographical prose to reflections on critical hermeneutics). But the passage is pertinent for another reason. It illustrates the futility of attempting to identify a foundational principle or objective structure that would be applicable to all of Benjamin's work, since the latter wants to be read as a configuration of reflections and ideas.[23] It is thus possible that Szondi quotes the passage for mere heuristic reasons, to prove just how impossible it is to reduce a work of such complexity and heterogeneity to a single definitive meaning. As Szondi stated before, violent shortcuts will not yield any authoritative reading, and hence he suspends any knowledge about how the different levels of meaning may interrelate. Moreover, the latent correspondences and deeper connections within the passage are almost immediately negated as the themes and figures are constantly changing. For lack of a basic, univocally defined kernel of thought, the citation does not provide guidance in defining Benjamin's terms but instead allows Szondi to trace the gradual and inexhaustible metamorphosis of a central trope in Benjamin's poetics. As Szondi quotes Benjamin once again, "Origin does not at all mean the formation or becoming of what has arisen *(Entsprungene)*, but rather what is arising *(Entspringendes)* out of becoming and passing away. The origin is a whirlpool in the stream of becoming and draws into its rhythm the material that is to be formed" *(HP, 158)*. Szondi has discovered a cogent and consistent way of approaching Benjamin's thought—namely, by retracing its underlying historicity, epitomized by the repeated use of the future perfect tense—a peculiar and somewhat contrived tense used to express that something will have happened before some other future time specified in the sentence. In short, the future perfect tense grammatically enables Benjamin's paradoxical trope of "hope in the past," which gave Szondi's speech its title.

Szondi knows that any attempt to sift through Benjamin's work to discover eternal values and an immanent essence (a strategy more akin to the ahistorical formalism of Staiger's *Werkimmanenz*) would run counter to that thinker's project. Instead Szondi adopts a key principle of Benjamin's hermeneutics—namely, the notion that each literary work possesses its own problematic historicity independent of which it cannot be understood.[24] In other words, Szondi breaks open the idea that history is a fixed content—rather than a necessary dimension—within a

---

23. This concept, long since established in the field of Benjamin studies, is supported by Benjamin's own essentially Neoplatonic distinction between ideas (i.e., being and essence) on the one hand, and concepts (i.e., their representation or manifestation) on the other.

24. Timothy Bathi writes that Szondi conceives of (literary) history as "a dialectical progression from *Wirkungsästhetik* through the tensions within and between various forms of classicism and historicism to dialectical aesthetics themselves . . . as if it were an instance where history acted itself out in accord with a structure of prefiguration and fulfillment—itself one of culture's most fundamental and enduring structures for making sense of events and their relations, especially those events called texts." Timothy Bahti, "Fate in the Past: Peter Szondi's Reading of German Romantic Genre Theory," *Boundary 2* 11, no. 3 (1983): 111–25, here 112–13.

literary text, a thesis he first articulated in his *Traktat über philologische Erkenntnis* (On Philological Knowledge): "The philologist searches for history in the work of art rather than searching for a work of art within history."[25] This insight explains why Szondi underscores Benjamin's effect and influence on other poets and thinkers, as well as his elective affinities, thereby suggesting that Benjamin's productivity is as much the result of his social and intellectual milieu as of his unique talent as a critical thinker. When Benjamin translated Proust, Szondi writes, he was so impressed with the French novelist that he feared for his own creativity and therefore resolved "[not] to read a word more of Proust than what he needed to translate at the moment, because otherwise he risked straying into an addictive dependency which would hinder his own production" (*HP*, 146).

By thus including the historical context and biographical details of the work's production in his reading, Szondi accomplishes his erstwhile intention to write not *about* literature but *with* it, "in retracing their mode of being, as being written" (*im Nachvollzug nämlich ihres Geschriebenseins*).[26] As Rainer Nägele writes, Szondi treats the biographical and historical facts not as concomitant, merely peripheral circumstances, but as the transcendable basis of any text.[27] Hence the phrase *im Nachvollzug des Geschriebenseins* must not be understood as synonymous with empathy or psychological penetration.[28] Rather Szondi is concerned with reconstructing the specific historicity inherent in every literary or philosophical work, that is to say, an antiessentialist historicity, which is initiated by the process of writing and reinitiated every time it is (re)read, and henceforth undergoes perpetual change.

Szondi's inaugural address thus privileges Benjamin's dialectical conception of historical experience and historicity over the traditional framework of philological inquiry. As Szondi writes, "Benjamin's last effort, undertaken in the face of the victory of national socialism and the failure of German and French social democracy, was devoted to formulating a new conception of history which would break with the belief in progress, with the notion of the progress of humanity in a 'homogeneous and empty time.' . . . Benjamin's new conception of history is rooted in the dialectic of future and past, of messianic expectation and remembrance" (*HP*, 157). Suggesting that Benjamin's texts, like any remnant of the past, contain a utopian, critical core that must be exposed by the critic or reader, Szondi's reading of Benjamin's work effectively mirrors Benjamin's methodology: "Benjamin listens for the

---

25. Szondi, *Schriften*, 1:275; my translation.

26. Peter Szondi, *Das lyrische Drama des Fin de Siècle*, ed. Henriette Beese, vol. 4, *Studienausgabe der Vorlesungen* (Frankfurt a. M.: Suhrkamp, 1975), 16; my translation. On the notion of *Nachvollzug des Selbsterlebten*, see Wilhelm Dilthey, "Entwürfe zur Kritik der historischen Vernunft," *Gesammelte Schriften*, vol. 7.2 (Leipzig: Teubner, 1958), 191–220.

27. See Rainer Nägele, "Text, History and the Critical Subject: Notes on Peter Szondi's Theory and Praxis of Hermeneutics," *Boundary 2*, 11, no. 3 (1983): 38.

28. Ibid., 39.

first notes of a future which has meanwhile become the past. . . . Benjamin's tense is not the perfect, but the future perfect in the fullness of its paradox: being future and past at the same time" (*HP*, 153). The figure of "Hope in the Past" and the juxtaposition of boding and insight ("the premonition of the child and the knowledge of the grown man") are Szondi's answer to Benjamin's paradoxical claim that prophecy is contained in remembrance (*HP*, 153). This figure of thought also exemplifies what both Szondi and Benjamin define as the ideal stance of the (literary) historian. As Szondi writes, Benjamin, whose writings progress in a nonlinear manner, epitomizes Friedrich Schlegel's definition of the historian as "a prophet facing backwards" (*HP*, 156). Looking back means, quite literally, comprehending and embracing the future.

Szondi fails to mention that this temporal paradox organizes and motivates much of Benjamin's oeuvre. Rather than explicating it, however, Szondi applies this paradox by casting it as the structuring principle of his own text about Benjamin and thereby carries on Benjamin's legacy through textual performativity. For Szondi not only takes interest in Benjamin's "lost time"—meaning the time that is, as Michael Hays has put it, "not the past but a future . . . that looks back on the shattered dream of an ideal world"—but he also reflects on how the historical events that obstructed Benjamin's future (will) affect the future—that is, *his* present.[29] For Szondi's inaugural address is of course located beyond the historical barrier that had shattered Benjamin's hopes. And yet the speech's title, *Hope in the Past*, should not be regarded as a pessimistic or even cynical gesture but rather as the expression of a dialectical tension between past and present, which ultimately conjures a utopian future perspective into the present-day reality of Szondi's public address. For the paradox of "hope in the past" contains within itself a call for reflection, criticism, and political responsibility that is ultimately addressed to Szondi's audience—but in the spirit of Benjamin.

It would not be off the mark to read Szondi's "excavatory" hermeneutics as a self-authenticating strategy that is conceived to mobilize his audience's investment in the role of the university within society. Charged with political content, Szondi's inaugural address is not a nostalgic retrospective but a way to make history meaningful. To cite Roland Barthes, who wrote in reference to the power of the spoken word in the context of 1968, the delivery of Szondi's speech indeed eliminates "the age-old distance between act and discourse, event and testimony."[30] Szondi's speech thereby gives way to what Barthes described as "a new dimension of history . . . immediately linked to its discourse."[31] Speech and writing, as well as their reception and interpretation, coincide in the spontaneous event of public speaking that

---

29. See Michael Hays, foreword to Szondi, *On Textual Understanding*, vii–xxi, here x.

30. Roland Barthes, "Writing and Event" (1968), in Barthes, *The Rustle of Language*, trans. Richard Howard (Berkeley: University of California Press, 1989), 150.

31. Ibid.

"makes" history. Given its nonconformist approach to public speaking as well as its oppositional relation to the academic public, Szondi's speech is linked to the other acts of discursive contestation treated in this book, which likewise instigated the formation of a counter-public sphere that beginning in the 1950s and throughout the 1960s challenged Germany's relative indifference toward Jewish marginalization and persecution. Like the other speakers discussed before, albeit (even) more cryptically, Szondi calls for a broader acknowledgment of the crimes committed by the Nazi regime—within and beyond the university.

The significance of dispensing with interpretation corresponds to the challenge of establishing Benjamin's work in the academy while at the same time protecting it from possible (mis)appropriations. By withholding his own theoretical apparatus and by confining himself to quoting Benjamin's work and scarcely commenting on it, Szondi underscores the primary role of reception—the pure act of *listening*—which precedes any hermeneutic or philological project. Szondi thus reverses the conventional path of literary scholarship by testing whether his audience might be able to complete, indeed *actualize*, the meaning of his public address as he enunciates it. In that way, the listeners take on the role of the third and thereby fulfill the critical potential of the speech—simply by listening. This process of critical reception is meant to occur despite, or precisely because of, the lack of a concrete agenda and without the conventional pathos and rhetorical tropes that are characteristic of public speech. The success of Szondi's inaugural speech then is independent of whether or not his audience can hear an "authentic" voice within the letter, the writing, or the spoken word. In a complete reversal of the logo- and phonocentric paradigm, Szondi's addressees no longer read a text that may originate from orality but instead listen to a piece of writing.[32] To put it another way, aural reception supersedes textual exegesis as Szondi reads Benjamin "aloud."

By implicitly emphasizing the immediate and thus arguably more "authentic" act of *listening*, Szondi shines the spotlight of his public address on his audience. Thus the inaugural speech shifts away from rhetorical persuasion and toward an experimental form of scholarly presentation that literally *includes* the listener—not in the sense of a transformative Buberian dialogue, of course, but in the sense of making the listener the *site* of Szondi's impassioned inaugural address. Instead of discussing Benjamin's thought discursively, Szondi presses the testimonial dimension of literature. He simply submits Benjamin's writings, in the hope that this might generate a process of understanding in some of his listeners, obliging them to witness experiences that would otherwise remain imperceptible to them.

---

32. As Derrida writes, "And the *first* convention, which would relate immediately to the order of natural and universal signification, would be produced as spoken language.... The voice is closest to the signified, whether it is determined strictly as sense (thought or lived) or more loosely as thing. All signifiers, and first and foremost the written signifier, are derivative to what would wed the voice indissolubly to the mind or to the thought of the signified sense.... The written signifier is always technical and representative." Derrida, *Of Grammatology*, 11.

Underneath his montage of citations, Szondi manifests his conviction that Benjamin's language—and specifically, his "metaphors based on twofold definitions"—can be deciphered only by a reader who conscientiously holds fast to the primary object of hermeneutic inquiry—namely, the citation from the text itself (*HP*, 154).

The Witness

Peter Szondi begins the radio adaptation of his inaugural address, *Hoffnung im Vergangenen*, as follows: "In 1962 Walter Benjamin would have turned seventy. It is a futile, unanswerable, and sad question to ask what else he would have accomplished in his life, what impact he was destined to have after the new beginning, had he not lain dead in Portbou since 1940. A victim of National Socialism."[33] By linking the thematic core of his speech, Benjamin's philosophy of history, with a deeply personal, biographical dimension, his suicide at the Franco-Spanish border at Portbou in 1940, Szondi's reading allows the autobiographical prose text *A Berlin Childhood around 1900* to function as the pivot between Benjamin's life and work. Long citations reveal how Benjamin experienced the seemingly mysterious world of the German Empire as an adolescent and how he sought to decipher the secret laws governing bourgeois life. His reflections on Berlin, a place that emerges as a mystifying urban cityscape, foreshadow Benjamin's future theory of Paris as the paradigmatic site of modernity. By drawing from Benjamin's biography and by attempting to capture his mentality and spirit—his *Lebensgefühl*—Szondi subverts the methodological framework of his otherwise highly objective and impartial textual analysis.[34] As a text that is permeated by a vague melancholy, *In Search of Lost Time in Walter Benjamin* is thus ultimately incompatible with Szondi's other writings.

Szondi, who significantly once referred to his inaugural speech as his "personal credo," here overtly reflects on his role as a literary scholar and a (public) intellectual.[35] The speech then is about more than staking out his academic niche. More fundamentally, Szondi interrogates his intellectual place of belonging, astonished as he was, according to Jean Bollack, "at having been admitted, such as he was, into the sacred college of 'full' professors."[36] That this process is mediated through Benjamin's prose is unconventional but perfectly within the logic of Szondi's argument.

---

33. Peter Szondi, *Hoffnung im Vergangenen: Walter Benjamin und die Suche nach der verlorenen Zeit* (Frankfurt a. M.: Hessischer Rundfunk, 1961), audio recording; my translation.

34. On the role of subjectivity in Szondi's inaugural address, see Thomas Sparr, "Peter Szondi," *Bulletin des Leo Baeck Instituts* 78 (1987): 62. See also Nägele, who concedes to the presence of a personal dimension in all of Szondi's writing. See Nägele, "Text, History and the Critical Subject," 38.

35. P. Szondi to Rudolf Hirsch, January 21, 1961, in Szondi, *Briefe*, 201.

36. J. Bollack, "Opening Remarks," *Boundary 2*, 8. On Szondi's role as a public intellectual, see Karl Grob, "Theory and Practice of Philosophy: Reflections on the Public Statements of Peter Szondi," *Boundary 2*, 169–230.

For in a passage about Rilke, Szondi notes that as a reader of Proust, the poet could not help but identify with the protagonist of the *Recherche du temps perdu*, and thus he became a "reader of himself" (*HP*, 148). There is an intrinsic link between the faculty of empathy and the act of reading as remembrance, which of course has ramifications for the act of writing as well. As the example of Rilke shows, it is hardly productive to write one's own biography, because the result of such an endeavor would be the story of someone else's life.[37] To learn about oneself, it is better to project oneself onto the fictitious character of a novel, such as, for instance, Proust's "Marcel." This is a strange assertion whereby Szondi suggests that in order to recover one's biographical reality, it is better to read than to write—since, apparently, truth resides elsewhere, in the life of others and not in oneself. That being the case, Szondi's montage reveals what is truly at stake for him in this form of biographical inquiry. If he decides to scrutinize Benjamin's autobiographical prose and to shed light on his predecessor's personal history, it is because his own life—his own destiny—is at the core of this investigation. Although Szondi makes no overt personal statement and never uses the first-person pronoun "I," his speech ostensibly pertains to his own life and survival as well.

Referring to "death" and "the dead," and, specifically, Benjamin's death, on six separate occasions, the speech becomes saturated with intimations of the theme of dying. This kind of insistence transforms seemingly random repetition into a compelling poetic gesture. Szondi clearly struggles to grasp the devastating reality of death—of Benjamin's death, the death of other victims of the Gestapo, and, by implication, his own fortuitously providential survival of the Holocaust. In a gesture that mirrors this recurrent invocation of death, Szondi ponders the meaning of love, an experience that, like death, is equally abstract and essential. What both figures have in common is that they resist any attempt at defining them. As Benjamin explains in a passage from *A Berlin Childhood* that recounts a foundational preverbal experience of his, "I . . . grasped . . . what only later came to me as a word: love" (*HP*, 146, 151). This is a crucial observation that Szondi—incidentally and significantly—quotes twice. Death by contrast has the opposite effect. We grasp it verbally as a mere concept and lacking substance until the moment in which we die and thereby lose our ability to communicate the experience. As a result, it is impossible to testify about death, be that one's own or the death of the other.

Szondi's inaugural speech is shaped by a way of thinking that privileges death—in which death is defined metaphorically as the loss of one's intellectual spirit, political integrity, and moral character. But the speech is also about literal death, and as

---

37. As Szondi argues, "[Rilke's] work differs fundamentally from that of *A la recherche*, for in contrast to Proust's thesis of involuntary remembering (*la mémoire involontaire*), Rilke's writing represents a conscious and assiduous effort to 'carry out' or 'realize' (*leisten*) his childhood once again. Later Rilke was to judge his own effort abortive because the place of his own childhood was taken by that of another, the fictional hero Malte" (*HP*, 148).

such it marks the beginning of commemoration. Szondi, to be sure, definitely holds out a modicum of hope for his audience: he demands only that they acknowledge the fact that Benjamin took his life in flight from the Gestapo. Although they could never truly understand what Benjamin endured in the final moments of his life as a refugee, it is nevertheless their ethical duty to attempt to do so. For a humble attempt by his listeners to confront one particular story of one particular victim of the Holocaust could begin the process of dismantling the topos of "unspeakability" and "incommensurability," which for many years had represented the standard academic response to justify the failure of establishing a discourse about the Nazi genocide in Germany.[38]

When books are burned, what remains of freedom of thought, the backbone of academic activity? When millions of people are murdered, what remains of humanistic thought and the very idea of humanity? In the case of Benjamin, there are texts, texts that survived and that survived him and thus allow him to survive, texts acting as placeholders for a person who no longer exists while at the same time functioning as a site of reflection, of coming to terms with the demise as it is unfolding in real time and in reality. This, then, is the substance of Szondi's indictment. Bearing a trace of death but also a trace of the struggle to make sense of it, Benjamin's texts (and in particular *German Men and Women*) serve as philological evidence: they are the primary and concrete facts of Szondi's critique of the German university and his indictment of those still existing anti-Semitic scholars who populate it. Hence the many citations in Szondi's speech indicate the testimonial aspect of Szondi's talk. They function as personal and legal guarantors, lending the text a dual hermeneutic impetus. On the one hand, they are the objects of the hermeneutic textual analysis, but on the other hand, they are the subjects of an imaginary tribunal. For every citation is a witness testimony and thus part of a trial, staged for the purpose of mobilizing a process of justice within the institutional framework of the university. Most significantly, the Wais citation exposes the continuing presence in the academy of individuals who embraced the Fascist ideology. Hence whereas Szondi cites Benjamin to compensate for his *absence*, Wais is cited even though (or precisely because) he may be present in the audience. In the latter case, citation thus serves to draw attention to the *presence* of a particular witness. Built on the tension between writing and speaking, life and death, the speech is structured as a hearing of witness testimonies, and thus it relies on the principles of orality and publicness. For the discipline of judicial hermeneutics is, as Rudolf Stichweh notes, "a hermeneutics of interaction, an exegesis of statements derived from public, dialogic speech."[39]

38. On the problem of the oft-cited "unspeakability" of the Holocaust, see Thomas Trezise, "Unspeakable," *Yale Journal of Criticism* 14, no. 1 (2001): 39–66.

39. Rudolf Stichweh, "Zur Subjektivierung der Entscheidungsfindung im deutschen Strafprozeß des 19. Jahrhunderts," in *Subjektivierung des justiziellen Beweisverfahrens: Beiträge zum Zeugenbeweis in*

In this way, Szondi's inaugural speech goes beyond textual analysis by considering a *case* that is suspended in the gray area between literary and judicial hermeneutics, between the academy and the public (political) sphere. Taking recourse to the testimonies of what would be more credible witnesses, Szondi quotes others in order to substantiate his case. This speaks to Arendt's definition of the rhetorical figure of citation, which "serves to have witnesses, and also friends."[40] Citations serve to continue a dialogue among friends after the conversation has been interrupted in the case of the death of one of its participants. At other times, the citations serve as a form of witness testimony calling absent witnesses back to life by literally "summoning" them. This also explains why citations are granted the quasi-judicial status of "testimony" and why they are accepted as a sign of presence and life. Unlike the "dead letter" on the page, Szondi's citations literally have a voice and are therefore associated with the individuals who have been or will be uttering them. Thus they secure the virtual survival of Benjamin and other thinkers within the framework of Szondi's text.[41]

Szondi brings into play two separate modalities of citation. By shifting between citations that signify either absence or presence (but never both), Szondi establishes a relationship between the *testis* and the *martis*, two different kinds of witnesses that derive from Latin and Greek etymology, respectively.[42] As a public speaker who cites extensively from a variety of sources, Szondi embodies both modalities. Serving as the mouthpiece of a figure like Benjamin, he speaks on behalf of the true witness, the *martis* (martyr), whose death is his credential par excellence, whereas Szondi is of course alive and thus figures as *testis* (witness)—a disinterested witness who assumes the stance of a neutral third party. What complicates Szondi's testimony, however, is that as he interrogates the conditions of possibility of Benjamin's survival within his text, he also draws attention to (and ultimately affirms the factuality of) Benjamin's passing. As a result, Szondi paradoxically inverts the way in which classical rhetoric uses citation—namely, by quoting a deceased person as if he were alive, and a renowned thinker as if he were an essential witness in his own tribunal. Szondi's speech thereby undermines the conventions of both judicial speech and the funeral oration or classical eulogy. In the former case he fails to provide sufficient forensic evidence, since the citations alone hardly prove anything; in the latter he speaks not about the *deceased* but about the dead person's *passing*.

Europa und den USA, ed. André Gouron (Frankfurt a. M.: Klostermann, 1994), 265–300, here 291; my translation.

40. Arendt, *Denktagebuch*, 756; my translation.

41. Derrida, *Of Grammatology*, 12.

42. Benveniste defines the *testis* as a witness "who attends as the 'third' person (*ter-stis) at an affair in which two persons are interested; and this conception goes back to the Indo-European community." Émile Benveniste, *Indo-European Language and Society* (Miami, FL: University of Miami Press, 1973), 526. The Greek notion of *martis* (martyr), by contrast, denotes a persecuted victim who bears witness with his own death. Agamben, *Remnants of Auschwitz*, 26.

No matter how emphatic and persuasive, Szondi's ventriloquy cannot raise Benjamin from the dead. And thus Szondi is and remains the hidden core of his inaugural address, the palpable presence behind the words of the other. What is at stake in the speech then is Szondi's struggle to understand Benjamin's writings in the context of his tragic death, and the possibility of recovering the thinker's voice by mobilizing his own (problematic) status as a witness. For Szondi was himself a victim of the Holocaust who had been deported to the concentration camp Bergen-Belsen at age fifteen from where he had escaped to Switzerland in 1944.[43] Deriving his enunciative authority from the fact that he saw, shared, and survived the experience to which he testifies, Szondi speaks in and through the voice of the *superstes* (survivor): he is the third, who, in Émile Benveniste's terms, "subsists beyond."[44] Personifying the possibility of surviving life-threatening conditions, the *superstes* remains in flux between the living and the dead. As he gives his testimony on behalf of a *martis*, an ideal and true witness who is, however, no longer able to testify, Szondi's position on the speaker's podium is inherently ambivalent, since he can only ever speak in the capacity of a secondary witness whose judgment is inevitably affected and thus potentially compromised. He is a witness of the second order whose testimony would require the testimony of a third-order witness willing to testify on his behalf. As Paul Celan once put it succinctly and pessimistically, "No one bears witness for the witness."[45]

As a *superstes*, Szondi is essentially speechless, since, as François Lyotard has argued, there is no language or discourse that would allow him to testify about his proper experience, for

> to the privation constituted by the damage there is added the impossibility of bring-
> ing it to the knowledge of others, and in particular to the knowledge of a tribunal.
> Should the victim seek to bypass this impossibility and testify anyway to the wrong
> done to him or to her, he or she comes up against the following argumentation: either
> the damages you complain about never took place, and your testimony is false; or else
> they took place, and since you are able to testify to them, it is not a wrong that has
> been done to you, but merely a damage, and your testimony is still false.[46]

43. In 1944, the Nazis agreed to exchange 1,683 Hungarian Jews who were detained at Bergen-Belsen for German citizens held by the Allied forces. Szondi's family was among this group of prisoners. Rolf Keller and Wolfgang Marienfeld, eds., *Konzentrationslager Bergen-Belsen: Berichte und Dokumente* (Hannover: Niedersächsische Landeszentrale für Politische Bildung, 1995), 21.

44. According to Benveniste, the *superstes* is a witness "'who has his being beyond', a witness in virtue of his surviving, or as 'the one who stands over the matter', who was present at it." Benveniste, *Indo-European Language and Society*, 526.

45. See Paul Celan, *Aschenglorie* [Ash-Glory], in Celan, *Selections*, 105. See also Jacques Derrida, *Sovereignties in Question: The Poetics of Paul Celan*, ed. Thomas Dutoit and Outi Pasanen (New York: Fordham University Press, 2005), 89.

46. Lyotard, *The Differend*, 5.

This is especially true for the scholar and scientist. Indeed, the status of the *super-stes* represents an impossible stance for someone whose traditional role it is to secure the objectivity of scientific knowledge and theory. This is at least true within the terms of classical rhetoric: according to Aristotle, witnesses involved in or present at a crime are simply not capable of giving objective testimony. While they can confirm "whether or not something has happened," they are incapable of evaluating "the quality of the act—of whether, for example, it was just or unjust or conferred an advantage or not."[47] For this reason, Aristotle deems "ancient" testimonies more coherent and impartial than those given by witnesses who are living and able to testify. As Szondi calls a contemporary thinker like Benjamin to the witness stand by quoting him, he draws on the rhetorical tradition of citing "the poets and other well-known persons"—but not without infusing historical momentum and actuality into his public address.[48] As a *superstes* who has acquired neither the authority of death nor that of old age, Szondi moves away from scholarly discourse in the attempt to reach out to a broader audience, West Germany's public sphere.

Was this cryptic effort to give voice to a *martis* conceived in response to a public defamation campaign carried out by Holocaust revisionist Paul Rassinier against concentration camp survivors in Germany? Between March 24 and April 8, 1960, and thus less than a year before Szondi arrived in Berlin, Rassinier held a series of lectures in twelve West German and Austrian cities, lectures that were sponsored by Rassinier's German publisher Karl-Heinz Priester, a former SS officer and propagandist for Josef Goebbels. During this lecture tour, Rassinier brought various revisionist claims to the attention of the German public, including the allegation that the "genocide myth" had been invented by the international Zionist movement.[49] Rassinier also argued that the testimonies of concentration camp survivors were grossly exaggerated: "You have to reckon with the complex of Ulysses' lie, the tendency of all world travelers to exaggerate their adventures. Every one has this complex, and so it is with the internees. Human beings need the miraculous, in the ugly as well as in the beautiful. Each internee hoped and wished to come out of this adventure with the halo of a saint, with the glory of a hero, or a martyr, and each one embroiders his own Odyssey without realizing that the reality is quite enough in itself."[50] What makes the case of Rassinier unique is that he was himself a detainee in the concentration and labor camps of Buchenwald and Dora, and a former Socialist who had been active in the anti-Nazi resistance. Hence Rassinier was a concentration camp survivor who accused other survivors of lying about

47. Aristotle, *On Rhetoric*, 113.
48. Ibid., 112.
49. Paul Rassinier, *Debunking the Genocide Myth: A Study of the Nazi Concentration Camps and the Alleged Extermination of European Jewry*, trans. Adam Robbins (Los Angeles: Noontide Press, 1978).
50. Paul Rassinier, *Was nun, Odysseus? Zur Bewältigung der Vergangenheit* (Wiesbaden: Karl Heinz Priester, 1960), 17; my translation.

their experience and who pitted his own testimony against that of other witnesses. "I did not see any gas chambers," Rassinier thus stated during his lecture tour in Germany, and went on to accuse other witnesses of lying: "It is a fact that not one single internee ever saw that this means was used for mass exterminations. . . . And yet there are time and again people who say that they had been witnesses."[51] The irony of Rassinier's argument is, of course, duplicitous: on the one hand, it neatly encapsulates a double bind that would soon be used by a number of Holocaust revisionists to discredit witnesses of the Holocaust, but on the other hand, Rassinier effectively fails to recognize that the double bind applies to him as well. After all, there is no difference in status between Rassinier and other concentration camp survivors (except for the fact that there really were no gas chambers at Buchenwald).

The double bind is as follows: having survived an extermination camp, survivors are faced with a formidable dilemma, since their very survival calls into question their claim that the conditions of their internment were deadly. As a result of this double bind, others, including Rassinier's academic successor Robert Faurisson, have fallaciously argued that the survivors are living "proof" that there was no "final solution" and that the Nazis never intended a complete extinction of the Jewish "race." As Lyotard paraphrases Faurisson, "The plaintiff complains that he has been fooled about the existence of gas chambers, fooled that is, about the so-called Final Solution. His argument is: in order for a place to be defined as gas chamber, the only eyewitness I would accept would be a victim of this gas chamber; now, according to my opponent, there is no victim that is not dead; otherwise, this gas chamber would not be what he or she claims it to be. There is, therefore, no gas chamber."[52]

There is no record of Szondi reacting to Rassinier's lectures in 1960, which, according to the author's claims, boosted the sales of his books and effectively raised the plausibility of revisionism among Germany's right-wing citizenry.[53] But there is documentation that during the time when Szondi took on his position at the Free University, Rassinier developed more contacts with Germany and began to publish with the *Deutsche Hochschullehrer-Zeitung* (Journal of German University Teachers), a journal that is a lot less respectable than its name would indicate.[54] Among other things, Rassinier requested that a committee of independent historians inquire into the truth about the concentration camps, thereby effectively challenging the German constitution. It says much about the mood of postwar Germany's academic and civic landscape that this extremist speaker was not stopped from his conspiratorial and fraud campaign. As a matter of fact, Rassinier and his entourage

51. Ibid., 27.
52. Lyotard, *The Differend*, 3–4.
53. Rassinier, *Was nun, Odysseus?* 17.
54. See Pierre Vidal-Naquet, *Holocaust Denial in France: Analysis of a Unique Phenomenon* (Tel Aviv: Tel Aviv University, Faculty of the Humanities, 1995), 32.

could be said to have created their own version of a counter-public sphere—one that was indeed tolerated as such until 1963, when the German authorities deported the extremist as he was attempting to enter Germany again, this time for the purpose of attending the Auschwitz trial. Ironically, as will be shown in the next chapter, the Auschwitz trial drastically raised the political stakes of testimony but at the same time worked against garnering respect for the claims of actual witnesses. Rassinier's campaign had not been without its successes.

Szondi never made a public statement about his internment at Bergen-Belsen, but his inaugural address at the Free University represents his attempt to circumvent the dilemma of providing a testimony that was simultaneously indispensable and impossible. For Szondi speaks through a strategy that allows him to draw authority from death and yet secure the actuality of orally performed and orally transmitted testimony, while speaking from the perspective of a victim without, however, having to articulate his proper experience. In other words, Szondi has surrendered his voice, but he is by no means speechless. His inaugural address links two concrete, unique but exemplary lives that occasionally intersect to shape the contours of a counterpublic anchored in oppositional acts of speaking and listening. Contrary to the traditional literary scholar then who abstracts, as Szondi writes, "due to a falsely conceived notion of science," from his personal experience, Szondi implicitly acknowledges his personal perspective and psychological reality but without giving in to a pathos of anguish (*HP*, 157). There are moments when he "believes to understand" Benjamin, moments when he is able to empathize with the experiences and desires of the other, such as, for instance, Benjamin's "strange wish to be able to lose himself in a city" (*HP*, 156). In these rare instances, two distinct perspectives coincide, that of the disillusioned adult and that of a hopeful child, that of responsibility assumed (or not) toward the dead and that of inexonerable guilt felt (or not) by the living.

Szondi reads Benjamin through the lens of himself, and himself through the lens of Benjamin. This is a two-pronged and reciprocal act of reading and listening that lays claim to two subject positions that are both sustained and threatened by the notion of empathy. Its effect is twofold. It raises the antipositivistic, politically committed, and self-reflexive quality of Szondi's scholarship, and it legitimizes an experimental act of witnessing through the immediacy and force of a public performance. As a textual and performative intervention, the speech further shows that Szondi's thesis about the relevance of the historical standpoint of the interpreter is applicable to the related domain of the judicial: "True objectivity is bound up with subjectivity" (*HP*, 157).[55]

---

55. Szondi writes: "The hermeneutics of our time is defined by this shattering of traditional philology, a philology that was historical and thus fancied itself to be independent of its own historical standpoint—a belief that went unchallenged by its practitioners and even seduced them to still greater confidence." Szondi, *Introduction to Literary Hermeneutics*, trans. Martha Woodmansee (Cambridge: Cambridge University Press, 1995), 12.

7

PETER WEISS

But the citizens must uphold the law
and there can be no deviation, for pure water
can never be drawn once the well has been fouled.

—Aeschylus, *The Oresteia*

Like Szondi's inaugural address, *Die Ermittlung* (The Investigation), Peter Weiss's theatrical representation of the Frankfurt or Auschwitz trial, solicits and draws its momentum from the simultaneity of collective reception. When the play was first staged on October 19, 1965, its premiere took place in sixteen theaters simultaneously, including four theaters in West Germany (West Berlin, Essen, Cologne, and Munich), eleven theaters in East Germany (Altenburg, East Berlin, Cottbus, Dresden, Erfurt, Gera, Halle, Leipzig, Neustrelitz, Potsdam, and Rostock), and one, under the direction of Peter Brook, in London.[1] Weiss's script was able to absorb a wide range of directorial approaches. While seven directors produced it in the form of a recitation, the nine others ventured often highly stylized theatrical

---

1. Peter Weiss, *The Investigation: A Play*, trans. Jon Swan and Ulu Grosbard (New York: Atheneum, 1966).

performances that ranged from minimalist and undramatic presentations to more pathos-laden interpretations of the script.

Given this high-profile set of simultaneous premieres, *The Investigation* is a hybrid that has as much in common structurally with public speech as it does with theatrical performance:[2] having convinced his publisher, Peter Suhrkamp, to release the work's copyright to the public domain for one day, Weiss staged a carefully orchestrated premiere that effectively disavowed the divide between sociopolitical reality and the domain of culture and art that by the 1960s had long been seen as characteristic of European capitalist society at least since the mid-nineteenth century.[3] *The Investigation* thereby subverts a set of conventional boundaries separating the real trial from its representation on stage: the boundary between history and drama, between the public sphere of social activity and the more narrowly defined literary sphere of art, and finally between political resistance and aesthetic practice. By delegitimizing the institutional base of the theater, Weiss's documentary play not only departs from the traditional understanding of what the status and properties of the *medium* of theater and perhaps of literature in general ought to be, but, more crucially, subverts the *institution* of the theater from within.[4] Hence the present chapter expands this book's scope of inquiry: extending the notion of politics to a cultural site of social interaction, it examines the perceived and actual limits of what has so far been delineated as an emerging counterpublic of discursive conflict and deliberation.

The premieres of *The Investigation* saw a range of experiments designed to bear out the idea of documentary theater, and many arrived at ironic reversals of theatric conventions. One production opened with the announcement "Court in Session: Please rise," while another featured displays indicating that applause was deemed inappropriate.[5] *The Investigation* was a spectacle that integrated art and political resistance, theater and public speech. To be sure, Weiss here released some of the tension that is reflected in the antithetical title of his major novel, *Ästhetik*

---

2. As a form of public speech, *The Investigation*, however, eschews any traces of classical judicial or forensic rhetoric. It is significant, for example, that Weiss dispenses with the *plaidoyers* that concluded the hearing of the evidence, some of which were published in book form shortly after the trial. See Hans Laternser, *Die andere Seite im Ausschwitz-Prozess 1963/65: Reden eines Verteidigers* (Stuttgart: Seewald, 1966).

3. See Peter Bürger, *Theory of the Avant-Garde*, trans. Michael Shaw and foreword by Jochen Schulte-Sasse (Minneapolis: University of Minnesota Press, 1984). Contrary to Weiss's play *Marat/Sade* (1963), which exemplifies what Peter Bürger has defined as the art of the neo-avant-garde that emerged after 1945, *The Investigation* is more closely associated with the historical avant-garde, whose tenets Weiss here revisits and renews by negating the category of individual reception and by striving toward the abolition of autonomous art (Bürger, 53–54).

4. See also Daniel K. Jernigan, who claims that "the stage setting in *The Investigation* creates the postmodern impression of an immediate event by suspending historical referents and minimizing the difference between stage and house." Daniel K. Jernigan, *Drama and the Postmodern: Assessing the Limits of Metatheatre* (Amherst, MA: Cambria Press, 2008), 214.

5. Christopher Innes, *Holy Theatre: Ritual and the Avant Garde* (Cambridge: Cambridge University Press, 1984), 223.

des Widerstands (The Aesthetics of Resistance, 1975–81)—the genitive construction proposing a dialectical tension that at once casts aesthetic practice as a form of resistance and deems political resistance to be potentially aesthetic.[6] For the duration of the gripping media event of the staging of *The Investigation*, these two poles coincided in an unprecedented intervention—a "collective manifestation" in the words of Peter Brook—that took place in the theater but had a much larger and more general audience in mind: Germany's public sphere broadly conceived.[7] And so although Weiss's theater audience epitomizes the Habermasian bourgeois public sphere, which is secluded from the political or "representative" sphere, it is potentially here, "in the institutions of art criticism, including literature, theater and music criticism, [that] lay opinion of the mature public or the public considering themselves as such organizes itself."[8] Depending on a public sphere in which individuals would debate contemporary issues and thus regulate civil society through constructive criticism, *The Investigation* bears directly on the political reality—it is indeed constructed to speak out against a major branch of the political sphere— namely, West Germany's jurisdiction in legal matters. By rejecting the illusionistic stage of classical theater, Weiss appeals to the theater audience to participate in the "investigation" and the process of judgment, for the legal issues negotiated during the "Criminal Case against Mulka et al." (as the Auschwitz trial was officially termed) should not be confined to the court. Instead, Weiss insists, they call for Germany's lay audience, considering that it shared some culpability or *Mitschuld* (shared guilt) with the Nazi regime.[9]

Just as the defendants are indicted for legal crimes but also accused of moral transgressions, the general public is thereby implicated in their indictment. The abbreviation "et al." of the "Criminal Case against Mulka et al." could be extended to the entire German citizenry. Still, according to Weiss, Germans had not been suitably scandalized by the dreadful information that had been revealed during the Frankfurt proceedings. As a result, *The Investigation* emerges as an ambitiously multilayered project that embraces culture, justice, and history. By involving the theatergoing public in Germany's legislation and by working toward a public

---

6. See Erika Salloch, *Peter Weiss' "Die Ermittlung": Zur Struktur des Dokumentartheaters* (Frankfurt a. M.: Athenäum, 1972), 42–46.

7. Michael Kustow, *Peter Brook: A Biography* (New York: St. Martin's Press, 2005), 157.

8. Habermas, *The Structural Transformation*, 59–60.

9. For Weiss's reflections on the notion of *Mitschuld*, see Peter Weiss, "Antwort auf eine Kritik zur Stockholmer Aufführung der 'Ermittlung'" (1966), in Weiss, *Rapporte* (Frankfurt a. M.: Suhrkamp, 1968–71), 2:45–50, here 49. On the moral implications of the problem of *Mitschuld*, see Karl Jaspers, *The Question of German Guilt*, trans. E. B. Ashton (New York: Capricorn Books, 1961). Katja Garloff has made the case that a certain complicity between the Nazi criminals and the German public is inscribed in the play, insofar as the sporadic laughter of the defendants, which is prompted by the stage directions, establishes a subtle link between the villains and the audience. Katja Garloff, "Peter Weiss's Entry into the German Public Sphere," *Colloquia Germanica* 30, no. 1 (1997): 62. See also Wilhelm Ungerer, "Auschwitz auf dem Theater?," in *Deutsche Nachkriegsliteratur und der Holocaust*, ed. Stephan Braese and Holger Gehle (Frankfurt a. M.: Campus, 1998), 71–97, here 83.

sphere that would be more actively involved in and consequently also more influential with regard to political matters, Weiss addresses the question of guilt, foregrounds a contemporary legal case, and simultaneously exposes a political crisis. For, as the play reveals, the Auschwitz trial was an ethical, political, and juridical failure. An endeavor conceived to help shape political reality, *The Investigation* actualizes, indeed it might be appropriate to say it *corrects*, the real-life trial by mirroring it and by putting on a second-order trial conceived to mobilize an ersatz *Öffentlichkeit*—the kind of counter-public sphere Buber, Celan, Bachmann, Arendt, Johnson, and Szondi had already begun to envision.

The present chapter reads the play as both a highly politicized response to the problems that characterized the process of West Germany's democratization and a historically significant and in key instances technically precise recapitulation of the judicial proceedings of the Frankfurt trial. As a comparative reevaluation of Weiss's play and the transcripts of the trial (derived from the original audio recordings) suggests, testimonial evidence played a substantial role in the Auschwitz trial.[10] Contrary to the Nuremberg prosecution, which had virtually shunned the testimony of survivors and based its case exclusively on documentary evidence and expert witnesses, the hearings in Frankfurt made extensive use of cross-examinations and testimonial evidence. The prosecution thus presented the testimony of over four hundred eyewitnesses, most whom were either former SS men who had served in Auschwitz or survivors of the concentration camps. Needless to say, the extensive and probing cross-examinations produced enormous tension in the courtroom. As Weiss noted after attending several sessions of the trial, "The confrontations of witnesses and the accused, as well as the addresses to the court by the prosecution and the replies by the counsel for the defense, were overcharged with emotion" (*IN*, 5). For witnesses like Dr. Konrad Morgen, a former SS judge, it took considerable strength of character to testify against former comrades and superiors. As for the survivor-witnesses who were confronted with their tormentors and torturers, the hearings may have seemed like a continuation or repetition of their traumatic experiences. Overwhelmed by their memories, these witnesses often found it very difficult to articulate experiences they had never shared with

<hr/>

10. In the 1990s, Rolf Bickel and Dietrich Wagner discovered audio recordings of the Auschwitz trial. Although the West German *Strafprozessordnung* (federal criminal procedure) prohibits the transcription of criminal procedures, the testimonies were audiotaped with the purpose of supporting the court's memory. Owing to the intervention of survivors, the tapes were not destroyed after the trial and were released once the protective time limit of thirty years had expired. A compilation of these audiotapes has been published as Rolf Bickel and Dietrich Wagner, *Der Auschwitz-Prozess—Tonbandmitschnitte, Protokolle und Dokumente*, ed. Fritz Bauer Institut, Frankfurt am Main und dem Staatlichen Museum Auschwitz-Birkenau (Berlin: Directmedia, 2004); and Bickel and Wagner, *Verdict on Auschwitz: The Frankfurt Trial 1963–1965* (Frankfurt a. M.: Hessischer Rundfunk, 2005), DVD. Contemporary scholarship on the subject of trials and witnessing, as well as history and memory, has generated increased scholarly interest in these tapes. See, for instance, Friedrich Hoffmann, *Die Verfolgung der nationalsozialistischen Gewaltverbrechen in Hessen* (Baden-Baden: Nomos, 2001); and Kerstin Freudiger, *Die juristische Aufarbeitung von NS-Verbrechen* (Tübingen: Mohr Siebeck, 2002).

anyone, not least because their statements were given in a German court and before a German public. This difficulty was compounded by the fact that the defendants denied their culpability until the very end, showed no sign of repentance, and never articulated a genuine word of compassion. As presiding judge Hans Hofmeyer asserted in his closing statement, "For the most part, the defendants kept silent or lied about and denied everything."[11]

Weiss tackles a variety of political and ideological issues in *The Investigation*, but it is his highly perceptive approach to the status and function of testimony in particular that makes the play an accurate interpretation of the Auschwitz trial. As with a good portion of Szondi's address, the text of *The Investigation* was not, strictly speaking, written by Weiss. Rather, he assembled a large number of citations taken verbatim from the Frankfurt proceedings, some of which he had transcribed himself in 1964 (Weiss was invested in seeing the procedures in person, rather than reading about them in the newspaper or seeing them represented in photographs).[12] In a move diametrically opposed to that of Szondi, who quoted extensively from literary prose in his inaugural address at the Free University, Weiss takes testimony from a public trial to be recited in the space of the theater. If, in Szondi's text, literary citations supplant commentary and scholarly exegesis, historical documentation in *The Investigation* takes the place of literature and imagination. Weiss, as it were, developed his own brand of *Dokumentartheater* (documentary theater), a genre in which historical material is adapted for dramatic and usually political ends. According to Weiss's definition, the documentary theater "abstains from any kind of invention, it adopts authentic material and presents it on the stage without any modification of its content."[13] In Weiss's case, this means that the play is not merely based on, but actually consists of, unaltered dialogues and authentic snippets from the trial. And yet Weiss never denied having selected, rearranged, and manipulated the documentary materials.[14] The result of an elaborate artistic process that involved selection and collage, *The Investigation* is of course an aesthetically enhanced, Dantesque "Oratorio in 11 Cantos" (hence the play's German subtitle) that self-reflexively exposes its own constructedness and thereby openly reveals itself as a work of fiction.[15]

11. Quoted in Bickel and Wagner, *Verdict on Auschwitz*; my translation.

12. For a detailed account of Weiss's artistic procedure, see Marcel Atze, " 'Die Angeklagten lachen': Peter Weiss und sein Theaterstück 'Die Ermittlung,' " in *Auschwitz Prozess 4 Ks 2/63 Frankfurt am Main*, ed. I. Wojak (Cologne: Snoeck, 2004), 782–807. Weiss drew additional information from historical documentation and from Bernd Naumann's coverage of the trial, published daily in the *Frankfurter Allgemeine Zeitung*. A first draft of the play is published in Weiss, *Rapporte*,1:113–24. An early version of it was published as Peter Weiss, "Frankfurter Auszüge," *Kursbuch* 1 (1965): 152–88.

13. Peter Weiss, "Notes on Contemporary Theater," in *Essays on German Theater: Lessing, Brecht, Dürrenmatt, and Others*, ed. Margaret Herzfeld-Sander, foreword by Martin Esslin (New York, NY: Continuum, 1985), 294–300, here 294.

14. See Weiss, "Frankfurter Auszüge," 202.

15. See Robert Cohen, "The Political Aesthetics of Holocaust Literature: Peter Weiss's 'The Investigation' and Its Critics," *Studies in the Representation of the Past* 10, no. 2 (1998): 47. Weiss once avowed

But Weiss nevertheless regarded the documentary form as a device for showing a more objective truth. The literalism of the recited testimonies was to counter the way in which historical reality was distorted during the trial, while the accuracy of the citations was directed against the defendants' lies and rhetorical ambiguity. This does not, however, mean that the play is predicated on the positivist generalizations of historiography, as some critics have argued.[16] As with Szondi's montage of Benjamin citations, Weiss's Auschwitz inventory, albeit premised on the power of testimony, openly acknowledges its legal and hermeneutic fallacies (they are indeed so significant and substantial that they lead to the failure of the trial). What makes this montage effective then is not the expressivity of the compiled testimonies, but the fact that the characters of the play are devoid of personal idiosyncrasies and that show no sign of emotional investment. As Weiss specified in the annotations to the play, "The variety of experiences can at most, be indicated by a change of voice or bearing" (*IN*, 5).[17] The language that is recited on stage is monotonous and void of punctuation, accents, or dialects. And while it retains a maximum of descriptive and graphic precision, it is neither rhetorically colorful nor psychologically evocative. As in Szondi's inaugural address, the citations in Weiss's play are not performed but quite simply recited. Thus the present chapter casts light on a significant formal parallel between Weiss's theatrical representation of a trial and Szondi's inaugural address: both take recourse to an array of citations that exemplify the problem inherent in survivor testimonies—namely, the gap between what was seen and what can then be said about such facts.

The present comparative analysis of Szondi's and Weiss's opposing approaches to evidentiary issues also examines their shared thematic concern with the repressed Nazi past. Like Szondi, whose Berlin speech anticipates the antirestorative thrust of the imminent student revolts, Weiss refuses to accept the denial and repression of the memory of Auschwitz in postwar Germany. But while both writers are early

---

that his play was but a mediated representation of the real event: "Instead of showing reality in its immediacy, the documentary theater presents an image of a piece of reality torn out of its living context." Weiss, "Notes on Contemporary Theater," 296. See also Christian Rakow, who considers the tension between its factualness and self-referentiality to be the essence of Weiss's documentary theater. Christian Rakow, "Fragmente des Realen: Zur Transformation des Dokuments in Peter Weiss' 'Die Ermittlung,'" *Weimarer Beiträge* 50, no. 2 (2004): 274–76.

16. Led by Lawrence Langer, the first generation of critics criticized the "factualism" of Weiss's documentary play, as well as its "endless cataloguing" (Rosenfeld) of "mere factual truth," stated "in the language of history" (Langer). Weiss was also accused of relying "uncritically on the Nazis' own bureaucratic rhetoric" and denying the incommensurability of the victims' real, lived experience. To some critics, this "rhetoric of fact" (James E. Young) revealed Weiss's "dispassionate" attitude toward their perspective. For a summary of these points, see Cohen, "The Political Aesthetics of Holocaust Literature," 51. See also James E. Young, *Writing and Rewriting the Holocaust: Narrative and Consequences of Interpretation* (Bloomington: University of Indiana Press, 1988), 78.

17. In an earlier version of the play, a fragment titled "Frankfurter Auszüge," Weiss instructs the actors to fully replicate the witnesses' emotional reaction, as, for example, their bursting into tears. Weiss, "Frankfurter Auszüge," 153.

advocates of political change who effectively write against the repression of the Nazi past, Weiss's play is clearly more confrontational than Szondi's address. The Swedish playwright reaches to new experimental registers for the utmost provocative effect. No playwright before him had explored the hidden repercussions of Auschwitz in contemporary German society.[18] Although the 1960s saw an explosion of plays that were inspired by trials against Nazi criminals and sought to represent Nazism and the Nazi genocide naturalistically, none of these plays were set in present-day Germany and none actually collided with the limits and exclusions imposed on them by hegemonic views of justice and history.[19] This is what guarantees the exceptional status of the 1965 productions of *The Investigation* among other contemporary plays: they demonstrate how theater as a discursive and social field can directly affect the public sphere by representing alternative actions poised at great distance from institutional authority.

Public Theater

Between December 1963 and August 1965, the Federal Republic witnessed the first and largest trial against Nazi criminals ever handled by German authorities. The "Criminal Case against Mulka et al.," otherwise known as the "Auschwitz" or "Frankfurt trial," targeted some of the key personnel of the Auschwitz concentration camp, including prison guards, SS commanders, medical staff, and members of the so-called Politische Abteilung (Political Section). Preceded by a five-year investigation during which over 1,400 Auschwitz survivors had been interrogated, the proceedings were an attempt to put the Nazi system as a whole on trial.[20] Given

18. See Julia Hell, "From Laokoon to Ge: Resistance to Jewish Authorship in Peter Weiss's 'Ästhetik des Widerstands,'" in *Rethinking Peter Weiss*, ed. Jost Hermand and Marc Silberman (New York: Peter Lang, 2000), 23. For Weiss, who essentially viewed anti-Communist Cold War politics as a continuation of Fascism, the concern about the Nazi past was of course coupled with a deep-seated rejection of capitalism. See Weiss, "Antwort auf eine Kritik," In 1968, Weiss joined the Swedish Communist Party, but nevertheless maintained a critical attitude toward official GDR ideology. For a discussion of Weiss's political aesthetics in relation to the problem of *Vergangenheitsbewältigung*, see also Alfons Söllner, *Peter Weiss und die Deutschen: Die Entstehung einer politischen Ästhetik wider die Verdrängung* (Opladen: Westdeutscher Verlag, 1988); R. Cohen, *Peter Weiss in seiner Zeit* (Weimar: Metzler, 1992); Jochen Vogt, "Treffpunkt im Unendlichen? Über Peter Weiss und Paul Celan," *Peter Weiss Jahrbuch* 4 (1995): 102–21; Irene Heidelberger-Leonhard, "Peter Weiss und sein Judentum: 'Die Ermittlung', die ihrer Ermittlung harrt," *Peter Weiss Jahrbuch* 11 (2002): 39–55.

19. See, most notably, Rolf Schneider's play *Prozeß in Nürnberg* (Trial in Nuremberg, 1967), Rolf Hochhuth's plays *Der Stellvertreter* (The Deputy, 1967) and *Soldaten: Nekrolog auf Genf* (Soldiers: An Obituary for Geneva, 1967), and Heinar Kipphardt's plays *In der Sache J. Robert Oppenheimer* (In the Matter of J. Robert Oppenheimer, 1964) and *Joel Brand: Die Geschichte eines Geschäfts* (Joel Brand: The Story of a Trade, 1965). Weiss himself deemed it impossible to represent a concentration camp on stage. See Wilhelm Girnus and Werner Mittenzwei, "Gespräch mit Peter Weiss," *Sinn und Form: Beiträge zur Literatur* 17, nos. 1–6 (1965): 678–88, here 687.

20. The analysis in this chapter is largely informed by Hermann Langbein's and Bernd Naumann's historical documentation of the Auschwitz trial, as well as by recent research conducted by Irmtrud

that it was covered in all the major newspapers (Bernd Naumann provided daily reports in the *Frankfurter Allgemeine Zeitung*), the trial also resulted in the long-overdue dissemination of extensive information about the Holocaust in the post-war period. Indeed, the Auschwitz trial was the only trial against Nazi criminals that had a significant impact on the public imagination in Germany. Whereas the Nuremberg (1945–49) and Eichmann (1961) trials had been received with a combination of indifference and antagonistic sentiment, the Auschwitz trial marked a historical watershed because it radically transformed German awareness and understanding of Nazi crimes.[21]

Although a variety of larger and smaller trials in and outside of Germany had already paved the way for the proceedings in Frankfurt, the "Criminal Case against Mulka et al." was a notable judicial event in that it coincided with the reinstatement of a German tribunal. During the Allied occupation, Nazi perpetrators had been tried by foreign authorities because the Allied Control Council Laws prohibited German courts from prosecuting crimes other than those "committed by persons of German citizenship or nationality against other persons of German citizenship or nationality, or stateless persons."[22] The Nuremberg trials, for instance, were conducted by an international tribunal and in accordance with the Allied jurisdiction. In the West Sector alone, 5,866 individuals had thus been put on trial by foreign administrations prior to 1955, when the sovereignty of the German judiciary (and with it the German penal code of 1871) was fully restored. After the foundation of the Zentrale Stelle der Landesjustizverwaltungen zur Aufklärung nationalsozialistischer Verbrechen (the West German Central Office for Prosecuting Nazi Crimes) in 1958, the Federal Republic initiated a series of investigations against former war criminals who had not yet been indicted by the Allied forces. In this

---

Wojak, Werner Renz, Rebecca Wittmann, and Devon O. Pendas. See H. Langbein, *Der Auschwitz-Prozeß: Eine Dokumentation*, 2 vols. (Frankfurt a. M.: Europäische Verlagsanstalt, 1965); Bernd Naumann, *Auschwitz; A Report on the Proceedings against Robert Karl Ludwig Mulka and Others before the Court at Frankfurt*, trans. Jean Steinberg, intr. Hannah Arendt (New York: Praeger, 1966); Wojak, *Auschwitz Prozess*; W. Renz, "Der erste Frankfurter Auschwitz-Prozeß," *1999: Zeitschrift für Sozialgeschichte des 20. und 21. Jahrhunderts* 2 (2000): 11–48; Rebecca Wittmann, *Beyond Justice: The Auschwitz Trial* (Cambridge, MA: Harvard University Press, 2005); Devon O. Pendas, *The Frankfurt Auschwitz Trial, 1963–1965: Genocide, History, and the Limits of the Law* (Cambridge, MA: Harvard University Press, 2006).

21. See Mark Osiel, *Mass Atrocity, Collective Memory, and the Law* (New Brunswick, NJ: Transaction, 1997), 192–93 and 207. Osiel also cites Ian Buruma, who described the Auschwitz trial as a cornerstone in West Germany's critical engagement with the legacy of the Third Reich, since it "was the one history lesson . . . that stuck." Ian Buruma, *The Wages of Guilt; Memories of War in Germany and Japan, 1960–66* (New York: Farrar, Straus & Giroux, 1994), 149.

22. See Allied Control Council Law No. 10, Punishment of Persons Guilty of War Crimes, Crimes against Peace and against Humanity, art. 2(a), December 20, 1945, 3, *Official Gazette Control Council for Germany* 50–55 (1946). It is only after 1958 that the prosecution of war crimes committed by German nationals was entrusted to German courts. See Adolf Schönke, *Strafgesetzbuch: Kommentar* (Munich: C. H. Beck, 1959), Vorbemerkung par. 3–7 II.1, "Nach dem Territorialprinzip." Unless otherwise noted, all quotes refer to the 1959 version of the *Kommentar*.

context, the Auschwitz trial takes on extraordinary significance insofar as it marks the institution of a sovereign West German judicial system. As historian Rebecca Wittmann notes, "The newly independent, democratic West German government [was] to demonstrate that it was capable on its own of coping with Nazi crimes."[23]

Around the time of—and almost certainly in reaction to—the Frankfurt trial, Weiss made a note in his diary of the imperative to compel the German public to acknowledge the Nazi genocide.[24] Shortly thereafter, Weiss resolved to draw additional attention to the already highly visible and momentous Auschwitz trial by restaging it in the theater. In so doing, he set out to confront the theatergoing public with a representation of events that had interested but not significantly altered the public sphere, which Weiss understood to function in a fundamentally restorative or stabilizing way: "In a country where there have transpired such monstrous, gruesome events, there must exist a collective trauma. This has hardly been touched upon. If one were to truly bring it to light, it would lead to a national crisis, a collapse."[25]

Like the Auschwitz trial itself, the theater premiere of Weiss's play received much attention from the media. It also drew a large number of spectators into the theaters—and provoked many to cancel their subscriptions in reaction to what would prove to be an upsetting experience. In fact, it is safe to say that no other play in the German postwar era caused as much controversy or was met with as much repugnance as *The Investigation*.[26] In addition to having to cope with the unexpectedly gruesome subject matter, which was presented in literally unheard-of detail, the audience was confronted with a play that radically subverted the formal conventions of theater. In most productions, there was hardly any stage set, and the play completely shunned any "characters" with whom the audience might identify. Stripped of individuality and emotions in Weiss's script, the actors abstained from performing naturalistically. Hence the productions seemed to most viewers both shocking and monotonous, offensive and dull.[27] Ultimately, many spectators were unable to aesthetically assimilate this extremely difficult and demanding piece. In an effort to counteract their disapproving reaction, guests of the Freie Volksbühne

23. Wittmann, *Beyond Justice*, 25.

24. Anticipating a question asked by the generation of 1968—"Was habt ihr getrieben?" (What where you doing?)—Weiss once noted the following in his notebook: "In this question there still lies a huge task, which so far has at best been neutralized by the notion of *Vergangenheitsbewältigung*—." Weiss, *Notizbücher*, 1:252; my translation. Weiss envisioned his documentary theater as "a critique of cover-ups . . . falsifications of reality . . . lies." See Weiss, "Notes on Contemporary Theater," 295.

25. Weiss, *Notizbücher*, 1:251–52; my translation.

26. See Klaus Wannemacher, "'Mystische Gedankengänge lagen ihm fern': Erwin Piscators Uraufführung der *Ermittlung* an der Freien Volksbühne," *Peter Weiss Jahrbuch* 13 (2004): 96–99. Christoph Weiß analyses the different reception of the play in East and West Germany, which he finds to be consistent with the distinct ways in which the respective countries instrumentalized the Nazi past. Weiß, *Auschwitz in der geteilten Welt*, 228–334.

27. See Vogt, "Treffpunkt im Unendlichen?," 102–21.

premiere were handed flyers kindly requesting that they stay until the end of the play.

It is true that the play's German title, *Die Ermittlung*, underscores the cognitive, indeed hermeneutic, dimension of a performance that is based on a trial. More than the English "investigation," the notion of *Ermittlung* places an emphasis on the scrutiny of facts and the active, rational attempt to uncover the truth of the matter at hand. And this also reflects the "inquisitorial" nature of the German court system, where the judge is an investigator rather than a referee who adjudicates disputes between opposing parties. In *The Investigation*, the only kind of judicial "speech" materializes in the form of unprompted speaking, specifically in the witnesses' and defendants' responses to the questions asked by the judge:

JUDGE:	Did you see anything of the camp
2ND WITNESS:	Nothing
	I was just glad to get out of there
JUDGE:	Did you see the chimneys
	at the end of the platform
	or the smoke and glare
2ND WITNESS:	Yes
	I saw smoke
JUDGE:	And what did you think
2ND WITNESS:	I thought
	those must be the bakeries
	I had heard
	they baked bread in there day and night
	After all it was a big camp (*IN*, 10)

By way of simulating the Auschwitz trial on a theater stage, the play confronts a lay audience with a set of legal predicaments that are specific to West Germany's juridical system. For instance, *The Investigation* situates the judge at the center of the trial, which is in accordance with German penal procedural code. Presiding over the proceedings, a German judge heads the investigation, initiates testimony, and evaluates the evidence as a disinterested officer of the court. Given that German criminal law is based on an inquisitorial (rather than antagonistic) legal system, it is the court and not the prosecution that gathers evidence and decides which evidence is or is not relevant to a case.[28] In the majority of German trials, it is also the judge and not (as in the Anglo-Saxon legal system) a jury who passes judgment on the accused. Accordingly, the judge embodies the law. As the only nonpartisan figure in the context of the trial, he serves as what Derrida calls "a witness of

---

28. Wittmann, *Beyond Justice*, 33–34.

the witness"—a witness, that is, of the eyewitnesses who testified during the court proceedings.[29]

Lending his ears to the witnesses and encouraging them to elaborate on their testimonies and clarify their statements, the judge in *The Investigation* holds the play together and occupies its center.[30] But while this emphasis on the judge is consistent with the organization of a regular German court, it is significantly at odds with the exceptional structure of the Auschwitz trial, since on that occasion, the regional court had created a *Schwurgericht* (temporary jury court) consisting of three professional judges and six lay jurors to better cope with the size and importance of the charge. By contrast, Weiss collapses these three judges into a single character and eliminates the jurors altogether. Moreover, *The Investigation* never reaches a final verdict but ends brusquely in midsentence:

ACCUSED #1: Today
when our nation has worked its way up
after a devastating war
to a leading position in the world
we ought to concern ourselves
with other things
than blame and reproaches
that should be thought of
as long since atoned for
[Loud approbation from the Accused] (*IN*, 270)

With this abrupt ending, the authority of the judge is annulled, and Weiss leaves open the question of how many defendants were convicted and of which crimes. Thus Weiss aims at a "realistic" depiction and yet conceals details that everyone was familiar with—the play was, after all, staged only two months after the Auschwitz trial had ended. Weiss alters, indeed eliminates, the trial's conclusion and omits a verdict because formally it would have created an ill-founded sense of stability and consistency, and thematically it would have provided a falsely redemptive resolution. Weiss's ending also suggests that it is the audience—an alternative, displaced jury of sorts—and not the judge who must pass judgment in the case. Indeed, when compared to the unfolding of the real trial, the trajectory of *The Investigation* generates a significant shift in agency away from the judge to the audience, a shift that echoes the transfer of agency from the speaker to the listeners in Szondi's inaugural address. But Weiss also makes an emphatic point about the judgment per se

29. See Jacques Derrida, "A Self-Unsealing Poetic Text: Poetics and Politics of Witnessing," in *Revenge of the Aesthetic*, ed. Michael P. Clark (Berkeley: University of California Press, 2000), 200.

30. See Benedikt Descourvières, "Annäherung an das Unsagbare: Skizzen einer symptomatischen Lektürepraxis von Peter Weiss' 'Die Ermittlung,'" *Peter Weiss Jahrbuch* 11 (2002): 85–104, here 96.

by raising a number of critical questions: Are the sentences that were imposed in Frankfurt just, and what do they tell us about Germany's penal code? Has the case against "Mulka et al." really been concluded? And, most importantly, what is and what ought to be the stance of the audience and the East and West German publics with respect to the trial and its verdicts?

Drama and Law

In presenting the Auschwitz trial to a theater audience, Weiss calls upon a long-standing structural affinity between drama and legal proceedings. Not only are their forms and themes similarly structured around dialogue that is completed by a witnessing third party, such as a judge or jury, as well as the audience, dramas in the Western tradition have often taken trials as their subject matter, which is an important reminder that dramas and trials fundamentally sustain one another.[31] In the Greek tragedy *The Eumenides* (458 BCE) by Aeschylus, Athena establishes the first known jury in ancient literature when she requests that a group of citizens sit alongside the gods in judgment of the Erinyes' case against Orestes.[32] By enacting the passage from archaic blood feuds and superstitious tribalism to the institutionalization of law and mercy, the tragedy establishes the formal structure of a democratic tribunal while simultaneously educating the citizenry about the meaning and implications of law.

From its inception, ancient tragedy sanctioned the legitimacy of the legal procedures of Greek democracy and served as a source of knowledge about those procedures for a theatergoing public. Taking its place in a tradition in which the practice of drama has acted as a model and testing ground for the ideal of a democratic judiciary, *The Investigation* likewise *enacts* the institution of West Germany's independent legal system rather than reflecting on it. What is decisive for Weiss's representation of the Auschwitz trial then is the novelty of a West German tribunal based on a judge. By taking recourse to both ancient and modern, Greek and German forms of trial and positing the audience as a jury while placing the judge at the center of its formal investigation, Weiss interrogates the democratic order in which justice is distributed in postwar Germany, while challenging the foundation and the very idea of legality in view of a Holocaust trial.

By omitting the judgments that ended the Frankfurt trial in August of 1965, Weiss explores the conditions of possibility of a political, if not revolutionary, form of documentary theater. Instead of staging an illusory drama for passive onlookers, Weiss's play appeals to the theater audience to revisit and critically assess the

---

31. On the "absolute dominance of dialogue" in the drama of modernity, see Peter Szondi, *Theory of the Modern Drama*, trans. Michael Hays (Minneapolis: University of Minnesota Press, 1987), 13.
32. Aeschylus, *The Oresteia*, trans. Peter Meineck (Indianapolis, IN: Hackett, 1998).

verdicts by literally withholding them. Weiss thereby compels his audience to consider the possibility of a fairer, more adequate trial by presenting, in the tradition
of the experiments associated with Bertolt Brecht's epic theater, a world that is
precisely not immutable but inherently *veränderbar* (alterable).[33] What is at stake
in *The Investigation* then is Weiss's refusal to exclude his viewers from his representation of a highly significant contemporary matter.[34] In breaking the imaginary
"fourth wall" at the front of the theater stage by presenting a completely dedramatized, hyperliteral, and issue-oriented performance that is further emphasized by
the bareness of the stage, Weiss clearly works in the tradition of Brecht.[35]

There are other connections between Weiss's concept of documentary theater
and Brecht's dramatic theory. For example, instead of provoking the audience to
empathize and identify with its characters, *The Investigation* produces a twofold
disidentification. As in Brecht's epic theater, the actors in the play are to dissoci-
ate themselves from their roles and stay permanently out of character ("The actor
speaks his part not as if he were improvising it himself but like a quotation"), while
the audience is to stand back from the action on stage and adapt a new, more reflective attitude toward the theater.[36] Furthermore, in both epic theater and documentary theater, a didactic potential is achieved by way of "alienation effects," which
make the language recited on stage seem conspicuous, and encourage audience and
actor alike to judge the social issues they invoke.[37]

There is, however, a significant difference between the uses to which Brecht
and Weiss put their respective techniques of estrangement. Brecht's epic theater is
marked by frequent and sudden interruptions that can occur in the form of cap-
tions, songs, political speeches, the Brechtian "gestic" language, or even a character's direct address to the audience.[38] All of these elements serve to bring the action
to a momentary halt in order to provoke *Befremden* (astonishment) in the spectator.
As Brecht explains, "The epic theater's spectator says: I'd never have thought it—
That's not the way—That's extraordinary, hardly believable—it's got to stop."[39]
Although Weiss also actively works against the illusory character of theater, he

33. Bertolt Brecht, "Indirect Impact of the Epic Theater," in *Brecht On Theatre: The Development of an Aesthetic*, ed. and trans. John Willett (New York: Hill and Wang, 1964), 57–62, here 60.

34. The exclusion of the spectator from the events on stage is a crucial characteristic of what Szondi dubbed "absolute drama." See Szondi, *Theory of the Modern Drama*, 7–11.

35. As Brecht notes, "It is of course necessary to drop the assumption that there is a fourth wall cut-ting the audience off from the stage and the consequent illusion that the stage action is taking place in reality and without an audience." Bertolt Brecht, "Short Description of a New Technique on Acting," in Willett, *Brecht On Theatre*, 136–47, here 136.

36. Brecht, "Short Description of a New Technique on Acting," 138.

37. Ibid., 136.

38. As Brecht notes, "It is possible for the actor in principle to address the audience direct." Brecht, "Short Description of a New Technique on Acting," 136.

39. Bertolt Brecht, "Theatre for Pleasure of Theatre for Instruction," in Willett, *Brecht On The-atre*, 69–76, here 71.

employs estrangement effects in a different manner: in *The Investigation*, estrangement is not based on the principle of interruption or momentary breaks in continuity.[40] Rather, the thought-provoking nature of Weiss's play is achieved without any apparent break in the play's cohesive texture or narrative consistency.[41] While *The Investigation* is marked by hair-raising strangeness and a self-conscious—as well as ironic—relationship to the laws and principles of theater (after all, this is a play with neither a proper ending nor a beginning nor a development), here it is not estrangement effects that punctuate the play but rather the "strange" documentary elements themselves that dominate the performance as a whole through Weiss's antiperformative, unrhetorical language and dedramatized mise-en-scène.

In this way, Weiss relocates the site of disruption from the stage to an extra-theatrical space—namely, the two Germanys' public spheres. By allowing two different registers—reality and fiction—to coexist, the theater ceases to function as an institution where politics are taught and reflected on, a Brechtian *politische Anstalt* (political institution). Instead, it gives shape to an *event* during which everyone (voluntarily or not) partakes in politics. By arranging a performance that is virtually coterminous both temporally and spatially with a real-life political event, Weiss all but eliminates the divide between illusion and reality, art and politics. Benjamin's statement on the leveling of spectator and spectacle in Brechtian theater has now acquired new significance: "The stage is still elevated. But it no longer rises from an immeasurable depth: it has become a public platform."[42] As a result of this "direct" intervention on a "public" stage, the theater then begins to function as the very site of the political, generating the audience's recognition and active recollection. While theater evokes "astonishment" in the spectator, this astonishment is not an end in itself. It serves to transform the spectator's interest into an "expert one."[43] After all, any "surprise" expressed by spectators upon hearing the truth about the concentration camps would belie that they had long been—or should have been—familiar with the historical reality. Instead of exonerating them of their repressed guilt (and thereby aligning them with the defendants, who keep denying that they have witnessed or consented to executions), *The Investigation* forces the audience to acknowledge—finally—that the barbaric events that were fully divulged in the

---

40. Benjamin makes a note of the frequent disruptions in Brecht's plays, which result in a "retarding quality of these interruptions and the episodic quality of this framing of action." Walter Benjamin, "Studies for a Theory of Epic Theatre," in *Understanding Brecht*, trans. Anna Bostock, intr. Stanley Mitchell (London: NLB, 1973), 23–26, here 24.

41. Though hardly noticeable to a live audience, the reflective, quasi-literary statement of Witness 5 in act 2 represents the only interruption of the monotonous conundrum of the investigation. According to Marita Meyer, it is a "monade" within the play. Marita Meyer, "Bergpredigt—Dante—Odysseus—Levi: Ein intertextueller Kommentar zu zwei Sätzen im 'Gesang vom Lager' in Peter Weiss' 'Ermittlung,'" *Peter Weiss Jahrbuch* 9 (2000): 102.

42. Walter Benjamin, "What Is Epic Theatre? [Second Version]," in *Understanding Brecht*, 15–23, here 22.

43. Walter Benjamin, "What Is Epic Theatre? [First Version]," in *Understanding Brecht*, 1–14, here 4.

Frankfurt courtroom had indeed transpired in the recent past and on German territory—and this would expand their horizon of experience in relation to the experiences their victims suffered. In that way, Weiss's play is prefigured by Benjamin's famous reflection on the normality and pervasive acceptance of the state of exception. As Benjamin wrote in his *Theses on the Philosophy of History*, "The current amazement that the things we are experiencing are 'still' possible in the twentieth century is *not* philosophical. This amazement is not the beginning of knowledge—unless it is the knowledge that the view of history which gives rise to it is untenable."[44]

Contrary to Brecht's allegorical theater then, which takes up a current affair by transposing it onto historical events (as in the role of the Thirty Years' War in *Mother Courage* or the Italian Renaissance in *Life of Galileo*), Weiss's play is openly and directly *about* a contemporary issue, even if the words "Auschwitz," "Germany," and "Jew" are not mentioned at any point in the play. And while Brecht often displaced his plays to remote settings (for example, *Man Equals Man* and *The Good Person of Szechwan* are set in colonial India and China, respectively), *The Investigation* insists on the geographic immediacy of the action displayed. In Brecht as in Weiss, the audience is familiar with the events represented on stage; however, Weiss's spectators are not asked to decipher the meaning of a political parable but to confront political reality in its unadorned, most literal condition.[45] As an essential dimension of both Brecht's epic theater and Weiss's documentary theater, their involvement (through "discussion and responsible decisions") is the condition sine qua non for "the mass of spectators [to] become . . . a coherent whole."[46]

The simultaneous premiere of *The Investigation* in different locations plausibly suggests the invasion of the public sphere by contemporary politics and the critical involvement of the German nation in a contemporary crisis that is as profound as it is acute. By compelling the theater audience to attest to the event of the performance, the play is a political intervention that seeks to reconstitute an omitted and repressed reality through the creation of alternative sites of discursive practice. "If I want anything from an audience," Weiss once explained, "it's that they listen very carefully and be completely awake, not hypnotized, absolutely alive, answering all the questions in the play."[47] But answering the questions raised by *The Investigation* is not a private matter. Rather the issues must be resolved collectively, which is why Weiss appeals to the audience either to publicly sanction or to veto the institution

---

44. Walter Benjamin, "On the Concept of History," in *Selected Writings*, ed. Marcus Bullock and Michael W. Jennings (Cambridge, MA: Belknap Press of Harvard University Press, 1999), 4:389–400, here 392.

45. Brecht writes: "Perhaps the incidents portrayed by the epic actor need to be familiar ones, in which case historical incidents would be the most immediately suitable." Bertolt Brecht, "The Question of Criteria for Judging Actors [Notes to *Mann ist Mann*]," in Willett, *Brecht On Theatre*, 51–56, here 56.

46. Benjamin, "What Is Epic Theatre? [First Version]," 10.

47. Peter Gray, "A Living World: An Interview with Peter Weiss," *Tulane Drama Review* 11, no. 1 (1966): 106–14, here 111.

of a legal system as it is being tested for the first time. What is at stake in this trial is not just the respective judgments but the very legality of the legal system that has issued them. By effectively putting West German democracy on trial, *The Investigation* itself becomes a trial. In other words, the play represents—*is*—itself. That said, it is also a drama par excellence: the drama that marries the institution of law with the invention of a new form of (documentary) drama.

In Athens, the Theater of Dionysos, commonly known as the birthplace of Greek tragedy, was adjacent to the court of justice, the "Areopagos," which had been host to the Erinyes' historic acceptance of the law. The Auschwitz trial likewise took place inside an actual theater, as the court was moved from the Römer (the Frankfurt city hall), to the much larger Haus Gallus (a civic auditorium), so that overflow crowds could be accommodated. Even if it was, strictly speaking, not planned as such, this alternative locality may have sensitized Weiss to the "theatrical" implications of a trial when he was himself attending sessions of the Frankfurt proceedings as an "audience-member" and "witness." Another layer of "drama" was added by the physical position of the judges who were seated on the stage of this modified theater, where they were dramatically framed by velvet drapes. Through a twist of fate, this new location of the Frankfurt court came to function as a symbolic reminder of the fundamental affinity between drama and law.

Matters of Definition(s)

Much of the scholarly debate on *The Investigation* has focused on the question of whether Weiss's representation of the trial does justice to the experience of the victims and survivors. Linked to the broader question of whether it is at all possible to bear witness to and aesthetically represent the experience of the Holocaust, this debate fails to do justice not only to the play's most urgent concern but also to its most innovative aspect. At the center of *The Investigation* is the investigation itself, and not the crimes that were under investigation or the historical event that gave rise to them.[48] To reiterate, *The Investigation* does not take Auschwitz or the unrepresentability of Auschwitz as its subject matter, but rather it engages the status and legitimacy of modern democracy with respect to this judicial and ethical burden. Working within a Marxist framework, the play combines a revolutionary impetus like that of Kluge and Negt with a profound commitment to get to the bottom of the disturbing legacy of the "final solution." As far as the obvious mediatedness of Weiss's documentary theater and his much-criticized attempt to "aestheticize" the

48. See Irène Tieder, "Reading or Listening: On Peter Weiss's 'The Investigation,'" in *Comprehending the Holocaust: Historical and Literary Research*, ed. Asher Cohen et al. (Frankfurt a. M.: P. Lang, 1988), 272; and, most recently, Robert Buch, "Zeugen und Zuschauer: Peter Weiss' 'Die Ermittlung,'" *parapluie, Elektronische Zeitschrift für Kulturen, Künste, Literaturen*, no. 22, http://parapluie.de/archiv/zeugenschaft/ermittlung.

Holocaust is concerned, it must not be forgotten that the Frankfurt trial was likewise a highly mediated event—it was indeed a *Schaugericht* (show trial) in the eyes of some critics.[49] It simply does not make sense to speak of authentic, unmediated testimony with regard to the Frankfurt proceedings, since the statements were the result of tedious cross-examinations and were recorded only once the judge had received permission from each witness. Moreover, the testimonies were hemmed in by the public, indeed theatrical, character of the trial on the one hand, and the rigorous legal structure of the proceedings on the other.

Hence by making his play look like "reality," Weiss reveals the trial as a fiction that is made up of theatrical signs. The use of testimonies from the actual trial in the play does not in fact increase the realism of the performance but rather makes the reality of the theater bear witness to the external world, which seems completely out of touch with the reality of the witnesses. In other words, there is significant tension between the formal facticity of the testimonies (i.e., the fact that they are taken from reality)—what Christopher R. Browning calls the "authenticity of the survivor accounts"—and the way in which their status as truth is constantly subverted.[50] For even if the referential status of the witnesses' statements is beyond doubt, the truth value of their testimonies is not irrefutable. This is because the numerous witnesses who had been examined in the course of the Frankfurt trial sink into anonymity as soon as they are given a voice on the theater stage. Represented by only nine actors in the play, they function as the mouthpieces for many others. To quote from Weiss's stage directions, "Inasmuch as the witnesses in the play lose their names, they become mere speaking tubes. The nine witnesses sum up what hundreds expressed" (*IN*, 5). This reduction in the number of witnesses is, however, consistent with the relatively small percentage of witnesses who actually testified during the Frankfurt trial. Just as nine actors represent over four hundred witnesses in the play, the latter had represented the approximately fifteen hundred potential witnesses who had come forward during the extended pretrial phase. The Frankfurt court selected only a fraction of applicants for a number of reasons, including the reluctance of many survivors to come forward for fear of SS organizations that were undoubtedly still active. Other witnesses felt they were incapable of facing a court because of the lasting effects of their traumatic experience. Finally, it is important to remember that the search for survivors had to fail on at least one level: Who could testify for those witnesses who did not live to see the Auschwitz trial? How was it possible to account for the millions of victims who could no longer bear witness?[51]

---

49. On the notion of a show trial, see Arendt, *Eichmann in Jerusalem*, 4.
50. Christopher R. Browning, *Collected Memories: Holocaust History and Postwar Testimony* (Madison: University of Wisconsin Press, 2003), 38.
51. On the inherently reductive nature of the play, see Weiss, *Notizbücher*, 1:271.

Given that not all potential witnesses could testify in court and that not all witnesses who testified could be represented on the stage, Robert Cohen aptly calls the anonymity of the witnesses in the play the "equivalent, in the literary sphere," of the dehumanizing effect of the concentration camps, where prisoners were tattooed with a number and deprived of distinguishing features such as their clothes, hair, and proper names.[52] In a broader sense, the nature of Weiss's literary adaptation suggests that a sense of realism persists precisely in its seeming "incongruousness." Being a prisoner in Auschwitz meant to be bereft of one's individuality. Hence it makes sense that in the play, the testimonies are void of personal agency and lacking in emotional and psychological substance. Submitted in the form of anonymous scraps of language, they are severed from the subjects who uttered them and who are in turn deprived of their status as reliable witnesses. It is precisely their unreliability then that presents another telling structural similarity between the actual trial and Weiss's documentary play. By desubjectivizing the witnesses in the play, Weiss points to the particular legal implications of testimony during the Auschwitz trial. The prosecution in Frankfurt often cast testimonies into doubt, arguing that the witnesses had fading memories and often lacked insight into the larger events that were unfolding in the concentration camps. And it is true that by holding them prisoner in barracks and restricted areas and by incarcerating them without timepieces or calendars, the SS had indeed made it difficult, if not impossible, for them to identify the locations and dates of individual crimes:

5TH WITNESS: When I look at their faces
I find it hard to tell
whether I recognize them or not
But that man there
looks familiar to me (*IN*, 14)

Another significant intervention by Weiss pertains to the impeccable German that is spoken by the witnesses in the play. During the Auschwitz trial, the majority of testimonies had to be translated into German from no less than nineteen different languages, and although the court provided simultaneous interpretation, it often proved challenging to offer adequate translations of each individual testimony.[53] By eliminating the multilingual dimension of the trial, Weiss seems to suggest that the philosophical and ethical problem of witnessing—more precisely, the challenge of giving testimony to the unspeakable—greatly transcends

---

52. Cohen, "The Political Aesthetics of Holocaust Literature," 49. Cohen supports his claim by citing Adorno's observation that "in the concentration camps it was no longer an individual who died, but a specimen." T. W. Adorno, *Negative Dialectics*, trans. E. B. Ashton (New York: Seabury Press, 1973), 362.
53. Langbein, *Der Auschwitz-Prozeß*, 16–17.

the (linguistic, communicative) problems commonly associated with the process of (literary) translation. The question of unanswered guilt and purposeless suffering cannot be reduced to a simple problem of miscommunication. At stake were arbitrary oppression and willful genocide, not linguistic fallacies and verbal misprision.

But there is another effect of reducing the trial's multiple languages to that spoken by the (German) perpetrators. Weiss has the witnesses reiterate the so-called *Lagersprache* (camp-speak), a language of euphemisms that by virtue of its bureaucratic blandness and sanitized technicality conceals the object of suffering. As the following quote shows, the absurd innocuousness of terms such as "crew" and "final search" neutralizes the acts of savagery they designate:[54]

7TH WITNESS: Each Special Commando was destroyed
after a few months
and replaced by a new crew (*IN*, 247)
... The Clearance Detail came in with hoses
and washed the corpses down
Then they were pulled
into the freight elevators
and taken up to the ovens (*IN*, 256)
... Before cremation
men of the Special Commando
conducted a final search (*IN*, 257)

By thus having the witnesses and the defendants employ the same language, and yet relentlessly contradict each other, the play exposes a fundamental contradiction of testimony that affected the outcome of the trial: while both parties adhered to their own subjective version of truth, their competing accounts of reality were linked by an oddly sympathetic language:

3RD WITNESS: We called [Boger]
the Black Death
ACCUSED #2: I've had a lot of nicknames besides that one
We all had nicknames
That doesn't prove anything (*IN*, 172)

Does this mean that the possibility of communication and consensus persevered on at least a linguistic level? Or does it not rather expose the semantic gap

---

54. Weiss, *Notizbücher*, 1:231. See also Langbein's description of how the judge struggled to prevent the use of the camp's jargon in court. Langbein, *Der Auschwitz-Prozeß*, 40. Robert Cohen terms their language "Nazi jargon" in reference to T. W. Adorno, *The Jargon of Authenticity*, trans. Knut Tarnowski and Frederic Will (Evanston, IL: Northwestern University Press, 1973). For an exhaustive list of linguistic elements that fall into this category, see Rakow, "Fragmente des Realen," 274–76.

between language and subjectivity, between personal experience and its divulgence and interpretation by an impassive court? Witness 5 unwittingly articulates this recurrent dilemma. Describing the atrocities she suffered in Auschwitz, she repeats seven times that such crimes were not deemed exceptionally cruel because they had become a function of everyday life: "It was normal . . . that was normal" (*IN*, 41–42). Such statements tend to cast significant doubt on the witnesses' credibility because it confounds the difference between victims and perpetrators, between crime and "normality." The problem of testimony is further underscored by citations that allude to the double bind mentioned in the previous chapter, a double bind according to which the survival of a witness is taken as proof that his testimony cannot be legitimate.[55] Asked about the practice of torture in the camp, Witness 8 describes how he was tormented with the "Boger's swing," a notorious torturing machine used by the "political section." In response, the defense attorney remarks that the witness himself is living proof that the torture could not have been too severe:

COUNSEL FOR
THE DEFENSE: Were you subjected to a session
on that swing too
8TH WITNESS: Yes
COUNSEL FOR
THE DEFENSE: Then it was possible
to survive it after all (*IN*, 82)
. . .

COUNSEL FOR
THE DEFENSE: It has been stated by the witness
that no one could survive
the swing
From all appearances
this claim would seem to be exaggerated (*IN*, 88)

Another key modification undertaken by Weiss was to eliminate testimonies from the trial that were given by legal experts, historians, and eyewitnesses who were neither Nazi criminals nor Auschwitz survivors. Of even greater significance is that the prosecution in Weiss's play presents no written, printed, or photographic evidence, even though the jury in Frankfurt had access to a significant amount of additional evidentiary material in various media, including film footage documenting the liberation of the concentration camp through the Red Army, death indexes

---

55. As Lyotard explicates this dilemma, "[For a Holocaust denier], the only acceptable proof that [a gas chamber] was used to kill is that one died from it. But if one is dead, one cannot testify that it is on account of the gas chamber." Lyotard, *The Differend*, 3.

from the camp's registry, transport permits for Cyklon-B that had been signed by Mulka, a collection of photographs documenting the construction of the crematorium, and drawings and photo albums documenting everything that transpired at Auschwitz.[56]

The main reason then why testimonies break down in the context of the play is that they are hopelessly overdetermined, while any other documentary evidence is copiously omitted. In its withholding of crucial evidence, the play accentuates a grave judicial problem encountered during the Frankfurt trial. Contrary to the mock trials performed by National Socialist "special courts," the prosecution in Frankfurt had to establish the guilt of the defendants through a complicated legal procedure and due process in accordance with West German law.[57] Hence conviction depended on lawful evidence, even though the latter proved difficult to recover. As Judge Hans Hofmeyer acknowledged in his closing statement, the prosecution had limited access to evidence other than testimony, yet it was forced to regard testimonial evidence as subordinate:

> In the experience of criminology, witness testimony is not among the best means of proof, particularly if the testimony of witnesses concerns events that took place more than twenty years ago and [are] seen by them in a setting of unbelievable unhappiness and suffering. Even the ideal witness who wished to speak only the truth and tries hard to search his memory is sure to suffer lapses after twenty years. He runs the danger of projecting things he himself experienced onto others and things others described very vividly in that setting as his own experience. Thus he may err in fixing the time and place of his own experiences.[58]

The elimination of nontestimonial evidence from the text and the staging of *The Investigation* emphasizes that the eyewitness testimonies, albeit insufficient as proof, were to perform the burden of the evidentiary work. For Weiss, it is a foregone conclusion that the witnesses would then not be able to give coherent testimony under this immense pressure. Ultimately, there is only testimony, which, independent of material evidence, accomplishes little.

As the machinery of the trial churns on, so the play suggests, the participants' statements are crushed under a convoluted indictment resulting from years of systematic research and hours of nitpicking cross-examinations. According to Weiss's retelling of the Auschwitz trial, the legal establishment buried the basic human experiences (an alternative form of historical evidence, so to speak) beneath the

---

56. Cornelia Brink, "Das Auschwitz-Album vor Gericht," in Wojak, *Auschwitz Prozess*, 148–59.
57. See Werner Johe, *Die gleichgeschaltete Justiz: Organisation des Rechtswesens und Politisierung der Rechtsprechung 1933–1945, dargestellt am Beispiel des Oberlandesgerichtsbezirks Hamburg* (Frankfurt a. M.: EVA, 1967), 159 and 66.
58. Naumann, *Auschwitz*, 416.

avalanche of bureaucracy that arose from the dense administrative process, thereby repeating the act of objectification and dehumanization. In the end, a case that some had thought to be self-evident seemed in fact almost impossible to prosecute under German law. But if it was true that the seemingly gratuitous intricacies of the legal debates and the procedural codes invoked by them did overwhelm the frail personal testimony of the survivors, the bureaucracy of the West German judiciary had to be cut from the same cloth as the Nazi bureaucracy. This was an appealing claim for Weiss and some of his contemporaries on the left.

Cruelty

During a roundtable discussion with director Peter Palitzsch, state attorney Fritz Bauer, as well as a number of critics and intellectuals, a discussion that took place in Stuttgart shortly after the play premiered, Weiss articulated the following critique of the Auschwitz trial: "The judge and the other assessors are no longer able to manage the facts of this trial in a judicial manner; as a result they have to assign punishment in the same way that this is done for an ordinary safecracker, which stands in no relation to the true events."[59] Resulting in what fits Ernst Bloch's notion of "scandalous acquittals or short sentences handed to Nazi murderers"—namely, seven convictions for murder, ten for aiding and abetting murder, and three acquittals— the trial seemed a failure to Weiss, a perfect mirror indeed of the vicissitudes and contradictions of history.[60] And it is true that with its excessively lenient verdicts, the trial effectively signified a series of legal and judicial setbacks in contrast to the groundbreaking proceedings in Nuremberg and Israel.[61] Clearly, the political climate of postwar Germany had ceased to be conducive to further Nazi trials. The Cold War had produced a significant shift in the political agendas of the day, forcing the Allies to curtail the denazification process, a decision that the West German government of Chancellor Adenauer was quick to adopt. As Prosecutor General of Hesse Fritz Bauer declared, the stakes of the Frankfurt proceedings were thus less legal than symbolic and political.[62] And the East German government, whose cultural policies and responses to Nazi trials in the West were grounded in a Marxist analysis of Fascism, simply regarded the trial as further proof that Fascism was a necessary historical consequence of capitalist development.

And yet the complications of the Auschwitz trial were more than just the by-product of conflicting ideologies. More significant than the political agendas of the

---

59. Ungerer, "Auschwitz auf dem Theater?," 86–87; my translation.

60. Ernst Bloch, "The So-Called Jewish Question" (1963), in *Literary Essays*, trans. Andrew Joron et al. (Stanford, CA: Stanford University Press, 1998), 488–91, here 489. The German original reads, "Streichel-Strafen für Mörder-Nazis," a much more polemical term.

61. See Shoshana Felman, *The Juridical Unconscious: Trials and Traumas in the Twentieth Century* (Cambridge, MA: Harvard University Press, 2002), 17 and 122.

62. See on this Bickel and Wagner, *Verdict on Auschwitz*.

Cold War were a number of specific legal restrictions concerning the indictment of
Nazi perpetrators in Germany, restrictions that Weiss's play successfully brings to
the fore. Indeed, Weiss has not been adequately credited for the political insight-
fulness and critical precision of his Auschwitz play. His intervention on the level
of choosing and arranging the materials from the trial makes significant headway
in the analysis of the precise legal restrictions that negatively affected the trial. For
instance, it is significant that the play, rather than concluding with the announcement of the verdict or a particularly persuasive testimony, culminates in Mulka's
final attempt to establish his innocence through an argument that encapsulates the
legal dilemmas the prosecution faced throughout the proceedings. First, Mulka
refutes the possibility of defying the rules and routines of the concentration camp:
"I was an officer / and I knew military law" (*IN*, 269). By thus stating that he had
no choice but to follow orders, Mulka has recourse to the *Befehlsnotstand* (defense
of superior orders), a legal principle according to which a person is not guilty of a
crime if in committing it he merely "obeys orders." How then is it possible for a
tribunal to try a war criminal who is oblivious to his wrongdoings and who vehemently denies his culpability? How does one judge potentially legal actions that
are at the same time immoral or unethical? How does one prosecute a crime that
embodies not a violation of, but rather *conformity to*, the "law" of a totalitarian
state?[63] As Arendt observed in her account of the Eichmann trial, the "defense
of superior orders" subverts the very notion of culpability because it casts mass
murderers as dutiful agents of a regime that was at the time considered legitimate.
Accordingly, Arendt writes, "[Eichmann's] guilt came from his obedience, and
obedience is praised as a virtue."[64]

Even more critical for the outcome of the case than the "defense of superior
orders" was that contrary to the precedent-setting Nuremberg trials, which had
instituted the jurisprudential concept of "crimes against humanity," the Auschwitz trial was restricted to pursuing "ordinary" crimes committed by individuals
who were said to have followed personal, rather than ideological, motives.[65] For

63. Although both the trial and the play were fraught with these questions, several witnesses successfully challenged the "defense of superior orders" by naming SS men who had refused to execute
or torture prisoners without being punished as saboteurs. And this is precisely why the judge pithily
refutes the "defense of superior order": "each one of the men in charge / could take a stand / against conditions in the camp" (*IN*, 58).
64. Arendt, *Eichmann in Jerusalem*, 247. For Arendt's seminal discussion of the Jerusalem court's
failure to address "distinctions between discrimination, expulsion, and genocide," see 268–69.
65. Setting down the laws and procedures by which the Nuremberg trials were to be conducted,
the "Charter of the International Military Tribunal" included a paragraph that outlawed the "murder,
extermination, enslavement, deportation, and other inhumane acts committed against any civilian population, before or during the war; or persecutions on political, racial or religious grounds in execution of
or in connection with any crime within the jurisdiction of the Tribunal, whether or not in violation of
the domestic law of the country where perpetrated." See par. 6.a ("Crimes against Humanity"), in "The
Charter and Judgment of the Nürnberg Tribunal," ed. United Nations Secretary-General—General
Assembly (New York: International Law Commission, 1949).

although in 1954 a statute against *Völkermord* (genocide) had been introduced into the German penal code (StGB § 220 a), the latter was superseded by a broader *Analogieverbot* (ban on retroactivity) (StGB § 2), which prohibited retroactive conviction for actions that became illegal only after they had been committed.[66] This then is the equivalent of the basic legal maxim *nullum crimen, nulla poena sine praevia lege poenali* (penal law cannot be enacted retroactively). Given that genocide had not been defined as a crime during the Third Reich, Nazi perpetrators could not be indicted for actions that had been legal—or rather, that had not yet been defined as *illegal*—when committed. Hence the Auschwitz trial did not provide for charges against organized state-sanctioned murder, and Nazi perpetrators were instead indicted on the basis of the existing murder statute instead of the newly established genocide statute. Pointing to the fact that the former had been in effect throughout the Nazi period, war criminals were thus tried for specific instances of "regular" murder. In the context of trials concerning the mass killings that took place during the Third Reich, these were, however, much harder to prove than industrial mass murder. To quote Arendt, "What the old penal code had utterly failed to take into account was nothing less than the everyday reality of Nazi Germany in general and of Auschwitz in particular."[67]

The difficulty in applying the murder charge stemmed from its dependence on the cruelty clause (StGB § 211 "Mord"), which stipulates that the subjective motivations that have led to the crime are central to the murder indictment: "A murderer is, whoever kills a human being out of murderous lust, to satisfy his sexual desires, from greed or otherwise base motives, treacherously or cruelly or with means dangerous to the public or in order to make another crime possible or cover it up."[68] Thus, in order to convict a defendant of murder, the prosecution had to prove that his actions had been inspired by base motives such as greed or *Mordlust* (bloodthirstiness), which in the case of SS commanders would have resulted from unrestrained racial hatred or anti-Semitism. In addition to demonstrating a defendant's cruelty, the prosecution had to lay unequivocal evidence of his murderous intention before the court. For paragraphs 16 and 46, on "Irrtum" (Mistake about Circumstances of the Act) and "Strafzumessung" (Principles for Determining Punishment), respectively, stipulate that the murder indictment depends on whether or not the defendant's actions are based on intent and subjective mental reasoning. Paragraph 46 states, "Consideration shall be given in particular to . . . the

66. Schönke, *Strafgesetzbuch*, 42 and 806. The constitution of the FRG likewise provides for a ban on retroactivity (*Grundgesetz für die BRD*, art. 103, sec. 2, "Verbot rückwirkender Strafgesetze und der Doppelbestrafung").
67. Hannah Arendt, "Auschwitz on Trial," in Naumann, *Auschwitz*, xxi–xxii.
68. Schönke, *Strafgesetzbuch*, 776. As promulgated on November 13, 1998 (*Federal Law Gazette*, 1:945, 3322); unless otherwise indicated, translation here and elsewhere provided by the Federal Ministry of Justice and reproduced with kind permission, http://www.iuscomp.org/gla/statutes/StGB.htm#211.

state of mind reflected in the act and the willfulness involved in its commission."[69] Hence an action that results in someone's death is defined as unlawful only if its agent gives sufficient indication of his awareness that it fulfills the definition of a crime. At the same time, he must be proven to have been in a position to judge and to consciously choose between lawful and unlawful conduct.

The defendants make use of such legal loopholes throughout *The Investigation*, but in the final portion of the play in particular these arguments effectively over-power the prosecution's allegations. The irony of Mulka having the last word fur-ther highlights the defense's eventual victory in the Auschwitz trial. Here then is how Mulka invokes the "cruelty clause" in his final statement:

> ACCUSED #1: I can say now
> that I was filled with revulsion (*IN*, 268)
> . . . I almost broke down
> The whole business made me so sick I
> had to be hospitalized (*IN*, 269)

Mulka further maintains that his actions do not meet the criteria of intentional-ity with respect to the crime. Aware that according to German law, an action must be committed willfully in order to be judged a crime, Mulka stresses that he was ignorant of the true nature of the "final solution." When the judge asks him, "You knew nothing / about the Extermination Program," he responds, "Only toward the end of my time in the service" (*IN*, 268). Finally, Mulka invokes the guilt principle by denying that his actions were based on choice or sadistic behavior on his part. He claims that he was simply not aware that the mass murder committed in Auschwitz was unlawful, and that he assumed that it was linked to a secret war objective:

> ACCUSED #1: We were convinced
> that our orders
> were all part of achieving some secret
> military objective (*IN*, 269)

Wittmann has pointed to a paradox inherent in the fact that the prosecution "had to use and therefore validate Nazi orders and regulations to show that the defendants had acted above and beyond the orders of the SS."[70] Even more so, it was absurd that the prosecution of Nazi criminals relied on laws that leading Nazi jurists had introduced when they amended the 1871 penal code in the 1930s and 1940s. These changes included a substantial revision of the *Tatbestandsrecht*

---

69. Schönke, *Strafgesetzbuch*, 90.
70. Rebecca Wittmann, "Indicting Auschwitz? The Paradox of the Frankfurt Auschwitz Trial," *German History* 21 (2003): 506.

(definition of perpetration) in 1941, which essentially required an element of subjective intent and placed significant emphasis on the offender's *Gesinnung* (fundamental moral disposition) to justify a murder indictment. As a result of this new
version of the murder statute, crimes were judged according to the "moral" quality
of the defendant's motivations.[71] Of course, in the context of the Nazi show trial
cases, substituting *täterbezogene* (subjective) for *tatbezogene* (objective) determinants greatly facilitated the indictment of political opponents or unwanted citizens.
The prosecution only had to argue that the defendant was by his very nature a
Tätertyp (prototypical criminal). As the 1944 amendment (= "Preliminary Remark
to 'The Doctrine of the Criminological Type,'" 1.II.2) states, "In some elements
of an offense and other elements of the penal code the designated punishment is
not based on a specific act, but on a specific idiosyncrasy of the offender, namely
his 'antisocial' existence (*Kohlrausch*). . . . Such characters who are by their very
nature felonious are referred to the criminological type."[72] What this means, however, is that the same law that was created during the Third Reich to legitimize
the serious charges brought against often innocent individuals who were either
considered *Staatsfeinde* (enemies of the state) or subject to racial persecution was
now used to thwart the indictment of major Nazi offenders.[73] Moreover, the focus
on the defendant's subjective motivations, which essentially depend on the attitude
he displayed during and after the actions in question as well as his conduct during
the trial, is intrinsically linked to the inherent problem of testimonial evidence.
As Devon O. Pendas has pointed out, these motivational factors concern "internal
states of affairs, [and] they can usually be demonstrated only on the basis of indirect
evidence (e.g. laughing while killing someone or acting in excess of one's orders),
except for those rare cases where direct statements made by the perpetrators at the
time of the crime are available."[74]

It seems dubious that witnesses who were subjected to intense psychological
scrutiny would be taken seriously when making claims about the defendant's internal, psychological, and, even more difficult to assess, moral dispositions.[75] Again,
they would face the seemingly impossible task of having to provide "hard facts"
about the subjective state of an individual's mind. How is it possible to determine,
let alone "prove," someone else's feelings and personal experience, especially if this
other person is so abysmally "other"? And how to prove what is merely subjective,
especially when one's own subjecthood was, and is again, disempowered? Weiss's

---

71. Schönke, *Strafgesetzbuch*, 771. As Pendas writes, guilt thus assumed "a direct, causal link
between free, subjective, individual decisions and behavioral outcomes in the world; motives, in this
sense, are held to cause results." Pendas, *The Frankfurt Auschwitz Trial*, 56.

72. See Schönke, *Strafgesetzbuch*, 8; my translation.

73. See J. Perels, "Juristische Grundlagen," in Wojak, *Auschwitz Prozess*, 124–47, here 139.

74. Pendas, *The Frankfurt Auschwitz Trial*, 58.

75. On the court's attempt to infer the credibility of the witnesses from their personality and psychological disposition, see Langbein, *Der Auschwitz-Prozeß*, 16.

play is the first theatrical representation of the Auschwitz trial to engage this paradox. *The Investigation* submits that the survivors, obliged to use the language of those in power, were consigned to relinquish their own subjective perspective, while the defendants had legal recourse to the subjective to "prove" their innocence. According to Weiss, this biased but legally acceptable distribution of subjectivity and subjecthood took the place of justice in the Auschwitz trial.

Mulka's final words are an allusion to the *Verjährungsfrist* (statute of limitation), which is yet another legal intricacy that had surfaced during the prosecution of former Nazis accused of having participated in mass extermination. Pursuant to paragraph 67 of the German penal code (StGB § 67 "Sequence of Execution"), individuals could not be charged with murders committed more than twenty years ago. With regard to the Auschwitz trial, this meant that after 1965, murder charges would have to be dismissed, an event that defendant Mulka confidently anticipates: "We ought to concern ourselves / with other things / than blame and reproaches / that should be thought of / as long since atoned for" (*IN*, 270). Although seven individuals were brought up on murder charges (Mulka was not among them), Weiss's "incomplete" version of the trial suggests that the court failed to confront the machinery of genocide. As Mulka's defense attorney recapitulates toward the end of the play, "In relation to this camp / not even the sum of 2 million dead / can be conclusively established" (*IN*, 267).

The play concludes with the defense's claims that mass liquidation was not equivalent to cruel treatment, that cruel treatment was never intended, and that genocide never took place. In this way, *The Investigation* suggests that the gigantic legal mechanism set in motion to try Nazi criminals failed to bring justice to the victims and survivors. Too many laws contained in the 1871 penal code had been revised, suspended, or perverted by Nazi judges, and too many of these revisions had not been repealed after World War II. Given that the 1871 penal code had been operative—and abused—during the Third Reich, recycling and rehabilitating it was the wrong way to approach West Germany's rebirth as a modern democracy, for the stakes of justice and historical responsibility would have been worth the effort of creating a novel, uncompromised, and improved judiciary system, one that would and could have been sanctioned by the German public. By embodying the institution of a legal system that would confront Nazi crimes, the Auschwitz trial is based on a tautology. In addition to having to try Nazi crimes according to Nazi rules, the indictment of Nazi perpetrators was assisted by former Nazi jurists—most notably Adolf Schönke, Nazi jurist and author of the primary commentary on the German penal code, titled *Kommentar zum Reichsstrafgesetzbuch*, of 1942, the postwar editions of which he supervised until 1952. Schönke and his National Socialist colleagues had created a legal setting that made it very difficult to call those who had tried to liquidate the entire Jewish race before a German court. And of course this, too, could be seen as a strategy by which the Nazi regime quite successfully planned to protect itself. For not only did the Nazis destroy evidence and exterminate eyewitnesses of the camps; they also sanctioned the abusive regulations that would protect them in future Nazi trials where these amendments would be treated as legitimate laws.

Although Weiss's play instigates a process by which the German legal system could potentially achieve a level of self-understanding, it is nonetheless extremely disapproving of the Auschwitz trial and utterly pessimistic about the future of West German democracy. Its critical potential lies in Weiss's attempt to put the contemporary definitions of legality on trial before the public through the overtly ambiguous status of testimony. By further opting for the radical ellipsis of an open ending, Weiss appeals to the theater audience to question the legitimacy of the 1871 penal code, which, albeit amended by the Nazis, was held to be legal in postwar Germany and the Frankfurt tribunal. *The Investigation* is thus not only about the legality of one particular trial but more generally about the status and the very legality of West Germany's entire legal system and by extension its moral system, which was itself on trial. The event-like nature of the play's simultaneous performance in sixteen theaters allowed Weiss to usher the topic of the reestablishment of a defective judicial system onto the stage of public debate.

Even though the play ends without positively establishing the litigation against "Mulka et al.," *The Investigation* nevertheless makes a coherent and authoritative claim that pertains to the Frankfurt proceedings as well. Indeed the distinction between a literary gesture and a political intervention is canceled out by the nature of the theater performance: for every single testimony that is uttered on stage is concurrently also imparted to the German public. In that sense, it does not matter that they are citations—not least because it was suggested that some of the testimonies given in court were themselves citations.[76] What is significant is that these citations are absolutely referential—not in reference to another testimony, that is, but in reference to the historically contiguous context of their enunciation. Accordingly, *The Investigation* is marked by the use of testimonies that, albeit too frail to bring about justice, serve as concrete, powerful agents that are actively recited and publicly announced, sometimes by actors who were sitting among the spectators, and sometimes even by actors who were themselves concentration camp survivors, as was the case in some of the performances produced in the GDR.

Might an upset and indignant theater audience take action in response to this injustice that is, according to the conceit of the performance, unfolding in real time and right in front of them? Would such a counterpublic provide the political base to facilitate a reversal of the Nazis' destruction of legality? And finally, could such a site act as a trigger for revolution? Weiss evidently takes the avant-garde position extremely seriously: the possibility of resistance persists in the space of rupture.

---

76. In his closing statement, Judge Hofmeyer addresses the possibility that some witnesses may have unconsciously quoted the testimonials of other witnesses. Naumann, *Auschwitz*, 276.

Aphasia

Terminated without a criminal indictment, the trial staged in *The Investigation* fails because the witnesses are unable to prove the defendants' subjective intentions but are nevertheless alone made responsible for providing the prima facie evidence of all facts essential to the case. By thus eliminating vital nontestimonial evidence, such as the printed, filmic, and photographic evidence that was presented during the real Auschwitz trial, Weiss poses the question of why the witness testimonies alone were not enough. During the Auschwitz trial, the defense easily repudiated testimonies because they were based on personal viewpoints and opinions ("We called [Boger] the Black Death"). But more than that, they were also able to successfully dispute the photographic evidence, arguing that the pictures taken in Auschwitz provided no proof that the SS officers had acted with premeditated malice. And it is true that these pictures, some of which showcase the bureaucratic selection process at Birkenau that served to implement the "final solution," fail to show any obvious sign of cruelty or murderous intent. As Harun Farocki writes in reference to the Nazis' protective strategy of erasing the traces of mass executions, "In their anticipated post-war future, the Nazis could have displayed these images; while here in the camp, there would be not a single kick, not a single dead person, to be seen—the extermination of the Jews would have the appearance of an administrative measure."[77]

Thus, even though *The Investigation* is stripped of nontestimonial evidence, the play lays no claim to the primacy of oral testimony. Rather it establishes a parallel between two kinds of evidence, one spoken and personal and hence grounded in perception and memory, the other documented in writing or print or even photographed by a camera—but both far from irrefragable. Weiss is not invested in pitting one form of evidence against another so as to test how the outcome of the case could have been affected through the employment of different kinds of proof. His approach to the question of testimony is more conceptual, indeed experimental: using eyewitness testimonies that are delivered by a number of "impersonators" who alternate between different "roles," *The Investigation* makes a case against the traditional assumption that spontaneous spoken language reveals essence and veracity. Aligning the witnesses' accounts with written, rehearsed text that is recited by anonymous performers, rather than with "spontaneous" utterance, the play accentuates the written-down, premeditated character of testimony. This is no longer the kind of drama that classical aesthetic theory had described as the literary genre closest to the visual arts because it translates the arbitrariness of verbal signs into corporeal existence and speech acts and thereby raises the genre's linguistic status to that of "natural" communication. For Weiss's avant-garde aesthetic effectively

---

77. Harun Farocki, "Reality Would Have to Begin," in *Working on the Sightlines*, ed. Thomas Elsässer (Amsterdam: Amsterdam University Press, 2004), 193–202, here 200.

denaturalizes the spoken language of theater and thereby underscores its intellectual, rational, and cognitive properties. Evidently, the testimonies recited on stage are not meant to affect our senses but to galvanize our ability to judge and evaluate.

That language is the archetypal medium of rationality and intellect is a point Weiss also makes in his *Laocoon or the Limits of Language*, a speech he gave in acceptance of the Lessing Prize in 1965, the same year in which *The Investigation* premiered.[78] In addition to evincing Weiss's intellectual autobiography, this speech contains a response to G. E. Lessing's essay *Laokoon oder Über die Grenzen der Malerei und Poesie* (Laocoön: An Essay on the Limits of Painting and Poetry, 1766), a compelling and influential critique of the ancient Greek sculptural grouping known as the "Laocoon group."[79] Weiss reiterates Lessing's contention that the literary, "temporal" arts such as music, poetry, and dance and the pictorial, "spatial" arts such as painting, sculpture, and architecture are incommensurable and inherently different: verbal description represents movement and narrative, while pictorial representation freezes time. As Lessing argues, literary texts unfold in the course of time and thus cannot be perceived or "taken in" all at once, while paintings and sculptures present themselves in their entirety to the beholder and hence they signify simultaneity and temporal stasis.

In his Lessing Prize address, Weiss goes beyond the deferential bow to the legacy of Lessing, a standing convention of this literary institution. Revisiting Lessing's claim that the Laocoon sculpture depicts the pregnant moment just before the climax of agony, and hence leaves the beholder without resolution, Weiss associates its static condition even more poignantly with death and aphasia: "[Laocoon's] mouth, and the mouth of the youngest son, are half open, not in a final scream but in a final exertion before wearing down. They have given up their voices. . . . They form nothing but a monument to their own demise. Never again will they make a sound" (*LL*, 180). Weiss's reading of the ancient sculpture offers a structure of paralysis that corresponds to what Lessing has defined as the stasis of visual representation, but at the same time it complicates Lessing's dichotomy between linguistic and pictorial art. Strangled by a giant sea snake, Laocoon and his younger son are figures of despair and defeat, for they are physically immobilized by their pain and verbally muted by their fear of the abject. The third figure in the sculpture, however, Laocoon's older son, embodies a different kind of response to the horrid spectacle. Although he is caught up in the same irreducible event, he has not yet collapsed under the destructive force of the constriction:

Only the oldest son indicates through his gestures that he is still capable of speaking, of communicating his "self." Contrary to Laocoon and his younger son, who

78. Peter Weiss, "Laokoon oder Über die Grenzen der Sprache" (1965), in Weiss, *Rapporte*, 1:170–87; my translation; hereafter this work is abbreviated as *LL*.

79. Gotthold Ephraim Lessing, *Laocoön: An Essay on the Limits of Painting and Poetry*, trans. and intro. Edward Allen McCormick (Baltimore: Johns Hopkins University Press, 1984).

are completely wrapped up in the process of perishing and are thus unable to make themselves noticed by anyone, the older son still refers to the event. He can survey it. . . . Posturing toward the outside world, he announces his intention to escape the embrace. [He] is still part of a living world, he breaks away from the statuary so as to give a report to those who might come to his rescue. (*LL*, 180)

By alluding to the possibility that the elder son might break away from the attack, Weiss puts pressure on Lessing's distinction between painting and poetry. In his view, the sculpture exceeds the corporeality of three human bodies by taking action (or the potential of it) as its object. Weiss indeed proposes that the Laocoon group possesses a communicative openness that belies the specificity of the visual arts. By suggesting that it is possible to escape and bear witness from inside the event, he effectively aligns the work with verbal expression and, by extension, narrative and literature. As Weiss contends, the medium of language will allow the elder son to draw near the psychological limit situation he is suffering without, however, reducing and belittling its intensity. Although Weiss here ostensibly describes the experience of a sculptural figure, his argument applies to the beholder of the sculpture as well. According to Weiss, pictorial art is perceived instantaneously and thus ultimately contemplatively, while textual and verbal forms of expression direct our thoughts away from musing and imagination toward explanation and definition. There is a continued invocation of dichotomies in Weiss's speech, and in particular the dichotomy between perception and reception, which are equated with seeing and speaking, respectively. According to Weiss, only the act of speaking—and writing—enables us to actively tackle a trauma, for contrary to images, words are retained, elaborated upon, and ultimately dissolved into a series of distinctive signifiers that clearly identify and trace the origins of pain: "Words orbit around the components of images and render them to pieces. Images content themselves with the pain, words want to know of the origin of pain" (*LL*, 182). Hence while visual forms of expression are apt to illustrate the general condition of trauma, language serves to painstakingly analyze every aspect of it, draw causal connections, and reflect on its significance.

Weiss's reference to the therapeutic character of language resonates with Freud and Breuer's assertion that language has the power to "cut the residues" of past traumatic experiences and thereby release the trauma that they may have caused. Here then is another speech that doubles as a "talking cure": stressing the importance of articulation and communication for traumatized individuals, Weiss proposes that there is but one way to overcome a personal tragedy or a traumatic experience—namely, by speaking about it, by listening and responding:[80] "Speaking, writing,

---

80. See Cathy Caruth, who speaks of "a speaking and a listening *from the site of trauma*," which "provides the very link between cultures: not as a simple understanding of the pasts of others, but rather

reading moves in time. Sentence meets countersentence, question meets answer, answer meets another question. A claim is revoked, the revoked is subject to new assessment. The writer and the reader are in motion, are always open to changes" (*LL*, 179). Language provokes dialogue and triggers change, but more than that: it represents the cognitive condition of possibility of the act of witnessing, and the latter in turn stabilizes the cognitive capacity of a traumatized person.[81] Hence where the other figures of the Laocoon sculpture embody the finality of death and aphasia, the elder son epitomizes the positive, transformative, and ultimately healing power of linguistic representation even though he is represented by a sculptural figure. What the elder son is witnessing he will commit to testimony, Weiss suggests, thereby reducing the distance between spatial and temporal forms of representation.

Weiss's Lessing Prize address is a speech about the problem of testimony that also seeks to overcome this problem by enacting it. For what is ultimately at stake for Weiss is his own attempt at testifying to his experience of being stigmatized and persecuted as a Jew in Nazi Germany—an attempt that is both embodied and made explicit in the text. Like Arendt, Weiss cannot accept the Lessing Prize without at least calling attention to his own historical status as a (former) German Jew, and like Arendt, he cannot take recourse to a simple, direct, first-person narrative to deliver his acceptance speech. Aware of the double bind that emerges when a subject bears witness to the loss of his subjecthood, Weiss deliberately curtails and withholds himself, transposing the experience of his loss (of language, of his identity) from the shifter "I" into an impersonal "he." Weiss's grappling with the problem of bearing witness is both thematized and played out performatively in his speech, although not of course theoretically resolved. As was the case in Arendt's Lessing Prize address, there is slippage in the speaker's capacity to repudiate his living body. While most of the speech is told in the disembodied voice of an impersonal third-person narrator, there is the occasional use of pronominal linguistic shifters that point to the presence of a subject of enunciation. A few paragraphs into the speech, Weiss thus reminisces about something that happened to him in early childhood—"das . . . mir selbst geschah" (*LL*, 171). Alluding to the moment when his nascent ego consciousness discovered that such events happened to himself as an "other," Weiss here uses the pronominal shifter "me" to allow a momentary

---

within the traumas of contemporary history, as our ability to listen through the departures we have all taken from ourselves." C. Caruth, ed., *Trauma: Explorations in Memory* (Baltimore: Johns Hopkins University Press, 1995), 11.

81. Yet according to Caruth, trauma can never be fully understood: "The trauma is repeated suffering of the event, but it is also a continual leaving of its site. The traumatic event thus *carries with it* what Dori Laub calls 'the collapse of witnessing,' the impossibility of knowing that which first constituted it. And by carrying that impossibility of knowing out of the empirical event itself, trauma opens up and challenges us to a new kind of witnessing—the witnessing, precisely, *of the impossible*." Caruth, *Trauma*, 10.

sense of biographical unity as the locus of subjective meaning. The final sentence of Weiss's Lessing Prize address, by contrast, marks the final and decisive split between the subject of enunciation and the subject of utterance. As in Arendt's phrase "I so explicitly stress," Weiss here cues us to perceive the nervous (and ultimately hostile) interplay between the grammatical first-person and its ever-elusive autobiographical subject: "But the writer whose experiences are the subject of my account was void of any sense of coherence" (*LL*, 185). Drawing attention to the absence of coherence between the "I" and "the writer," this sentence both shows and says what it does.

Arendt presented the experience of loss as the loss of identity; her speech was organized around the question posed to Nathan: "Who are you?" In contrast, Weiss—whose speech bears the title *On the Limits of Language*—figures loss as a loss of language, a problem less existential and universal perhaps, but infinitely more poignant for an aspiring literary artist. A point Weiss emphasizes in his speech is how the entirely unknown and alien language of National Socialism invaded and overpowered his native German tongue: "The meaning of the words is shifting. Uncertainty takes hold. New words appear overnight, everyone repeats them without comprehending, they no longer possess the words, the words possess them" (*LL*, 175). Weiss continues to describe how he abandoned his native language when, after emigrating to London in 1935 and to Prague in 1937, he again emigrated to Stockholm, where he was forced into the speechlessness of exile: "Only a minority were able to flee. They left the space from where every one of their words had once emerged and ended up in territories where they were overcome by speechlessness" (*LL*, 176). As a result of this alienating and disparaging experience, Weiss chose to forsake his native tongue and immersed himself in the study of Swedish. Crucially for Weiss, the loss of his native German was linked to a complete loss of subjectivity—the equivalent of the "undoing of the self" in trauma. For Weiss, this meant that he experienced a radical reconfiguration, even disruption of life: "Being outside of language signified death" (*LL*, 182–83).[82] Weiss's autobiographical account raises a problem that is familiar to trauma theorists: trauma occurs when a person is unable to register and assimilate certain events, events that consequently also exceed his linguistic faculties and hence elude thematization and iterability. In Weiss's case this results in a double bind: the very thing that has caused his trauma—the loss of language, of his mother tongue—is also that which prevents him from overcoming it. The loss is therefore inscribed in the process of coming (or not) to terms with it, while language in its very elusiveness is both the medium and the object of representation.

---

82. As Garloff has pointed out, Weiss in his notebooks "draws an analogy between the situation of the witnesses and that of the returning exile, who is subject to the same discursive strategies of scrutiny and denial that devaluate the witnesses' voices." Garloff, "Peter Weiss's Entry into the German Public Sphere," 50.

192   *Speaking the Unspeakable in Postwar Germany*

Weiss's autobiographical account is exact in some ways, but omissive in others. One important aspect of his trajectory that is absent in the speech is the fact that Weiss, who was trained as a painter, turned away from the visual arts and immersed himself in the production of literature despite his linguistic exile. As a matter of fact, Weiss wrote his first prose work *Från ö till ö* (From Island to Island) in Swedish—the work was published shortly after he was married to the Swedish painter Helga Henschen in 1943—and then, in 1950, switched back to his native German tongue with his first produced play, *Der Turm* (The Tower). Replicating the logic of Weiss's autobiographical account, the Lessing Prize address is a speech about language, not visual imagery, despite its apparent focus on the Laocoon sculpture.[83] As a matter of fact, the speech endorses a process of identification away from Laocoon's paralysis, from the bondage with a reality he cannot bear, toward the elder son and the possibility of bearing witness—through literature. As Weiss points out, he is himself Laocoon's elder son, and thus he eschews the static world of the sculpture for the temporal reality of narrative: "He was Laocoon's oldest son. He was yet granted a grace period, but he and his family were entangled in the event. He saw what happened next to him and what could happen to him any instant" (*LL*, 184). Comparing himself to Laocoon, who is about to bear witness, Weiss tells his own story, a story that revolves around the loss of his German mother tongue before and during his exile from Germany. Paradoxically however, Weiss employs an eloquent and connected prose style to describe an existential crisis that allegedly left him in a speechless limbo. The speech abounds with evocative and indeed poetic passages like the following: "Everywhere mouths are moving, emitting words, everywhere ears are fluttering and catching the words, as if that was the easiest thing in the world" (*LL*, 170). As in Hugo von Hofmannsthal's *A Letter* (1906), in which a fictitious "Lord Chandos" explains to his friend the philosopher Francis Bacon why he is supposedly no longer able to write, but does so in a prose that is both graceful and highly articulate, Weiss here pairs linguistic skepticism with rhetorical eloquence.[84] But Weiss makes a rhetorical move that allows him to circumvent the paradoxical problem of testifying, in German, to the alleged loss of his native tongue: he adopts the viewpoint of a third-person narrator. As in Szondi's inaugural address, Weiss's Lessing Prize address thereby testifies to the absence of a dead person, yet this person is not a friend or an intellectual predecessor like Walter Benjamin, but Weiss's own former self, a young Jewish art student who was forced to relinquish his mother tongue, his country, and his German citizenship (and identity). In contrast to Szondi's attempt to resuscitate Benjamin's person by lending him his living voice, Weiss thus stages his own linguistic

---

83. See Martin Rector, "Laokoon oder der vergebliche Kampf gegen die Bilder: Medienwechsel und Politisierung bei Peter Weiss," *Peter Weiss Jahrbuch* 1 (1992): 40.
84. Hugo von Hofmannsthal, "Letter," in *The Lord Chandos Letter and Other Writings*, trans. Joel Rotenberg, intr. John Banville (New York: New York Review Books, 2005), 117–28.

suffocation. For not a single utterance announces the survival of his original self; not one word identifies the victim with the voice of the speaker. Thus the logic of ventriloquy described above is completely reversed: while Szondi ventriloquized Benjamin to afford him a voice, and while the actors on Weiss's theater stage ventriloquized eyewitnesses who had fallen into a silence that lasted for twenty years, Weiss now uses self-ventriloquy to communicate the agony of being silenced and draw attention to the mutilating effect of verbal exile.

In view of the space given to myth and the precise political function it seems to fulfill, did Peter Weiss deliver a funeral oration in honor of Peter Weiss? The speech is certainly not a traditional epideictic address designed to publicly and ritualistically affirm a mainstream historical narrative. For Weiss scorns his listeners in Hamburg, intimating that they are complicit or perhaps, in effect, identical with those who are responsible for "his" traumatic fall from the German language. As a public speaker and recipient of the Lessing Prize, Weiss is (or pretends to be) radically disconnected from Germany's cultural landscape and the domain of the German language. To repeat the passage cited before, "But the writer whose experiences are the subject of my account was void of any sense of coherence [with the German language and culture]" (*LL*, 185). Hence Weiss's Lessing Prize address is organized as a double distancing act. In addition to refusing to personally address his audience throughout the speech, the speaker thematizes the seeming "abyss" that separates him and them. Indeed Weiss simultaneously dissociates his former self from his present "I," suggesting that "he who is the subject of this speech" is by no means identical with the "I" who delivers this public speech (*LL*, 174). Having been erased from the German geopolitical map, the former "he" has returned to haunt the autobiographical discourse of the expatriate, who comes to function both as his own ventriloquist and as the witness of a witness from beyond. If it is true that, as W. G. Sebald notes, "all of [Weiss's] work is designed as a visit to the dead," this implicit elegy to himself might indeed be considered a central node of Weiss's entire œuvre.[85]

Enacting the conflict within Weiss's linguistically fractured mind, the Lessing Prize address is an experiment located on the nexus between language and identity, death and witnessing. Weiss proposes that he will testify—for he *is* the elder son—by passing through death and aphasia. However, he also claims to speak on behalf of himself, even though his undeniable corporeal presence on the speaker's podium of course belies this effort at concealing what is so ostensibly there. Given these contradictions and the speaker's reluctance to solve or even acknowledge them, Weiss's Lessing Prize address is arguably without the therapeutic value Weiss attributes to the act of witnessing. Despite Weiss's eloquence, nothing is said but the unsayability

---

85. W. G. Sebald, "The Remorse of the Heart: On Memory and Cruelty in the Work of Peter Weiss," in *On the Natural History of Destruction*, trans. Anthea Bell (New York: Random House, 2003), 169–91, here 176.

of his personal experience, which keeps ramifying the harder he tries. The speech is thus a symbolic representation of unspeakability; it is, like the Laocoon group, an aesthetic "object" that thematizes the theoretical possibility of testimony without, however, actualizing this vital potential.

Weiss thus speaks from a displaced, indeed shifting, Archimedean point that allows him to navigate the boundaries between different psychological states and identities as he confronts the difficult task of confronting postwar Germany's public sphere. Like Buber in 1953, or Arendt in 1959, Weiss can speak neither as a native German nor as a foreigner, neither as the prodigal son nor as a neutral arbiter of history and collective memory. Taking on an ambiguous subject position that is situated beyond the psychological status quo of German society, but still within its moral and legal parameters, Weiss eschews the rhetorical constraints involved in a high-profile award ceremony and the arguably hypocritical implications that arise from it, as well as the futility of speaking about a calamity that he and millions of others failed to prevent from happening.

Needless to say, from such an arcane perspective, neither Weiss nor any public speaker for that matter could possibly alter the course of history or "move the Earth," as Archimedes had proclaimed. And yet the theoretical possibility and practical necessity of such an aporetic stance is intertwined with another equally ambiguous and receding space, which is located not in Germany but within what the Nazis termed the *Eingegliederte Ostgebiete* (Incorporated Eastern Territories): Auschwitz, as the Germans called Oswiecim, in Poland, was a place that was visible but not seen, concealed yet sufficiently evident. For Weiss, who had fortuitously escaped the concentration camps, it reportedly represented the sole "firm position in the topography of [his] life."[86] What Weiss (like the other figures discussed in this book) understood was that denying the existence of Auschwitz was hardly empowering. For it is only from this impossible space and from the radical break it marks that we can begin to imagine the possibility of a counter-public sphere that valorizes rather than vilifies the witness-survivor.

---

86. Peter Weiss, "My Place," in *German Writing Today*, ed. and trans. Christopher Middleton (Baltimore: Penguin, 1967), 20–29, here 20.

CONCLUSION: SPEAKING OF THE NOOSE IN THE COUNTRY OF THE HANGMAN (THEODOR W. ADORNO)

I deny that there has ever been such a German-Jewish dialogue in any genuine sense whatsoever, i.e., *as a historical phenomenon*. It takes two to have a dialogue, who listen to each other, who are prepared to perceive the other as what he is and represents, and to respond to him. Nothing can be more misleading than to apply such a concept to the discussions between Germans and Jews during the last 200 years.

—Gershom Scholem, *Against the Myth of the German-Jewish Dialogue*

This book would not be complete without a consideration of Theodor W. Adorno's role in the formation of a public discourse on the Holocaust in postwar Germany. There are multiple reasons for this. Adorno's presence loomed large in the new republic's sociopolitical and intellectual landscape. During the 1950s and 1960s he gave over three hundred public speeches and delivered about as many radio lectures, prompting some to speak of a veritable Adorno-inflation.[1] Adorno could be heard—and was indeed listened to—on an almost weekly basis.[2]

---

1. Quoted in Michael Schwarz, "'Er redet leicht, schreibt schwer': Theodor W. Adorno am Mikrophon," *Zeithistorische Forschungen/Studies in Contemporary History*, Online-Ausgabe, 8 (2011): 1, http://www.zeithistorische-forschungen.de/16126041-Schwarz-2-2011.

2. Schwarz, "'Er redet leicht, schreibt schwer.'"

Evidently this aural and performative aspect of his public engagement was important to Adorno, who did not want to be reduced to the role of a writer. As Jaimey Fisher has demonstrated, Adorno not only took his role as an academic
teacher quite seriously but effectively viewed himself as a public (re)educator.[3]
Another key reason is that Adorno made a significant and, compared to the
other public speakers under discussion here, more consistent and systematic contribution to the postwar debate on the denazification process and the aftermath
of the Holocaust. And it was in this capacity that he was in demand as a public
speaker, not as a formidable thinker of the Frankfurt school or one of the most
iconic figures of critical theory.[4] As a former exile who was extremely critical of
the repressive climate of postwar Germany but had nevertheless returned as early
as 1949 and stayed, Adorno seemed like an obvious choice to lecture on the subject, even if his questions and explications were by no means always comfortable.
Stunned by the Germans' ostensible unawareness of their past misdeeds and their
unwillingness to accept and act on them, Adorno repeatedly decried his fellow
citizens' morally irresponsible and psychologically and intellectually inadequate
flight from reality. Like Arendt, he was appalled by the extensive disavowal of
guilt he witnessed in Germany, as well as the pervasive habit of brokering one's
own wartime suffering against the suffering one had "unwittingly" inflicted on
Jewish victims.

This diagnosis was also the starting point of Adorno's famous lecture *Was
bedeutet: Aufarbeitung der Vergangenheit* (The Meaning of Working through the
Past), which he delivered in 1959 in response to a new wave of anti-Semitic attacks
against synagogues and Jewish community institutions in West Germany.[5] The
opening paragraph of the lecture is worth citing in full, as it eloquently articulates
Adorno's powerful message:

> The question "What does working through the past mean?" requires explication.
> It follows from a formulation, a modish slogan that has become highly suspect dur-
> ing the last years. In this usage "working through the past" does not mean seriously
> working upon the past, that is, through a lucid consciousness breaking its power to
> fascinate. On the contrary, its intention is to close the books on the past and, if possi-
> ble, even remove it from memory. The attitude that everything should be forgotten

3. Jaimey Fisher, "Adorno's Lesson Plans? The Ethics of (Re)education in 'The Meaning of Working through the Past,'" in *Language without Soil: Adorno and Late Philosophical Modernity*, ed. Gerhard
Richter (New York: Fordham University Press, 2010), 76–98.

4. See Klaus Reichert, "Adorno und das Radio," *Sinn und Form* 62 (2010): 454–65, here 462.

5. T. W. Adorno, *The Meaning of Working through the Past*, in Adorno, *Critical Models: Interventions and Catchwords*, trans. Henry W. Pickford (New York: Columbia University Press, 1998), 89–103;
hereafter abbreviated as *WP*. Adorno presented this paper on November 6, 1959, during a conference
on education hosted by the Deutsche Koordinierungsrat der Gesellschaften für Christlich-Jüdische
Zusammenarbeit in Wiesbaden.

and forgiven, which would be proper for those who suffered injustice, is practiced by those party supporters who committed the injustice. I wrote once in a scholarly dispute: in the house of the hangman one should not speak of the noose, otherwise one might seem to harbor resentment. However, the tendency toward the unconscious and not so unconscious defensiveness against guilt is so absurdly associated with the thought of working through the past that there is sufficient reason to reflect upon a domain from which even now there emanates such a horror that one hesitates to call it by name. (*WP*, 89)

Adorno rejects the notion of "working through the past" (*Aufarbeitung der Vergangenheit*) as one that is tendentious and dangerously misleading. It is certainly less contentious than the term "mastering the past" (*Vergangenheitsbewältigung*), which in the public parlance of the 1950s connoted—and concealed—just another, different form of violence (*Gewalt*) toward Jewish victims. After all, the term captured the idea of a political and administrative imperative to make amends in the form of legislative and diplomatic measures that were ultimately dictated by the German state. The term "working through," however, was problematic in its own right. Adorno regarded the phrase as nothing more than a slogan or catchphrase that suggested one thing but meant another. Although Adorno does not explain as much, the word *Arbeit* (work) implies that the Germans made a sustained and labored effort to reevaluate the past, if in reality this task was more likely considered an unpleasant chore to be checked off a list. It certainly did not receive the kind of sincere and conscious attention that Adorno would have deemed essential. Uncannily echoing the slogan *Arbeit macht frei* (Labor makes [you] free), which was placed at the entrance of a number of concentration camps, the term *Aufarbeitung* suggests that the Germans would be quick to accomplish their task and hence be freed from any obligation toward their victims.

Equally problematic was the fact that the term *Aufarbeitung* resonated with the Freudian notion of "working through" (*durcharbeiten*), thereby holding a promise it could not keep. When Freud coined the term *durcharbeiten* in an article titled "Erinnern, Wiederholen und Durcharbeiten" (Remembering, Repeating and Working Through, 1914), he stressed the extraordinary effort required of both patient and analyst in their struggle against repression and defense mechanisms.[6] In other words, Freud truly conceived of "working through" as a form of "work" that had to cut "through" deep layers of resistance in order to allow the patient to get in touch with and submit to his deepest and perhaps most hurtful feelings. As Freud's language suggests, there is nothing trivial or easy about it: "One must allow the patient time to become more conversant with this resistance with which

---

6. Sigmund Freud, "Remembering, Repeating and Working Through (Further Recommendations on the Technique of Psycho-Analysis II)" (1914), in Freud, *The Standard Edition*, 12:145–56.

he has now become acquainted, to *work through* it, to overcome it, by continuing, in defiance of it, the analytic work according to the fundamental rule of analysis."[7] As a superficial and reluctant practice marked by denial and omissions, the postwar German practice of *Aufarbeitung* was diametrically opposed to *durcharbeiten*, defined by Freud (and by extension, Adorno) as "working upon" and coming to terms with the past through guided analysis and (in the case of Adorno) critical reflection.

A similarly suspicious and inadmissible assertion was that the Germans suffered from a so-called *Schuldkomplex* (guilt complex; *WP*, 90). Like *Aufarbeitung, Schuldkomplex* is a pseudopsychological notion; it is borrowed and adapted from the vocabulary of Jungian psychoanalysis, where the term "complex" refers to sometimes a conscious or semiconscious, but usually an unconscious pattern of feelings, memories, thoughts, and desires organized around a common theme. It is crucial to note that Jung found complexes perfectly normal. As an intrinsic part of psychic life, they were the building blocks of the psyche, derived from emotional experience. The use of the term in the context of the postwar debate concerning the German nation's psychic state (which ultimately represents a "collective unconscious" in the Jungian sense), however, suggests that this particular complex was considered a pathological and thus ultimately perilous element. As Jung writes, "While the contents of the personal unconscious are felt as belonging to one's own psyche, the contents of the collective unconscious seem alien, as if they came from outside. The reintegration of a personal complex has the effect of release and often of healing, whereas the invasion of a complex from the collective unconscious is a very disagreeable and even dangerous phenomenon."[8] Adorno, who at an earlier point in his career had denounced Jungian theory for justifying Fascist tendencies, disparages the claim that Germans suffered from a guilt complex, because it aligned this very concrete and real form of historical guilt toward the Jews with the symptoms of neurosis and mental disturbance.[9] It thereby not only invoked another version of the argument that Germans were suffering as well, but also insinuated that the cause of this complex was not real but pathological, an ultimately treacherous illusion. In other words, it suggested that the very notion of a German "guilt" was simply not tenable.

A third point Adorno makes with respect to the language of *Aufarbeitung* concerns the "mitigating expressions and euphemistic circumlocutions" postwar Germany had inherited from the Nazi period, a language that was also the subject

---

7. Ibid., 155.

8. Carl Jung, "The Psychological Foundations of Belief in Spirits," in *Collected Works* (Princeton, NJ: Princeton University Press, 1948), 8:301–18; here 312.

9. On the critical assessment of Jung's theory by Benjamin, Adorno, Horkheimer, et al., see Richard Wolin, *Labyrinths: Explorations in the Critical History of Ideas* (Amherst: University of Massachusetts Press, c1995), 70.

of the previous chapter on Weiss (*WP*, 90). As Adorno notes in *The Meaning of Working through the Past*, group experiments conducted by the Institute for Social Research had shown that Germans frequently used rhetorical strategies that would allow them to shield themselves from the reality and soften the truth of their involvement in German crimes against the Jews. Adorno in his lecture deliberately works against such forms of rhetorical denial. Like Buber, who already in 1953 had confronted his German audience with the primal facts about Auschwitz, Adorno takes care to call things as they are. The issue was not whether it had been five or six million people who had been gassed, but that millions of innocent people had become victims of the most ghastly form of (administrative) mass murder: *Vergasung* (gassing). Here as in other places in his lecture, Adorno can barely contain his contempt for the "idiocy," "blindness," and "lax consciousness" of those Germans who still had the audacity to trivialize or deny this fact (*WP*, 91). Clearly Adorno employs this kind of language not solely for informational and heuristic purposes but also as an emotional outlet for his ongoing frustration with the German people.

Adorno's other key argument, already hinted at in the first paragraph of the lecture, concerns the question of whether or not the Germans' pervasive "mechanisms used to defend against painful and unpleasant memories" were the result of unconscious psychological processes or merely a self-serving strategy aimed at simply moving on (*WP*, 91). Although he often took recourse to psychoanalytical concepts, Adorno here leans to the side of the less charitable proposition, according to which these defense mechanisms are "the achievement of an all too alert consciousness" and serve "highly realistic ends" (*WP*, 91, 92). Refusing to consider psychology as an exculpating or mitigating factor, Adorno rigorously insists that the cause of forgetting points beyond the individual and hence must be explained objectively: "The forgetting of National Socialism surely should be understood far more in terms of the general situation of society than in terms of psychopathology" (*WP*, 91). Too conducive for forgetting were the objective social conditions that had caused the emergence of Fascism in the first place. Revealing the nightmare horizon of Enlightenment ideology, these conditions epitomized three core research problems informing the political project of critical theory: capitalism, the culture industry, and Cold War politics. It was part of Adorno's intellectual endeavor to seek out and define the concrete practical measures that would ensure the Germans' gradual development toward emancipation. *The Meaning of Working through the Past* was only one in a series of such educational efforts.

People Who Do Such Things

The concerns of Adorno's *Erziehung nach Auschwitz* (Education after Auschwitz), which was initially delivered as a radio lecture in 1966, are consonant with those of *The Meaning of Working through the Past*, not the least because both speeches are polemical and prescriptive in intent.[10] It was no small accusation to argue (as Adorno did in *Education after Auschwitz*) that the conditions that had led to the Nazi genocide had remained largely unchanged in postwar Germany. And it was a doomful prediction to suggest that the barbarism of Auschwitz could easily be repeated in the future if Germany failed to grapple with the relationship between education and morality. On the other hand, Adorno does propose a series of practical educational measures by which German society might prevent Auschwitz from repeating itself. Implicit in this proposal is the conviction that such a recurrence could be prevented. Adorno's speech thus holds an emancipatory promise, suggesting that education as a critical practice could foster a climate wherein "the motives that led to the horror would become relatively conscious" (*EA*, 194).

What then are these educational measures? Crucially targeting the youth but extending to adulthood, they entail instruction in- and outside the traditional classroom setting. Adorno speaks quite literally of "mobile educational groups and convoys of volunteers"—traveling cadres, presumably consisting of the same class of individuals whom he defined in *The Meaning of Working through the Past* as those Germans who are "hardly susceptible to fascism" (*EA*, 196; *WP*, 100). Adorno believes in the value of guided, structured discussion groups and open debates that are informed by scientific analysis and an intellectual understanding of Germany's humanistic tradition as well as its long-held cultural practices. At once opposed to and dependent on the mainstream media, Adorno's educational measures also involve high-quality television broadcasts that would work against the narrow, consciousness-distorting framing mechanisms of the mass media, controlled as they were by Christian conservative policy-making and capitalist market forces. Finally, Adorno recommends that these educational measures should be concentrated primarily on the *platten Land* (literally, "flat land," a pun that associates dullness with the open country), where barbarism more widely prevails, thereby undermining the sentimental view of the countryside as an idyllic alternative to the iniquitous city (*EA*, 196).

Where Adorno agrees with other speakers considered in this study is in his call for a turn to the perpetrating subject, for a consideration of the sociological and, even more importantly, psychological processes that led to the systematically administered genocide. As for Arendt and Weiss, sustained reflection on the Nazis' symptoms reinforced Adorno's conviction that "the roots must be sought in the persecutors, not in the victims" (*EA*, 193). As Adorno elaborates, "One must

10. T. W. Adorno, "Pädagogik nach Auschwitz," Hessischer Rundfunk, April 18, 1966; published as "Erziehung nach Auschwitz," first in *Zum Bildungsbegriff der Gegenwart*, ed. Heinz-Joachim Heydorn et al. (Frankfurt a. Main: Verlag Moritz Diesterweg, 1967), 111–23; and subsequently in Adorno, *Gesammelte Schriften*, ed. Rolf Tiedemann (Frankfurt a. M.: Suhrkamp, 2003), 10.2: 674–91; see also Adorno, "Education after Auschwitz," in Adorno, *Critical Models*, 191–204; hereafter abbreviated as *EA*.

come to know the mechanisms that render people capable of such deeds, must reveal these mechanisms to them, and strive, by awakening a general awareness of those mechanisms, to prevent people from becoming so again" (*EA*, 193). How was it possible that so many German citizens had participated in the destruction of European Jewry? In answering this question, Adorno emphasizes a point similar to that made by Arendt in her much-contested *Eichmann in Jerusalem*: it is these individuals' inability to think and reflect for themselves that produces the conditions for a mindless (and ultimately stupid) submission to the facile "truths" promulgated by the culture industry. Then and now, public education was failing the German people.

Hence Adorno's lecture takes on a performative impetus that is proportionate to his cause but different from previously discussed attempts at acting on it. Contrary to other public speakers who adopted extremely self-conscious modes of rhetorical and aesthetic presentation that made the gap between truth and demonstrability painfully clear, Adorno seizes on the opportunity of reaching a mass audience by opting for the (arguably reductive) simplicity and clarity of style that he was otherwise deeply suspicious of. Attesting to Marie Luise Kaschnitz's observation that Adorno "speaks with ease but writes heavily," the lecture (and other similarly educational pieces by Adorno) stands in contrast to the pointedly oblique and dense nature of his philosophical writings.[11] But because Adorno presents his ideas in an accessible and transparent form, he is able to illustrate his points in a way that the general public would be sure to understand—an essential attribute of the lecture, given that his point was to educate *them* toward personal and political maturity. This is not to say that *Education after Auschwitz* complies with the quasi-literary form of the radio essay as it was cultivated, first by Alfred Andersch, and subsequently by other members of the Gruppe 47 during the 1950s and 1960s. Quite the opposite is true. Adorno's radio lectures, most of which he recorded himself, are marked by the precise and methodical language of philosophy spoken in absolute sincerity and without vocal inflections or other aural effects. Clearly, as Michael Schwarz notes, Adorno wanted foremost to be understood.[12]

Adorno spoke publicly, often in a semi-improvised manner, to develop new ideas and at the same time test their effect before publishing them. This explains the discrepancies between the recorded and the published versions of his *Education after Auschwitz* lecture. For instance, the published essay opens with a powerful adaptation of Adorno's new categorical imperative, previously published in his *Negative Dialectics*, where Adorno had decreed with utmost authoritative finality "that Auschwitz will not repeat itself."[13] As a command that is unconditionally and

---

11. Quoted in Schwarz, "'Er redet leicht, schreibt sich schwer,'" 4; my translation.
12. Schwarz, "'Er redet leicht, schreibt sich schwer,'" 3. This is not to deny that Adorno was often criticized for the recondite and oblique style of his lecturing.
13. Adorno, *Negative Dialectics*, 365.

universally binding, Adorno's categorical imperative obliges without any other condition than the rightful authority of (moral) philosophy, even if Adorno of course writes from a postmetaphysical stance, raising awareness, as Gerhard Richter puts it, "of the difficult impulse in post-Hitlerian thinking of seeking a universalizable morality of action even when we have no secure metaphysical or universal ground on which to stand."[14] Like Buber, who in his Peace Prize speech had drawn attention to a moral abyss that was absolute and categorical in its terms, Adorno postulates a truth that is beyond doubt because (or even though) it is rooted (negatively) in the fundamental condition of human ethicality turned inside out. It is the smallest common denominator of even the most divergent statements about post-Nazi Germany. Why then does Adorno mitigate this crucial point in his radio lecture?

There are two changes, both of which exemplify how scrupulously Adorno met the difficult challenge of educating his postwar German audience about their Nazi past. The first change occurs in the rephrasing of the *Negative Dialectic*'s categorical imperative for the purpose of a public lecture. The original phrase is worded in strong, menacing language that is dominated by words such as *Frevel* (outrage) and *leibhaft* (bodily) that are drawn from a biblical—indeed satanic—register: "A new categorical imperative has been imposed by Hitler upon unfree mankind: to arrange their thoughts and actions so that Auschwitz will not repeat itself, so that nothing similar will happen. When we want to find reasons for it, this imperative is as refractory as the given one of Kant was once upon a time. Dealing discursively with it would be an outrage, for the new imperative gives us a bodily sensation of the moral addendum—bodily, because it is now the practical abhorrence of the unbearable physical agony to which individuals are exposed even with individuality about to vanish as a form of mental reflection."[15] How much more cautious is the wording of Adorno's radio lecture: "The premier demand upon all education is that Auschwitz not happen again. Its priority before any other requirements is such that I need not and should not justify it. I cannot understand why it has been given so little concern until now" (*EA*, 191). While this reiteration effectively evokes the universality and normative prescription of a categorical imperative, it avoids both the use of philosophical terms ("categorical imperative") and the invocation of Hitler as the paradoxical root of the imperative's prescriptive morality. The second major change is from presentation script to script presentation. When Adorno recorded the radio lecture, he further weakened the categorical imperative of his *Negative Dialectics* by qualifying it twice with the ostensibly spontaneously uttered phrase *scheint mir* (it seems), while also relativizing his supposed incomprehension at his contemporaries' lack of interest in it by employing the adverb *recht* (quite).

---

14. Gerhard Richter, "Nazism and Negative Dialectics: Adorno's Hitler," in *Unmasking Hitler: Cultural Representation of Hitler from the Weimar Republic to the Present*, ed. Klaus Leo Berghahn and Jost Hermand (Bern: Peter Lang, 2005), 105–46, here 119.

15. Adorno, *Negative Dialectics*, 365.

Moreover, Adorno adds the flavoring particle *doch* to a factual, assertive statement as if to preemptively respond to disagreement on the part of his listeners. Here is a transcript of the radio lecture's opening paragraph: "*To me it seems* that the premier demand upon all education is that Auschwitz not happen again. Its priority before any other requirements *seems to me* such that I need not and should not justify it. I cannot *quite* understand why it has been given so little concern until now, which is *indeed* the case" (*EA*, 191; emphasis added).

Through these rhetorical devices, Adorno significantly softens his stance and admits to his own ambiguity and struggle with the issue at hand. At the same time, he opens his statement up for debate, thereby undermining the very notion of a categorical imperative. In that way, Adorno's opening paragraph sets the stage for a radio lecture that is at the same time incontrovertible and heuristic, prescriptive and participatory. Its fairly spontaneous character is carried through the entire lecture, which is permeated by a range of qualifiers and flavoring particles that mark content as opinion rather than passing it off as fact, while also indicating how the speaker thinks that it relates to his listener's knowledge. Thus Adorno through his speech performs what it means to think critically within and despite the constraints of radio, a mass medium that had for all too long been (and was still) gravely misused by political and commercial forces. It shows that although he was at least initially more skeptical of the radio than his prewar collaborator Benjamin, who had actively employed radio plays as an instrument of enlightenment and social change during the 1930s, Adorno eventually came to concur with the conviction that mass media could help cultivate a more critical and progressive society.

The Radio Voice

It is essential to read *Education after Auschwitz* through the lens of Adorno's early writings on the radio, and in particular his essay "The Radio Voice" to fully appreciate what the speaker set out to accomplish.[16] Finished in 1939 and hence under the influence of the Nazis' rise to power, and conceived, more specifically, in response to Hitler's uncannily "successful" deployment of both rhetoric and radio as his propaganda media, Adorno issues a critique of the radio "voice"—embodied and monopolized at this historical moment by the "frightening" sound of Hitler's "barking" and "howling" speech.[17] Of course Adorno's critique extends beyond the particulars of a dictator's sound and tonality in its most extreme historical incarnation. It is based on a phenomenological description of the act of listening to

---

16. T. W. Adorno, "The Radio Voice," in *Current of Music: Elements of a Radio Theory*, ed. Robert Hullot-Kentor (Cambridge: Polity Press, 2009).
17. These are the words with which Virginia Woolf responded to the live transmission of Hitler's Nuremberg rally speech, which she listened to on the radio; quoted in Anne Karpf, *The Human Voice: The Story of a Remarkable Talent* (London: Bloomsbury, 2006), 223.

music and speech, and in particular *live* music and speech on the radio. As Adorno points out, during a live broadcast the act of listening is simultaneous with the performance, thereby creating an illusion of immediacy and presence that to his mind concealed its reified nature. One fundamental problem of radio as a mechanized form of communication was that it encouraged people to listen alone. While the performance of a symphony was socially integrating in that it brought people together inside a music hall, this "power to build a community" was positively lost in the radio transmission of the same symphony, as it failed to join people in space (even if it did join them in time).[18] Falsely promoting "the idea of allowing huge masses to 'participate' in the original events from which they are actually excluded," radio broadcasts thus created a false sense of community binding the listener to the particular moment of the event and, more importantly, tying him to the act of listening:[19] "The listener remains the slave of radio's immediacy, of the simultaneity of the performance."[20] In that sense, radio was analogous to the service of public utilities over which the consumer had no control. Having little power to regulate the flow of power, water (or for that matter, ideas), in his private space, the consumer can only turn it off, and only with dire consequences: "The individual is at the mercy of society even within the sphere of his extreme privacy; and that subjectively this dependence causes a perpetual state of fear within him."[21]

So much is at stake for Adorno in the radio voice. It is structurally related to dictatorship because it likewise reflects a unidirectional, centrally controlled, and hierarchical authority: "The individual has no chance to raise his voice against the super-voice addressing him."[22] Like Alexander Kluge and Oskar Negt, who would later caution that in television "the wealth objectified in social production appears so omnipotent that relationships between individuals fade into insignificance," Adorno thinks that radio broadcasting bears witness to the reification of society:[23] "Just as these authorities alienate themselves from men, regarding men as a mere material for the realization of their will, so does the radio voice. It is its alienation, its reification in virtue of which it appears to speak itself."[24] And yet Adorno was to become attuned to the radio as a pedagogical tool in the postwar period. Another way of counteracting the "shouting of the commentator" on the radio and with it the indelible memory of Hitler's fanatic voice and his demagogic speeches, which were still considered by some Germans as the standard for an effective and

18. T. W. Adorno, "Radio Physiognomics," in *Current of Music*, 50.

19. Adorno, "The Radio Voice," 387.

20. Ibid., 379.

21. See Adorno's as yet unpublished "Memorandum: Music in Radio," microfilm copy, Paul Lazarsfeld Papers, CRBM, 17; cited in David Goodman, *Radio's Civic Ambition: American Broadcasting and Democracy in the 1930s* (London: Oxford University Press, 2011), 171.

22. Adorno, "The Radio Voice," 376.

23. Kluge and Negt, *Public Sphere and Experience*, 100.

24. Adorno, "The Radio Voice," 391.

enthralling rhetoric, was to answer them with a similarly sweeping and forceful negative.[25] This is not to claim that Adorno's radio lectures were anything close in impact or magnitude to what Hitler's speeches had been. But they do constitute Adorno's earnest effort at multiplying his audience and reaching thousands of listeners with the purpose of educating—rather than manipulating—them in the intellectual and moral virtues of critical thinking. Adorno's radio voice was even, not loud, and his delivery of *Education after Auschwitz* in particular was sober and instructive, offering insight in a self-effacing, nonpatronizing way that shows just how careful he was not to exhibit any similarity to the voice of a dictatorial commentator or a dictator *tout court*. As Klaus Reichert writes, "Instead of pontificating he simply articulated."[26]

In *Education after Auschwitz* Adorno performs a tricky balancing act. He speaks calmly so as not to shout, but vehemently enough not to be swallowed up by (or simply ignored within) the culture industry's economy of kitsch production. And while he has to be attuned to his listeners as well as to his particular individuality, he must also maintain a philosophical grasp of the objective conditions of his subject matter. Otherwise he would inevitably fail to bridge the gap between the "hard" materiality of scientific and theoretical knowledge and the "soft" practice of public education. As Kluge and Negt put it in their homage to Adorno, "A production process such as one that is stringently theoretical tears the researcher apart to a certain extent. Or, to use a different image: this mode of production can only be realized along a narrow range of possibilities. . . . Only in a social form, with an alternatively configured collective practice of theory, can the extreme labor process of theory and scholarship be adequately linked to the productive labor that defines the whole of society."[27] Foreshadowing Kluge and Negt's notion of a counter-public sphere, Adorno's radio lecture simulates a discussion that would be based on "a face-to-face relation" and consequently "subject to discursive conflict and negotiation."[28] Instead of resisting the reach of mass media, Adorno hopes to invigorate a community of "belonging" from within. It is entirely without irony or subversiveness that Adorno, the ardent critic of mass-mediated technologies, uses the latter as tools in the formation of a contingent, alternative public.

On July 7, 1967, Adorno delivered a lecture on Goethe's *Iphigenie in Tauris* at the Free University in Berlin.[29] Given by invitation of Peter Szondi, the talk is a passionate reinterpretation of Goethe's play, which Adorno reads as a prophecy of the

---

25. Ibid., 377.
26. Reichert, "Adorno und das Radio," 464.
27. Kluge and Negt, *Public Sphere and Experience*, 24–25 n. 42.
28. Hansen, foreword, xxxvi.
29. "On the Classicism of Goethe's *Iphigenie*," in Adorno, *Notes to Literature*, ed. Rolf Tiedemann, trans. Sherry Weber Nicholsen (New York: Columbia University Press, 1992), 2:153–170.

Enlightenment's reversal into myth. Initially entitled "Against Barbarism," the *Iphigenie* lecture offers a prime example of Adorno's critical method: "In its fragmentary quality, Goethe's classicism proves its worth as correct consciousness, as a figure of something that cannot be arbitrated but which its idea consists of arbitrating. Goethe's classicism is not the resolute countermovement of a chastened man to his early work but rather the dialectical consequence of that early work."[30] Yet despite the lecture's critical import, which was directed against one of the foremost classical works of the German canon and with it, as Ulrich Plass observes, "the very institution the students were invested in changing," a group of left-wing students attempted to sabotage it.[31] It was only after Szondi asked those students who did not wish to listen to leave the hall that Adorno was able to deliver his lecture.[32] Adorno was exasperated by the event, which is believed to have greatly contributed to his exhaustion in face of the increasingly irrational, indeed nonacademic and anti-intellectual attitude propagated by the *Studentenbewegung* (student movement).[33]

Why then did the students disrupt a lecture by one of the few professors who never distanced himself from the movement as a whole and who officially condoned their fight for university reforms while seeking out dialogue with them about the contemporary political situation? A professor and uncompromising thinker, too, whose teachings had provided them with the theoretical tools for their critical theory–inflected, antiauthoritarian opposition? There is little doubt that the students in question had been bitterly disappointed in Adorno, who had, as Richard Langston observes, "withheld his validation and defense of their victimology," because he was opposed to the students' arguably regressive brand of direct action through provocation and civil disobedience.[34] After repeated unanswered calls for a declaration of Adorno's allegiance to Fritz Teufel, a member of the left-wing splinter group Kommune 1 (Commune 1), who had been arrested during the demonstrations of June 2, a few students marched up to the lectern and unfurled banners, one of which declared, "Berlin's left-wing Fascists welcome Teddy the classicist." Describing the obvious sarcasm of this message, Langston rightly suggests that

30. Ibid., 2:159.

31. Ulrich Plass, *Language and History in Theodor W. Adorno's "Notes to Literature"* (New York: Routledge, 2007), 157.

32. See Szondi, *Über eine "freie (d.h. freie) Universität,"* 55–59.

33. Despite his frustration, Adorno agreed to meet with members of the SDS shortly thereafter to discuss the contemporary political situation. See John Abromeit, "The Limits of Praxis: The Social-Psychological Foundations of Theodor Adorno's and Herbert Marcuse's Interpretations of the 1960s Protest Movements," in *Changing the World, Changing Oneself: Political Protest and Collective Identities in West Germany and the U.S. in the 1960s and 1970s*, ed. Belinda Davis, Martin Klimke, and Wilfried Mausbach (New York: Berghahn Books, 2010), 13–40.

34. Richard Langston, *Visions of Violence: German Avant-Gardes after Fascism* (Evanston, IL: Northwestern University Press, 2008), 129. In a letter to Gabriele Henkel, Adorno wrote that the campaign against him expressed the students' ambivalence toward a father figure. See Stefan Müller-Doohm, *Adorno: A Biography* (Cambridge: Polity Press, 2005), 459.

"the communards were as sympathetic to the humanitarian aspirations of Goethe's Iphigenia—in whom Adorno saw a premonition of modernity's collapse into myth—as they were earnest about identifying themselves as Fascists."[35] If these agitators called themselves Fascists, it was to put precisely their anti-Fascism on display, which would in turn serve to refute Habermas who had recently imputed a form of "leftist Fascism" to their leader Rudi Dutschke.[36] Whatever their motivation, the effect of this ironic self-attack is perplexing: it implicitly accuses one of the leading anti-Fascist thinkers whose analysis of the "authoritarian character" was a foundational concept in the theory of anti-Fascism of the same heresy to which they had so candidly and falsely confessed. (In a letter to Samuel Beckett, Adorno would later note his surprise at "the feeling of suddenly being attacked as a reactionary."[37]) Already we have in this strategy—in the convoluted attempt at assigning Fascistic tendencies to a declared enemy—the inflationary use of a term that quickly led to a spiraling of its diffusion and simplification. If Adorno is a Fascist, then aren't we all? This is not only an outrageously unjust accusation but also an empty rhetorical gesture that strips the term of any descriptive value.

Even more problematic was the fact that by fashioning themselves as the victims of a new Fascist order, these young gentiles implicitly equated anti-Fascism with Jewish suffering. Appropriating the roles of the victim ("long-haired Ersatz Jews" was a common descriptor in the ensuing years), the students began to consider themselves targets of anti-Communist repression—and hence the equivalent of the Jews in Nazi Germany. Of course Adorno and Szondi, who were both Holocaust survivors, regarded this as a dangerous and unacceptable move. In a similar vein, the slogan *Nous sommes tous des Juifs allemands* (We are all German Jews), adopted by French students to express their solidarity with Daniel Cohn-Bendit, a Jewish-born leader of the movement who had been denied reentry into the republic, equates the French government with the Nazi regime and thereby downplays the uniqueness of the Holocaust and diminishes the suffering of its victims.

If figures like Adorno, Arendt, Buber, Szondi, and Weiss had put their identity as members of the persecuted minority of the Jews on the line to defend and possibly even resurrect a German-Jewish dialogue, if it ever existed, while Bachmann and Johnson had expressed their support for and solidarity with this group while

35. Langston, *Visions of Violence*, 129.

36. See Jürgen Habermas, spoken contribution to the forum "Bedingungen und Organisation des Widerstandes," Hanover, June 9, 1967, reprinted in Wolfgang Kraushaar, *Frankfurter Schule und Studentenbewegung: Von der Flaschenpost zum Molotowcocktail 1946–1995* (Hamburg: Rogner & Bernhard, 1998), 2:250–51. See also Rudi Dutschke, "Vom Antisemitismus zum Antikommunismus," in *Die Rebellion der Studentenbewegung oder die neue Opposition*, ed. Rudi Dutschke (Reinbek bei Hamburg: Rowohlt, 1968), 58–93, here 58; quoted in Michael Schmidtke, *Der Aufbruch der jungen Intelligenz: Die 68er Jahre in der Bundesrepublik und in den USA* (Frankfurt a. M.: Campus Verlag, 2003), 149.

37. Quoted in Simon Critchley, *The Book of Dead Philosophers* (New York: Vintage Books, 2008), 215.

calling for a process of critically confronting the Nazi past from within the German people themselves, the students now turned their backs on these pioneering efforts. Hence if there was any momentum gained from the critical interventions described in this book, it was lost by the time the new generation of rebellious and increasingly militant students began to articulate their ambitious political agenda. For while the new Left surely reckoned with the sins of their fathers, they were only marginally concerned with understanding the specificity of the disaster that had unfolded through the hands of the "Auschwitz generation." Focused on the structural, political, and moral *continuities* between Nazism and West German democracy at the expense of the radical *break* in history constituted by Auschwitz, the 1968ers' attitude to the Nazi past was marked by ambivalence and contradiction. In the words of Hans Kundnani, it "both intensified the engagement with the Nazi past and drew a line under it."[38]

What happened to the spirit of rapprochement between Jewish and non-Jewish students who had protested jointly against the German government's (and societies') failure to openly address and acknowledge the horrendous crimes committed during the Nazi period? The initial consensus about shared political purposes was not only heavily compromised by what Langston terms the "phantasms of the Holocaust" that were woven into the new Left's politics, but effectively put to an end by the massive criticism aimed at Israel's handling of the Six-Day War against Egypt.[39] One aim of this book has been to show the emergence of a counter-public sphere that formed around the speeches of a set of exiled or formerly exiled intellectuals who insisted on the reality of Auschwitz, even if it did not easily lend itself to articulation. The student movement's reaction to Adorno's *Iphigenie* lecture shows the risks and questions that attend this emergence of a counterpublic devoted to the memory of the Jewish victims of Nazism. While it is true that the students expanded and consolidated this oppositional discursive space through their own critical interventions, their activism took a decidedly different turn in the period of radicalization after 1968, when the ubiquity of public speech, now recognized as a distinct form of social and political action, replaced the tacit search for sometimes as little as a single deviant word—"Auschwitz," "death," or even just "I" and "Thou." Having found their cause, the students no longer needed to search for a common ground or a possible "ground" tout court—be that religious or ethical, sociopolitical or epistemological—to articulate what had seemed virtually "unspeakable" to their intellectual mentors. Obviously, this shift in process also implies a shift in substance and ideas. As a new generation of German intellectuals began to contextualize the political and economic legacy of the nation's totalitarian past within a current and

---

38. Hans Kundnani, *Utopia Or Auschwitz? Germany's 1968 Generation and the Holocaust* (New York: Columbia University Press, 2009), 308.

39. Langston, *Visions of Violence*, 129.

global horizon, the subjective experience of individual Jewish survivors and other victims and witnesses began to seem an inadequate basis for the collective experience of marginalization, oppression, and persecution.[40] But while the development of a counterpublic that would oppose the official interpretation of the Nazi past was temporarily stalled by the student revolts at the end of the postwar era, the public speeches that are the focus of this book nevertheless laid the seeds for what would in the following decades become Germany's "culture of memory," whereby Germans have, in the words of one commentator, "adopted an acute historical sensitivity, making expressions of genuine sorrow and shame longstanding fixtures of German identity."[41] It is important to remember that the broad and sweeping expressions of guilt and responsibility taking place in today's Germany would not have been possible without the individual subjective interventions by a number of (often Jewish and not always German) intellectuals whom the hegemonic discourse had rendered as outsiders.

---

40. As Bettina Warburg writes, "In the late 1960s and early 1970s, the reconsideration of the Holocaust by the younger generation allowed for the generalization of the Nazi past to move away from a specific debt to the Jews and move the focus on moral debt owed to the Jewish community." Bettina Warburg, "Germany's National Identity, Collective Memory, and Role Abroad," in *Power and the Past: Collective Memory and International Relations*, ed. Eric Langenbacher and Yossi Shain (Washington, DC: Georgetown University Press, 2010), 51–70, here 55.
41. Warburg, "Germany's National Identity," 41.

Bibliography

Recordings

Adorno, T. W. *Pädagogik nach Auschwitz*. Frankfurt a. M.: Hessischer Rundfunk, 1966. Audio recording.

Bachmann, Ingeborg. *Georg-Büchner-Preis 1964 der Deutschen Akademie für Sprache und Dichtung an Ingeborg Bachmann, Dankesrede*. Frankfurt a. M.: Hessischer Rundfunk, 1964. Audio recording.

Bickel, Rolf, and Dietrich Wagner. *Der Auschwitz-Prozess—Tonbandmitschnitte, Protokolle und Dokumente*. Edited by Fritz Bauer Institut, Frankfurt a. M./Staatliches Museum, Auschwitz-Birkenau. Berlin: Directmedia, 2004. Audio recording.

———. *Verdict on Auschwitz: The Frankfurt Trial, 1963–1965*. Frankfurt a. M.: Hessischer Rundfunk, 2005. DVD.

Buber, Martin. *Verleihung des Friedenspreises des deutschen Buchhandels 1953 in der Frankfurter Paulskirche and den Religionsphilosophen Martin Buber*. Frankfurt a. M.: Hessischer Rundfunk, 1953. Audio recording.

Celan, Paul. *Georg-Büchnerpreis 1960 der Deutschen Akademie für Sprache und Dichtung an Paul Celan, Laudatio und Dankesrede "Der Meridian."* Frankfurt a. M.: Hessischer Rundfunk, 1960. Audio recording.

Szondi, Peter. *Hoffnung im Vergangenen: Walter Benjamin und die Suche nach der verlorenen Zeit*. Frankfurt a. M.: Hessischer Rundfunk, 1961. Audio recording.

Books and Articles

Abromeit, John. "The Limits of Praxis: The Social-Psychological Foundations of Theodor Adorno's and Herbert Marcuse's Interpretations of the 1960s Protest Movements." In *Changing the World, Changing Oneself: Political Protest and Collective Identities in West Germany and the U.S. in the 1960s and 1970s*, edited by Belinda Davis, Martin Klimke, and Wilfried Mausbach, 13–40. New York: Berghahn Books, 2010.

Adorno, T. W. *Critical Models: Interventions and Catchwords*. Translated by Henry W. Pickford. New York: Columbia University Press, 1998.

———. *Current of Music: Elements of a Radio Theory*. Edited by Robert Hullot-Kentor. Cambridge: Polity Press, 2009.

———. *Gesammelte Schriften*. Edited by Rolf Tiedemann. 20 vols. Frankfurt a. M.: Suhrkamp, 2003.

———. *The Jargon of Authenticity*. Translated by Knut Tarnowski and Frederic Will. Evanston, IL: Northwestern University Press, 1973.

———. "Memorandum: Music in Radio." Microfilm copy. Paul Lazarsfeld Papers. CRBM.

———. *Negative Dialectics*. Translated by E. B. Ashton. New York: Seabury Press, 1973.

———. *Notes to Literature*. Edited by Rolf Tiedemann, translated by Sherry Weber Nicholsen. 2 vols. New York: Columbia University Press, 1992.

Aeschylus. *Oresteia*. Translated by Peter Meineck. Indianapolis, IN: Hackett, 1998.

Agamben, Giorgio. *Remnants of Auschwitz: The Witness and the Archive*. Translated by Daniel Heller-Roazen. New York: Zone Books, 2002.

Albrecht, Monika, and Dirk Göttsche, eds. *Über die Zeit schreiben*. Vol. 2, *Literatur- und Kulturwissenschaftliche Essays zum Werk Ingeborg Bachmanns*. Würzburg: Köngshausen und Neumann, 2000.

Arendt, Hannah. "Adolf Eichmann: Von der Banalität des Bösen." *Merkur* 186, no. 17 (1963): 759–76.

———. "The Aftermath of the Nazi-Rule: Report from Germany." *Commentary* 10 (1950): 342–53.

———. *Between Past and Future: Six Exercises in Political Thought*. New York: Viking Press, 1961.

———. *Denktagebuch*. Edited by Ursula Ludz and Ingeborg Nordmann. 2 vols. Munich: Piper, 2002.

———. *Eichmann in Jerusalem: A Report on the Banality of Evil*. New York: Penguin, 1963.

———. *Essays in Understanding, 1930–1954: Formation, Exile, and Totalitarianism*. Edited by Jerome Kohn. New York: Harcourt Brace, 1996.

———. *Hannah Arendt/Karl Jaspers Correspondence, 1926–1969*. Edited by Lotte Kohler and Hans Saner, translated by Robert Kimber and Rita Kimber. New York: Harcourt Brace Jovanovich, 1992.

———. *Men in Dark Times*. New York: Harcourt, Brace & World, 1968.

———. *Nach Auschwitz: Essays und Kommentare 1*. Translated by Eike Geisel. Berlin: Edition Tiamat, 1989.

———. *The Origins of Totalitarianism*. New York: Harcourt Brace, 1966.

———. *Rede am 29: September 1959 bei der Entgegennahme des Lessing-Preises der Freien und Hansestadt Hamburg*. Hamburg: EVA, 1999.

———. *Vita Activa oder vom tätigen Leben*. Munich: Piper, 1960.

———. *Was ist Politik?* Munich: Piper, 2003.

Arendt, Hannah, and Uwe Johnson. *Der Briefwechsel*. Edited by Eberhard Fahlke and Thomas Wild. Frankfurt a. M.: Suhrkamp, 2004.

Aristotle. *On Rhetoric: A Theory of Civic Discourse*. Translated by George A. Kennedy. Oxford: Oxford University Press, 1991.

Auerochs, Bernd. " 'Ich bin dreizehn Jahre alt jeden Augenblick': Zum Holocaust und zum Verhältnis zwischen Deutschen und Juden in Uwe Johnsons 'Jahrestagen.' " *Zeitschrift für deutsche Philologie* 112, no. 4 (1993): 595–617.

Austin, J. L. *How to Do Things with Words*. Cambridge, MA: Harvard University Press, 1962.

Bachmann, Ingeborg. *Nachlass*: TA1/ 175. Österreichische Nationalbibliothek, Vienna.

———. *"Todesarten"-Projekt*. Edited by Monika Albrecht and Dirk Göttsche. Munich: Piper, 1995.

———. *Werke*. Edited by Christine Koschel, Inge von Weidenbaum, and Clemens Münster. 4 vols. Munich: Piper, 1978.

———. *Wir müssen wahre Sätze finden—Gespräche und Interviews*. Edited by Christine Koschel and Inge von Weidenbaum. Munich: Piper, 1983.

Bachmann, Ingeborg, and Paul Celan. *Correspondence: Ingeborg Bachmann and Paul Celan*. Translated by Wieland Hoban. London: Seagull Books, 2010.

———. *Herzzeit: Ingeborg Bachmann—Paul Celan; Der Briefwechsel*. Edited by Bertrand Badiou, Hans Höller, and Andrea Stoll. Frankfurt a. M.: Suhrkamp, 2008.

Barner, Wilfried, and Christoph König, eds. *Zeitenwechsel: Germanistische Literaturwissenschaft vor und nach 1945*. Frankfurt a. M.: Fischer, 1996.

Barthes, Roland. *The Rustle of Language*. Translated by Richard Howard. Berkeley: University of California Press, 1989.

Bathi, Timothy. "Fate in the Past: Peter Szondi's Reading of German Romantic Genre Theory." *Boundary 2* 11, no. 3 (1983): 111–25.

Ben-Chorin, Schalom. *Zwiesprache mit Martin Buber: Erinnerungen an einen großen Zeitgenossen*. Gerlingen: Bleicher, 1978.

Bender, John, and David E. Wellbery, eds. *The Ends of Rhetoric: History, Theory, Practice*. Stanford, CA: Stanford University Press, 1990.

Benhabib, Seyla. *The Reluctant Modernism of Hannah Arendt*. New York: Rowman & Littlefield, 2003.

Benjamin, Walter. *The Arcades Project*. Translated by Howard Eiland and Kevin McLaughlin. Cambridge, MA: Belknap Press of Harvard University Press, 1999.

———. *Gesammelte Schriften*. Edited by Rolf Tiedemann and Hermann Schwepphäuser. 7 vols. Frankfurt a. M.: Suhrkamp, 1972.

———. *Selected Writings*. Edited by Marcus Bullock and Michael W. Jennings. 4 vols. Cambridge, MA: Belknap Press of Harvard University Press, 1999.

———. *Understanding Brecht*. Translated by Anna Bostock, with an introduction by Stanley Mitchell. London: NLB, 1973.

Benveniste, Émile. *Indo-European Language and Society*. Miami, FL: University of Miami Press, 1973.

———. "Language and Human Experience." *Diogenes* 51 (Fall 1965): 1–12.

———. *Problems in General Linguistics*. Miami, FL: University of Miami Press, 1973.

Bernstein, Richard J. *Hannah Arendt and the Jewish Question*. Cambridge, MA: MIT Press, 1996.

Bird, Stephanie. *Women Writers and National Identity: Bachmann, Duden, Özdamar*. Cambridge: Cambridge University Press, 2003.

Blanchot, Maurice. "The Last One to Speak." Translated by Joseph Simas. In "Translating Tradition: Paul Celan, in France" edited by Benjamin Hollander, 229–39. Special issue, *ACTS: A Journal of New Writing* 8/0 (1988).

Bloch, Ernst. *Literary Essays*. Translated by Andrew Joron et al. Stanford, CA: Stanford University Press, 1998.

Bollack, Jean. "Opening Remarks." *Boundary 2* 11, no. 3 (1983): 5–10.

———. *Paul Celan: Poetik der Fremdheit*. Translated by Werner Wögerbauer. Vienna: Zsolnay, 1999.

———. "Paul Celan und Nelly Sachs: Geschichte eines Kampfs." *Neue Rundschau*, 1994, 119–34.

Borch-Jakobsen, Mikkel. *Remembering Anna O: A Century of Mystification*. Translated by Kirby Olson. New York: Routledge, 1996.

Böschenstein, Bernhard, and Sigrid Weigel, eds. *Ingeborg Bachmann und Paul Celan: Poetische Korrespondenzen*. Frankfurt a. M.: Suhrkamp, 1997.

Braese, Stephan, and Holger Gehle, eds. *Deutsche Nachkriegsliteratur und der Holocaust*. Frankfurt a. M.: Campus, 1998.

Brecht, Bertolt. *Werke: Große kommentierte Berliner und Frankfurter Ausgabe*. Edited by Werner Hecht et al. 30 vols. Frankfurt a. M.: Suhrkamp, 1988–.

Browning, Christopher R. *Collected Memories: Holocaust History and Postwar Testimony*. Madison: University of Wisconsin Press, 2003.

Buber, Martin. *An der Wende: Reden über das Judentum*. Cologne: J. Hegner, 1952.

———. *Between Man and Man*. Translated by Ronald Gregor Smith. New York: Macmillan, 1965.

———. *Briefwechsel aus sieben Jahrzehnten*. Edited by Grete Schaeder. 3 vols. Heidelberg: Lambert Schneider, 1972.

———. *Das Problem des Menschen*. Gütersloh: Gütersloher Verlagshaus, 2000.

———. *Der Jude und sein Judentum: Gesammelte Aufsätze und Reden*. Gerlingen: Lambert Schneider, 1993.

———. *The Eclipse of God: Studies in the Relation between Religion and Philosophy*. New York: Harper and Brothers, 1953.

———. *I and Thou*. Translated by Walter Kaufmann. New York: Charles Scribners' Sons, 1970.

———. *The Knowledge of Man: Selected Essays*. Edited by Maurice Friedman, translated by Maurice Friedman and Ronald Gregor Smith. New York: Harper & Row, 1965.

———. *The Letters of Martin Buber: A Life of Dialogue*. Edited by Nahum N. Glatzer and Paul Mendes-Flohr. New York: Schocken Books, 1991.

———. *Men of Dialogue: Martin Buber and Albrecht Goes*. New York: Funk & Wagnalls, 1969.

———. *Nachlese*. Heidelberg: Lambert Schneider, 1965.

———. *On Judaism*. Edited by Nahum N. Glatzer. New York: Schocken Books, 1972.

———. *Pointing the Way: Collected Essays*. Edited and translated by Maurice Friedman. London: Routledge and Kegan Paul, 1957.

———. *Reden über Erziehung*. Heidelberg: Lambert Schneider, 1953.

———. *Werkausgabe*. Edited by Paul Mendes-Flohr and Peter Schäfer. 8 vols. Gütersloh: Gütersloher Verlagshaus, 2001–.

———. *Werke*. 3 vols. Munich: Kösel/Lambert Schneider, 1962.

Buch, Robert. "Zeugen und Zuschauer: Peter Weiss' 'Die Ermittlung.'" *parapluie:* Elektronische Zeitschrift für Kulturen, Künste, Literaturen, no. 22. http://parapluie.de/archiv/zeugenschaft/ermittlung.

Büchner, Georg. *Complete Works and Letters*. Translated by Henry J. Schmidt, edited by Walter Hinderer and Henry J. Schmidt. New York: Continuum, 1986.

———. *The Major Works*. Edited by Matthew Wilson Smith, translated by Henry J. Schmidt. New York: Norton, 2012.

———. *Werke und Briefe*. Münchner Ausgabe. Munich: Deutscher Taschenbuch Verlag, 1988.

Bürger, Peter. *Theory of the Avant-Garde*. Translated by Michael Shaw, foreword by Jochen Schulte-Sasse. Minneapolis: University of Minnesota Press, 1984.

Burke, Kenneth. *The Philosophy of Literary Form*. Berkeley: University of California Press, 1967.

———. *A Rhetoric of Motives*. New York: Prentice-Hall, 1950.

Buruma, Ian. *The Wages of Guilt: Memories of War in Germany and Japan, 1960–66*. New York: Farrar, Straus & Giroux, 1994.

Caruth, Cathy, ed. *Trauma: Explorations in Memory*. Baltimore: Johns Hopkins University Press, 1995.

Celan, Paul. *Collected Prose*. Translated by Rosmarie Waldrop. Manchester: Carcanet, 1986.

———. *Der Meridian: Endfassung, Vorstufen, Materialien*. Edited by Bernhard Böschenstein and Heino Schmull. Tübinger Ausgabe. Frankfurt a. M.: Suhrkamp, 1999.

————. *Die Gedichte: Kommentierte Gesamtausgabe*. Edited by Barbara Wiedemann. Frankfurt a. M.: Suhrkamp, 2005.

————. *Gesammelte Werke in fünf Bänden*. Edited by Beda Allemann and Stefan Reichert. 5 vols. Frankfurt a. M.: Suhrkamp, 1983.

————. *Lightduress*. Translated by Pierre Joris. Los Angeles: Green Integer, 2005.

————. *The Meridian: Final Version—Drafts—Materials*. Edited by Bernhard Böschenstein and Heino Schmull, translated by Pierre Joris. Stanford, CA: Standford University Press, 2011.

————. *Paul Celan: Selections*. Edited by Pierre Joris. Berkeley: University of California Press, 2005.

Celan, Paul, and Gisèle Celan-Lestrange. *Correspondence (1951–1970)*. Edited by Bertrand Badiou and Eric Celan. 2 vols. Paris: Seuil, 2001.

Celan, Paul, and Nelly Sachs. *Briefwechsel*. Edited by Barbara Wiedemann. Frankfurt a. M.: Suhrkamp, 1999.

"The Charter and Judgment of the Nürnberg Tribunal." Edited by United Nations Secretary-General—General Assembly. New York: International Law Commission, 1949.

Cissna, Kenneth N., and Rob Anderson. *Moments of Meeting: Buber, Rogers, and the Potential for Public Discourse*. Albany: State University of New York Press, 2002.

Cohen, Robert. *Peter Weiss in seiner Zeit*. Weimar: Metzler, 1992.

————. "The Political Aesthetics of Holocaust Literature: Peter Weiss's 'The Investigation' and Its Critics." *Studies in the Representation of the Past* 10, no. 2 (1998): 43–67.

Corngold, Stanley. *Lambent Traces: Franz Kafka*. Princeton, NJ: Princeton University Press, 2004.

Critchley, Simon. *The Book of Dead Philosophers*. New York: Vintage Books, 2008.

Czubaroff, Jeanine. "Dialogical Rhetoric: An Application of Martin Buber's Philosophy of Dialogue." *Quarterly Journal of Speech* 86, no. 2 (2000): 168–89.

Dahrendorf, Ralf. *Society and Democracy in Germany*. Garden City, NY: Anchor Books, 1969.

Daiya, Kavita. *Violent Belongings: Partition, Gender, and National Culture in Postcolonial India*. Philadelphia: Temple University Press, 2008.

Däufel, Christian. *Ingeborg Bachmanns "Ein Ort für Zufälle": Ein interpretierender Kommentar*. Berlin: de Gruyter, 2013.

Derrida, Jacques. *Limited Inc*. Evanston, IL: Northwestern University Press, 1988.

————. *Of Grammatology*. Translated by Gayatri Chakravorty Spivak. Baltimore: Johns Hopkins University Press, 1997.

————. "A Self-Unsealing Poetic Text: Poetics and Politics of Witnessing." In *Revenge of the Aesthetic*, edited by Michael P. Clark, 180–207. Berkeley: University of California Press, 2000.

————. *Sovereignties in Question: The Poetics of Paul Celan*. Edited by Thomas Dutoit and Outi Pasanen. New York: Fordham University Press, 2005.

————. *The Work of Mourning*. Edited by Pascale-Anne Brault and Michael Naas. Chicago: University of Chicago Press, 2001.

Derrida, Jacques, and Gianni Vattimo, eds. *Religion*. Stanford, CA: Stanford University Press, 1998.

Descourvières, Benedikt. "Annäherung an das Unsagbare: Skizzen einer symptomatischen Lektürepraxis von Peter Weiss' 'Die Ermittlung.'" *Peter Weiss Jahrbuch* 11 (2002): 85–104.

Dilthey, Wilhelm. *Gesammelte Schriften*. 26 vols. Leipzig: Teubner, 1914–2006.

Diner, Dan, ed. *Zivilisationsbruch: Denken nach Auschwitz*. Frankfurt a. M.: Fischer, 1988.

Dischereit, Esther. *Übungen jüdisch zu sein*. Frankfurt a. M.: Suhrkamp, 1998.

Documents on the Foreign Policy of Israel. Vol. 6: *1951*. Jerusalem: Government Printer, 1991.

Dutschke, Rudi, ed. *Die Rebellion der Studentenbewegung oder die neue Opposition*. Reinbek bei Hamburg: Rowohlt, 1968.

Eich, Günther. "Rede zur Verleihung des Georg-Büchner-Preises" (1959). In *Jahrbuch: Deutsche Akademie für Sprache und Dichtung Darmstadt*, 170–82. Heidelberg: Lambert Schneider, 1959.

Eigen, Sara. "Hannah Arendt's 'Lessing Rede' and the 'Truths' of History." *Lessing Yearbook* 32 (2000): 309–24.

Eitz, Thorsten, and Georg Stötzel. *Wörterbuch der "Vergangenheitsbewältigung": Die NS-Vergangenheit im öffentlichen Sprachgebrauch*. Hildesheim: Georg Olms Verlag, 2007.

Farocki, Harun. "Reality Would Have to Begin." Translated by Marek Wieczorek. In *Working on the Sightlines*, edited by Thomas Elsaesser, 193–202. Amsterdam: Amsterdam University Press, 2004.

———. *Working on the Sightlines*. Edited by Thomas Elsaesser. Amsterdam: Amsterdam University Press, 2004.

Felman, Shoshana. *The Juridical Unconscious: Trials and Traumas in the Twentieth Century*. Cambridge, MA: Harvard University Press, 2002.

Felstiner, John. *Paul Celan: Poet, Survivor, Jew*. New Haven, CT: Yale University Press, 1995.

Fetcher, Iring. *Joseph Goebbels im Berliner Sportpalast 1943: "Wollt ihr den totalen Krieg?"* Hamburg: Europäische Verlagsanstalt, 1998.

Fickert, Kurt. "The Identity of 'Der Genosse Schriftsteller' in Johnson's *Jahrestage*." *Monatshefte für deutschsprachige Literatur und Kultur* 91, no. 2 (1999): 256–67.

Fine, Robert, and Charles Turner, eds. *Social Theory after the Holocaust*. Liverpool: Liverpool University Press, 2000.

Fisher, Jaimey. "Adorno's Lesson Plans? The Ethics of (Re)education in 'The Meaning of Working through the Past'." In *Language without Soil: Adorno and Late Philosophical Modernity*, edited by Gerhard Richter, 76–98. New York: Fordham University Press, 2010.

Fontanille, Jacques. *The Semiotics of Discourse*. Translated by Heidi Bostic. New York: Peter Lang Publishing, 2006.

Foucault, Michel. *The Archaeology of Knowledge*. Translated by A. M. Sheridan Smith. London: Tavistock Publications, 1972.

Freud, Sigmund. *An Autobiographical Study*. Edited by James Strachey. New York: W. W. Norton, 1952.

———. *The Standard Edition of the Complete Psychological Works of Sigmund Freud*. Edited and translated by James Strachey. London: Hogarth Press, 1959.

———. *Studienausgabe*. Frankfurt a. M.: S. Fischer, 1971.

———. "The 'Uncanny.'" Translated by Joan Riviere. In *Collected Papers* 4:368–407. New York: Basic Books, 1959.

Freudiger, Kerstin. *Die juristische Aufarbeitung von NS-Verbrechen*. Tübingen: Mohr Siebeck, 2002.

Friedmann, Maurice. *Buber's Life and Work: The Later Years, 1945–1965*. New York: E. P. Dutton, 1983.

Fries, Ulrich. *Uwe Johnson's "Jahrestage": Erzählstruktur und politische Subjektivität*. Göttingen: Vandenhoeck u. Ruprecht, 1990.

Gadamer, Hans-Georg. *Truth and Method*. Edited by Garrett Barden and John Cumming. New York: Continuum, 1975.

Garloff, Katja. "Peter Weiss's Entry into the German Public Sphere." *Colloquia Germanica* 30, no. 1 (1997): 47–70.

Gaus, Günther. *Was bleibt, sind Fragen: Die klassischen Interviews.* Edited by Hans-Dieter Schütt. Berlin: Das neue Berlin, 1996.

Geissner, Hellmut. *Rede in der Öffentlichkeit: Eine Einführung in die Rhetorik.* Stuttgart: Kohlhammer, 1969.

Gente, Peter, and Peter Weibel, eds. *Deleuze und die Künste.* Frankfurt a. M.: Suhrkamp, 2007.

Girnus, Wilhelm, and Werner Mittenzwei. "Gespräch mit Peter Weiss." *Sinn und Form: Beiträge zur Literatur* 17, nos. 1–6 (1965): 678–88.

Goltschnigg, Dietmar, ed. *Georg Büchner und die Moderne: Texte, Analysen, Kommentar.* 2 vols. Berlin: Erich Schmidt Verlag, 2002.

Goodman, David. *Radio's Civic Ambition: American Broadcasting and Democracy in the 1930s.* London: Oxford University Press, 2011.

Goschler, Constantin. *Schuld und Schulden: Die Politik der Wiedergutmachung für NS-Verfolgte seit 1945.* Göttingen: Wallenstein, 2005.

Gray, Peter. "A Living World: An Interview with Peter Weiss." *Tulane Drama Review* 11, no. 1 (1966): 106–14.

Grieswelle, Detlef. *Politische Rhetorik.* Wiesbaden: DUV, 2000.

Habermas, Jürgen. *Philosophical-Political Profiles.* Cambridge, MA: MIT Press, 1983.

———. *The Structural Transformation of the Public Sphere: An Inquiry into a Category of Bourgeois Society.* Translated by Thomas Burger and Frederick Lawrence. Cambridge, MA: MIT Press, 1989.

Hahn, Barbara. *Die Jüdin Pallas Athene: Auch eine Theorie der Moderne.* Berlin: Berlin Verlag, 2002.

———. *Hannah Arendt—Leidenschaften, Menschen und Bücher.* Berlin: Berlin Verlag, 2005.

"Hannah Arendt." *Frankfurter Allgemeine Zeitung*, September 29, 1959, 10.

Hansen, Miriam Bratu. *Cinema and Experience: Siegfried Kracauer, Walter Benjamin, and Theodor W. Adorno.* Berkeley: University of California Press, 2012.

Hasenclever, V. F. W. *Denken als Widerspruch: Plädoyers gegen die Irrationalität oder ist Vernunft nicht mehr gefragt?* Frankfurt a. M.: Eichborn, 1982.

Hausmann, Frank-Rutger. *Die Rolle der Geisteswissenschaften im Dritten Reich 1933–1945.* Munich: R. Oldenbourg, 2002.

Heidelberger-Leonhard, Irene. "Peter Weiss und sein Judentum: 'Die Ermittlung', die ihrer Ermittlung harrt." *Peter Weiss Jahrbuch* 11 (2002): 39–55.

Hell, Julia. "From Laokoon to Ge: Resistance to Jewish Authorship in Peter Weiss's 'Ästhetik des Widerstands.'" In *Rethinking Peter Weiss*, edited by Jost Hermand and Marc Silberman, 21–44. New York: Peter Lang, 2000.

Herzfeld-Sander, Margaret, ed. *Essays on German Theater: Lessing, Brecht, Dürrenmatt, and Others.* Foreword by Martin Esslin. New York: Continuum, 1985.

Hesse, Hermann. *Gesammelte Werke.* 12 vols. Frankfurt a. M.: Suhrkamp, 1951.

Hetzel, Andreas. "Das schöpferische Wort: Bubers Sprachdenken und die Tradition der Logosmystik." *Im Gespräch: Hefte der Martin Buber-Gesellschaft* 8 (2004): 41–47.

Heusen, Sarah von der. "Mascha Kaléko und der Fontane-Preis: Ein Fallbeispiel." *Berliner Hefte zur Geschichte des Literarischen Lebens* 8 (2008): 222–31.

Hinderer, Walter. *Deutsche Reden.* Stuttgart: Reclam, 1973.

Hitler, Adolf. *My Struggle.* Translated by Edgar Dugdale. London: Hurst & Blackett, 1937.

Hoffmann, Friedrich. *Die Verfolgung der nationalsozialistischen Gewaltverbrechen in Hessen.* Baden-Baden: Nomos, 2001.

Hofmann, Michael. "Das Gedächtnis des NS-Faschismus in Peter Weiss' *Ästhetik des Widerstands* und Uwe Johnsons *Jahrestagen.*" *Peter Weiss Jahrbuch* 4 (1995): 54–77.

———. "Die Schule der Ambivalenz: Uwe Johnsons 'Jahrestage' und das kollektive Gedächtnis der Deutschen." *Johnson-Jahrbuch* 10 (2003): 109–19.

Hofmannsthal, Hugo von. *The Lord Chandos Letter and Other Writings.* Translated by Joel Rotenberg, with an introduction by John Banville. New York: New York ReviewBooks, 2005.

Höller, Hans. *Ingeborg Bachmann: Das Werk von den frühesten Gedichten bis zum "Todesarten"-Zyklus.* Frankfurt a. M.: Athenäum, 1987.

Horman, Yasco. *Theaters of Justice: Judging, Staging, and Working through in Arendt, Brecht, and Delbo.* Stanford, CA: Stanford University Press, 2011.

Horwitz, Rivka. *Buber's Way to "I and Thou": The Development of Martin Buber's Thought and His "Religion as Presence" Lectures.* Philadelphia: The Jewish Publications Society, 1988.

Innes, Christopher. *Holy Theatre: Ritual and the Avant Garde.* Cambridge: Cambridge University Press, 1984.

Isenschmid, Andreas. "Emil Staiger und Peter Szondi." In *1955–2005—Emil Staiger und Die Kunst der Interpretation heute,* edited by Joachim Rickes, Volker Ladenthin, and Michael Baum, 173–88. New York: Peter Lang, 2007.

Jaspers, Karl. *The Question of German Guilt.* Translated by E. B. Ashton. New York: Capricorn Books, 1961.

Jaspers, Karl, and Hannah Arendt. *Reden zur Verleihung des Friedenspreises des deutschen Buchhandels.* Munich: Piper, 1958.

Jens, Walter. *Von deutscher Rede.* Munich: Piper, 1969.

Jernigan, Daniel K. *Drama and the Postmodern: Assessing the Limits of Metatheatre.* Amherst, NY: Cambria Press, 2008.

Johe, Werner. *Die gleichgeschaltete Justiz: Organisation des Rechtswesens und Politisierung der Rechtsprechung 1933–1945, dargestellt am Beispiel des Oberlandesgerichtsbezirks Hamburg.* Frankfurt a. M.: EVA, 1967.

Johnson, Uwe. *Anniversaries: From the Life of Gesine Cresspahl.* Translated by Leila Vennewitz and Walter Arndt. 2 vols. New York: Harcourt Brace Jovanovich, 1975–87.

———. *Begleitumstände: Frankfurter Vorlesungen.* Frankfurt a. M.: Suhrkamp, 1980.

———. *Berliner Sachen.* Kursbuch. Frankfurt a. M.: Suhrkamp, 1975.

———. *Jahrestage: Aus dem Leben von Gesine Cresspahl.* 4 vols. Frankfurt a. M.: Suhrkamp, 1970–83.

———. *Mutmassungen über Jakob.* Frankfurt a. M.: Suhrkamp, 1959.

———. *Uwe Johnson: Speculations about Jakob and Other Writings.* Edited by Alexander Stephan. New York: Continuum, 2000.

Jung, Carl. *Collected Works.* Princeton, NJ: Princeton University Press, 1948.

Kacandes, Irene. *Talk Fiction: Literature and the Talk Explosion.* Lincoln: University of Nebraska Press, 2001.

Kaiser, Alfons. "Der 16. Januar 1967 oder Können wie uns auf Johnson verlassen?" *Johnson-Jahrbuch* 2 (1995): 256–58.

Karpf, Anne. *The Human Voice: The Story of a Remarkable Talent.* London: Bloomsbury, 2006.

Kaufmann, Walter. *Discovering the Mind*. New York: McGraw-Hill, 1980.

Keller, Rolf, and Wolfgang Marienfeld, eds. *Konzentrationslager Bergen-Belsen: Berichte und Dokumente*. Hannover: Niedersächsische Landeszentrale für Politische Bildung, 1995.

Kittler, Friedrich, Thomas Macho, and Sigrid Weigel. *Zwischen Rauschen und Offenbarung: Zur Kultur- und Mediengeschichte der Stimme*. Berlin: Akademie Verlag, 2002.

Klages, Wolfgang. *Gefühle in Worte gießen: Die ungebrochene Macht der politischen Rede*. Würzburg: Deutscher Wissenschafts-Verlag, 2001.

Kluge, Alexander, and Oskar Negt. *Geschichte und Eigensinn*. Frankfurt a. M.: Zweitausendeins, 1981.

————. *Public Sphere and Experience: Toward an Analysis of the Bourgeois and Proletarian Public Sphere*. Translated by Peter Labanyi, Jamie Owen Daniel, and Assenka Oksiloff. Minneapolis: University of Minnesota Press, 1993.

König, Christoph, Werner Röcke, and Hans-Harald Müller, eds. *Wissenschaftsgeschichte der Germanistik in Porträts*. Berlin: de Gruyter, 2000.

König, Jan C. L. *Über die Wirkungsmacht der Rede: Strategien politischer Eloquenz in Literatur und Alltag*. Göttingen: Vandenhoeck & Ruprecht, 2011.

Kraushaar, Wolfgang. *Frankfurter Schule und Studentenbewegung: Von der Flaschenpost zum Molotowcocktail 1946–1995*. Hamburg: Rogner & Bernhard bei Zweitau-sendeins, 1998.

Krick-Aigner, Kirsten A. *Ingeborg Bachmann's Telling Stories: Fairy Tale Beginnings and Holocaust Endings*. Riverside, CA: Ariadne Press, 2002.

Krimmer, Elisabeth. *The Representation of War in German Literature: From 1800 to the Present*. Cambridge: Cambridge University Press, 2010.

Kundnani, Hans. *Utopia or Auschwitz? Germany's 1968 Generation and the Holocaust*. New York: Columbia University Press, 2009.

Kustow, Michael. *Peter Brook: A Biography*. New York: St. Martin's Press, 2005.

Lacoue-Labarthe, Philippe. *Poetry as Experience*. Translated by Andrea Tarnowski. Stanford, CA: Stanford University Press, 1999.

Langbein, Hermann. *Der Auschwitz-Prozeß: Eine Dokumentation*. 2 vols. Frankfurt a. M.: Europäische Verlagsanstalt, 1965.

Langston, Richard. *Visions of Violence: German Avant-Gardes after Fascism*. Evanston, IL: Northwestern University Press, 2008.

Laternser, Hans. *Die andere Seite im Auschwitz-Prozess 1963/65: Reden eines Verteidigers*. Stuttgart: Seewald, 1966.

Leahy, Caitríona, and Bernadette Cronin. *Re-acting to Ingeborg Bachmann: New Essays and Performances*. Würzburg: Königshausen und Neumann, 2006.

Lessing, Gotthold Ephraim. *Laocoön: An Essay on the Limits of Painting and Poetry*. Translated and with an introduction by Edward Allen McCormick. Baltimore: Johns Hopkins University Press, 1984.

Levinas, Emmanuel. *Proper Names*. Translated by Michael B. Smith. Stanford, CA: Stanford University Press, 1996.

Lindner, Burkhard. "Habilitationsakte Benjamin: Über ein 'akademisches Trauerspiel' und über ein Vorkapitel der 'Frankfurter Schule' (Horkheimer, Adorno)." *LiLi: Zeitschrift für Literaturwissenschaft und Linguistik* 53/54 (1984): 147–65.

Lockwood, Richard. *The Reader's Figure: Epideictic Rhetoric in Plato, Aristotle, Bossuet, Racine and Pascal*. Geneva: Librarie Droz, 1996.

Lyon, James K. *Paul Celan and Martin Heidegger: An Unresolved Conversation, 1951–1970*. Baltimore: Johns Hopkins University Press, 2006.

Lyotard, Jean-François. *The Differend: Phrases in Dispute*. Minneapolis: University of Minnesota Press, 1988.

Margalit, Gilad. *Guilt, Suffering, and Memory: Germany Remembers Its Dead of World War II*. Bloomington: Indiana University Press, 2010.

Mattenklott, Gert. "Benjamin als Korrespondent, als Herausgeber von *Deutsche Menschen* und als Theoretiker des Briefes." In *Walter Benjamin*, edited by Uwe Steiner, 273–82. Bern: Lang, 1992.

Mayer, Hans. *Georg Büchner und seine Zeit*. Frankfurt a. M.: Suhrkamp, 1972.

McVeigh, Joseph G. "Ingeborg Bachmann as Radio Scriptwriter." *German Quarterly* 75, no. 1 (2002): 35–49.

Meier, Georg Friedrich. *Versuch einer allgemeinen Auslegungskunst*. Edited by Axel Bühler and Luigi Cataldi Madonna. Hamburg: Felix Meiner, 1996.

Mein, Georg. "Fermenta cognitionis: Hannah Arendts 'Hermeneutik des Nach-Denkens.'" *DVjs* 77, no. 3 (2003): 481–511.

Mendes-Flohr, Paul. *From Mysticism to Dialogue*. Detroit: Wayne State University Press, 1989.

Meyer, Marita. "Bergpredigt—Dante—Odysseus—Levi: Ein intertextueller Kommentar zu zwei Sätzen im 'Gesang vom Lager' in Peter Weiss' 'Ermittlung.'" *Peter Weiss Jahrbuch* 9 (2000): 102–14.

Middleton, Christopher, ed. *German Writing Today*. Baltimore: Penguin, 1967.

Mitscherlich, Alexander, und Margarete Mitscherlich. *Die Unfähigkeit zu trauern: Grundlagen kollektiven Verhaltens*. Munich: Piper, 1967.

———. *The Inability to Mourn*. Translated by Beverly R. Placzek. New York: Grove Press, 1975.

Moltmann, Günter. "Goebbels' Rede zum totalen Krieg am 18. Februar 1943." *Vierteljahreshefte für Zeitgeschichte* 12, no. 1 (1964): 13–43.

Moore, Donald J. *Martin Buber: Prophet of Religious Secularism*. New York: Jewish Publication Society of America, 1974.

Mosès, Stéphane. "Émile Benveniste et la linguistique du dialogue." *Revue de Métaphysique et de Morale* 4 (2001): 93–109.

———. "Wege, auf denen die Sprache stimmhaft wird." In *Argumentum e silentio*, edited by Amy C. Colin, 43–57. Berlin: W. de Gruyter, 1987.

Müller, Lothar. "Der abgesperrten Weltluft den deutschen Raum weit öffnen." *Frankfurter Allgemeine Zeitung*, July 1, 1999, 44.

Müller-Doohm, Stefan. *Adorno: A Biography*. Cambridge: Polity Press, 2005.

Nägele, Rainer. "Text, History and the Critical Subject: Notes on Peter Szondi's Theory and Praxis of Hermeneutics." *Boundary 2* 11, no. 3 (1983): 29–41.

Naumann, Bernd. *Auschwitz: Bericht über die Strafsache gegen Mulka und andere vor dem Schwurgericht Frankfurt*. Translated by Jean Steinberg. Frankfurt a. M.: Athenäum, 1968.

———. *Auschwitz: A Report on the Proceedings against Robert Karl Ludwig Mulka and Others before the Court at Frankfurt*. New York: F. A. Praeger, 1966.

Osiel, Mark. *Mass Atrocity, Collective Memory, and the Law*. New Brunswick, NJ: Transaction, 1997.

Pakier, Małgorzata, and Bo Stråth, eds. *A European Memory? Contested Histories and Politics of Remembrance*. New York: Berghahn, 2010.

Parkes, Stuart, and John J. White, eds. *The Gruppe 47: Fifty Years on a Re-appraisal of Its Literary and Political Significance*. Amsterdam: Rodopi, 1999.

Pavsek, Christopher. "History and Obstinacy: Negt and Kluge's Redemption of Labor." *New German Critique* 68 (1996): 137–63.

Pendas, Devon O. *The Frankfurt Auschwitz Trial, 1963–1965: Genocide, History, and the Limits of the Law*. Cambridge, MA: Harvard University Press, 2006.

Perloff, Marjorie. *Wittgenstein's Ladder: Poetic Language and the Strangeness of the Ordinary*. Chicago: University of Chicago Press, 1996.

Pitkin, Hanna Fenichel. *The Attack of the Blob: Hannah Arendt's Concept of the Social*. Chicago: University of Chicago Press, 2007.

Plass, Ulrich. *Language and History in Theodor W. Adorno's "Notes to Literature."* New York: Routledge, 2007.

Plato. *Phaedrus*. Translated by C. J. Rowe. London: Aris & Phillips, 1999.

Poag, James F., and Claire Baldwin. *The Construction of Textual Authority in German Literature of the Medieval and Early Modern Periods*. Chapel Hill: University of North Carolina Press, 2001.

Pöggeler, Otto. *Spur des Worts: Zur Lyrik Paul Celans*. Freiburg: K. Alber, 1986.

Rakow, Christian. "Fragmente des Realen: Zur Transformation des Dokuments in Peter Weiss' 'Die Ermittlung.'" *Weimarer Beiträge* 50, no. 2 (2004): 266–79.

Rassinier, Paul. *Debunking the Genocide Myth: A Study of the Nazi Concentration Camps and the Alleged Extermination of European Jewry*. Los Angeles: Noontide Press, c1978.

———. *Was nun, Odysseus? Zur Bewältigung der Vergangenheit*. Wiesbaden: Karl Heinz Priester, 1960.

Rector, Martin. "Laokoon oder der vergebliche Kampf gegen die Bilder: Medienwechsel und Politisierung bei Peter Weiss." *Peter Weiss Jahrbuch* 1 (1992): 24–41.

Reichert, Klaus. "Adorno und das Radio." *Sinn und Form* 62 (2010): 454–65.

Renz, Werner. "Der erste Frankfurter Auschwitz-Prozeß." *1999: Zeitschrift für Sozialgeschichte des 20. und 21. Jahrhunderts* 2 (2000): 11–48.

Revesz, Eva B. "Poetry after Auschwitz: Tracing Trauma in Ingeborg Bachmann's Lyric Work." *Monatshefte für deutschsprachige Literatur und Kultur* 99, no. 2 (Summer 2007): 194–216.

Richter, Alexandra. "Die politische Dimension der Aufmerksamkeit im *Meridian*." *DVjs* 77 (2003): 659–76.

Richter, Gerhard. "Nazism and Negative Dialectics: Adorno's Hitler." In *Unmasking Hitler: Cultural Representation of Hitler from the Weimar Republic to the Present*, edited by Klaus Leo Berghahn and Jost Hermand, 105–46. Bern: Peter Lang, 2005.

Richter, Hans Werner, ed. *Almanach der Gruppe 47*. Reinbek: Rowohlt, 1962.

———. *Im Etablissement der Schmetterlinge: Einundzwanzig Portraits aus der Gruppe 47*. Munich: Hanser, 1986.

Rosenzweig, Franz. *The Star of Redemption*. Translated by Barabara E. Galli. Madison: University of Wisconsin Press, 2005.

Salloch, Erika. *Peter Weiss' "Die Ermittlung": Zur Struktur des Dokumentartheaters*. Frankfurt a. M.: Athenäum, 1972.

Salzmann, Bertram. "Literatur als Widerstand: Auf der Spur eines poetologischen Topos der deutschsprachigen Literatur nach 1945." *DVjs* 2, no. 77 (2003): 331–47.

Santner, Eric L. *Stranded Objects: Mourning, Memory, and Film in Postwar Germany*. Ithaca, NY: Cornell University Press, 1990.

Schäfer, Martin Jörg, and Ulrich Wergin, eds. *Die Zeitlichkeit des Ethos: Poetologische Aspekte im Schreiben Paul Celans*. Würzburg: Königshausen & Neumann, 2003.

Schestag, Thomas. *Buk*. Munich: Boer, 1994.

―――. *Die unbewältigte Sprache: Hannah Arendts Theorie der Dichtung*. Basel: Engeler, 2006.

Schilpp, Paul Arthur, and Maurice Friedman, eds. *Martin Buber*. Stuttgart: Kohlhammer, 1963.

Schlinsog, Elke. *Berliner Zufälle: Ingeborg Bachmanns "Todesarten"-Projekt*. Würzburg: Königshausen und Neumann, 2005.

Schmidt, Thomas. "'Es ist unser Haus, Marie': Zur Doppelbedeutung des Romantitels Jahrestage." *Johnson-Jahrbuch* 1 (1994): 143–60.

Schmidtke, Michael. *Der Aufbruch der jungen Intelligenz: Die 68er Jahre in der Bundesrepublik und in den USA*. Frankfurt a. M.: Campus Verlag, 2003.

Schmitt, Carlo. *Wegmarken der Freiheit: Essays zur Literatur und Politik*. Tübingen: Klöpfer und Meyer, 2001.

Schnell, Rüdiger. "Von der Rede zur Schrift: Konstituierung von Autorität in Predigt und Predigtüberlieferung." In *The Construction of Textual Authority in German Literature of the Medieval and Early Modern Periods*, edited by James F. Poag and Claire Baldwin, 91–123. Chapel Hill: University of North Carolina Press, 2001.

Schönke, Adolf. *Strafgesetzbuch: Kommentar*. Munich: C. H. Beck, 1959.

―――. *Strafgesetzbuch für das Deutsche Reich: Kommentar*. Munich: C. H. Beck, 1944.

Schuppener, Georg, ed. *Jüdische Intellektuelle in der DDR: Politische Strukturen und Biographien*. Leipzig: Arbeitskreis Hochschulpolitische Öffentlichkeit beim StuRa der Universität Leipzig, 1999.

Schwarz, Michael. "'Er redet leicht, schreibt schwer': Theodor W. Adorno am Mikrophon." *Zeithistorische Forschungen/Studies in Contemporary History*, Online-Ausgabe, 8 (2011): 1. http://www.zeithistorische-forschungen.de/16126041-Schwarz-2–2011.

Schwerbrock, Wolfgang. "Literaturpreise und Öffentlichkeit." *Frankfurter Allgemeine Zeitung*, November 4, 1961.

Sebald, W. G. *On the Natural History of Destruction*. Translated by Anthea Bell. New York: Random House, 2003.

Seemann, Silke. *Die politischen Säuberungen des Lehrkörpers der Freiburger Universität nach dem Ende des Zweiten Weltkriegs (1945–1957)*. Freiburg i. Breisgau: Rombach, 2002.

Simon, Ernst. *Aufbau im Untergang*. Tübingen: Mohr, 1959.

Söllner, Alfons. *Peter Weiss und die Deutschen: Die Entstehung einer politischen Ästhetik wider die Verdrängung*. Opladen: Westdeutscher Verlag, 1988.

Spang, Kurt. *Rede*. Bamberg: C. C. Buchners, 1987.

Sparr, Thomas. "Peter Szondi." *Bulletin des Leo Baeck Instituts* 78 (1987): 59–69.

Staiger, Emil. *Die Kunst der Interpretation: Studien zur deutschen Literatur*. Zurich: Artemis, 1950.

Stichweh, Rudolf. "Zur Subjektivierung der Entscheidungsfindung im deutschen Strafprozeß des 19. Jahrhunderts." In *Subjektivierung des justiziellen Beweisverfahrens: Beiträge zum Zeugenbeweis in Europa und den USA*, edited by André Gouron, 265–300. Frankfurt a. M.: Klostermann, 1994.

Storz, Gerhard. "Zur Diskussion über die verachtete Rhetorik." *Stuttgarter Zeitung*, November 31, 1964; January 9, 1965; March 27, 1965.

Sulzer, Dieter, Hildegard Dieke, and Ingrid Kußmaul. *Der Georg-Büchner-Preis 1951–1978*. Marbach am Neckar: Deutsche Akademie für Sprache und Dichtung Darmstadt, 1978.

Szondi, Peter. *Briefe*. Edited by Christopher König and Thomas Sparr. Frankfurt a. M.: Suhrkamp, 1993.

———. *Celan Studies*. Edited by Jean Bollack, translated by Susan Bernofski with Harvey Mendelsohn. Stanford, CA: Stanford University Press, 2003.

———. *Das lyrische Drama des Fin de Siècle*. Edited by Henriette Beese. Studienausgabe der Vorlesungen 4. Frankfurt a. M.: Suhrkamp, 1975.

———. *Introduction to Literary Hermeneutics*. Translated by Martha Woodmansee. Cambridge: Cambridge University Press, 1995.

———. *On Textual Understanding and Other Essays*. Translated by Harvey Mendelsohn. Minneapolis: University of Minnesota Press, 1986.

———. *Schriften*. Edited by Jean Bollack. 2 vols. Frankfurt a. M.: Suhrkamp, 1978.

———. *Theory of the Modern Drama*. Translated by Michael Hays. Minneapolis: University of Minnesota Press, 1987.

———. *Über eine "freie (d.h. freie) Universität."* Frankfurt a. M.: Suhrkamp, 1973.

Tieder, Irène. "Reading or Listening: On Peter Weiss's 'The Investigation.'" *Comprehending the Holocaust: Historical and Literary Research*, edited by Asher Cohen et al., 267–78. Frankfurt a. M.: P. Lang, 1988.

Trezise, Thomas. "Unspeakable." *Yale Journal of Criticism* 14, no. 1 (2001): 39–66.

Ueding, Gert. *Deutsche Reden von Luther bis zur Gegenwart*. Frankfurt a. M.: Suhrkamp, 1999.

Ulmer, Judith S. *Geschichte des Georg-Büchner-Preises: Soziologie eines Rituals*. Berlin: de Gruyter, 2006.

Ungerer, Wilhelm. "Auschwitz auf dem Theater?" In *Deutsche Nachkriegsliteratur und der Holocaust*, edited by Stephan Braese and Holger Gehle, 71–97. Frankfurt a. M.: Campus, 1998.

Vidal-Naquet, Pierre. *Holocaust Denial in France: Analysis of a Unique Phenomenon*. Tel Aviv: Tel Aviv University, Faculty of the Humanities, 1995.

Vogt, Jochen. "Treffpunkt im Unendlichen? Über Peter Weiss und Paul Celan." *Peter Weiss Jahrbuch* 4 (1995): 102–21.

Wais, Kurt. *Die Gegenwartsdichtung der europäischen Völker*. Berlin: Junker und Dünnhaupt, 1939.

Wannemacher, Klaus. "'Mystische Gedankengänge lagen ihm fern': Erwin Piscators Uraufführung der *Ermittlung* an der Freien Volksbühne." *Peter Weiss Jahrbuch* 13 (2004): 89–102.

Warburg, Bettina. "Germany's National Identity, Collective Memory, and Role Abroad." In *Power and the Past: Collective Memory and International Relations*, edited by Eric Langenbacher and Yossi Shain, 51–70. Washington, DC: Georgetown University Press, 2010.

Weigel, Sigrid. *Ingeborg Bachmann: Hinterlassenschaften unter Wahrung des Briefgeheimnisses*. Vienna: P. Zsolnay, 1999.

Weiser, Peter. *Wien: Stark bewölkt*. Vienna: Christian Brandstätter, 1984.

Weiß, Christoph. *Auschwitz in der geteilten Welt: Peter Weiss und die "Ermittlung" im Kalten Krieg*. 2 vols. St. Ingbert: Röhrig Universitätsverlag, 2000.

Weiss, Peter. "Frankfurter Auszüge." *Kursbuch* 1 (1965): 152–88.

———. *The Investigation: A Play*. Translated by Jon Swan and Ulu Grosbard. New York: Atheneum, 1966.

———. *Notizbücher: 1960–71*. 2 vols. Frankfurt a. M.: Suhrkamp, 1981.

———. *Rapporte*. 2 vols. Frankfurt a. M.: Suhrkamp, 1968–71.

———. *Stücke 1*. Frankfurt a. M.: Suhrkamp, 1976.

Wetters, Kirk. *The Opinion System: Impasses of the Public Sphere from Hobbes to Habermas*. New York: Fordham University Press, 2008.

Wiedemann, Barbara. *"Ein Faible für Tübingen": Paul Celan in Württemberg; Deutschland und Paul Celan*. Tübingen: Klöpfer und Meyer, 2013.

———. *Paul Celan—Die Goll-Affäre: Dokumente zu einer "Infamie."* Frankfurt a. M.: Suhrkamp, 2000.

Willet, John, ed. *The Development of an Aesthetic*. New York: Hill and Wang, 1964.

Wittmann, Rebecca. *Beyond Justice: The Auschwitz Trial*. Cambridge, MA: Harvard University Press, 2005.

———. "Indicting Auschwitz? The Paradox of the Frankfurt Auschwitz Trial." *German History* 21 (2003): 505–32.

Wojak, Irmtrud, ed. *Auschwitz Prozess 4 Ks 2/63 Frankfurt am Main*. Cologne: Snoeck, 200

Wolin, Richard. *Labyrinths: Explorations in the Critical History of Ideas*. Amherst: University of Massachusetts Press, c1995.

Wrede, Wilhelm. *Das Messiasgeheimnis in den Evangelien: Zugleich ein Beitrag zum Verständnis des Markusevangeliums*. Göttingen: Vandenhoeck & Ruprecht, 1901.

Wyman, David S., and Charles H. Rosenzveig, eds. *The World Reacts to the Holocaust*. Baltimore: Johns Hopkins University Press, 1996.

Yitzhak, Arad, Israel Gutman, and Abraham Margaliot, eds. *Documents on the Holocaust: Selected Sources on the Destruction of the Jews*. Lincoln: University of Nebraska Press, 1999.

Young, James E. *Writing and Rewriting the Holocaust: Narrative and Consequences of Interpretation*. Bloomington: Indiana University Press, 1988.

Young-Bruehl, Elisabeth. *Hannah Arendt: For the Love of the World*. New Haven, CT: Yale University Press, 1982.

INDEX

absence: of Benjamin in postwar Germany, 153; and citation, 154; of a dead person, 192; of God, 32; of "I," 191; of Jews in Germany, 4; and presence, 44–46; of rules and certainty, 13

academy: anti-Semitism of, 18, 153; Arendt and, 88; Benjamin's status in, 140–42, 150; Buber's critique of, 30; and the public sphere, 154; Szondi and, 142. *See also* university

addressee(s): absence in process of writing, 19; allocutions postulating, 43; as dialogic other, 39–40; distance between speaker and, 68; impact of speech on, 42; interaction with, 20; involvement of, 57; Johnson's, 120, 125; Szondi's, 140, 150; worthy and unworthy, 45

Adenauer, Konrad, Chancellor: admission of German guilt, 129; Christian-conservative politics, 4; curtailing of denazification, 180

Adorno, Theodor W., 3; abdication of poetry, 75; authoritarian character, 207; breach in historical continuity, 42; and Celan, 12; citizenship, 11; conditions of repression, 10; *Deutsche Menschen,* 138; as editor of Benjamin, 140; *Erlebnis* vs. *Erfahrung,* 53; *Iphigenie* lecture, 205–6, 208; *The Jargon of Authenticity,* 177n54, 201–2; as mentor of Szondi, 143; *Minima Moralia,* 140; *Negative Dialectics,* 176n52; radio lectures, 8; student revolts, 22

Aeschylus, *The Eumenides,* 170

aesthetics: aesthetic assimilation of *The Investigation,* 167; *Aesthetics of Resistance,* 161; boundaries between political resistance and aesthetic practice, 160; classical theory of, 187; and event, 16; Laocoon group as aesthetic object, 194; public speech as aesthetic practice, 3, 10; and *Vergangenheitsbewältigung,* 165n18; *Wirkungsästhetik,* 147n24

Agamben, Giorgio: ethics, 4n8; *martis,* 154n42; subject of enunciation, 108–10; survivor as witness, 106n31

Aichinger, Ilse, 111

alterity. *See* otherness

Andersch, Alfred, 201

anti-Semitism, 1–2, 4, 57, 104–5, 110, 113, 153, 182, 196

aphasia, 68, 97n18, 155, 158, 187–88, 190–93

aporia, 69, 110

apostrophe, 20, 35–36, 57n8, 59, 63. *See also* figure, rhetorical

Archimedes: theory of the lever, 13, 194

Arendt, Hannah, 2–3, 87–113; atomic weapons, 10; Bachmann, 12; breach of tradition, 42; *daimōn,* 96, 98–99, 120; discovery of Auschwitz, 4; friendship, 93, 134; *The Human Condition,* 8, 10n25, 11n28, 92–93, 95, 101, 103, 110; influence on Habermas, 8; in Johnson's *Anniversaries,* 87–96; *Karl Jaspers: A Laudatio,* 96–100; labor, work, and action, 97; Lessing Prize address, 20, 91, 93, 95, 97, 100–112, 118, 131, 190; *Origins of Totalitarianism,* 28n11, 132n32; pariah, 21, 91, 97, 102–7, 111–12, 118; plurality, 10, 12, 93, 95, 97–98, 110, 118, 121, 132; political engagement, 34; repatriation, 11; and rhetorical tradition, 15; self-revelation, 12, 21, 91–92, 94, 97–101, 111; the social, 91–92, 94, 97n17; space of appearance, 9–11, 91, 97–98, 103; speech, 95–96; *vita activa,* 88, 99; Zionist movement, 13

Aristotle: deliberative rhetoric, 33n32; *ethos* of speaker, 35; *On Rhetoric,* 16; plurality, 12; testimony, 156

atomic weapons, 10

audio technology, 66, 68, 71–72

Auschwitz, 37, 45, 124, 173; caesura of, 29, 116, 208; education after, 199–205; language and, 54, 125; Oswiecim, 194; poetry after, 27, 75n12; reality of, 199, 208; shock of discovery, 4, 8; survivor of, 93, 174–87

Auschwitz trial, 158, 160–70, 180–82, 183

Austin, J. L., 17, 33, 37–38

Austria, 13; Bachmann and, 70–71, 73–74, 83, 156; Buber and, 26

avant-garde, 10, 140, 160n3, 186–87

awards. *See* literary prizes